Gavin Mortimer is a bestse t
who has published over thi ,
including The Men Who e
leading authority on World d
over one hundred veterans from the SAS, SBS and LRDG. As well as appearing on numerous TV and radio programmes, Gavin was the consultant for the National Army Museum's 2018 exhibition about the history of Britain's special forces and he has guided several serving members of the SAS around the sites in France where their predecessors fought in 1944.

David Stirling

The Phoney Major: The Life, Times and Truth about the Founder of the SAS

Gavin Mortimer

CONSTABLE

CONSTABLE

First published in Great Britain in 2022 by Constable
This paperback edition published in 2023 by Constable

1 3 5 7 9 10 8 6 4 2

A CIP catalogue record for this book is available from the British Library.

Paperback ISBN 978-1-47213-457-8

Typeset in Bembo by SX Composing DTP Ltd, Rayleigh, Essex
Printed and bound in Great Britain by Clays Ltd, Elcograf S.p.A.

Papers used by Constable are from well-managed forests and other responsible sources.

Constable
An imprint of
Little, Brown Book Group
Carmelite House
50 Victoria Embankment
London EC4Y 0DZ

An Hachette UK Company
www.hachette.co.uk

www.littlebrown.co.uk

For Bill and Blair, perpetually at odds with the trivialities and meanness of modern life

If you know a man in peace, you know him in war.

Lord Moran, *The Anatomy of Courage*

Prologue

On the evening of Wednesday 14 December 1955 Father D. J. Crowley arrived in Belfast from his home in Crossgar. He had recently returned to Northern Ireland from London, having retired from his post as an under-secretary at the Ministry of Labour. For Crowley it was a day to catch up with old acquaintances, and one in particular – Col Blair Mayne, war hero, rugby star and one of the most famous men in the country. The pair had arranged a meeting to discuss a forthcoming reunion dinner for the Paratroop Old Comrades' Association and men of the Special Air Service.

Shortly after his arrival in Belfast, Crowley saw the front page of the evening paper, the *Belfast Telegraph*. There was a photo of Mayne, under the headline 'Colonel Blair Mayne, 4 times winner of DSO, dies in crash'.

The inside pages described Mayne's exploits in *Boy's Own* prose: how he fought the Nazis in North Africa, Italy and France. There was hyperbole in the report – such as the claim that Mayne was 6ft 6in when he was 6ft 2in – but most of it was factually accurate: Britain's greatest guerrilla fighter was dead. 'It may seem a strange fate that Col. Blair Mayne should have survived so many hazards as a soldier, and at 40 lose his life in a motor accident,' said the *Belfast Telegraph*. 'But he lived hard in peace, as well as in war. Forced by an injury to give up the life of action in which he shone, he became restless and without purpose. Men like him are made for conflict, and 1939 came as a happy release from his solicitor's desk.'

The hard living was a veiled reference to Mayne's drinking. Everyone in Belfast and beyond knew of his fondness for a binge. In February 1952 he had been fined £15 for a fracas outside the Dublin home of Senator William Quirke when, in his cups, he had assaulted the senator's son as he searched in vain for the Old Belvedere rugby clubhouse so he could carry on drinking.

On Thursday 15 December the papers described the events surrounding Mayne's death in greater detail. No reference was made to drink being involved but people who knew the deceased could again read between the lines.

The inquest had been held on the day of Mayne's death. There was no mention of the Masonic dinner he had attended in his home town of Newtownards, nor the hand of poker he had played afterwards with friends. He dropped one of those friends, Mr J. A. Auterson, at his house in Bangor and said he was 'going straight home'.[1] He didn't. The night was still young, and he called in on a fellow Mason, George Matthews, for a nightcap or two.

Mayne climbed into his cherished red two-litre Riley a few minutes before 4 a.m. for the drive back to the family home at Mount Pleasant. He lost control of his automobile one mile from his destination. The vehicle struck a stationary lorry in Mill Street, careered across the road, scraped along the sides of a number of houses and crashed into an electric standard pole. The commotion woke James Alexander and his wife in their Mill Street home. Alexander, a local bus driver, told the inquest that when he opened the front door he 'saw lights flashing from overhead electric wires and a car sitting on the footpath with headlights on and engine running'.[2] Asked why he did nothing other than return to bed, Alexander said that he thought it was electricity board men working on the overhead wires.

Mayne lived for a short while, though he was dead by the time Alexander left for work at 6.40 a.m. He saw that the Electricity Board vehicle was still there. When he approached, Alexander realised his initial error and he then saw a man lying on the front seat. Dr William Glover examined the body of Blair Mayne in Ards hospital and estimated that death had occurred one to four hours previously.

Mayne was laid to rest at Movilla Cemetery in Newtownards on 16 December.

The cortège was more than a mile long, a procession of mourners that reflected the accomplishments of Mayne over the course of his forty years. Dozens of his former rugby teammates from Ards, Ireland and the British Lions attended, including Sam Walker, who had captained the Lions to South Africa in 1938, a tour in which Mayne distinguished himself as one of the finest players of his generation.

There were numerous luminaries from the legal profession, including officials of the High Court, Mr Justice Shield, Mr Thomas King, president of the Incorporated Law Society Northern Ireland, and employees of G. L. MacLaine & Co., the solicitors where Mayne had begun his legal career in the summer of 1939.

The mayor of Newtownards was in attendance; so, too, representatives from the Queen's University Services Club and Queen's University Officer Training Corps, the borough council and the church.

Of military men there were many. From brigadiers to privates, they took their place in the procession to pay their respects to a warrior of peerless courage. Col Brian Franks represented the 2nd Special Air Service Regiment, and Sgt Maj Bob Bennett, who had gone into battle alongside Mayne on numerous occasions, represented the 1st SAS Regiment. Col Ian Lapraik, who had served in the Special Boat Squadron (SBS) in the war, attended on behalf of the 21st SAS (Territorial) Regiment, and Maj Stewart Macbeth, another SBS officer of note, was also present.

The Reverend Fraser McLuskey, MC, padre to the SAS in 1944, conducted the service at the graveside. Four years earlier McLuskey had published his wartime memoirs, devoting a chapter to 'Paddy' Mayne, his hero, a cultured and compassionate man who 'possessed more than his fair share of the wit and charm that come from Ireland'.[3]

Many of the men who had served in the SAS were absent. Some had not the means to afford the passage from Britain, and others hadn't been able to arrange time off work at such short notice. A number had scattered to the four winds in the decade after the war, emigrating to Australia, America, Canada and southern Africa. A few had rejoined the SAS and were fighting communist insurgents in Malaya.

David Stirling, the man credited with forming the SAS, had settled in Rhodesia shortly after the war. He returned to Britain frequently to raise funds for an initiative he had started in southern Africa, but his absence from the funeral of Mayne wasn't particularly noteworthy.

Nonetheless, it was curious that when *The Times* ran a tribute to Mayne in its edition of 24 December 1955, it was written by Col Brian Franks. Franks was a fine soldier, a brigade major in the Commandos before taking command of 2nd SAS in June 1944. Yet he didn't know Mayne that well. He hadn't witnessed his ferocity in battle or seen how in the early days Mayne had almost single-handedly saved the SAS from extinction. It was an elegant eulogy, all the same, which began:

> The death of Paddy Mayne has been a great shock to all those who knew him, both during and after the last war. Those who served under him came to regard him as indestructible, and it is a tragedy that he should meet his end in a motor car accident. The gift of leadership and his ability to inspire complete devotion and loyalty were his to an exceptional degree.

Franks had honoured Mayne in person, at his funeral, and in print. Yet from David Stirling there was silence. But what could he have said about a man he feared and envied in equal measure? Mayne was one of the few men who had seen through Stirling and recognised him for what he was.

But now that Mayne was dead, Stirling saw his opportunity. He would return from his self-imposed exile and stake his claim to be the father of British special forces. He had the connections and the cunning. Within weeks of Mayne's death Stirling contacted the socialite author Virginia Cowles with a proposal for a book. It would be called 'The Phantom Major' and it would transform Stirling into a dashing guerrilla legend and Mayne into a dark, intemperate Irishman.

PART I

1

Contrary to received opinion,[1] Archibald David Stirling was not born at the family's ancestral home of Keir House in the beautiful Perthshire countryside. Instead, 'The Hon Mrs Stirling of Keir gave birth to a son on Monday November 15 1915, at 15 Cambridge Square, London,' announced the *Scotsman* newspaper on 20 November.

Archibald David was named after his father, although from an early age he was called just David. He was the fourth child delivered to the Stirlings, and the third boy. His mother Margaret had no birthing ritual. Her eldest child, William, or Bill, as he was known to his friends and family, who had inherited his paternal grandfather's name, was born in Grosvenor Gardens, London, in May 1911, and a brother, Peter, followed in February 1913. Peter was delivered at Keir House and Margaret, who arrived on 4 July 1914, at Cawder House, the Stirlings' summer retreat in Lanarkshire.

After David, two more children followed, both born in London: Hugh, in May 1917, and the last of the brood, Irene, in March 1919.

David's father was overseas when his son was born. Brig Gen Archibald Stirling had commanded the 1st Lovat Scouts Yeomanry in the latter part of the Gallipoli campaign in 1915 and in February 1916 the Scouts were amalgamated with several other yeomanry regiments to form the

2nd Dismounted (Yeomanry) Brigade, part of the Western Frontier Force under the command of the Egyptian Expeditionary Force.

Archibald Stirling remained with the Frontier Force for only a short time. He was approaching fifty, and was sick and worn out. This had been his third war and he was feeling his age. Nonetheless he returned in the summer of 1916 a hero, learning shortly after his arrival at Keir that he had been Mentioned in Despatches for a second time.

Vivid reminders of the war greeted the brigadier upon his arrival. He and his wife had transformed Keir House into a hospital for wounded officers and men in the winter of 1914–15; the fervour with which Margaret went about the task may have been her way of coping with the grief of losing her brother Hugh, killed at Ypres in October 1914 fighting with the Scots Guards.

David Stirling's mother, Margaret Mary Fraser, known to her close friends as Peggy, was a force of nature, an alpha female, the embodiment of the Victorian values of duty, virtue and vigour. Her father, the 13th Lord Lovat, had been aide-de-camp to Queen Victoria when, in 1887, he died aged fifty-eight. Her mother remained a widow until her death fifty-one years later. Religion dominated Margaret's life. Two of her brothers were monks at Fort Augustus Abbey, and two of her sisters worked for the Catholic Church.

Mrs Stirling's self-assurance dazzled her children, particularly David, who in his own words held her 'in a respect which was tinged with awe'.[2] Furthermore, like many children in a large brood, he felt overlooked and undervalued by his parents, especially his mother. He craved her attention and her approval.

His mother was no dour zealot. A contemporary described her as 'immensely warm-hearted and sociable, alive to the arts … she carried her public work lightly with zest and a great sense of fun'.[3]

She came of age in the Edwardian era, *La Belle Époque*, that brief and gloriously carefree interlude before the War to End All Wars. An eye-catching woman, if not a beautiful one, Margaret had poise, elegance and a cool self-confidence. It was during this epoch that Margaret met Archibald Stirling.

Little is known of their courtship, other than their engagement was announced in January 1910. On the surface one might surmise it was a marriage of convenience; he was forty-two and in need of an heir, and she was in her twenty-ninth year and conscious that her child-bearing years wouldn't last for ever.

Contemporary newspaper reports of the wedding – which took place at the Lovats' ancestral home at Beaufort Castle in Scotland that April – were concerned more with the couple's lineage than with their love. In submitting the toast of the Stirling family, John Hurll declared: 'Another notable alliance has been made, this time with another historic house, that of the Frasers of Lovat, and I am sure that it is our fervent hope, that the union may be a long and happy one. The motto of the Stirlings is "Gang Forward", and it is our wish that they may continue to gang forward through the coming centuries as they have through the past.'[4]

To win the hand of Margaret, Archibald Stirling had converted to Catholicism. Neither he nor his father, Sir William Stirling-Maxwell, 9th Baronet, had been devout Protestants. Sir William's devotion was art. On graduating from Trinity College, Cambridge, in 1839, he had embarked on a Grand Tour. Spain entranced him and he used his wealth to amass the most noteworthy collection of Spanish art outside Spain. His collection included works by Goya, Murillo, Zurbarán and at least eight El Grecos.

Archibald Stirling, the younger son, lacked his father's intellect and charisma. He was a soldier and landowner, straightforward and a little dull. His wife provided the sparkle. She was a society hostess whose balls were the talk of the town; in June 1913 she arranged the eightsome reels for the Caledonian Ball at the Hotel Cecil in London's Strand, which included among the fifteen hundred guests the cream of Britain's aristocracy.

Margaret Stirling was a celebrity, a woman of refinement who rubbed shoulders with royalty. But to the constituents of Kinross and West Perthshire, what mattered most was her religion, and the fact she had converted her husband to Rome. When the brigadier-general contested the general election of December 1918, popularly known as the khaki election, as the Unionist candidate he suffered a shock defeat. The reason? As one correspondent wrote to the local paper, the *Strathearn Herald*, Stirling was a 'distinguished pervert' on account of his Catholicism.

The old soldier never fully recovered from the humiliation. His health slowly deteriorated throughout 1919 and that winter he suffered a severe bout of pleurisy. As part of his recuperation, he and his wife spent three months in Argentina, returning in April 1920 to learn that Margaret had been appointed an Officer of the Order of the British Empire for the valuable work she had accomplished during the war.

The noise that greeted the Stirlings as they walked through the front door of Keir must have been deafening: Bill was eight, Peter seven, Margaret six, David four, Hugh nearly three and Irene had recently celebrated her first birthday.

Bill was his mother's favourite. He was her first, of course, but already he was a strapping and accomplished young gentleman, bright and outgoing and adventurous, the apple of any mother's eye. Peter was also well rounded, a quick learner and a sociable boy, and he and his elder brother spent many afternoons racing each other around the estate. The worry for Mrs Stirling was David. He seemed a little overawed by his rumbustious brothers and preferred the company of Margaret. She was kinder and more sensitive; indeed, for nearly two years she had been David's interpreter.

For the first four years of his life David Stirling lived in a world of his own. His elder sister was his conduit to those on the outside. Try as he might, he was unable to articulate himself properly; the words he wanted to say remain trapped on his lips and only gibberish emerged. Margaret alone understood what he wanted, and interpreted his demands and desires to the rest of the family. David was four when doctors diagnosed a 'restricted tongue' – it was probably ankyloglossia, more commonly known as tongue-tie, a result of an abnormally short frenulum attaching the tongue to the floor of the mouth. The cure is simple – a frenotomy, the snipping of the frenulum – and once David had been treated he left his own world.

It took him a while to adjust to his new one. By his own admission, his inability to make himself understood had made him sulky and irritable; these traits remained, as did a vivid imagination and a strong independence.

Keir was an ideal home for such a boy. He could incorporate its extensive grounds into his fantasy world. Keir House was built on high ground looking out over the Carse of Lecropt, rising from land on which had once stood Arnhall Castle. A couple of miles north-west of Bridge of Allan and one and a half miles south-west of Dunblane, Keir had been in the Stirling family since the middle of the fifteenth century.

Sir William Stirling-Maxwell had brought an artistic touch to the remodelling of Keir between 1847 and his death in 1878. He expanded the gardens, constructing them around a centuries-old Spanish chestnut tree, and over time further steps, terraces and fountains in the grand style were added. He enlarged the estate's parklands and woodlands so that it became an idyll for a young boy where his imagination, and legs, could run wild.

If Keir wasn't adventure enough, the Stirlings spent summers with their cousins, the Lovats, in the village of Morar, a mile south of Mallaig in the north-west of Scotland. Keir and Morar provided physical and mental stimulation for David and his five siblings, and yet he alone appeared not to be thriving in this privileged upbringing. He was 'regarded as something of a problem child',[5] and his parents hoped that boarding school would straighten him out.

Ampleforth had been founded by Benedictine monks at the start of the nineteenth century but it was not until 1900 that it was officially constituted as a Catholic boarding school. Nine years later a theatre was built, but pupils had to wait until 1923 before Ampleforth installed electric lighting and central heating.

David arrived at the prep school the following year, following the path taken by Bill and Peter. The boys' father had been educated at Eton College, but their mother was insistent that her sons must be educated as Catholics. Much would have been expected of the third Stirling boy, given the manner in which his brothers had wholeheartedly embraced Ampleforth life.

Peter shone academically from the start, winning a literary prize, but he was also 'tried on a number of minor charges connected with railway travelling'.[6] The school magazine didn't elaborate on the charges, noting only that the accused was acquitted.

Bill, meanwhile, was settling into the senior school, securing the position of librarian and enlisting in the cadets. He was also a fanatic on the sports field; not a great one for team sports, he enjoyed athletics, contesting the high jump and half-mile in the school sports. Peter moved to the senior school at the start of the 1923–4 academic year, having won the prep-school French prize.

For a sensitive, insecure and diffident boy like David, the train journey from Scotland to Ampleforth must have been one of anxiety and foreboding. A bond was being severed; not the one with his parents, who had after all left him and his siblings in the care of nurses and governesses when they went to South America for three months in 1920, but his attachment to Keir.

Keir was his sanctuary. Its vast estate comforted and protected him; it had an abundance of nooks and crannies where a sulky and confused young child could seek refuge. The household staff were unfailingly kind and compliant, even obsequious. He had never experienced hostility. He was now on his way to an environment where not everyone would be so accommodating.

Douglas Brown, one of David's contemporaries at Ampleforth,

later recalled his first day at the school and how it left him with a 'feeling of a gloomy sanctum straight out of Dickens'.[7] On their arrival, Brown and his parents were welcomed by two monks: 'The shorter, stouter figure was Abbot Edmund Matthews who had recently been succeeded by the tall man with horn-rimmed spectacles, standing beside him as Headmaster, Fr Paul [Nevill],' he wrote.

Matthews and Nevill were responsible for the transformation of Ampleforth from a small boarding school into the 'Catholic Eton'. A pupil himself in the 1890s, Nevill was appointed headmaster in 1924, a position he held for thirty years. The school was already in the process of modernising and Nevill was asked to push through further reforms. He soon introduced the house system (there were four houses in 1926: St Cuthbert's, St Oswald's, St Bede's and St Aidan's); built new science buildings and refectories; improved the quality of the food; provided more extracurricular activities and recruited more lay staff. A nine-hole golf course was created by the senior boys in their spare time, a cinder running track was laid and a stop butt was built for the rifle range.

Also at Ampleforth at this time was the Stirlings' cousin, the Honourable Simon Fraser, the Master of Lovat. He described the school as 'avant-garde and unconventional', and although there was corporal punishment bullying was non-existent. Lovat attributed this to 'the self-reliance which characterized the school'.[8]

In Father Paul's long reign he saw many boys blossom into confident young men, among them Bill and Peter Stirling. In 1925 Bill was voted onto the hunt committee, won the Spanish prize and finished second in the under-sixteen mile race at sports day; in 1926 Bill was appointed master of hounds and passed his school certificate, gaining a 'with credit' in English, French and Spanish.

In his final year at Ampleforth, 1928–9, Bill was a school monitor – one of Father Paul's innovations – master of hounds, a member of the second XV rugby team, a keen runner, a prize winner in the fishing club and a member of the senior literary and debating society. In one debate he argued for the motion that 'while a Conservative government is in power, the prosperity of the British Empire is assured'. Though his team lost, the school magazine said that Bill 'could always be relied on to produce weighty, and usually lengthy, arguments. He is at his best when fighting a losing battle.'[9]

There were some pursuits that Bill concealed from the Ampleforth staff. He and Simon Fraser bought rabbits from a local poacher and the pair sometimes got into fights outside the school grounds. On one occasion they were set upon by some boys on the train between York and Edinburgh. Lovat had his cap thrown out of the window but Bill came to his cousin's rescue, flattening two of their assailants.

Peter also prospered. Like his elder brother, Peter was an enthusiastic runner and the pair clashed in the half-mile at the 1929 sports day, reprising all the times they had raced one another around the Keir estate. A boy called Hammon crossed the line first in two minutes and seventeen seconds, with Peter just pipping Bill to second. As a junior, Peter had set a new college record for the mile while also dominating the 440 yards and half-mile in his age group.

It was no great surprise that Peter was appointed head monitor in his last year at Ampleforth. It was a recognition of his outstanding contribution to college life. He was an astute captain of the second XV and, like Bill, a driving force on the hunt committee. Academically, he edged his brother, passing the school certificate 'with credits' in Latin, elementary mathematics, English, French and Spanish. Of Peter's oratory skills in the debating society, the school magazine said: 'Stirling spoke impressively without notes and stated the case for his party with seriousness and deep thought.'[10]

Bill continued the family tradition of going up to Trinity College, Cambridge. Ampleforth kept a note of his progress, relaying in the school magazine of 1930 that Bill had 'made memorable his Mastership of the Trinity Foot Beagles by killing an unprecedented number of hares'.

Peter, the cleverest of the brothers, broke with tradition in going up to Magdalen College, Oxford, from where he sent the occasional despatch to the *Ampleforth Journal* informing them of his progress as he read Politics, Philosophy and Economics.

David Stirling left Ampleforth in 1934 after ten undistinguished years. Unlike his brothers, who boarded at St Cuthbert's, David was a member of St Oswald's. According to Douglas Brown, St Cuthbert's was the house for the rough-and-tumble types, those who adored country pursuits. Not surprisingly their house colour was green, whereas maroon denoted an Oswald's boy. 'The master of hounds and winner of the point-to-point was more often than not provided by Cuthbert's,' recalled Brown. 'Oswald's was a complete contrast. Maroon seemed just the right shade for their studious, artistic and musical talents.'[11]

The housemaster of St Oswald's was Father Stephen Marwood, or 'Steenie', as he was known to the boys. Father Paul described him as possessed of a 'a marvellous mixture of strength and uprightness', and Brown recalled that '"Steenie" had a warm outgoing personality who gave affection liberally and this was returned.'[12]

He nonetheless failed to bring David out of his shell. In his authorised biography, written six decades later, Stirling's schooldays were covered in a page and a bit, the chief reflection being that his favourite pastime was solitary hikes across the Yorkshire countryside imagining he was hunting wild animals. Despite the presence of his brothers David was homesick at Ampleforth; the long walks may have been an opportunity to release his unhappiness without the worry of his tears being spotted by taunting classmates.

In the prep school he played for the second XV rugby team and the second XI in cricket, alongside Miles Fitzalan-Howard, later the 17th Duke of Norfolk. But on starting the senior school in September 1927 his name vanished from the school magazine for two years. David claimed that he contracted typhoid in his early teens, which entailed a long recovery during which time he was taught at Keir by a private tutor.

In 1930 David joined the Officer Training Corps (OTC), of which Peter was a lance corporal in his final year at Ampleforth (Bill had attained the rank of sergeant). According to David, one of the OTC's under officers was Francis (Freddie) de Guingand, who as chief of staff to Gen Bernard Montgomery in the Second World War, gave Stirling invaluable assistance in raising the Special Air Service.

In fact, Freddie de Guingand had left Ampleforth more than a decade earlier and in 1930 was in Nyasaland with the King's African Rifles; the de Guingand who was a contemporary of Stirling's was Geoffrey; he was also in St Oswald's House and was a talented thespian.

David followed Bill and Peter into the debating society and successfully argued for the motion that 'women are taking too great a part in public life'. Meanwhile his younger brother, Hugh, was also now at Ampleforth and described by a contemporary as 'a boy of more than average intellectual attainments … he combined charm of manner and a nimbleness of wit and tongue with a humorous outlook on life that made him an agreeable and amusing companion.'[13]

Hugh, in other words, was as popular as Bill and Peter, a boy of many talents and one 'who thought for himself and was not afraid of questioning accepted conclusions until he had satisfied himself of their validity'.

A good pianist who performed Schubert's Ländler in the inter-house music competition, Hugh also impressed as an aspiring soldier, passing the examination for the Officer Training Corps at the same time as David (despite their eighteen-month age difference) and being promoted lance corporal. He also surpassed David academically, gaining credits in his School Certificate in English, history, geography, oral French and general science; David managed credits in history, geography and oral French. The high point of David's career at Ampleforth was when, in his last year, he was appointed master of beagles having previously served on the hunt committee. Subsequently, he claimed that his schooldays were marked by mischief and that he broke the rules with abandon, accepting stoically the six of the best he received as punishment for poaching and adventuring. In reality, the word that best describes David's schooldays is 'anonymous'. He seems to have left little imprint on Ampleforth or on his peers, in stark contrast to his brothers.

His mother must have felt a sense of disappointment that Ampleforth had failed to achieve with David what it had done with Bill, Peter and Hugh and instilled a sense of purpose and responsibility into his character. David was sybaritic, a dreamer, but also prone to bouts of depression, incapable of devoting himself to a cause or task. For Mrs Stirling, David remained a great source of worry, but now she no longer had the wise counsel of her husband to call on.

2

The 1920s was the decade of flappers, jazz, 'talkies' and the Charleston; to the Americans the years were 'roaring' and to the French the '*années folles*'. To Brig-Gen Archibald Stirling they were years of cruel decline.

Archibald Stirling was a Victorian and the mores of the Britain that rose from the ruins of the Great War baffled him; Keir became his fortress against the outside world, where he could roam the gardens and woodland taking comfort in the reliability of nature. He limited his public engagements and didn't enjoy publicity. In 1926 the Stirlings hosted Prime Minister Stanley Baldwin and his wife at Keir during their brief visit to the region; the appearance of the PM caused a flurry of excitement in the local press, and the society magazine *Tatler* published a photograph of Mr Baldwin and his wife chatting to Mrs Stirling in the grounds of the house, but of the brigadier there was no sign.

As the decade wore on his health deteriorated; his wife, on the other hand, was rarely out of the newspapers as she organised fêtes, whist drives and balls. Anyone who considered themselves anyone in Scotland wanted a ticket to Mrs Stirling's Gleneagles Ball; it was the perfect way to bring down the curtain on the season, in the opulent splendour of the Gleneagles Hotel in September.

In 1929 – the year he left Ampleforth – Bill Stirling attended the Gleneagles Ball along with his cousin the Honourable Simon Fraser, two eligible young bachelors whose photographs appeared in *Tatler* a week later.

In November 1929 Bill was appointed second lieutenant in the Lovat Scouts, the territorial unit to which his father had belonged twenty years earlier, and two months later he went up to Trinity College, Cambridge, to read for the Historical Tripos.

On his infrequent returns to Keir his father was always a little weaker, and the end came in February 1931 when the brigadier-general died in an Edinburgh nursing home. Among the telegrams of condolence was one from His Majesty King George V and Queen Mary.

Bill's father left £9 million in his will, most of which went to him now he was laird of Keir. Because of his new duties as laird, Bill was absent for much of the Easter term of 1932 when examinations for Part II of the Tripos took place. He was 'allowed' the term in the vernacular of the university, however, and graduated *in absentia* in June.

By then he was undergoing officer training at the Royal Military Academy, Sandhurst, together with Simon Fraser. The pair were commissioned in the Scots Guards in September and five months later Fraser became the 15th Lord Lovat on the death of his father. In the years that followed Bill juggled his army career with his responsibilities at Keir. It was a demanding life, one that rarely allowed him the chance to enjoy some time to himself, or acquire a wife.

He hosted shooting parties on the estate, attended local bazaars, presided over the Dunblane Agricultural Show and in May 1935, to mark the King's Silver Jubilee, he and his mother put on a lavish spread for four hundred underprivileged children. Before lighting the bonfire, Bill gave a short address 'on the liberties enjoyed in this country' and then presented each child with two jubilee pennies and a commemorative mug.

In January 1936 Bill resigned his commission in the Scots Guards, having reached the conclusion that he could no longer perform both roles adequately. He did so reluctantly but with no deep regret, and was put on the Reserve of Officers. As laird, Bill was concerned with the welfare of his employees and his tenants; as the eldest of six fatherless siblings, he also had to look out for his brothers and sisters. Peter was fine. He was preparing for the exams to enter the diplomatic service and none of the family had any doubt he would pass with flying colours; Hugh was still at Cambridge, but had already decided to follow family tradition and join the Scots Guards. Margaret was enjoying the life of a single girl, and at the Coronation Ball in May 1937 she would be one of several 'Mayfair beauties' to parade before King George VI and Queen Elizabeth at the Albert Hall. Irene was in her last year of school and would be presented to the King and Queen at Holyrood House in the summer of 1937.

The problem was David.

David left Ampleforth in April 1934 aged eighteen and a half, the same month that his mother arrived in London with her elder daughter. Mrs Stirling had taken house in the capital for the season, and she was hosting a dance for Margaret in a Mayfair ballroom with May Day as the theme. The guest list of five hundred was a *Who's Who* of high society: the Duke and Duchess of Norfolk, the Duchess of Rutland, the Marchioness of Salisbury, Countess of Dalhousie, Viscount Fincastle, the 15th Lord Lovat – the list went on.

None of Mrs Stirling's boys were present. Bill was with the army, Peter at Oxford and Hugh at Ampleforth. David must have had an excuse not to attend; in truth he had never cared for the balls that so enraptured his mother. He was neither good at dancing nor enjoyed it. But of course the dancing was secondary to the main purpose of a society ball: to be married off. The pressure was intense, particularly with a mother as well connected as his. David later told his biographer that he found coquetry intolerable and would flee the moment he found himself the target of any woman on the hunt for a husband.

He even managed to avoid the Gleneagles Ball on 3 October. Margaret, Bill and Peter were there (Hugh and Irene were too young) but David once more had eluded the clutches of any predatory female.

In January 1935 David went up to Cambridge to study for a Certificate of Proficiency in Architecture; there were no predatory females at Trinity, but plenty of predatory males, sexually and ideologically. One of the most notorious was Anthony Blunt. He had become a Fellow of Trinity College in 1932 and it's believed he was recruited by the Soviet intelligence service at the end of the following year, or in early 1934. He subsequently groomed one of his undergraduates, John Cairncross, to become the fifth member of the Cambridge spy ring.

Blunt and David Stirling had some mutual acquaintances – Blunt's mother was the second cousin of the Earl of Strathmore, who with his wife, the Countess, attended some of Mrs Stirling's balls – and as an art historian Blunt would have known of some of the works hanging at Keir.*

There is no evidence, however, that Stirling and Blunt formed any sort of relationship at Cambridge.

In his authorised biography, David Stirling devoted little space to his brief period at Cambridge. Like Ampleforth, it was not an edifying experience. He recalled that most of his time at Trinity was spent at parties or the nearby racecourse at Newmarket, where he usually lost more than he won. He claimed he was sent down after racking up twenty-three misdemeanours. His tutor enumerated his offences and 'invited' Stirling to choose three on which to be sent down. Stirling told his biographer he couldn't remember the three he selected.

* In the October 1939 *Journal of the Warburg and Courtauld Institutes*, Anthony Blunt wrote an essay on 'El Greco's "Dream of Philip II": An Allegory of the Holy League', in which he mentioned the Stirling collection and he thanked Mrs Stirling for access to her husband's correspondence on the subject.

On the train back to Keir Stirling decided that he would become an artist. He went to Paris and for a year and a half lived the life of a bohemian on the Left Bank, complete with beret. But his paintings were bland and his tutor advised him to look for alternative form of self-expression. He returned to Cambridge, who must have believed he was now a reformed character, but instead of studying he again spent most of his time at Newmarket, or in White's, the private club in St James's. After a year back at Trinity he quit.

That was Stirling's version. According to the college records, however, he was resident for three terms, Lent (January to March) and Michaelmas (October to December) 1935, and Lent 1936. He had been 'allowed' Michaelmas 1934 and Easter (April to June) 1935, though no reason for his absence was recorded. He sat no university examinations and did not graduate.

When David's time at Trinity finally petered out in March 1936, he was twenty. School and university had failed to rouse him from his torpor, so perhaps it was time for him to be put to work. Mrs Stirling and Bill contacted Reginald Fairlie, an Edinburgh architect who had designed the new Catholic church at Dunblane that had been consecrated in December 1934 and was a result of the munificence of Mrs Stirling.

David was soon on his way to Edinburgh in the hope that some of what he had learned on his proficiency in architecture course at Cambridge could be put to good use. Where he lodged is unknown; Fairlie shared a house with James Smith Forbes, one of his former partners at James Smith Forbes architects. One of their neighbours was the flamboyant artist Francis Cadell, who lived alone save for his faithful manservant. Asked to list his recreations in *Who's Who*, Cadell limited himself to 'bed and billiards'.

Stirling arrived in Edinburgh with unrealistic expectations of what awaited him. He was a novice, and a lazy one at that, not to be entrusted with anything important. When Stirling realised he would have to start at the bottom and that there would be little scope for creativity, he quit.

On returning to Keir he was asked by his mother to accompany her on a tour of the grounds. Mrs Stirling gave her son the most 'shocking wigging'.[1] It was 1937, Bill was a respected laird of Keir, Peter had joined the diplomatic service, Hugh had been commissioned in the Scots Guards and what, she demanded to know, was David going to do with his life? She was no doubt worried that David was, in the words of the former Prime Minister David Lloyd George, the embodiment of a generation that was 'soft, slack and self-indulgent'.[2]

The army might make a man of him, if only the supplementary reserve of officers. The *London Gazette* of 23 July 1937 announced that the Scots Guards had a new recruit: 'Archibald David Stirling (late Cadet Lce.-Corpl., Ampleforth Coll. Contgt., O.T.C.), to be 2nd Lt.'

He undertook some military training that summer, but in the winter he was off again, heading to Switzerland, where he climbed a few peaks and enjoyed the freedom of being plain David Stirling rather than the errant son of the Honourable Mrs Stirling, OBE.

When he reappeared at Keir in 1938, as feckless and aimless as ever, drastic action was required. Bill had recently returned from a working holiday in the USA, Mexico, Cuba, Guatemala, El Salvador and Venezuela with Lord Lovat. They had been exploring business opportunities in Latin America but had also paid a visit to El Paso, where a family friend owned a ranch.

Charles William Urmston – Bill to his friends and family – was the son of Augustus Brabazon Urmston, an acquaintance of Brig-Gen Stirling. The Urmstons were from Doune, four miles west of Keir, and Augustus had immigrated to Mexico in 1890 after five years of service in the Gordon Highlanders. Within six years he owned more than two hundred thousand acres in the state of Chihuahua, which he called the Hacienda de San Pedro, and Bill Urmston inherited the ranch on the death of his father in 1931.

Bill Stirling and Bill Urmston had been contemporaries at Cambridge, and the former asked his friend for a favour: would he hire David as a ranch hand? Work him as hard as you like; the harder the better, for he needs knocking into shape.

It was agreed that David would spend a year on the ranch. He was happy with the arrangement. He had outgrown Keir, and Scotland. It was too small-town. As a young boy Keir had protected him; now it suffocated him. He was oppressed, too, by his mother. He could sense he was a disappointment to her, and that in comparison to his three brothers he was, in the parlance of the day, a 'lounge lizard'. The opportunity to reinvent himself thousands of miles away appealed to David.

There was, however, one last duty before he unfettered himself from Keir: tea with Queen Mary. To great excitement, King George VI's mother visited Stirling Castle in September 1938 and then paid a visit to Keir at the invitation of her old friend, the Hon Mrs Stirling. 'Hundreds of people lined the road between Stirling and Bridge of Allan, and others congregated at the south entrance of Keir to await the Royal party,' reported the *Strathearn Herald* on 17 September 1938. 'Her Majesty was welcomed by the youthful Mr William Stirling, and his mother … there were also present Miss Margaret Stirling, Miss Irene Stirling, Mr Hugh Stirling, Mr Peter Stirling, and Mr David Stirling.'

Among the entourage of Queen Mary were the King and Queen of Bulgaria, the Earl and Countess of Athlone, Lady Cynthia Colville and the Honourable Sir Gerald Chichester, the Queen's Private Secretary.

Tea was served and afterwards the Queen was given a tour of the house and the grounds. She found Keir charming and 'showed great interest in some of the artistic treasures of the house, particularly the Stuart paintings'.

David sailed from Glasgow on the evening of 11 November on board the SS *Cameronia*, a large ocean liner belonging to the Anchor Line. On arrival at Ellis Island nine days later he was required to complete the standard immigration form. He was aged twenty-two, 6ft 4½in tall, eyes and hair both brown. He had been born in London and his last residence was Dunblane, where lived his next of kin, the Honourable Mrs Stirling.

In the column marked occupation he wrote 'nil' and asked his race or people he submitted 'English', in contrast to most of his fellow passengers who stated they were Scottish. His final destination was El Paso, Mexico, but his temporary residence was the Pierre Hotel in New York City.

David wasn't the only one of the Stirling clan to be despatched overseas. Drawing on more of her family connections, Mrs Stirling packed off Irene, now eighteen, to Japan to broaden her horizons. While in Tokyo she was the house guest of the Morlands; Oscar Morland was in the diplomatic service and his wife, Alice, was Mrs Stirling's niece, a woman famous for being 'the youngest hostess who ever entertained Royalty'.[3] The *Tatler* gossip columnist stifled a smirk as he penned his 'And the World said ...' column for the 14 December issue. 'Mrs Stirling of Keir has speeded three of her six children,' he wrote. 'David to Mexico where he is working on "Bill" Urmston's ranch; Irene to Japan, where she will stay with the Oscar Morlands [...] and Hugh to Egypt with the 1st Battalion Scots Guards. Conversely, the Lovats are settling down to their duties with a good grace.'

One wonders how the elegant putdown was received at Keir. Not well. Perhaps Mrs Stirling took one of her long walks around the gardens to let off steam.

She would have been even more infuriated had she known that David had yet to set a foot in a stirrup and was still ensconced at the Pierre, a luxury forty-one-storey hotel of cream-coloured brick on the corner of Fifth Avenue and Sixty-first Street.

But David couldn't hide his whereabouts for long; he required money from his mother, which he received, along with a telegram informing him Margaret was on her way to New York to straighten out her errant brother. David had tried to excuse his extended stay in New York on the grounds of illness, but his mother was not fooled. She could imagine what *Tatler* might write if they got wind of her son's idleness.

Mrs Stirling's manoeuvre worked. So frightened was David of his mother, even when she was venting her fury through an emissary, that he checked out of the Pierre and rode the railroad west. He subsequently sent his sister a letter in which he said he hoped she understood why he had fled New York the moment she arrived.

He was suffering now, however, as his brother and mother had intended. It was a tough life in the saddle, and camping in a tent was no fun because of the cold nights.

David told his sister that he was about to embark on a cattle drive to a ranch seventy miles away. He had then to ride to Bella Coola, on the west coast of Canada, a distance he estimated to be about 215 miles. From there he would help drive fifty horses from their winter pasture to the home ranch in El Paso.

It must have been early spring when David wrote to his sister, and life on the prairie got easier as the summer arrived. He was a wrangler, working alongside men who didn't care for titles or money, but judged a man by how tough he was in the saddle and in the mind. David prospered. He was physically brave, and he enjoyed the sensation of being plain David and not a Stirling, the son of the Honourable Mrs Stirling. He also discovered for the first time that he had a power over people; he could bend them to his will, not by force but by charm. No matter if it was insincere flattery; it worked. He had the gift of making people feel so important they would do whatever he asked, regardless of the validity of his request. His technique was simple: stooping to their eye level, he flashed his diffident smile and in his quiet, cultured voice enquired with hesitant courtesy if they wouldn't mind awfully helping him out.

David was in Montana, driving the horses towards the ranch in El Paso, when he learned that Britain and Germany were at war.

He telegraphed Keir and was ordered to return home by his mother. He wasted no time. He secured a cabin-class passage on the luxury liner SS *Manhattan* from New York to Southampton, arriving in England on 16 September 1939. There were forms to fill before disembarkation. This time, in the column marked occupation he proudly wrote 'rancher', and as an address he gave 'Dumbland, Scotland'. He had returned home with his hatred of Keir and Dunblane still burning.

3

Only ten months separated Blair Mayne and David Stirling in age but in youthful accomplishments the difference was so great as to be embarrassing. Stirling, the younger of the pair, was a quitter, a 'lounge lizard', one who on entering the United States of America in 1938 had listed his occupation as 'nil'.

Blair Mayne had also voyaged overseas in 1938, to South Africa as a member of the British and Irish Lions rugby squad. His selection for the tour was the climax to an outstanding sporting career that had started in earnest a decade earlier when he enrolled at Regent House grammar school in Newtownards. Mayne was made for sport; from an early age he showed exceptional hand-eye coordination. He also had balance, rhythm and reflexes so swift he seemed always to be a half-step ahead of his opponent, whatever the sport. At school he played cricket and rugby, and in his spare time enjoyed golf and swimming. He also shot, rode and fished.

Mayne possessed a physique that was as powerful as it was agile, and in adolescence he grew upward and outward. But what distinguished Mayne from his peers was his temperament. Physique alone doesn't make a great athlete; without a strong mind a strong body is useless. Some sportsmen thrive only as part of a team, finding courage in camaraderie, but Mayne excelled in individual sports as well as team ones. He had the self-discipline and iron determination to train on his own, in all weathers, pushing himself to the limits of his mental and physical endurance. He coped with the pressure of competition, thinking with clarity and processing information with such speed it appeared he knew what his opponent was going to do before they did.

When he was only seventeen Mayne was playing senior rugby for his local club, Ards, and by the time he was nineteen he was captain, issuing instructions to teammates ten years his senior. He led by example more than by words. He never bawled at his teammates; he cajoled and encouraged.

Mayne was appointed captain of the Ards cricket team for the 1934 season but that September he embarked upon a new challenge as an undergraduate at Queen's University in Belfast. He played another season of rugby at Ards before deciding to focus on university sport.

Ards's loss was Queen's gain, and in November 1935 Mayne played in the second row of the Queen's side that beat University College Dublin 11–3. That same week he was among thirteen candidates who stood for election to the Students' Representative Council; Mayne was one of eight chosen to sit on the council.

There were barely enough hours in the day: as well as studying for a law degree, playing for the rugby team, sitting on the students' council and drilling with the Officer Training Corps, Mayne also won the heavyweight division of the Irish junior inter-university boxing championships in Dublin, beating an opponent from University College Dublin in the final in February 1936. That victory secured him a place in the British universities' championships in London. He reached the final but lost on points to a boxer called Luntz from Liverpool University.

So Mayne was human after all. But he was soon in the ascendant once more, in October 1936 earning a place in the North of Ireland

XV against a West of Ireland XV in Galway, an indication that he was being considered for the national rugby team. In announcing Mayne's selection, a local paper described the 6ft 2in and 15 stone Mayne as 'a big, solid forward who learned the game in Regent House'.[1]

Mayne won his first cap for Ireland in April 1937, playing in the second row against Wales in Belfast, a match the hosts lost but one in which the debutant 'showed up well', according to one newspaper report.[2] The following season he played against England and Wales, and impressed enough to earn a place among the twenty-nine players selected to tour South Africa with the British and Irish Lions in the summer of 1938. Two of his fellow tourists were Queen's men, Harry McKibbin and George Cromey, and the Ulster prop Sammy Walker was captain.

Mayne and the seven other Irish Lions were given a 'cordial send-off' when they sailed for England on 18 May on the first leg of their voyage to South Africa.[3] It would be four and a half months before they returned.

When Mayne did come home it was with the reputation as the pre-eminent player of the tour. The Lions had lost the series two Test matches to one, but they acquitted themselves creditably against a South Africa side that in 1937 had gone to New Zealand and beaten the All Blacks on their own soil. In total, the tourists had played twenty-four matches and Mayne had featured in all but four. The hard grounds and fast pace had been too much for most of his teammates, who kept the physiotherapist busy throughout with a succession of injuries. Mayne alone of the forwards had remained free from injury. He hadn't just been durable; he had been consistently at the top of his game. Some of the tourists had been found wanting, mentally and physically, against the relentless aggression of their opponents. Not Mayne. The more ferocious the match, the better he played. 'Prominent', 'outstanding', 'magnificent' and 'best in the pack' were among the descriptions bestowed by the British and Irish newspapers on Mayne's performances. One South African paper went so far as to suggest he 'was the equal of any British forward ever seen in the Union'.[4]

The physical confrontation stimulated Mayne, as did the company of his fellow tourists. He had enjoyed a comfortable middle-class upbringing and although sport had broadened his social horizons, as had, to an extent, university, in South Africa he was living cheek by jowl with men from a diverse range of backgrounds.

His particular friend was the Welsh hooker, Bill 'Bunner' Travers, a coal trimmer from Newport who shared Mayne's love of combat. They were also united by their distaste for the stuffy formality that accompanied any major overseas rugby tour, where local dignitaries, swollen with self-importance, hosted interminable receptions. At one such function in Durban, Mayne and Travers slipped out of the country club and went drinking in establishments in which they felt more at home, among the city's working men.

Vivian Jenkins, the Lions' vice-captain, described Mayne as 'immensely popular' with his teammates. Jenkins also said, 'He was a very quiet chap. He was a bit of a loner in one way … at first glance you would think he wouldn't hurt a fly, but we soon discovered that when he got steamed up, he would do anything.'[5]

There were two things that got Mayne steamed up: alcohol and injustice. He had an acute sense of right and wrong, and reacted badly, and often violently, if he judged something was blatantly unfair. When the tourists arrived at their hotel in Pietermaritzburg in Natal they were unimpressed with their accommodation. The rooms were small and cramped, and their chagrin intensified when they discovered that the best rooms had been reserved for the Natal Rugby Union's officials and their wives, evidently intent on turning the midweek match into a mini holiday. 'Blair wasn't happy,' recalled Jenkins. 'So he decided to stage a one-man protest.'

Mayne smashed up everything in his room. The bed, the wardrobe, the chest of drawers and the bedside table. 'He broke the whole bloody lot and then piled it in a heap in the middle,' said Jenkins, who could hear the destruction from his room. 'I might have been vice-captain of the tour, but I kept very quiet because there was no way I was getting involved.'

The return to the mundanity of everyday life must have been hard for all the tourists after nearly five months away. They had visited vineyards, safari parks and swum in the Indian Ocean; they'd been wined and dined from Rhodesia to Cape Town, met some delightful young women, and now it was back to the nine to five.

For Mayne, that entailed practising with the Belfast solicitors G. L. MacLaine & Co., advising clients on matters relating to their cases or making the odd appearance in court as a witness to the signing of a contested will.

Rugby remained his outlet, his means of escaping the humdrum office life of the young solicitor. The physical challenge excited him, and there was nothing comparable to the adrenalin rush of running onto a pitch to the roar of thousands of voices. In South Africa thirty-six thousand spectators had watched the first Test match at Ellis Park, Johannesburg, and in February 1939 a capacity crowd of forty-three thousand saw Ireland beat England at Twickenham. Among the spectators was a correspondent for *Tatler*, the society magazine that a couple of months earlier had sniggered at the indolence of David Stirling.

There was nothing inert about the Ireland performance, they wrote, which was 'due almost entirely to a forward display of the real old-fashioned type'. The victory was Ireland's first at Twickenham since 1931 and while the correspondent thought it invidious to single out individuals, 'J. W. S. Irwin was a splendid leader, and was wonderfully supported by R. B. Mayne'.

The *Belfast Telegraph* agreed. Mayne had been superb, and he and David O'Loughlin were 'two giants for work' in a team performance the paper described as 'guerrilla-like rugby'.

On 28 March Mayne's name once more appeared in print, but this time in the *London Gazette* announcing his commission in the reserve of the Royal Regiment of Artillery:

> 8th A.A. Regt.—Robert Blair MAYNE (late Officer Cadet, Queen's Univ. Belfast Contgt, O.T.C.) to be 2nd Lt. 27th Mar. 1939, with regtl. seniority 6th Mar. 1939.

At first life continued as normal. On Monday 3 April 1939 the Lions reunited for a match at Ravenhill against an invitational XV, a chance for Belfast fans to get a glimpse of the players who had performed so respectably in South Africa. It was a thumping victory for the Lions, but a good-natured one, and Mayne provided the denouement when, 'amid uproarious merriment', he kicked the final conversion between the posts 'at the second attempt and with much difficulty'.[6]

There was a sinister stillness to the summer of 1939. Twenty-five years earlier, flaming June had been a month of parties and picnics in Britain and the terrible storm that broke in August caught the continent unawares. In 1939, life went on but few people made long-term plans.

On 28 June Mayne was introduced as a new solicitor to Judge John McGonigal at a sitting of the Belfast Quarter Sessions. Informed that Mayne had served his apprenticeship with Mr. T. C. G. Macintosh of Newtownards, before joining MacLaine & Co., the judge replied that he 'knew Mr Macintosh very well, and he was sure that Mr Mayne would do both firms every credit'.[7]

Nine weeks later Britain declared war on Germany, but as autumn became winter the conflict was dubbed 'phoney'. For Mayne, the only combat was on the rugby field, representing assorted army teams whenever invited. On 16 December he was selected to play for a combined Scotland/Ireland XV against an England/Wales team in a services international at the Richmond Athletic Ground in Surrey, with all gate receipts from the five-thousand-strong crowd going to the Red Cross. Mayne was on the losing side, but it was an occasion when the result was irrelevant.

PART II

4

The ideal role for David Stirling upon his return to Britain in September 1939 would have been a desk job in the Ministry of Information. As the government began plotting a strategy of national propaganda to boost morale on the home front and influence opinion abroad, a man of Stirling's fertile imagination would have been welcome. As it was, he travelled to the Guards training battalion at Pirbright in Surrey.

He had been there before, briefly in the summers of 1937 and 1938, having joined the supplementary reserve; but that was part-time soldiering in peacetime. Now the Guards were training for war. Stirling struggled from the start. At Ampleforth he had shown little aptitude for soldiering in the OTC, only ever attaining the rank of lance corporal. Too uncoordinated for the parade ground and too listless in the field, Stirling had little to recommend him to the Guards' training instructors.

The parade ground training was monotonous, but Stirling lacked the discipline to knuckle down and submit to the drudgery of drilling. According to his biography, he answered back to his drill sergeant and fell asleep in lectures because he was unafraid of authority. Part of this disdain for military discipline came from his character but Stirling also knew the weight that the family name carried. His mother was one of the best-connected women in Scotland; at some stage or another she had hosted every senior officer in the Scots Guards at one of her legendary balls. She was a friend to Queen Mary and Stanley Baldwin, and was an acquaintance of Queen Elizabeth. Stirling may not have liked his mother, but he was quite prepared to exploit her status for an easier life.

Another young Scots Guards officer at Pirbright was Willie Whitelaw,* who had the misfortune to be put under Stirling for instruction. It was not an edifying experience, he recalled: 'He would simply ignore the duties and go off to a party in London ... he was quite, quite, irresponsible.'[1]

Guardsmen shared that view. Archie Gibson grew up in Crieff, sixteen miles north of Keir, and joined the 2nd Battalion Scots Guards on the outbreak of war. A few weeks later he encountered Stirling when the battalion went on manoeuvres in Hampshire. 'I was detailed to go to the station and pick up a Guards officer,' he recalled. 'No one came off that train and no one came off the next train, and I thought this is rather a nice way of getting off manoeuvres so I'll wait for the third train.'[2]

Stirling stepped off that train, and Gibson winced when he saw the tall officer coming towards him. 'He was wearing his Guards checkered hat, service dress and Sam Browne belt, everything was wrong for manoeuvres.' Stirling climbed into the passenger seat and told Gibson to 'waken me up if anything exciting happens'. When they arrived at the site of the manoeuvres there wasn't a soul to be found. 'He slept for two hours,' said Gibson. 'It was just as well he missed manoeuvres because some higher-up officers would have bollocked him for turning up in the wrong gear.'

Stirling could always blame his lethargy on the state of the war. The initial excitement of early September slowly dissipated throughout the winter of 1939–40. The British Expeditionary Force in France

* Later Viscount Whitelaw, and Home Secretary in Margaret Thatcher's first government.

numbered more than 150,000 but had nothing to do other than dig ever deeper defensive positions on the eastern border. The Luftwaffe air raids that the British people had been warned by their government to expect never materialised and thousands of children who had been evacuated to the countryside in the first week of September returned to their cities. Only at sea was there any fighting. On land life was often more agreeable. 'I went hunting in borrowed clothes on a troop horse called Number Nine,' wrote Hermione Ranfurly in her diary on 20 November 1939.[3]

Born Hermione Llewellyn in 1913 to a wealthy father, who squandered his money gambling, and a mother who suffered from manic depression, Ranfurly's troubled upbringing had forged a character that was resilient and self-sufficient.

Her mother was an Elwes, some of whom were contemporaries of the Stirlings at Ampleforth, and her husband was Daniel, the 6th Earl of Ranfurly, an officer in the Sherwood Rangers Yeomanry whom she had married in January 1939.

Lady Ranfurly was staying at Brocklesby Hall in Lincolnshire, a large house whose twenty-seven thousand acres had been given over to the Sherwood Rangers Yeomanry for training. On 1 December she joined her husband and a group of his fellow officers on a hunt. When she returned to Brocklesby Hall she learned that Russia had invaded Finland.

What became known as the Winter War proved harder for the Russians to win than they had envisaged. The Finns were indeed brave, and their courageous resistance against the invader inspired Britain and France to offer assistance.

The French mobilised their Chasseurs Alpins with a view to sending them north to fight alongside the Finns, and Britain promised two divisions, including a battalion of soldiers with winter skills.

Designated the 5th (Special Reserve) Battalion Scots Guards, volunteers were chosen on their skiing ability and they began reporting for duty in January 1940 at Quebec Barracks in Bordon, Hampshire.

In command of the 'Snowballers', as the new unit was nicknamed, was Lt-Col Jimmy Coats, MC, Coldstream Guards, a famous bobsledder in the 1930s, while Maj Bryan Mayfield, Scots Guards, was appointed second-in-command.

Col Coats had instructions to have the battalion ready for active service by 1 March, so time was of the essence. The priority was to select the right personnel from the one thousand volunteers, who included civilians as well as soldiers, six hundred of whom were commissioned officers.

Coats and Mayfield interviewed them all and eventually appointed four company commanders and fifteen subalterns. Those not chosen had the choice of relinquishing their commissions and serving in the ranks, while continuing to receive their officer's pay. Among those who accepted this proposal was David Stirling, who enlisted on 25 February, and Andrew Maxwell, his cousin. Stirling was no expert on skis. The family had never skied in Scotland and so what experience he had would have consisted of the rudimentary skills he had learned from his time in Switzerland in the winter of 1937–8. That Stirling had scant experience of real winter conditions was evident in his letter to his sister while ranching in America, when he complained of the cold nights and snowstorms.

Most of the Snowballers, however, were inured to snow and ice. There were competitive skiers, Arctic explorers and renowned mountaineers. Freddie Spencer Chapman was the holder of the Polar Medal and a veteran of two explorations of Greenland, and Jim Gavin had been a member of the eight-strong 1936 Everest expedition.

The Snowballers embarked at Southampton on 2 March and landed in France the following day, taking the train onward to Chamonix in the Alps. Their training time in the Alps was brief and they were back in England just over a week later, hurriedly preparing to head to Finland where the Russians had launched a spring offensive. Before the

Snowballers could sail from Scotland the Winter War ended in defeat for Finland. 'We were all set to go when the Finnish Armistice came,' recalled George Jellicoe, one of the officers. 'It was an extremely lucky thing for us that there was that armistice, I think. Our bones would be bleaching on some sort of tundra very quickly. But it was a rather pleasant interlude, and I went from that straight away to our training battalion at Pirbright.'[4]

Stirling also returned to Pirbright, and, in his recollection, to White's, which had become a second home since his commission in the Scots Guards.

5

London was a city of liberation for David Stirling. He could lose himself in its anonymity, as well as its bars, clubs and nightspots. Physically and temperamentally, Stirling didn't have the feeling that he stood out in the capital. He could be himself.

He was also far removed from the influence of his family but, as he had demonstrated in New York in the winter of 1938–9, Stirling had neither the maturity or the self-discipline to stand on his own two feet. Left alone in a big city he invariably got up to mischief, like a child who has crept into the pantry. Mrs Stirling had sent Margaret to America to take David in hand; in London it would require the intervention of Bill to save David from himself.

After a brief foray into politics in November 1937, when he had unsuccessfully stood as the Progressive Party candidate in the Glasgow council elections (coming second to the incumbent Socialist Party in the left-wing stronghold of Provan), Bill had concentrated on business and his duties as laird of Keir.

Like his father, Bill was a popular master with the household and estate staff. He had his father's integrity and fairness, but was less patrician and more personable. He talked to his employees man to man, and not master to servant, as had been the way with the brigadier-general. His charm and humour were a maternal inheritance. His green fingers came from the paternal side. The Stirlings had always been enthusiastic horticulturalists and Bill was no different. In April 1939 he opened Keir's grounds to the public – at a cost of a shilling's entrance fee – as part of Scotland's Garden Scheme. Visitors had the opportunity to enjoy some of the most celebrated private gardens, with all proceeds going to the Queen' s Institute of District Nursing. The *Scotsman* newspaper visited Keir and congratulated Bill on 'his fine rock garden, shrubs, and walled garden'.

Unlike his father, Bill had an eye for a business opportunity, a quality he shared with his mother. Together they formed the Coal Company, and in April 1939 acquired Blackhill Colliery in Bishopbriggs, raising £7500 of capital by selling shares at £1 each.

The outbreak of war was an inconvenience for Bill, who as a reserve officer had been called up on 15 June 1939 and then released from duty on 15 July after a month's training at Windsor. With the grouse season under way, he rented land on Edinample Moors, twenty-five miles north of Keir. But on 1 September he was ordered to report for duty at Chelsea Barracks with the 1st Battalion Scots Guards. Six weeks later Bill joined the Scots Guards training battalion.

All the while he kept an eye on his business affairs. Early in 1940 Bill and his mother acquired another business, a quarrymaster and sand merchant in Renfrew, which they named the Houston Quarry Company Ltd. The capital was £500 in £1 shares, and this time there was a third director, Maj Bryan Mayfield.

Mayfield was a career soldier. He had been commissioned into the Scots Guards in 1918 aged nineteen and for the last three years he had been stationed in Palestine and North Africa. He was recently divorced so a business opportunity represented a new chapter in his life, and Bill was an old friend he knew he could trust from their time together in the Scots Guards.

When Bill and his mother made public the formation of the Houston Quarry Company Ltd, Mayfield was on his way to Chamonix with the Snowballers. Bill had been invited to join the battalion but he laughed off the idea; he had never skied in his life. But when presented with another invitation, again from Mayfield, he accepted.

Bill was asked if he would like to join an organisation called Military Intelligence Research, known as MI (R). In view of the internecine warfare that would bedevil British intelligence in the first two years of the war, it is worth examining the roots of MI (R) to better understand how this came to pass.

In 1909 the Secret Intelligence Service (SIS) was formed as a section of the Secret Service Bureau. In *The Special Operations Executive 1940–46*, M. R. D. Foot – himself a wartime intelligence officer – wrote of SIS, 'From 1921 it was under Foreign Office control,* though it also included sections from the navy, the army and the air force. Its job was to secure secrets from abroad. Founded in parallel with it, the security service (MI5) looked after preserving secrets at home, and came under the Home Office.'[1]

In 1938 three new sections were formed; one was concerned with propaganda and was known as Department EH, on account of its location in Electra House on London's Embankment. Another was Section D, headed by Maj Lawrence Grand. According to Foot, its *raison d'être* 'was to look into the theory of secret offensives: how could enemies be attacked, otherwise than by the usual military means?'

The third was known as GS (R), and initially comprised Maj Joe Holland and a typist. Holland was a decorated soldier from the Great War, who had been wounded in Ireland during the 1919–20 War of Independence. The guerrilla tactics of the Irish Republican Army (IRA) roused in Holland a deep fascination with irregular warfare, and by 1939 he was Britain's foremost expert in the field. M. R. D. Foot

* It is better known today as MI6.

recalled that he had collated reports on Boer tactics in the South Africa War of 1899–1902; T. E. Lawrence in the Great War; the Russian Revolution; the Spanish Civil War; the Sino-Japanese War; and the Arab–Jewish conflict in Palestine.

Described by Foot as 'a bald, burly, short-tempered, large-hearted man', Holland was a rarity in the conservative British military in being an unconventional theorist. Fortunately, in Frederick Beaumont-Nesbitt, the deputy director of military intelligence, Holland had a like-minded ally. In the spring of 1939 GS (R) was renamed MI (R), and Holland and Lawrence Grand began a close collaboration that ultimately resulted in the formation of the Special Operations Executive in July 1940. 'It was eventually formed by combining section D, MI (R) and EH,' wrote Foot, 'a combination approved by C [the head of SIS], by the Foreign Office, and by the army high command.'

In the interim, Holland moved into the main War Office building in Whitehall, and one of the men who joined MI (R) was Colin Gubbins, described as a 'small, slight, wiry Highlander'. Born in Japan in 1896, Gubbins was as independent and audacious in intellect as his chief. Together, Holland and Gubbins wrote two pamphlets, 'The Art of Guerrilla Warfare' and the 'Partisan Leaders' Handbook', and they then began to put into practice their theories. 'Holland spent the winter of 1939–40 starting up various parts of the secret war and finding the right men to take them over,' recalled Foot.[2] One of these 'parts' was Operation Knife.

On 9 April 1940 Germany invaded Norway, occupying the capital, Oslo, as well as Bergen, Trondheim and Narvik. There was spirited resistance from the Norwegians, however, assisted by an Allied expeditionary force, especially in western Norway where the cities of Bergen and Stavanger were of particular strategic importance. MI (R) hatched a plot to land a small party of men in Sognefjord, north of Bergen,* who would then work with the Norwegian resistance in sabotaging German railway communications.

Bryan Mayfield was chosen to lead the party, which consisted of Bill Stirling, Peter Kemp, Ralph Farrant, David Stacey and Jim Gavin. Mayfield and Gavin had been Snowballers, and the latter was a tough and experienced mountaineer, as well as a regular officer in the Royal Engineers and something of a demolitions expert. On coming down from Cambridge Kemp had felt compelled to go to Spain to fight in the civil war. Unlike most international volunteers, however, Kemp fought not for the Republicans but for the Nationalists. One of the few foreign officers in the elite Spanish Legion, his war ended in 1938 when shrapnel from a mortar round lacerated his face and hands.

Stacey had been a stockbroker before the war and was as inexperienced in clandestine warfare as Farrant – an artillery officer who had competed in the 1939 Fastnet yacht race – and Stirling.

What they did possess, however, was good breeding. 'England in the late 1930s and early 1940s was run, almost entirely, by an educated governing class drawn from headmasters' conference public schools,' reflected M. R. D. Foot. 'To know which school a man had been at was to know something about his probable competence and character.'[3]

Farrant had been to Rugby, Kemp to Wellington, Gavin to Uppingham and Stirling to Ampleforth. Furthermore, Kemp, Gavin and Stirling were Trinity men. David Stacey might have owed his place to Lawrence Grand, who, with the support of Sir Stewart Menzies, the new head of the SIS, tended to recruit his friends who worked in the City of London.

Kemp recalled that they were assembled in London in April 1940 and briefed on their mission. They would be transported to

* Some sources claim their destination was Hardangerfjord, thirty miles east of Bergen, but Peter Kemp stated in his 1958 memoirs that it was Sognefjord.

Norway by submarine and would have with them a substantial supply of explosives, grenades and weapons with which to equip the local resistance, who would be waiting to greet them at Sognefjord. Their initial task was to ski south to the Bergen-Oslo railway and sabotage it. Then they were to assess the German occupation of Norway and either organise local resistance or make their way to Sweden.

Kemp was promoted to captain, but he still considered himself the pup of the party. 'After me the most junior was Bill Stirling, at this time a captain in the Scots Guards,' he recalled. 'A man of six foot five and proportionately broad.'[4]

It had been four years since Bill had resigned his commission, and undoubtedly he owed his place on the party to the old-boy network. Nonetheless he had plenty of suitable traits: physically fit and temperamentally strong, he had power of command and 'was one of the best shots in the country'.[5] On the form he was required to complete on joining SOE, Bill listed his competency in driving a car or lorry, riding, swimming, mountaineering, shooting and running. But he answered 'no' when asked if he could ride a bike, ski or sail.

Once briefed on their mission, the six men of Operation Knife had a short audience with Joe Holland, who told them, 'I say, you know, it's frightfully nice of you chaps to go on this show.'

They caught the train from King's Cross to Edinburgh, and from there to the Rosyth naval base on the Firth of Forth. Their stores had gone before and were already stowed on HMS *Truant*, one of the new T-class submarines under the command of Lt-Cdr Christopher Hutchinson. 'At Rosyth these brave soldiers came on board,' he recalled. 'I say brave because they probably never volunteered to dive in a submarine to start with. Secondly, not perhaps in war, and thirdly, having got them to their landing place I was to forsake them, and leave them with such weapons as they had: plastic explosive, cheesewire for silencing sentries, ghastly-looking knives. I'd never seen such a bunch of cut-throats, but I must say, I did admire them.'[6]

Hutchinson observed that the seven men were all officers except one. When Hutchinson 'queried' the seventh man, he was told that he was Stirling's ghillie, Adam, brought on the mission by Bill as a condition of his participation. 'The ghillie was disguised as a corporal in the Lovat Scouts,' said Hutchinson.

Hutchinson had already acquired a reputation as an outstanding commander, having sunk and damaged two enemy vessels. However, months of constant patrolling had taken their toll and in a recent action HMS *Truant* had been hunted by three German torpedo boats, which between them dropped thirty-one depth charges at their prey, 'most of them unpleasantly close'. Consequently, Hutchinson could sleep only with 'fairly powerful drugs, drugs that I dare not take at sea'.

The *Truant* departed Rosyth at 5 p.m. on 24 April 1940 with the seven soldiers permitted to stay on deck until the submarine was clear of the estuary. Hutchinson then ordered them below and they turned in for the night. At 3.41 the next morning Mayfield and his men were talking to the commander in the ward room when two loud explosions shook the *Truant* as it sailed on the surface of the North Sea. Hutchinson made his way to the bridge, where the officer of the watch said he had seen 'a great red flash'. The bridge was cleared and the submarine dived. Hutchinson then began to assess the damage. 'One battery appeared to be in a very parlous state,' he recollected. 'Several cells were broken and chlorine gas was apparent. The forehatch had jumped open against its clips and shut again, and had let in quite a bit of water. What a mercy it did shut again. I was surprised it didn't fracture the clips.'

Hutchinson's initial assessment was a torpedo from an enemy submarine or torpedo boat, although the explosion was subsequently attributed to a mine. Whatever the cause, it was evident that the *Truant* was incapable of continuing to Norway. 'It was on my way back to Rosyth that I realised that my nerve had gone,' said Hutchinson.

He had discovered what his father's generation had learned: that men are like clothes, and no matter how tough they will eventually wear out. 'Courage is will power,' wrote Charles Wilson, a medical officer in the First World War, who in May 1940 was appointed Winston Churchill's personal physician. 'The story of how courage was spent in France [in the Great War] is a picture of sensitive men using up their will power under discouraging circumstances while one by one their moral props were knocked down. The call on the bank might be only the daily drain of the trenches, or it might be a sudden draft which threatened to close the account.'[7]

For Hutchinson, it may have been the sight of the forehatch that drained the last of his courage. It had been a lucky escape; on another day it might not have shut, and they would have foundered at night in the North Sea. Understanding that he was now a liability to his crew, Hutchinson exhibited impressive moral fortitude in signalling Rosyth that he was returning to base, 'and on arrival the commanding officer required a relief. So back we went and I could barely face any of my crew.'[8]

On arrival at Rosyth at 5.30 p.m. on 25 April Hutchinson was taken to hospital and he never returned to the *Truant*.*

The Admiralty promised Mayfield and his men that there would be a second attempt to transport them to Norway, but it might take a day or two to provide a replacement submarine. Rather than loiter on the Rosyth base, Bill invited his companions to Keir House to recuperate, where they were joined by Simon Fraser, 15th Lord Lovat, who had been taken on by Mayfield as 'an extra hand'.[9] Peter Kemp found the experience delightful. 'Exhilarated by the recollection of our recent escape and stimulated by the hope of another, more successful venture, we were yet able to relax enough to enjoy the

* Hutchinson recovered, and resumed his naval career, retiring a rear-admiral with a DSO and OBE in 1962.

superb hospitality which the Stirlings, undismayed by the imminent conversion of Keir into a hospital, lavished upon us,' he recalled.[10]

In fact, a wing of Keir had already been converted into a hospital, as it had a quarter of a century earlier. Age had not withered Mrs Stirling, now in her fifty-ninth year, and her patriotic fervour burned as brightly as ever. The previous March several Scottish newspapers had run stories about the house's conversion, including one in the *Dundee Courier* headlined 'Tommy's Hospital is Mansion', alongside which was a photograph of one of Keir's patients.

The appearance of Bill was a double cause for celebration for Mrs Stirling; not only was her firstborn back, but his timing couldn't have been better: the annual Scottish Gardens Scheme was upon them and his presence at Keir on Sunday 28 April would be greatly appreciated. Despite the dreary weather, reported the *Perthshire Advertiser*, 'those who visited the policies and gardens admired the beautiful spring flowers, the Alpine garden, rare Japanese shrubs, etc. ... The Hon Mrs Stirling gave personal welcome to many of the guests, while the young laird, Captain William J. Stirling, was also present prior to leaving the same evening to rejoin his regiment.'

But Bill wasn't rejoining his regiment; he was heading south to London. The previous day he and his comrades had been informed that there would be no second attempt to launch Operation Knife: the Norwegian campaign was unwinnable and Allied command had decided to withdraw troops from southern and central Norway. The news was a heavy blow to the men, but Bill alone was undeterred. His mind had been opened to the potential for irregular warfare; the reason he had insisted on taking his ghillie on Operation Knife was because Adam was an expert in fieldcraft, a man capable of moving swiftly and noiselessly across extreme terrain.

'It was thanks to Stirling's imagination and initiative that our partnership was not, in fact, immediately dissolved,' said Kemp. 'Accompanied by Mayfield he preceded us to London for conferences with Col Holland, the head of MI (R), and a number of influential friends of his own.'[11]

Bill arrived in London with the zeal of a convert. As he explained in his conferences, this war would be ample in opportunities for partisan warfare but at the moment the British approach was characteristically amateurish. He pointed to the fact that he had been obliged to take his ghillie to Norway because the rest of the party lacked fieldcraft experience. It was this and other skills that would make a good partisan, and not whether one had been to Eton or Oxford.

Bill presented a five-point charter:

(1) To command and train Independent Companies which had been operating in Norway.
(2) To train personnel for special missions.
(3) To instruct in Guerrilla warfare, demolitions, sabotage, secret micro-wave W/T communications.
(4) To conduct an experimental establishment in the security of a Protected Area.
(5) To rehearse and practise with security operations of the type undertaken by S.O.2.[12]

Holland, always one for innovation, saw immediately the good sense in Stirling's proposition, and forwarded it to the War Office with the recommendation that an irregular warfare training centre should be opened; he added that Stirling had suggested locating the centre in the north-west of Scotland, an area he knew well from family holidays. Mayfield was to be the director and Stirling his chief of staff.

Bill had in mind the area around Morar, topographically a smorgasbord for the student of irregular warfare. Within easy reach were the sea, beaches, a large freshwater loch, mountains and moorland. The land belonged to the Lovats but Simon Fraser readily agreed to its loan. He also suggested an HQ: Inverailort House, a large three-storey building of imposing brickwork that was currently unoccupied.

The house wasn't owned by the Lovats but by the Cameron-Heads, who signed it over to the army on 30 May and it was designated the Commando STC (Special Training Centre) Lochailort.

In the intervening period Bill, who was officially released from the Scots Guards for 'special duties' on 3 June, having received the go-ahead from Col Holland, had recruited a team of specialists for his training staff: he, Adam, Peter Kemp and Lord Lovat would teach students the art of fieldcraft, with the last the senior instructor. Lovat and Bill had fished, shot and hunted together since they were thirteen. They usually started the day by stalking roe bucks and then moved on to pigeon shooting. This was Bill's speciality, and he used a single-barrelled 16-bore Purdey to great effect. Lovat's weapon was a 20-bore double-barrelled and he believed himself superior to his cousin in bagging deer.

One time, Lovat had played a joke on his cousin by suggesting 'a trial by ordeal to decide the penetrating power of our respective weapons'.[13] Standing a hundred yards apart on a newly cut corn field, they took it in turns to fire at each other's backsides. After each shot, the pair advanced five yards. 'At fifty yards the salvos must have started to sting,' recalled Lovat. 'Past the halfway stage Bill started to rub his bottom.' What Stirling didn't know, until Lovat confessed years later, was that his adversary had taken the precaution to pad his bottom with a game bag before the firing commenced.

Other instructors at Lochailort included Ralph Farrant, and he called up an erstwhile comrade in the artillery, a Maj John Munn, whose forte was map-reading. Jim Gavin* did something similar, inviting a fellow Sapper officer, Mike Calvert, to join him at Lochailort as a demolitions instructor. Together they produced an 'Offensive Demolitions' handbook, which ran to forty-two pages and

* In 1941 Gavin was posted to Singapore where he established 101 Special Training Centre, from where graduated several men who proved magnificent guerrilla fighters, notably Ivan Lyon, who in 1943 led a canoe raid on Japanese shipping in Singapore that was one of the most audacious and successful commando attacks of the war.

was distributed to every student who attended the five-day explosive course. This was a mixture of lectures, practical demonstrations and exercises, such as pairing up and setting a dummy charge on a nearby stretch of railway line.

Calvert was another Snowballer, and a man as attuned to the potential of irregular warfare as Bill Stirling. In 1940 he had with the encouragement of Joe Holland written a paper for the War Office entitled 'The operations of small forces behind the enemy lines supplied and supported by air'.

Also recruited were Freddie Spencer Chapman and Capt Jimmy Scott, fellow Arctic explorers, who would help in the instruction of fieldcraft. Spencer Chapman, who would spend more than two years fighting a guerrilla war against the Japanese in Occupied Malaya, recalled how Stirling had come up with the idea 'to start a training centre for smash-and-grab raids on targets in enemy-occupied territory, a sideline which, after Dunkirk, seemed the only possible form of offensive warfare'.[14]

There was a sergeant-major appointed to the centre, remembered the actor David Niven, who returned from Hollywood to 'do his bit'. He was 'a huge man, brought by Bryan Mayfield and Bill Stirling from their parent regiment, the Scots Guards'.[15]

Kemp arrived at Inverailort House in the last week of May and judged it an austere location. The house, which was at the head of Lochailort on the south shore, was plain greystone and its colour matched the sky overhead. At the back of those was an imposing black cliff surmounted by a sinister wall of trees.

It surprised neither Kemp nor the rest of the instructors to learn that the rainfall in this corner of Scotland was the highest in the British Isles. The staff had a few days to get their bearings before the first intake of students arrived at the start of June. They were, wrote Kemp, 'twenty-five keen but puzzled subalterns, some of them volunteers, others arbitrarily despatched by their commanding officers. Among them was Stirling's brother, David.'[16]

6

Another popular myth about David Stirling was that he was one of the founders of the Special Training Centre at Lochailort, and a noted instructor in fieldcraft. He wasn't. He knew little about the art, having never shown much interest in shooting or stalking in the rare times he had lived at Keir in his adolescence. Lord Lovat remembered that his cousin had been a menace with a gun in his hand. 'He had a passion for pulling back hammers and stroking his trigger in the cold half-light, waiting for the geese to come over the sea wall,' said Lovat. 'Sometimes the pressures were the wrong way round and a premature explosion startled the Estuary. The gun was cocked when it should have been on safe, and loaded when believed empty.'[1]

David's skiing experience had been similarly limited but he had nonetheless contrived to use his charm and his contacts to wangle a place in the Snowballers battalion. There was no way he could hoodwink his big brother.

Bill had heard on the military grapevine that David and the Guards were not a good match. Since rejoining the regiment from the Snowballers, David had frittered away his time and his money in exclusive London clubs at the expense of his military reputation. Since 1 May, David had been with the Holding Battalion, stationed in the Tower of London. On 3 June, Bill took his brother under his wing, to the relief of the Scots Guards. Once he had completed the course at Lochailort, David was given a job as his brother's adjutant.

Another early recruit was Tommy Macpherson, a nineteen-year-old from Edinburgh, who thrived on the two-week course. 'There was a wide range of people and we got pretty good training, particularly night work and small patrol work,' he recalled.[2] As well as fieldcraft, navigating and seamanship, there were lessons in unarmed combat from William Fairbairn and Eric Sykes, two former Shanghai policemen. Fairbairn's instruction proved so popular that in 1942 he published a manual – *All In Fighting* – in which he wrote in the introduction, 'When dealing with an utterly ruthless enemy who has clearly expressed his intention of wiping this nation out of existence, there is no room for any scruple or compunction about the methods to be employed.'

An Olympic shooting gold medallist and graduate of Trinity College, Cyril Mackworth-Praed, had been hired by Bill to improve the recruits' shooting. '[Mackworth-Praed] had to be the finest shot I've ever seen,' said Macpherson. 'With a .303 standard bolt action, he could get three magazines off in a minute and they would all be on or beside the bullseye at 300 yards. He used his third finger on the trigger and he flicked he bolt which had an easy action, with his second finger after each shot. The speed of it was astonishing.'

Many failed to last the pace and Lord Lovat recalled that the drop-out rate of students was 30 per cent. But those who came through the ordeal were all the better for it. 'Several hundred junior leaders had survived the gruelling fortnight course, emerging fitter, more determined to succeed and with the self-confidence to do so,' reflected Lovat.[3]

Freddie Spencer Chapman was soon promoted assistant chief fieldcraft instructor to Lord Lovat. 'The fieldcraft training was based on the traditional lore of the Lovat Scouts,' he remembered. 'Plenty of practical map reading and direction finding, especially at night, stalking

– the enthusiasm of students being first aroused with deer stalking – long-range observation with the telescope, and a minute study of the technique of ambush assisted by lively demonstrations.'

Bill and Lord Lovat had quickly discerned that the standard army equipment was not adequate for their school, so, said Spencer Chapman, 'our patrols were given rubber footwear, the mountaineer's rucksack and light-weight tent, and the Polar explorer's concentrated rations'.[4]

Bill Smallman, an officer in No. 3 Commando, recalled practising amphibious landings on the nearby islands of Rum and Eigg, during his instruction at Lochailort. He described it as an excellent course, and he graduated 'ready to kill'.[5] An officer from No. 4 Commando, Bertram Boucher-Myers, said that after the Blitz started, students were sent down to London, to a bombed-out street in Battersea that had been commandeered for instruction in street-fighting.

The course concluded with a challenging forty-eight-hour march across rugged and difficult terrain around Lochs Beoraid and Morar. David Niven said that after weeks of 'running up and down the mountains of the Western Highlands, crawling up streams at night, and swimming in the loch with full equipment, I was unbearably fit'. He was also unbearably libidinous, and in desperate need of an assignation with a flaxen-haired Danish nymphomaniac he had met in London shortly before his posting to Lochailort. 'I spoke to Bill Stirling about my problem,' said Niven. 'And he, most understandingly, allowed me forty-eight hours' leave in London to rectify the situation.'[6]

In August 1940 Spencer Chapman left Lochailort to prepare for a posting to Australia to train troops in commando techniques. An instructor short, Bill Stirling asked David to start training students in fieldcraft while continuing to work as his adjutant. In September David was stopped by police in Dunblane for driving a private automobile without a licence. When the case was heard at the town's sheriff court on 2 October, Lt Stirling's defence was that 'he acted as an adjutant at a training centre, and regularly drove a military vehicle for which the ordinary licence was not required, and when he took out his own car he forgot about the licence'.[7] He was fined ten shillings.

Bill had discovered what the Guards had known for several months: David Stirling was indolent and temperamental, a disruptive influence for any commanding officer. Now it was his turn to look for a way to offload his wastrel sibling. The man who would, indirectly, prove his salvation was Winston Churchill.

Churchill had replaced Neville Chamberlain as Prime Minister the week after Bill Stirling had pitched his idea for an irregular warfare instruction school to the War Office. With Churchill now in power there was never any doubt that the school would be authorised. Since his days as a reporter and a soldier in the South African War of 1899–1902, Churchill had appreciated the methods of guerrilla warfare.

In June 1940 the Prime Minister sent a memorandum to his chiefs of staff instructing them to establish Britain's first special-forces units: 'We have always set our faces against this idea but … enterprises must be prepared, with specially trained troops, who can develop a reign of terror down these coasts, first of all on the "butcher and bolt" policy, but later on, or perhaps as soon as we are organised, we should surprise Calais or Boulogne, kill or capture the Hun garrison.'[8]

The 'Leopards' had been mooted initially as the name for the nascent force but this was dropped in favour of 'Commandos', and recruitment was soon under way. One of the commandos, raised on 7 July, was designated No. 8 and was commanded by Lt-Col Robert (Bob) Laycock. His breeding was impeccable; born in 1907, he had followed the well-worn path for young men of his caste: Eton, Sandhurst and a commission in the Royal Horse Guards (The Blues). He had a house in Mayfair and was a habitué of several clubs, one of which was White's.

It would be an exaggeration to claim that No. 8 Commando was formed in White's, but a great many of the officers who joined were members. Indeed, the preponderance of aristocrats led to it being christened 'The House of Lords' by rival units.

In fact one its officers was the Conservative MP for Farnham, thirty-nine-year-old Godfrey Nicholson, whose father-in-law was the 27th Earl of Crawford. There was a trio of lords, however, George Jellicoe, Richard Sudeley and Harry Stavordale, and the senior liaison officer was Philip Dunne, a former Tory MP.

Each of the ten troops comprised fifty men and was commanded by a captain; in charge of No. 6 Troop was Ralph Milbanke, Toby to his friends, the younger brother of Sir John Milbanke, the 11th baronet. He liked to ride across London on his horse Tiger, and in 1939 had attempted to win a bet by hitting a golf ball from Tower Bridge to the steps of White's.

A few officers were selected for reasons other than membership of White's: Jock Lewes, for example, of the Welsh Guards, a twenty-six-year-old Anglo-Australian who had won a rowing blue for Oxford and worked for a spell at the British Council in Berlin.

Some of No. 8 Commando's officers were sent to Lochailort, among them George Jellicoe. 'In September I went on a course in Lochailort, commando training,' he recounted. 'It was a rather good course and again extremely hard physically. Lord Lovat was the instructor and Bill Stirling was also in the instruction staff ... some of it was deer stalking and poaching, and hunting deer.'[9]

Some of the No. 8 Commando's officers were unused to taking orders, particularly from their social inferiors. But woe betide those who could not control their sense of entitlement. Randolph Churchill, the Prime Minister's son, was uppity with a gunnery instructor during a lesson in firing the new Bren gun. He was sent to explain himself to Lord Lovat and Bill Stirling; when he couldn't explain his behaviour he was expelled from Lochailort.

On 7 November David Stirling was posted to No. 8 Commando, then at Largs on the Ayrshire coast.

Stirling had little to recommend him, other than the four months he had spent as his brother's adjutant. He knew Jellicoe and several other of No. 8's officers, so in all probability he (or Bill) asked them to put in a word with Laycock. Stirling was posted to No. 4 Troop as a subaltern in charge of twenty-three soldiers.

After six days, another latecomer arrived: Evelyn Waugh. He was accepted because Laycock was a fan of his novels and he assumed that the thirty-seven-year-old could 'not fail to be an asset in the dreary business of war'.[10]

Waugh was shocked by what he found. 'Discipline was already deteriorating when I joined,' he later reflected. 'The indolence and ignorance of the officers seemed remarkable.'[11]

In a letter to his wife not long after his posting, Waugh categorised the likes of David Stirling, Randolph Churchill, Lords Sudeley and Stavordale and Viscount Milton as the 'Smart Set'. He described how they 'Drink a very good deal, play cards for high figures, dine nightly in Glasgow … the officers have very long hair & lap dogs & cigars & they wear whatever uniform they like.'[12]

Laycock recognised that ennui had spread throughout No. 8 Commando. He organised a war game, but it was cancelled. Waugh wrote to his wife on Christmas Day 1940 and described David Stirling as a 'gentleman obsessed by the pleasures of chance. He affectively wrecked Ludo as a game of skill and honour. Now we race clockwork motor cars.'[13]

Eventually, in January, it was decided to despatch three commando units to the Middle East, where they would be more gainfully employed than in Occupied Europe. After several aborted operations, including a planned assault on the Mediterranean island of Pantelleria, the War Office concluded that Britain was not yet in a position to launch any large-scale commando attack against German forces. In North Africa, however, Italy's long lines of communications along the coast were believed to be susceptible to amphibious assault.

On the night of 31 January/1 February 1941, under the codename Force Z, Nos 7, 8 and 11 Commando sailed for North Africa on board the troop ships *Glengyle* and *Glenroy*, while a third vessel, *Glenearn*, carried an overflow of officers and men bound for the same theatre.

No. 8 Commando were on the *Glenroy*, a former cargo ship that was, once clear of the River Clyde, converted into a casino. Seventeen days into their voyage, Evelyn Waugh wrote home: 'As the voyage goes on gambling gets formidably high. Chemin de Fer most nights with banks never lower than £50. Randolph [Churchill] lost over £400 [£22,500 today] last night. I do not play at this table but have a little poker game with the poor from whom I consistently win small sums ... David Stirling rarely appears before dinner.'[14]

Stirling's languor was impressive, so much so that his fellow officers christened him the 'Giant Sloth'.

7

On board the *Glenroy* were five troops of No. 11 Commando with the other five sailing to North Africa in the *Glengyle*. Among their officers was Lt Blair Mayne. He had come a long way, figuratively and literally, in the last year; for the first few months of 1940 he had remained more a rugby player than a soldier. On 21 February he played in a star-studded British Army XV against their French counterparts at the Parc des Princes in Paris in front of twenty-five thousand spectators.

More invitational matches followed throughout the spring. The army was happy to release him now and again, bathing in the reflected glory of having one of the nation's top athletes representing them. In addition, rugby matches were a good way of raising money and when, on 20 April, Mayne was part of an army side that beat a Great Britain XV 23–15 at the Richmond Athletic Ground, the gate money from the four thousand spectators was donated to the Army Recreation Equipment Fund.

For Mayne, however, life was increasingly unsatisfactory. Six months into the war and, although he wore khaki, he didn't feel much like a soldier. Playing rugby with his former Lions teammates was fun but it wasn't exactly doing his bit for the war effort. He applied for a transfer from the Royal Regiment of Artillery in search of some more stimulating soldiering. On 4 April he was transferred to the Royal Ulster Rifles. Among his fellow officers were Ambrose and Eoin McGonigal, two of the three sons of Judge John McGonigal, to whom Mayne had been introduced at a sitting of the Belfast Quarter Sessions the previous June. Mayne and Ambrose had also met before. Their paths had crossed at Queen's University in 1936 and 1937, and also probably at some point on a muddy rugby field; McGonigal had won a Leinster Schools cap before prioritising his studies in order to achieve his ambition of becoming a lawyer. Eoin was only nineteen but shared much in common with his older brother: a keen rugby player and cricketer, he followed Ambrose to Queen's in September 1938 to read law.

Mayne hadn't been long in the Royal Ulster Rifles when he responded to a request from the Cameronians (Scottish Rifles) for officers to join them on secondment. His decision was a desire to see some action and with him went a handful of other officers, including Eoin McGonigal.*

Shortly after Mayne arrived in Scotland, the Commandos were raised and among them was No. 11 Scottish Commando. Their commanding officer was Lt-Col Richard Pedder, a career soldier who had been commissioned into the Highland Light Infantry in 1924. He was a punctilious and driven man, intolerant of fools and frippery. He established his HQ in a hotel in Galashiels, a Scottish border town, and then began the process of weeding out the physically and temperamentally unfit from among the many hundreds of volunteers with exhausting route marches. Among the officers who made the grade were Mayne, McGonigal, Tommy Macpherson and Bill Fraser, a wiry man with a fresh complexion. The twenty-four-year-old Fraser was not long returned from France, where, as an officer in the 1st Battalion the Gordon Highlanders, he had been one of the few

* Ambrose later distinguished himself in the SBS, ending the war with an MC and bar.

members of the 51st Highland Infantry Division to escape capture at St Valery. Fraser's grandfather and father had served in the Gordons, but he was the first officer in the family, having been commissioned in 1940 after four years in the ranks.

Pedder had a good eye for character; his chose his officers well, except in the case of Lt Geoffrey Keyes of the Royal Scots Greys. He may have been pressured into accepting the Old Etonian son of Sir Roger Keyes, war hero, erstwhile Admiral of the Fleet, former Member of Parliament and, in July 1940, the Director of Combined Operations, whose remit included planning commando raids. Young Geoffrey had grown up in the shadow of his father, and he was desperate to emerge into the sunlight. 'He was not a natural athlete and did not look a strong chap and he didn't impress,' remarked Macpherson. 'But he had enormous personal determination and he wanted to be remembered.'[1]

Keyes wasn't suited to the special forces in any respect, but if he had to be accommodated then No. 8 Commando was his natural home, among his own kind. He didn't belong in No. 11 Scottish Commando, whose officers were middle class or, in a few cases, such as Bill Fraser's, working-class men who had risen from the ranks.

Unlike Keyes, whose burning (but unfulfilled) ambition at Eton had been to win his rugby colours, Mayne was in his element in the commandos. In letters to his mother he described the enjoyable rigour of endurance marches, of wading through rivers in the teeth of a gale. It was a good life.

There was a freedom to commando life that exhilarated Mayne. He had escaped the fetters of polite society, and all the artificiality that encompassed. Mayne had an interest in Polar exploration and had probably read Apsley Cherry-Garrard's stirring account of the ill-fated *Terra Nova* expedition to Antarctica in 1910, *The Worst Journey in the World*, which ended with the deaths of Captain Scott and four of his men on their way back from the South Pole. One of the dead was

Henry Bowers, a man whose description by Cherry-Garrard could also have applied to Mayne: 'To those accustomed to judge men by the standards of their fashionable and corseted drawing-rooms Bowers appeared crude … such men may be at a discount in conventional life; but give me a snowy ice-floe waving about on the top of a black swell, a ship thrown aback, a sledge-party almost shattered, or one that has just upset their supper on to the floorcloth of the tent, and I will lie down and cry for Bowers to come and lead me to food and safety.'

The commandos replicated the camaraderie of a rugby team: men of different shapes, sizes and intellects, but of a similar discipline and determination, all bound together in the pursuit of one goal. But the fraternity of a rugby team evaporated after the final whistle, when wives and sweethearts intruded on their brotherhood. Not so in the commando. Here the *esprit de corps* was inviolate. 'I like this place – we are very comfortable here and the mess is fine,' Mayne wrote to his mother in another letter. 'This is the sort of place I'll live in. No women about it, and clothes lying about all over the place, dirty teacups on the floor, wet boots in the oven, a rugby jersey over one armchair and your feet on the fender, a perfect existence.'[2]

His mother would have spotted the playfulness in her son's comment about absent females; numerous were the times when Mrs Mayne and her three daughters had admonished Blair for leaving a trail of wet rugby kit around their Mount Pleasant home.

Mayne was unusual among most of his fellow officers in being totally at ease in the presence of females. He had grown up in a house full of women and had gone to a co-educational school. Unlike most of his contemporaries in the commandos, who had been privately educated, Mayne found no mystery in the opposite sex. He enjoyed their company, although he was shy when sexually attracted to a woman.

A village dance was not such an occasion, and No. 11 Scottish Commando were invited to several during their time in Scotland in the autumn and early winter of 1940. According to Tommy Macpherson, Mayne and Eoin McGonigal would hunt together: 'They had slightly different tastes in young ladies,' he said. 'Blair liked dark ones and Eoin liked fair ones.'[3]

At other times, Mayne's idea of fun was an evening of hard drinking. He had enjoyed the odd 'thrash' in South Africa with the British Lions and the habit hadn't left him. 'When sober, a gentler, more mild-mannered man you could not wish to meet,' recalled one of his fellow commando officers, Gerald Bryan. 'But when drunk, or in battle, he was frightening. I'm not saying he was a drunk, but he could drink a bottle of whisky in an evening before he got a glow on.'[4]

Mayne and his fellow commandos bound for North Africa arrived at Geneifa, Egypt, on 11 March. They marched into a camp where they were inspected by Gen Sir Archibald Wavell, Commander-in-Chief Middle East, a man who believed that the ideal infantryman was 'a cross between a poacher and a cat burglar'.[5] Wavell told the new arrivals that two further units of commandos had been raised in the Middle East and would be added to Nos 7, 8 and 11 Commando to form 'Layforce' under the command of Lt-Col Robert Laycock. At this time No. 7 Commando became A Battalion, No. 8 Commando became B Battalion and No. 11 Commando became C Battalion. Two locally raised commandos, Nos 50 and 52, merged to become D Battalion.

Lt-Col Pedder issued a Special Order to No. 11 Commando, reminding his men of the need for security and secrecy. He also cautioned them that they would soon embark on some specialised training, some of which might not be to their liking. 'Constructive criticism and reasonable discussion are to be encouraged,' he stated. 'But only in the right place and on the right occasion.'[6]

8

The Hon Mrs Stirling had two additions to her family at the close of 1940. In July her eldest daughter Margaret had married Capt the Hon Simon Ramsay, The Black Watch, younger son of the late Earl of Dalhousie and the Countess of Dalhousie.

The ceremony was at Keir and it was not ostentatious on account of the house being in use as a hospital. There was a smattering of titled guests and Capt Bill Stirling gave his sister away.

Four months later it was Bill's turn. It was a low-key affair at St Mary's Cadogan Gardens in London, although *Tatler* published a photograph of the couple tying the knot, Bill in his Scots Guards uniform and his bride in a simple outfit. Her name was Susan Bligh, the twenty-four-year-old younger daughter of Maj the Hon Noel Bligh, DSO and the late Mrs Bligh, and a niece of the Earl of Darnley. Susan and her sister Jasmine – one of the first BBC announcers – were prominent London socialites, and like many of that station Susan had enrolled as a student nurse in the Voluntary Aid Detachment on the outbreak of war.

If there was a honeymoon, it was brief. While in London Bill had several conferences with Special Operations Executive, which had been formed the previous July by amalgamating Section D and

MI (R) at the suggestion of Lord Hankey, the Chancellor of the Duchy of Lancaster. It made more sense, in his view, that the two organisations should pool their intelligence resources rather than work as separate entities in pursuit of the same objective. SOE's first director was Sir Frank Nelson and he answered to Hugh Dalton, the Minister of Economic Warfare, who had political responsibility for the organisation. Two casualties of the shake-up were Maj Lawrence Grand and Col Joe Holland, who left intelligence and returned to the regular army.

One who remained was Colin Gubbins. In November 1940 he was appointed SOE's Director of Operations with the rank of acting brigadier. It had been a busy few months for the Scot. In Norway he had commanded the Independent Companies, specially trained troops, many of whom subsequently joined the commandos. On returning to Britain Gubbins had been instructed to raise auxiliary units, guerrilla fighters who in the event of a German invasion would wage an irregular war against the Nazis. Gubbins leaned heavily on the knowledge of Peter Fleming, who had already started training men as guerrilla troops, and Mike Calvert was posted from the Special Training School at Lochailort.

With Gubbins now in charge of the auxiliary units, Fleming was given another mission by Hugh Dalton, codenamed 'Yak'. He was to assemble a small team and take them to Egypt, where they would trawl the prisoner-of-war camps in search of anti-fascist Italians. Those judged physically, emotionally and ideologically suitable would join SOE for operations inside Italy. Indeed, Fleming was informed, if the POW camps proved a fertile recruiting ground they might even form a 'Garibaldi' Division that could be sent into battle against Mussolini's forces.

Fleming was allocated a room in the War Office, from where he began to recruit his team. A fellow officer in the Grenadier Guards was selected, Norman Johnstone, and also chosen was Lt Mark Norman, who 'didn't have a clue what it was about',[1] but who was related to Montagu Norman, the then Governor of the Bank of England and a member of the same social circle as Fleming's mother.

Bill Stirling also received an invitation. He knew Fleming from way back, and Peter had been to one of Mrs Stirling's balls in 1934, the year before he married the actress Celia Johnson. But Bill now had more to recommend him than merely his social status. Fleming himself had passed through Lochailort and it was logical to recruit its chief, a man who possessed authority, efficiency and determination.

In all Fleming recruited eight men, but Bill Stirling was the hardest to winkle out of his position because of his importance to the training centre. As telegrams were sent back and forth among various departments of the War Office, Fleming took his men to Lochailort for a course in irregular warfare.

Eventually, on 21 January 1941, Bill Stirling's participation in the Yak Mission was confirmed in a cable: 'W. J. Stirling, Scots Guards, RARO [Regular Army Reserve Officers] has been selected for a special appointment with the Inter-Services Research Bureau.* Please instruct this officer to report forthwith to Room 055a, War Office, Whitehall, London to assume the duties of the appointment.'[2]

Eleven days later Bill Stirling and the rest of the Yak Mission sailed from the Clyde on the *Glenearn*, carrying among their stores £40,000 in notes and gold sovereigns, and one ton of plastic explosive. Their vessel was part of the convoy that included the *Glenroy*, on which was David and No. 8 Commando. On 10 February there was a brief stop at Freetown, on the west coast of Africa, but there was no opportunity for Bill and David to meet. Troops were forbidden from leaving their vessels as they anchored under the burning sun. Bill did go ashore, however, along with Peter Fleming, to report to Gen Christopher Woolner, the Area Commander.

---

* One of the many cover names for SOE.

Once in Egypt, the Yak Mission swiftly learned that there would be no 'Garibaldi' Division; the prisoners were apathetic to the idea of taking up arms against Mussolini. They were interested only in sitting out the war and then returning to their families.

By the start of March 1941 the Allies believed they had all but won the Desert War; in two months Gen Richard O'Connor's Western Desert Force (subsequently the Eighth Army) had beaten an army of four corps during an advance of 500 miles, capturing 13,000 Italians, 400 tanks and 1290 field guns. The Allies were now in possession of the Libyan ports of Bardia, Tobruk and Benghazi, with their enemy dug in at El Agheila, a bottleneck from where they hoped to block an advance from Cyrenaica (eastern Libya) into Tripolitania (the western region of Libya).

O'Connor wanted to press home his advantage and annihilate his opponent but on 12 February Winston Churchill had sent a telegram to Sir Archibald Wavell, instructing him to transfer the preponderance of his army to Greece (under the command of Gen Henry Wilson) in readiness for a German invasion. Churchill's view was that the Italians were defeated, and therefore Egypt and the Suez Canal were no longer threatened. A token presence in North Africa would be enough to keep the Italians corralled in western Libya. But he had reckoned without the Germans. Hitler was initially reluctant to get involved in North Africa, his focus being on the Balkans and Russia, but he had been persuaded by Grand Admiral Erich Raeder, head of the Germany navy, to sign 'Führer Directive No. 22', authorising the raising of a force to be sent to North Africa. Raeder had argued that if the British controlled the Mediterranean it would hinder the Führer's plans for conquest in the East. On 6 February Hitler appointed Gen Erwin Rommel the force's commander, and by the time the advance elements had reached Tripoli in Libya in late February, they had been reconstituted as the Afrika Korps.

Meanwhile in Cairo the Yak Mission was, as Peter Fleming wrote in a letter to his wife, 'in a state of stagnation'. He was writing from the celebrated Shepheard's Hotel, where he and the team 'live expensively ... and I spend my time flapping around and trying to fix things up'.[3]

The hotel was the favourite venue for Cairo's chic society, its terrace the meeting place for old friends, new friends, lovers and business associates. Army officers recently arrived from Britain believed it offered an authentic taste of Africa, but others were more sceptical. The Scottish-born American war correspondent Allan Michie was a regular at Shepheard's, but only because he was gathering material for a forthcoming book.

'[It] is the greatest disappointment in Egypt,' he would write in *Retreat to Victory*. 'The interiors of the salons, with their Byzantine columns, mosque-like domes, and low couches covered with mounds of pillows, look like Hollywood's conception of a harem. On the terrace, leering dragomans sidle up to every newcomer and offer to escort him to the pyramids.'

It was tawdry but enticing, particularly for the soldiers, nurses and intelligence staff, most of whom had known only the commonplace of pre-war Britain.

Fleming was a seasoned adventurer and, like Bill Stirling, a man of the world. They sensed the undercurrent of dissolution, the cliques and intrigues that invariably follow expatriates around the world. Nowhere was this more evident than within SOE headquarters at the Rustum Buildings on Kasr el-Aini Street, in the Garden City district.

The unification that had occurred in SOE in London in July 1940, merging MI (R) and Section D, had not been replicated in Cairo. These two factions – known in North Africa as G (R) (General Research) and D/H respectively – were barely on speaking terms.

So London sent a renowned London lawyer, George Pollock, to take over D/H and establish a good working relationship with G (R).

In November 1940 Pollock had hired as his secretary Hermione Ranfurly, wife of Daniel, the 6th Earl of Ranfurly. A year earlier she had been living at Brocklesby Hall in Lincolnshire, close to her husband's regiment, the Sherwood Rangers Yeomanry. When the regiment was shipped to the Middle East in January 1940, she had on her own initiative followed her husband to Palestine, and thence to Cairo, to the consternation of the British military, who unsuccessfully tried to remove her from Cairo

Using her husband's connections, Ranfurly persuaded Pollock to employ her at SOE headquarters and she became a welcome addition to Cairo's social scene. A frequent guest at the British Embassy, Ranfurly dined with everyone from generals to the prime minister of Australia, Bob Menzies.

She was also familiar with the parties thrown in the first-floor flat of No. 13, Sharia Ibrahim Pasha Naguib, a wide tree-lined street in Garden City, close to the Embassy. The ground-floor flat belonged to Adam Watson, Second Secretary at the British Embassy, and he had as lodgers in 1941 the novelist Olivia Manning and her husband, Reggie. It was a well-located flat, but Watson warned his guests about the noise from the flat above.

It belonged to Peter Stirling, Third Secretary at the Embassy, and a man with a reputation for throwing Bacchanalian parties. Peter had been posted to Cairo in 1940; since joining the Foreign Office in 1937 he had impressed his superiors with his grasp of detail, his social graces and his delightful wit. Another of the Embassy's secretaries, Charles Johnston, who arrived in Cairo in early 1942, recalled of Peter that 'in sophistication and panache he outdid his brothers and everyone else in sight'.[4] Johnston described the atmosphere of the flat as 'raffish', with its 'floating population of officers on leave from the Desert', all of whom were desperate to forget the war for a few gloriously decadent days.

The ambassador, Sir Miles Lampson, and his wife were friends of Peter Stirling's mother and had been in her party at the 1936 Gleneagles Ball. Peter was known to accompany Sir Miles on shooting parties at the invitation of King Farouk of Egypt, and the younger man held his own against the best Egyptian marksmen.

By the end of February 1941 Hermione Ranfurly was confiding to her diary her concerns about the 'non-existent' security at SOE headquarters. When she got in a taxi and gave the address, the driver would grin and say, 'Oh, you want to go to the secret office!'[5]

On 24 March, Ranfurly told Anthony Eden, Secretary of State for War, of her fears when he visited Cairo. A few hours later Peter Fleming entered her office. He had been present when Eden was informed that Ranfurly wished to see him and wanted to know the subject of their conversation. Ranfurly knew Fleming socially, so over supper at Shepheard's that evening she took him into her confidence. He expressed his gratitude for her trust and advised that she continue to keep her ear to the ground. Fleming told Ranfurly that he was leading the Yak Mission to Greece the following day – minus one member. Bill Stirling was remaining in Cairo and he might prove a useful ally.

Bill had requested his release from the Yak Mission on 13 March, having grown disillusioned with the futility of their existence. He was given a position within SOE Cairo, but that dampened his spirits further. The arrival of George Pollock had only served to deteriorate relations; he had tried to reorganise SOE Cairo, designating the factions SO1 (semi-secret propaganda) and SO2 (sabotage operations).

Bill Stirling summed up SO2 as 'thoroughly rotten' and blamed Pollock.[6] To an extent, it wasn't his fault, he was a lawyer not a soldier, but nonetheless he had become a victim of Shepheard's Hotel syndrome, succumbing to the 'widespread delusion you can become a Lawrence of Arabia by sitting in offices and bars in Cairo'.[7]

Tired of the intrigues and in-fighting, Bill Stirling re-enlisted in the Scots Guards. It helped that the commanding officer of the Second Battalion was his friend, comrade-in-arms and business partner Lt-Col Bryan Mayfield, who had returned to his regiment after Operation Knife. One of Mayfield's lieutenants was Bill's youngest brother, Hugh.

Bill joined the battalion at Tahag camp, a city of military tents forty miles from Cairo, but he was soon appointed liaison officer of the 22nd Guards Brigade commanded by Ian Erskine, one of Bill's officers when he was commissioned in 1932.

On 6 April the 2nd Battalion Scots Guards entrained for Mersa Matruh, where they were one of five battalions dug in defensively around the Matruh Fortress. For the next fortnight they conducted reconnaissance patrols, probing west to see if another German advance was likely. On the night of 19 April Hugh Stirling – attached to the Durham Light Infantry – led a patrol into the desert. He didn't return. The Scots Guards' war diary noted on 20 April:

'Further news was received that Lieutenant H. J. STIRLING had been wounded having been fired on by Machine Gun on fixed line. He had not so far been brought in. 1st Battalion DURHAM LIGHT INFANTRY are sending out patrol night 20/21 April to attempt to locate and bring him in.'[8]

The Durham infantrymen returned from their patrol empty-handed. On 22 April Hugh was posted 'Missing and Wounded'.

Four days later, the war diary reported, 'Captain W. J. STIRLING, Liaison Officer, arrived from Brigade HQ.' The Second Battalion was preparing to pull back, and Bill may have been despatched with instructions from the brigadier, but it was also a chance to ask in person if anyone had news of his brother. It was a mystery. Witnesses reported seeing him wounded but no trace of him had been found. No one could shed any light on Hugh's likely fate. Bill returned to Brigade HQ to write to his mother at Keir.

★ ★ ★

On 2 May Hermione Ranfurly moved in with Gen Wavell and his wife. Evidently, Wavell had an ulterior motive in agreeing to take a lodger and on 4 May he expressed his doubts to Ranfurly about SOE's reliability; he then asked if she would copy any documents she thought might be of interest to him and deposit them in the care of the Chief of the General Staff, Lt-Gen Arthur Smith. Ranfurly replied that she was willing to smuggle material out of SOE headquarters when she left work each evening, but she would need help in copying them if she was to have them back in their files first thing the next morning. 'Fine,' said Wavell. 'I'll fix it.'[9]

The next morning, Hermione Ranfurly knocked on the door of the Stirlings' flat and was greeted by Peter's furious housekeeper, Mohammed Aboudi, known to one and all as Mo. He looked ready to do someone a mischief with the dustpan clasped in his hand. The reason for his rage, Mo explained, was that the previous evening Peter and Bill Stirling had arrived home from a party on the back of a donkey, which they then invited up to the flat. The donkey was still in residence and had made itself comfortable in the most pungent way imaginable.

There may have been a reason for the Stirlings' debauchery; Bill had recently returned from the front with the news that Hugh was missing in action. All he could tell Peter for certain was that their younger brother had been wounded; whether he had been taken prisoner by the Germans or whether he had crawled into a desert cranny to die, only time would tell.*

Another reason for Bill's excess was the pressure of juggling two roles: liaison officer of the 22nd Guards Brigade and SOE operative. Eventually, he reached the end of his tether with the latter. 'Bill Stirling, who works for SOE, appeared and told me he is so disgusted

---

* Hugh Stirling's body was never found, and he is commemorated on the Alamein Memorial. An obituary in the *Ampleforth Journal* of 1943 stated: 'Though he never attained "high office" his seriousness of purpose, his natural charm and above all his solid goodness and piety were a real contribution to the general good.'

with our office that he walked out,' wrote Ranfurly in her diary on 5 May. Bill returned to the Scots Guards, but on 17 May the war diary recorded that Capt W. D. M. Raeburn was 'ordered to relieve Captain W. J. Stirling as liaison officer at Brigade HQ. The latter officer left to take up an appointment at GHQ Middle East.'

Bill Stirling's role at GHQ was in the 'personal service' of Lt-Gen Arthur Smith.[10] Smith was a dry, intense man, who carried a bible in his hip pocket because it had stopped a German bullet from doing him harm in the Great War. He answered to Gen Wavell, and had been instructed to devise a plan to keep tabs on SOE. Wavell feared their lax security could have ramifications for the army unless action was taken. Wavell would have loved to storm into SOE HQ himself but they weren't under his control, so espionage was the order of the day.

In late May Ranfurly was summoned to Gen Smith's office in GHQ, where she found Bill Stirling. The general explained to the pair that he wanted to compile a dossier of evidence (this came to be known as the 'Anti-SO2' dossier) for the Minister of State, Oliver Lyttelton, due in Cairo shortly.

Stirling and Ranfurly devised a scheme for smuggling out evidence from SOE, one that proved foolproof even if it did leave Ranfurly feeling sordid. 'Mine is a horrible job,' she noted on 5 June. 'I leave the office last and lock up the safes and filing cabinets, hide key papers in my bra and depart … I walk across Garden City to the Stirlings' flat where I type copies of the papers I brought.'[11]

It took Ranfurly many hours each night to copy the papers she had smuggled out of SOE, which she then gave to Bill Stirling. He handed them to Gen Smith, while Ranfurly arrived at her office at the crack of dawn to put back the originals.

Smith was so grateful he took Ranfurly to lunch. He was less of a prig than she'd thought, and he was 'amazed' at the papers she had smuggled out. Wavell now described SOE as a 'Cairo Racket'.[12]

The dossier compiled by Bill Stirling was brutal in its assessment of SO2's many failings. 'An unfavourable view of the activities of SO2, Middle East, has for some time been taken by GHQ, Middle East, and indeed by most of the diplomatic and military personnel who have had dealings with this organisation,' he said in the introduction. He criticised everything, from the personnel to the supply to the training and concluded by stating that its members were 'incompetent' and their methods 'wasteful'.[13] Reform was urgently required, and Stirling attached a programme to effect such a change.

In late July Sir Frank Nelson, the head of SO2 in London, flew to Cairo with two of his operatives, Terence Maxwell and Bickham Sweet-Escott. The latter found an 'atmosphere of suspicion and jealousy' which embittered the relations between the various secret and semi-secret departments.[14]

Nelson was shown the Anti-SO2 dossier compiled by Smith, Stirling and Ranfurly, but he had already taken the decision to replace George Pollock with Maxwell. Although Nelson was dismayed by the indolence within SOE Cairo, he also believed that GHQ had 'conducted a propaganda exercise to denounce SOE operations by instigating the writing of false reports, as they wanted the office merged into their organisation'.[15] Maxwell brokered a compromise: SOE would retain their Cairo outpost but focus their activity on Turkey and the Balkans.

Maxwell had been briefed about GHQ's skulduggery by Peter Wilkinson, who had been sent to Cairo on the orders of Colin Gubbins to investigate the deteriorating relations. Wilkinson had a foot in both camps, as a member of SOE and a former regular army officer.

Wilkinson had arrived in Egypt in April 1941, shortly after Gen Erwin Rommel had launched his first offensive. His Afrika Korps had taken the port of Benghazi on 3 April and eight days later the British had been pushed out of Cyrenaica and back into Egypt, save for the garrison holding out in Tobruk.* This reverse was a shock for Churchill, who weeks earlier had assumed that victory in the Desert War was guaranteed. Now British forces were on the defensive against an aggressive, powerful and innovative opponent. A fresh strategy was required, involving new units, and this realisation only served to deepen GHQ's hostility towards SOE. 'Everyone was very much jumping onto this irregular wagon,' recalled Wilkinson. 'GHQ Middle East, seeing themselves slightly isolated, were very, very keen to set up all sorts of private armies … they at least were part of the regular army and really all hands were turned to squashing SOE.'[16]

Wavell already had one such 'private army' at his disposal, the Long Range Desert Group. Formed in June 1940 by Ralph Bagnold, a renowned desert explorer in the inter-war period, it had achieved much in its short existence. In November Wavell instructed Bagnold to enlarge his unit because their exploits had been 'most valuable and shows skill and enterprise of a high order'.[17]

Bagnold had sold the concept to Wavell with a promise to wage 'piracy on the high desert',[18] and the LRDG did just that, sallying forth from Cairo in 30-cwt Chevrolet trucks to ambush Italian vehicles, overrun their remote forts, lay mines and bring back prisoners for interrogation. But the true value of the LRDG lay in its unsurpassed skill in navigating into the interior of the Western Desert to carry out deep reconnaissance patrols and surveillance operations, in the process pioneering new routes across what was, for Europeans, terra incognita.

Bill Stirling knew much about the LRDG, not just from the reports he read in GHQ but from the first-hand accounts he received from one of its officers, Capt Michael Crichton-Stuart, whose family were long-standing friends of the Stirlings.

* During this advance Daniel Ranfurly was taken prisoner, along with Lt-Gen Philip Neame and Gen Richard O'Connor.

From Eton, Crichton-Stuart had been commissioned into the Scots Guards; he joined G [Guards] Patrol of the LRDG in December 1940 and adapted well to his new unit. The discipline required was personal, not regimental; there was no bawling, no drilling, no Blancoing. Soldiers sported beards and wore sandals in the LRDG. What mattered wasn't the outer man but the inner one.

Individual initiative and a strong self-discipline were the guiding principles of the Commando Special Training Centre at Lochailort; what Bill Stirling and Lord Lovat had striven to instil in all of their students. It must have gladdened Bill's heart to see his principles being put into practice.

The LDRG was a brilliant example of a private army whose return far exceeded its investment; in other words, its operational effectiveness – particularly intelligence-gathering and reconnaissance – came at little expense, either materially or in manpower for the conventional army.

GHQ was on the lookout for more irregular units as a means of asserting their dominance over SOE in North Africa and undermining their existence in Cairo.

9

On 6 May 1941 Col Bob Laycock wrote a letter to Lt-Gen Arthur Smith. The pair had recently met at GHQ in Cairo, when Laycock had aired his frustration at the inaction of his Layforce Commando. He wanted to put in writing the gravity of the situation. He wrote:

> Since our arrival here … we have pursued the same heart-breaking course of working the men up to concert pitch for projects which have eventually been cancelled … unless we are actively employed soon I anticipate a serious falling off in morale which was at one time second to none.
>
> The effect on the troops may be summed up by an inscription found written up on a partition in the mess decks of one of the Glen ships (the culprit was never apprehended), which read: – 'Never in the history of human endeavour have so few been b—ed by so many'.

Laycock concluded his letter by stating that 'if the higher authorities consider our useful employment to be problematical then it would be better to disband the Special Service Brigade now rather than to see it deteriorate'.[1]

Only evenings in Alexandria or weekends in Cairo broke the monotony for the Layforce commandos. The other ranks sampled the pleasures of Cairo's many brothels or drank in bars such as the Anzac, the Spitfire and the Churchill Bar. 'Egyptians don't like the war but they want to make as much money out of it as possible,' remarked Allan Michie.

Many establishments were out of bounds to the other ranks. Officers were willing to see their men die for their country but not gain entry to the Royal Automobile Club, the Turf Club, the Mohammed Ali Club or, heaven forbid, Shepheard's Hotel. They were allowed into the Gezireh Sporting Club, which liked 'to boast that generals and privates rub elbows in its grounds'. But, as Michie remembered, 'Actually, troops are banned from every part of the club except the cricket ground and are allowed in the swimming pool only after six in the evening.'[2]

One of the few places where officers and men could mix was the race track, a favourite haunt of David Stirling. On one occasion, Stirling encountered some of his men at the track and gave them the name of a dead certainty for an upcoming race. A few put their faith in Stirling's tip but others followed the advice of Dave Kershaw, a Liverpudlian who had fought for the Republicans in the Spanish Civil War; the 'hot tip' was in fact hopeless, he told them, and he advised backing another horse. Those who took his advice were rewarded and the men who trusted in Stirling were not.

Commando officers in Cairo soon understood that Shepheard's was the redoubt of staff officers, whom they christened 'Gaberdine swine or members of the Short Range Shepheard's Group'.[3] They looked elsewhere: the Mena House Hotel; the roof of the Hotel Continental, where they were entertained by 'the jelly-bellied wriggles of Hekmet Fahmy, a lissom Oriental dancer';[4] or the Dugout of the Metropolitan Hotel, where they bought expensive drinks for expensive hostesses of every colour and creed.

One of the most popular destinations for the well-heeled Layforce officers was the elegant house of Mrs Maud Marriott, the wealthy American wife of Brig John Marriott, commanding the 22nd Guards Brigade. Known as Mo-Mo to her admirers, Mrs Marriott lived in Gezirah, an island in central Cairo, and according to Evelyn Waugh her house 'gave back an echo of pre-war Mayfair in the London season'.[5]

Waugh was a regular, so too Lord Stavordale, Philip Dunne and Christopher Sykes, then working in the propaganda section of SOE Cairo. The Stirling brothers also attended from time to time; Bill was a good friend of both Waugh and Sykes, and one of the few men who brooked no nonsense from the acidic Waugh.

David said he used Peter's flat as a haven during his frequent trips to Cairo. It was a useful base from which to make sorties into the city's night spots. On more than one occasion, he was late back to camp the morning after a night of revelry but Stirling said he charmed his commanding officer into overlooking his tardy appearance. Eventually, the bon vivant in David decided it would be more practical to be based permanently in the city, so he checked himself into hospital, where he could recover from his roistering.

Peter and Bill were adolescent drunks; alcohol brought out the schoolboy in them and they indulged in high jinks, such as leading a donkey home. For David, drunkenness revealed a darker side.

'David had been known to knock down cab horses as a postprandial relaxation,' according to one of his fellow Layforce officers, Carol Mather. 'Of the particular one that I remember, I can't quite recall whether he ran behind and tripped it up, as one would a boy at school, or hit it in the face with his fist. At any rate down it came bringing with it a fair sample of gharrymen's oaths – Alexandria type.'[6]

To attack a harnessed and blinkered horse was a cruel and curious prank for any man to commit, none more so than Stirling. Hadn't he an affection and respect for the animal he had herded hundreds of miles across America? The violence may have been an expression of deep frustration with his life.

Stirling later claimed that his drunken escapades, together with two spells in hospital on account of dysentery and an eye injury, prompted the commissioning of a Board of Officers to consider whether he should face a court martial on a charge of malingering. His service record noted that he was 'Reported Wounded' at this time (the exact date was not stated) but there was no reference to disciplinary action of any kind.

On 20 May Stirling was one of eleven officers and ninety-nine other ranks who embarked on HMS *Aphis* bound for Ain el-Gazala. Their orders were to raid the airfield on the night of 21/22 May, and Stirling was to lead one of seven detachments comprising eleven men. 'Advance along western edge of Wadi … and neutralize enemy defensive fire'[7] was his instruction, but he never got the chance to go into action. The landing of *Aphis* was postponed because of strong winds and a heavy swell, and so the raid was rescheduled for 25 May. En route to the target the ship was attacked by several Savoia medium bomber aircraft and the mission was abandoned.

On 29 May Laycock informed No. 8 Commando that Layforce's dissolution was inevitable. What the future held, he couldn't say with certainty; there was the possibility of raising a small force to go to the Bush Warfare School in Burma, and Laycock hoped there would be opportunities for some form of commando-type raids in North Africa. However, many men would be obliged to return to their parent regiment.

The prospect of regular soldiering was welcomed by some guardsmen for whom the commando lustre had long since faded; others were dismayed at the thought of a return to drilling and Blancoing. Among the latter was Jock Lewes, although he too was fed up with the inertia he had experienced since joining the commandos. 'We still continue to do nothing with that ease and grace achieved only after long practice,' he had written to his father on 27 April.[8]

Lewes was an outsider in No. 8 Commando. He was well educated and well off but not from the same strata of society as most of his peers. Hollywood-handsome with strong, confident features, Lewes was an intellectual, an idealist and an aesthete. He was also courageous and innovative, and a bit of a prig. 'Our Christmas was a motley affair that didn't hang together or have much meaning beyond an occasion for eating and drinking too much,' he wrote to his sweetheart, Mirren, on 26 December 1940. 'We were very well looked after, but the men's existence is sordid at the best of times, and with the over-indulgences of Christmas Day cooped up on the troop deck, there was little room for good will or the exercise of the finer sensibilities to which the feast should make us prone.'[9]

The other factor that marked out Lewes from most of No. 8 Commando's officers was his determination to join the battle. Many appeared to regard the war as an exotic vacation, and they were damned if they would let Rommel interfere with their drinking and gambling; Lewes called it 'playboy soldiering'. He was desperate to test himself in battle. 'Just the sight, or even the sound of just one bullet fired in anger might have saved us from this decadence,' he told Mirren in a letter dated 5 May 1941. 'The sight of one dead man would have filled every fainting heart with zeal.'[10]

A few days later an idea began to take shape in his head, one to which he alluded in a letter to Mirren on 25 May. He couldn't go into the specifics for obvious reasons, but 'it is frighteningly exciting in preparation but gives me just that for which I have longed all my soldier days – a team of men, however small, and complete freedom to train and use them as I think best'.[11]

The idea was parachuting, but it wasn't his innovation. On 11 May Col Laycock had cabled Maj Dermot Daly, commanding officer of No. 8 Commando, advising him of impending RAF raids on Gazala and Derna. 'Consider every advantage would accrue from raids taking place simultaneously,' wrote Laycock. 'If you are prepared drop party of four all ranks by parachute near Derna … please say if you consider Derna parachute raid possible.' Laycock ended by suggesting that if Daly considered a parachute raid was impractical he should despatch two of his officers, George Jellicoe and Carol Mather, with a small party to 'raid Gazala earliest moon suitable'.[12]

The parachute raid never materialised but Lewes evidently heard of Laycock's idea. He approached his colonel and obtained permission to assemble a handful of men to begin training with a view to a parachute operation against an Axis target in Syria: Sgt Sid Stone* and Guardsmen R. D. Evans, Roy Davies and Mick D'Arcy.

At this point David Stirling appeared, quite insistent that he be allowed to join the experiment. He was bubbling with enthusiasm after a recent encounter with Bill's friend Michael Crichton-Stuart of the LRDG. David had mooted the idea of forming another unit similar to the LRDG but Crichton-Stuart had expressed doubt that GHQ would sanction such a force – unless it could offer something new, such as parachuting. The Germans were ahead of the British in this form of warfare and GHQ would surely be tempted by the prospect of having their own airborne force. The idea seized Stirling's imagination.

'He persuaded me to let him in on it in the last days when all arrangements were made,' Lewes explained in a letter to his father. 'I let him come reluctantly. He was interfering with my task in hand. I resented the strength of his persuasion and despised a little his colossal confidence.'

There was, he added, a further reason why he allowed Stirling to join his party. 'I did it as a means to a very approximate end.'[13]

Lewes and Stirling had nothing in common. One was austere, the other extravagant; one had graduated from Oxford with a degree in philosophy, politics and economics, and a rowing blue, and the other had quit Cambridge after three terms. Lewes was aware that Stirling

* Sgt Stone died of wounds sustained in the inaugural SAS operation.

was a man who overindulged every day, not just Christmas Day. But he also knew Stirling was terribly well connected.

On 11 June Lewes, Stirling and George Jellicoe made a call on Peter Oldfield, who was working for the Air Reconnaissance Unit at Middle East HQ. It was a meeting probably facilitated by Bill Stirling, who also worked at HQ. 'Grey Pillars', as the nerve centre of the British military was known, was situated in the Garden City district of Cairo. Once past the guards, visitors were greeted with an interior that had 'disintegrated into a warren: doors and sections of corridors were boarded up, while people came and went through adjoining bathrooms, knocked together to form passages between one flat and another'.[14]

Oldfield noted in his diary that the trio of commando officers requested 'a mosaic of Gazala' and afterwards 'had a demonstration of parachute jumping from the old Valencia'.[15] In fact it was only Stirling and Lewes who had the demonstration, along with Sgt Stone, all hopeful of carrying out a raid in Syria. Once airborne in the Valencia, they heaved out a dummy constructed of sandbags and tent poles. The parachute opened without a hitch. Once they had landed, the three men had a lesson in landing technique and parachute control from an RAF officer.

Stirling saw Oldfield again the following day and viewed some reconnaissance photos of Aleppo, but these 'could not help him'. Then, noted Oldfield, he and Jock Lewes went off 'to practise parachuting'.

They flew inland in the Valencia and reached a landing ground shortly before dusk. After a brief conflab they decided to jump that evening and an RAF officer agreed to despatch, although he urged them to hurry as the light was fading. As they fitted their parachutes, the officer reminded them to 'dive out as though going through water'. It was arranged that Lewes and his servant, Guardsman Roy Davies, would jump first, which they did without mishap. The aircraft circled and Stirling and Mick D'Arcy steeled themselves to jump, checking a final time that the static lines that ripped open their parachutes were correctly tied to the metal legs of the seat inside the Valencia's fuselage. D'Arcy went first, diving out as if going through water. Moments later he was 'surprised to see Lt Stirling pass me in the air'.[16]

Stirling hadn't dived as instructed, but rather flopped out, and consequently his parachute had caught on the tailplane and ripped two panels from the canopy. He accelerated past D'Arcy and hit the earth with great force. He may have suffered concussion and even temporary paralysis of his legs. His back hurt like hell. Nonetheless, he felt able the next day to pay another visit to Middle East HQ. 'Lt Stirling came in with wounds from his parachute jump,' noted Oldfield in his diary on 13 June.[17]

As Stirling limped into GHQ, Lewes and the rest of the party went up for a second jump. Evans, D'Arcy, Davies and Stone all executed perfect landings but Lewes 'in trying to avoid some oil barrels, rather badly injured his spine'.[18]

On 15 June David Stirling was admitted to hospital 'suffering from contusion of the back'.[19] It didn't take GHQ long to cancel the intended parachute operation against Vichy French forces in Syria. When Lewes had recovered he sailed for the besieged port of Tobruk with a contingent of Layforce volunteers. He consigned his idea of a parachute unit to history, and on 7 July wrote to Mirren: 'I have been working this afternoon with the men, digging trenches against the bombers … I feel well and strong.'[20]

'Bill Stirling and I went to Heliopolis Hospital to see his brother David who has injured his back making a parachute jump,' wrote Hermione Ranfurly in her diary on 22 June. 'I asked David what he would do when he is better and he told me that he belongs to Bob Laycock's Commandos but they are being disbanded shortly. "When I have got my legs to function again I have a scheme to put to headquarters," he said in his quiet voice. "It may be difficult to get them to accept it, but it is vital they do.'"[21]

On 12 August Ranfurly received a letter from David in which he told her he'd convinced GHQ of the validity of his proposition and was now about to start training his force at Kabrit.

He had his brother Bill to thank for his victory. On his release from hospital in the second week of July David had continued his convalescence at Peter's flat. Bill was already lodging. For the first time the brothers were free from maternal control, and they made hay. At Keir everything had been neat and tidy; bookshelves were ordered, Persian rugs were straight and herbaceous borders were immaculate. In the first-floor flat at No. 13 Sharia Ibrahim Pasha Naguib, it was bedlam. Charles Johnston lodged at the flat when he was posted to the Embassy in 1942 and described it as a typical bachelor pad, where everything was filthy, save for the food, and where officers on leave from the desert would arrive unannounced at all hours. The custom on gaining entry when there was no one at home was to break down the frosted glass window to the right of the front door. In the hallway was a long table on which were scattered letters sent from Britain for officers who had given the flat as their correspondence address. On a smaller table was the telephone with a worn telephone directory and several numbers scrawled on the whitewashed wall above.

The sitting room was lined with grey sofas pock-marked by cigarette burns, which created, in Johnston's eyes at least, the impression of a 'salon of a medium-grade bordel'.[22] Photographs of the King and Queen torn from *Tatler* covered one wall, not so much a touching gesture of patriotism as an attempt to conceal the bullet holes from the time Bill had given Peter a lesson in revolver shooting.

There were three bedrooms, each containing several camp beds. There were often queues for the two bathrooms, and performing one's ablutions required negotiating a route through the piles of tin uniform cases, ammunition boxes and elephant tusks.

Bill was still working for Lt-Gen Arthur Smith, and was therefore well informed about the failure of Layforce. He also had access to intelligence about the overall situation in North Africa, so he was aware of the army's strong points and its weak links, and any potential opportunities for his brother. Back in December 1940 Ralph Bagnold, the founder of the LRDG, had submitted a memorandum to the General Staff in which he recommended the raising of a desert striking force, based either at Wadi Halfa or Kano. This was a slimmed-down version of an idea that Maj Orde Wingate had proposed to GHQ the previous October in which he envisaged a mechanised force equivalent in strength to a division attacking Italian coastal targets from a base in the desert interior. It was wildly unrealistic, proof of Wingate's ignorance of the terrain of the Libyan desert.

Bagnold's proposal had been rejected but in May 1941 the 'same idea was raised in a different form'. The arrival of the Afrika Korps had caused the rethink. 'The German lines of communication were now of ever-increasing length,' ran the memo. 'The coast road from Tripoli to Sollum was 900 miles long; and with Kufra [Oasis] in our hands, constant raids against it by us should be quite possible, and would certainly tie up large numbers of enemy troops in its defence.'[23]

On 22 May, at a general staff conference at GHQ, a decision in principle was taken to form five units. In June, Bagnold relinquished command of the LRDG to Lt-Col Guy Prendergast and proceeded to Cairo 'to take up a new staff appointment as colonel in charge of a special section of the operations staff, to organise the raising of the new units and to control all independent desert operations'.[24] He had hardly the time to get his feet under his desk before another decision was reached: the LRDG would be placed under the command of the newly formed Eighth Army; as a result, the idea to establish five new strike units within the LRDG was shelved as the Eighth Army wanted to retain its strength rather than lose its best soldiers to a 'private army'.

Bill briefed David thoroughly on the situation and explained that there remained a need for a desert strike force; however, it would have to be small, or else it would be pooh-poohed by Eighth Army.

There was another factor to consider; while David was in hospital Wavell had been replaced by Gen Claude Auchinleck as commander-in-chief after the foundering of Operation Battleaxe, an offensive that had failed to oust the Germans from the Egyptian/Libyan border. However, Lt-Gen Arthur Smith was still CGS and Bill was confident he could at least pitch the idea to Auchinleck.

Of greater concern to Bill was David himself. His conduct since joining the commandos had conformed to type: an inability to knuckle down, a disdain for authority, an insufferable arrogance, the histrionics and immaturity. He had shown courage in jumping out of an aeroplane, but what was his motivation? Had David at last found a purpose or was he simply back in his fantasy world, this time playing the tough paratrooper, like those Germans on Crete? Bill had instructed hundreds of young men in the arts of irregular warfare at Lochailort and he knew a guerrilla fighter when he saw one; his gangly, uncoordinated, frail younger brother, who couldn't even jump out of an aeroplane without doing himself a mischief, was not one of them.

David was wan, listless and despondent, shorn of much of his self-confidence. Bill coaxed a letter from him to send to their mother, via Bob Laycock, who had been instructed to return to Britain by air to report on the Crete debacle and discuss the future of the commandos post Layforce.

Requesting that she address her future correspondence to Peter's flat as the commandos had been disbanded, David told his mother he was unsure what the future held but he was attempting to raise a parachute unit that would be more amusing than regular soldiering. He then apologised for having asked her to wire him £100, but explained this was to cover the 'absurd number of extra expenses I have had as a result of my various health setbacks'.[25] These included his parachute injury, a damaged eye and three weeks in hospital with dysentery.

Bill wanted to help David's parachute idea; he recognised that his brother needed a project to lift his spirits. Time was short. On 19 July a signal had been sent from GHQ to London, which began: 'Glad if you would consider early return to UK of the u/m [undermentioned]'.[26] It then listed virtually the full complement of No. 8 Commando officers, including David Stirling. Three days later, according to Stirling's service record, he was posted to No. 1 Special Service Unit from Layforce with the acting rank of captain.

Ensconced in Peter's flat, Bill and David developed the idea and then began drafting a memorandum. It was titled 'Training of Parachute Troops (Suggestions from Lieut. D. A. Stirling, Scots Guards)' but Bill's fingerprints were everywhere: in the analysis of the Greek campaign (intelligence provided by Peter Fleming, who had recently returned from Greece with the Yak Mission); in the suggestion to establish a training centre run on similar lines to Lochailort; and in the proposal to use submarines for exfiltration.

The next step was for Bill to submit the memorandum to his boss, Lt-Gen Arthur Smith, which he did swiftly. Smith read it and passed it to Gen Auchinleck. Allan Michie had trailed 'The Auk', as Auchinleck was nicknamed, throughout July. 'He blew into easy-going Cairo like a breath of Arctic air and began slashing through the slothful red tape of Middle East GHQ,' he wrote.[27]

One of the first ports of call for the fifty-seven-year-old Auchinleck was Shepheard's. Having surveyed a terrace replete with British staff officers enjoying an afternoon cocktail, Auchinleck returned to his office determined to cull GHQ of what the LRDG nicknamed the 'Short Range Shepheard's Group'.[28] According to Michie, within days scores of officers were ordered to rejoin their units in the desert.

Auchinleck drove himself hard, shunning the afternoon siesta that was a Cairo tradition and ordering his staff officers to 'cut down' on theirs.[29]

Asked by Michie if he had principles by which he commanded, Auchinleck replied that he had just one: 'There are no closed hours for an officer during a war. He must be thinking of his job and his men all the time, and his men come first.'[30] Oh, and there was one other: he didn't like verbosity in memorandums – the shorter, sweeter and pithier the better.

Auchinleck began his day with a staff conference attended by a small coterie of officers including Brig Gen John Shearer, Director of Military Intelligence, 'his Chief of the General Staff, stodgy old General Arthur Smith',[31] and Smith's deputy, Gen Neil Ritchie, who had arrived in Cairo in June believing he would be working for Wavell.

Ritchie was one of several senior officers who boarded with Auchinleck. He had left his American wife in India as the war raged in North Africa. Michie found that Ritchie shared his commander's pugnacious spirit, but he hid it well.

Auchinleck appreciated the memorandum submitted by the Stirling brothers and David was summoned to Ritchie's office: 'He took me along to the C-in-C [Auchinleck] and CGS [Smith] and after some discussion they agreed that the unit should be formed forthwith'. David was authorised to recruit six officers and sixty men.

'At the time of the unit's formation, about the end of July 1941, Brig Dudley Clarke was responsible for a branch in the Middle East which dealt among other things with military deception,' continued Stirling. 'One of his objects was to persuade the enemy that there was a fully equipped parachute and glider brigade in the Middle East … to humour him we agreed to name our unit "L" Detachment, SAS Brigade. Thus was the origin of the name, Special Air Service.'[32]

The joke at GHQ, however, was that SAS stood for 'Stirling and Stirling'.[33]

Bill knew Dudley Clarke well; the latter fulfilled a similar role for Wavell and then Auchinleck as he did for Smith.

Clarke's job title was Intelligence Officer (special duties) to the Commander-in-Chief, and his was a roving brief, as was Stirling's. It had been Wavell's way of circumventing SOE, who were in his opinion unreliable and inimical to the interests of his army. Bill persuaded Lt Ian Collins to act as L Detachment's unofficial administrative officer. The thirty-eight-year-old Collins, a member of the publishing family, had been one of Britain's leading tennis stars of the 1930s, winning the Scottish championship three times and representing Great Britain in the Davis Cup. He had joined No. 8 Commando but soon realised that time had caught up with him and soldiering was best left to younger men. Bill Stirling and Collins knew each other socially; the annual Gleneagles Hotel tennis tournament, a prestigious event on the circuit, coincided each autumn with Mrs Stirling's Gleneagles Ball in aid of the Perthshire and Kinross Nursing Association.*

The first task facing the Stirlings was to select the officers, and here once again Bill's influence was evident. David's inclination was to pick men of his social class regardless of their suitability, but Bill knew a parachute unit was no place for 'playboy soldiering'. Only the first recruit was David's choice: Jock Lewes.

In a letter to his father Lewes described how he had met David Stirling while on leave in Cairo. Stirling told him about L Detachment and asked him to join as chief instructor, 'supervising and to a large extent undertaking the training of the men and officers'. Lewes asked if he could sleep on it. 'When David came again in the morning I said "yes",' Lewes informed his father. 'Though I don't know why for I had made no decision in the night.'[34]

For a second time Lewes had succumbed to Stirling's powers

* Subsequently, when Bill Stirling formed 2SAS he ensured that Ian Collins was the liaison officer between the SAS and the Airborne Corps.

of persuasion. Lewes was not the first to find Stirling's charming entreaties irresistible despite doubts in his head. Why had he ceded, wondered Lewes. He listed David's qualities: 'His enthusiasm, his energy, his confidence, his courage in any undertaking to which he gave himself ... he is an all-in fighter.'

Of course, David had faults, but Lewes was prepared to overlook these. There was another reason why he had accepted the invitation: necessity. 'Layforce has finally disintegrated altogether since our return from confinement and I have thrown in my lot with David Stirling in a new venture, since I received a categorical refusal to my application to return to my unit in the UK,' he wrote to Mirren on 2 September. 'I will have you know that my position of chief instructor and second in command of this detachment is one of no little responsibility and social consequence!'[35]

Lewes was the perfect foil to David Stirling, his methodical and imperturbable nature a counterbalance to his commander's immaturity and impetuosity.

The next officer recruited was an old school friend of Bill Stirling's, the only boy at Ampleforth who had surpassed him in all-round ability. His name was Charles Bonington, the son of a German called Maximilian Bonig, who in 1914 had deemed it prudent to change the family name to the more British-sounding Bonington.

Bonington hadn't attended Ampleforth prep school; he had arrived at the senior school in 1924, a shock to the system having grown up in the Andaman Islands in India. From his first day at Ampleforth Bonington shone; in 1925 he was elected onto the council of the Medievalists' Society and gave an outstanding address on Saladin; he was one of three nominated school librarians; he was promoted to Under Officer in the OTC; he played Duke Orsino in the school's production of *Twelfth Night*; he was commended by the History Society for his paper on 'Soviet Intrigue in Asia'; he was the star player in the first XV and captained the team in his final year; he was in the cricket XI; and he was the dominant member of the debating society, with the school magazine stating that 'he is gifted with a wonderful flow of language, which is a great help in debate'.[36]

As well as being brilliant, Bonington, a 'small man with small eyes',[37] was selfish and egotistical. He read law at Oxford, from where he entered the Indian Government Service. He married Helen and in August 1934 she gave birth to their son, Christian (Sir Chris Bonington, one of Britain's greatest mountaineers). Nine months later Bonington abandoned his family and ran off to Australia with the ambition of becoming a journalist. It was tough at first: in September 1936 his name did appear in the newspapers but only because he had been fined £1 for travelling on a train without a ticket. The arresting officer told the court he had discovered Bonington 'under a motor car in a truck attached to a tram which arrived from Gympie'.[38]

By 1939 Bonington was writing feature articles for newspapers and appearing on radio to discuss history and the arts. On the outbreak of war he enlisted as a private in the Australian Imperial Force, but in July 1940 one of his former employers, the *Courier-Mail* newspaper, reported: 'There is only one AIF man attached to British Middle East headquarters in Cairo. He is sergeant Charles Bonnington [*sic*], BA, of Oxford, a Fellow of the Royal Anthropological Institute. His work has proved so valuable that he is being transferred from the AIF and granted a commission in the British army.'[39]

According to a letter from Bonington's father published in the *Ampleforth Journal*, Charles was wounded in Libya and 'was unconscious for days on end and did not expect to get over it, but a trip to Australia in a hospital ship and five months there set him up again'.[40] When Bonington returned to North Africa in the summer of 1941 every officer and all but eighty-nine men of his old battalion had been killed or captured in Crete. It was around this time that he encountered Bill Stirling, and in August Charles Bonington became one of L Detachment's six officers.

As to the three other officers, Bill Stirling had read the report on No. 11 Commando's action at Litani River in June, a tougher than expected fight against Vichy French troops. It had been one of the very few Layforce successes, attributable to the courage, resolve and initiative of the commandos, and Bill Stirling reasoned that in their ranks he would find the right type of officer for the parachute unit. One in particular he had in mind, a man whose name was known to him before the war through his feats on the rugby field: Blair Mayne.

10

The thirty-three officers and 513 other ranks of No. 11 Commando had spent March and April getting to know the Middle East. From their quarters in Cairo they were transported to Geneifa and thence to Alexandria for an attack on the port of Bardia. That operation was aborted and so it was back to Alexandria, and from there in late April to Palestine. By May, No. 11 Commando were encamped in Cyprus, disheartened and increasingly disillusioned with commando life. None more so than Blair Mayne. 'He had not been an enormously heavy drinker before, but a mixture perhaps of boredom and Cyprus wine … tempted him,' recalled Tommy Macpherson. 'And when he was in his cups he really was extremely difficult to deal with.'[1]

On one occasion a group of commandos went to a nightclub in Nicosia and opened a tab. The wine flowed and at the end of the evening the owner presented Mayne with the bill. He'd overcharged them, assuming the soldiers were in no fit state to remember how many bottles they'd drunk. But Mayne had kept count and he was unimpressed to discover he'd been heavily overcharged in the bill. This was unfair, and his response was similar to his reaction at the hotel in Pietermaritzburg during the Lions tour three years earlier:

Mayne pulled out his revolver and fired several rounds into the floor at the feet of the owner, making the man dance as his penance.

Mayne was sentenced to forty-eight hours' open arrest, with Macpherson as his supervising officer. He took his punishment without complaint and he and Macpherson got on well because of their shared interest in rugby.

The other person to whom Mayne listened was Eoin McGonigal. He was an anchor to Northern Ireland; when he looked at Eoin Mayne saw his brother Ambrose, and remembered his rugby days, and he saw also his father, John, the judge who had wished him well as a solicitor in the summer of 1939.

The incident in the nightclub may have been the final straw for Mayne, as far as No. 11 Commando was concerned. When word reached Cyprus that a military mission was being raised to go to the Bush Warfare School in Burma, and then on to China, Mayne applied to join, intimating his decision to his father in a letter dated 2 June.

The next day No. 11 Commando received a rush order to embark. As the men filed up the gangplanks of the destroyers *Hotspur* and *Ilex* there was more scepticism than excitement; they had been here before and the usual outcome was cancellation.

From Cyprus the commandos sailed to Port Said in Egypt, minus their commanding officer, Lt-Col Richard Pedder, who was in Jerusalem receiving his briefing from Gen Henry Wilson, commanding officer of British forces in Palestine and Trans-Jordan.

Wilson explained that Vichy French forces in Syria had acceded to a German request to use their aerodromes as launchpads for attacks on the British in Iraq, who were battling to quell a pro-Axis revolt. But it wasn't Iraq that concerned the British so much as the ramifications for Egypt; if Syria was controlled by the Germans, Winston Churchill informed parliament, this 'constituted very great dangers to the whole Eastern flank in our defence in the Nile Valley and the Suez Canal'.[2]

Wilson told Pedder that the Vichy French had an army of thirty-five thousand, while he had at his disposal the 7th Australian Infantry Division, part of the 1st Cavalry Division, a brigade of Indian troops and a small number of Free French soldiers. And Pedder's No. 11 Scottish Commando.

Pedder was ordered to come ashore north and south of the Litani River, where it debouched into the sea, to seize the bridge and facilitate the rapid advance along the coast road of the 21st Australian Infantry Brigade. Wilson said that the bridge had probably been destroyed and added that the scarce intelligence they'd obtained suggested that two colonial battalions of the enemy were holding a position on the right bank of the Litani River facing south.

No. 11 Commando approached the beach early on the morning of 9 June, wading towards Syria through a light surf from eleven landing craft. Pedder had split his force in three: a northern party, Z Force, commanded by Capt George More and comprising No. 4 Troop (Eoin McGonigal) and No. 10 Troop (Tommy Macpherson); a southern party, X Force, commanded by Maj Geoffrey Keyes; and Y Force, in the centre, under the command of Pedder and composed of Nos 1, 7 and 8 Troops.

It was Y Force that bore the brunt of the enemy resistance. 'Immediately the boat beached we came under very heavy machine gun, rifle and mortar fire from a point about three hundred yards south or right of our landing point,' recalled RSM Lewis Tevendale, who was with Pedder's party. 'We crawled off the beach and advanced along a dried river bed thus breaking through the enemy's first line of defence without sustaining one casualty.'[3]

For Lt Bill Fraser of 8 Troop it was a return to battle one year after being blooded at St Valery with the Gordon Highlanders. For Lt Blair Mayne of 7 Troop it was a baptism of fire; all the training, the self-examination, the questions posed to the likes of Fraser and other Dunkirk veterans – now he would see how he stood up to an opponent armed with more than a well-timed tackle, and whether his mind would cope with the thump of heavy machine guns, the sight of friends falling and the screams of the wounded.

One troop of Y Force advanced down a dry river bed. They cut some barbed wire and probed further. Dawn broke, and the enemy snipers went to work. Lt Gerald Bryan's corporal was shot in the head. Then Lt Alistair Coode was hit in the chest. His sergeant ran to his aid and was dropped by the same marksman. Bryan's men charged a battery of 75mm guns and despatched the crew with their bayonets.

Pedder instructed Bryan to provide fire support while he led his HQ section toward the enemy barracks east of Aiteniye farm. They took their objective, and twenty-five (mostly Senegalese) prisoners. Pedder led his men on. A bullet grazed his helmet. He turned to his sergeant and remarked he'd had a close shave. The next bullet killed him. Gerald Bryan was shot in the legs and taken prisoner. A bullet bowled over Bill Fraser. He lay among some scrub, not sure if he was alive or dead. His sergeant, Jock Cheyne, dashed over and examined him. The bullet had hit the chin strap of Fraser's helmet. His senses would take time to unscramble. He ordered Cheyne to take command but insisted on joining the advance despite his mild concussion.

Mayne's troop had lost one man coming ashore and another as they crossed the coastal road, following the route taken by Pedder. They encountered the prisoners seized by their CO and continued on. The terrain became more rugged and as they followed a path they saw some mules. Mayne told his men to be on their guard: the enemy was close. They pressed on and, turning a corner, Mayne came face to face with thirty enemy soldiers; they were sitting or squatting, not primed for action. In French, Mayne ordered them to the ground. One raised his rifle. Mayne shot him dead.

Mayne and his men had seized a command post. There was a quantity of ammunition and a telephone, but more importantly supplies of food and drink.

As they refreshed themselves the telephone rang. Mayne let it ring and then trailed the wire to another command post where he collected fifty more prisoners and several mortars and light machine guns.

Mayne lost another man in his troop in the afternoon, killed by Australians in one of several friendly fire incidents. Overall, however, it had been a satisfactory initiation for Mayne, and for No. 11 Commando. At midday on 10 June the 21st Australian Infantry Brigade crossed the Litani River and began the advance towards Damascus, which fell on 21 June.

The cost had been heavy. Pedder and four officers were dead and in total 104 commandos out of the 395 who had landed had been killed or wounded. Maj Keyes was now in command and, after submitting his report in person in Jerusalem, he wrote a raft of recommendations for gallantry awards, including several Military Crosses. Mayne's bold initiative was rewarded only with a Mention in Despatches.

Keyes had never liked the Irishman; he felt inadequate and intimidated in his presence, and he sensed – perhaps it was imagination, but he thought not – that Mayne had no respect for him.

It was more the fact that Mayne felt Keyes didn't belong in No. 11 Commando. He was an upper-class Englishman who had climbed the ladder of life not through skill or endeavour but by using the family name. Tommy Macpherson recalled that Keyes 'didn't get on with Blair Mayne'; he regarded him as uncouth and 'unreliable'.[4]

Keyes's greatest failing was his insecurity; he knew he was Mayne's inferior as a man and as a commando. But he had the rank. Back in Cyprus on garrison duty after Litani River, he attempted to assert his authority as Mayne and McGonigal chatted in the officers' mess. Mayne rose and fended off Keyes as if he were an opponent on the rugby field. Keyes fell back, grazing his head on the edge of a table.

Mayne had committed a serious offence and Keyes slunk out promising punishment. There was no official reprimand but on 23 June Mayne left No. 11 Scottish Commando and returned to

Egypt. At Geneifa he fell ill with malaria; during his convalescence he wrote to his brother on 15 July, informing him he had left the commandos because 'it wasn't the same since our CO [Pedder] got written off'.[5] He still held out hope, he added, that his request to be posted to the Far East would be granted.

Mayne enjoyed being pampered by the nurses during his recuperation. Their presence was not a disruptive influence; on the contrary, a hospital was a place for men to heal and not bond. He formed a friendship with an Irish nurse called Jane Kenny, who later corresponded with Mayne's sister.

No. 11 Commando were officially disbanded on 6 August when they were billeted at Abbassia Barracks in Cairo. The timing couldn't have been better for David and Bill Stirling. How exactly they recruited McGonigal, who joined on 15 August, and Fraser, who followed three days later, to L Detachment isn't known. McGonigal had acquitted himself well in command of No. 4 Troop at Litani River, while Fraser's war record spoke for itself. He was a Scot, too, undemonstrative, unflappable and unyielding. Bill Stirling's influence is evident in the selection of Fraser; he didn't care about his background, only his suitability for irregular warfare.

Similarly, the acquirement of Blair Mayne suggested Bill Stirling had made the initial approach. Had the invitation come from David, Mayne would have almost certainly rejected it. He had recently escaped from one weak and foppish upper-class commander in Geoffrey Keyes: why throw in his lot with a man who was a replica in personality and temperament?

So much about David was affected: the accent, the charm, the body language. Yet it seemed to bewitch most people. 'He was invested with this sort of magnetism and I fell very much under the spell,' admitted George Jellicoe.[6] Not Mayne. One SAS officer, Peter Davis, described what it was like to encounter Mayne for the first time: 'He was one of those people with the dead straight forehead, so that from the top of his head to the tip of his nose was a straight line. Under great jutting eyebrows, his piercing blue eyes looked discomfortingly at me, betraying his remarkable talent of being able to sum a person up within a minute of meeting him.'[7]

Mayne had the measure of David Stirling within the minute. The only superiority he had was his class. Otherwise Stirling was his inferior in every manner. Stirling knew it too.

He would command L Detachment in name only; psychologically, Mayne would lead. Bill Stirling understood this. It is why he wanted Mayne. He knew David did not have it in him to lead a guerrilla unit by example. When Bill scrutinised Mayne, when he observed his graceful movements, his calm and penetrating gaze, those eyes that missed nothing, he was reminded of his ghillie, Adam. L Detachment would succeed if Mayne was sent out to stalk and kill, while David remained in the big house, waiting to mount the trophies on the wall.

The Stirlings recruited in total nineteen other ranks from No. 11 Commando, among them Sgt John 'Jock' Cheyne, corporals Jeff Du Vivier and Bob Tait, and privates Cornelius 'Maggie' McGinn and John Byrne.

Jock Lewes brought with him from Tobruk Jim Almonds, Pat Riley, Jim Blakeney and Bob Lilley, all of whom had been with him in No. 8 Commando. Ernie Bond, Bob Bennett, Johnny Rose, Dave Kershaw and John Cooper were also recruited from David Stirling's former commando. Only a handful of the sixty men recruited to L Detachment came from neither No. 8 nor No. 11 Commando. Among them was Reg Seekings, a fenman who had served in No. 7 Commando and was selected by Stirling on the back of his impressive pre-war sporting prowess, notably as a heavyweight boxer.

Seekings rarely lost, but one opponent he could not get the better of was a local policeman and former Coldstream Guardsman called Pat Riley, who beat him twice. Sgt Riley's presence in L Detachment may have been a contributory factor in Seeking's selection; Riley was a favourite of Stirling's, and he in turn was fiercely loyal to his officer, and a word from him would have carried weight with his commanding officer.

Mayne's reputation had gone before him; the Guardsmen in particular awaited his appearance in Kabrit with anticipation. Pat Riley was eager to size up the Irishman. He considered himself a prime physical specimen and couldn't believe any man was his superior in that respect. The guardsmen were big men, and there was much discreet comparison. Jim Almonds sidled up to Mayne and judged him to be about his own height, 6ft 3in, and a little heavier than his own fifteen stone.

Reg Seekings said Mayne's 'appearance was a bit over-awing and he had a very powerful presence'.[8] Nowhere was Mayne's presence felt more than on the miniature rugby pitch that had been staked out at Kabrit. Here the guardsmen witnessed Mayne's extraordinary athleticism, the nimbleness and the lightning reflexes. And his strength. Jim Almonds received a pass and sprinted for the try line, only to have one of Mayne's 'huge ham-like hands'[9] rip the ball from his grasp.

David Stirling and Jock Lewes devised the parachute course that each man had to undertake, and the rest of the training programme took its inspiration from what had been taught at Lochailort by Bill Stirling: expertise in small arms, close combat, explosives and navigation.

The men were already proficient in these arts from their commando training but they practised and perfected the techniques learned in Scotland a year earlier. There were also regular route marches, mostly at night, carrying packs that became heavier as the weeks passed. Throughout this time Mayne, who had been appointed commander of 2 Troop, tightened his grip as the psychological leader of the unit. Jock Lewes, CO of 1 Troop, informed his father in a letter dated

25 September, 'I spend a great deal of time planning programs [*sic*] and writing reports, but I find quite enough time to keep pace with the training.'

Some of the men called Lewes 'The Wizard'. For hours each day he mixed ingredients and potions in a 'makeshift shack of a laboratory'.[10] 'To us Lewes was the brain and David had the power to get things done,' said Jimmy Storie, one of the sixty recruits to L Detachment. 'Jock liked things right. He was a perfectionist. He thought about things in greater depth than Stirling, who was more carefree.'[11]

Lewes eventually produced a bomb that proved devastatingly effective. The bomb – which Charles Bonington called 'Lewesite' – was unprepossessing at first sight. A stodgy lump weighing just 1lb, the plastic explosive and thermite was rolled in motor-car oil and then Lewes added a No. 27 detonator, an instantaneous fuse and a time pencil. It was all contained in a linen bag about the size of a glove.

Lewes colour-coded the time pencils according to the length of fuse: white was a two-minute fuse; green five minutes; black ten; yellow fifteen; brown twenty; blue twenty-five; and red thirty minutes. Over time Lewes developed a series of 'delay acid' fuses, specially designed for enemy aircraft. A red fuse meant the acid would take six and a half hours to eat through the wire if the air temperature was 40 degrees Fahrenheit – in other words, on a cold desert night. If the temperature was 88 degrees Fahrenheit, the acid would take three hours to eat through the wire. Violet was the longest delay fuse produced by Lewes, taking eight and a half days for the acid to activate the striker.

Lewes was at his happiest in his laboratory. His experiments were intellectually stimulating, and he enjoyed the solitude. Naturally aloof, Lewes was incapable of communicating with his men other than as their officer. He didn't have the social dexterity, the empathy, the inclination, to try to form a human bond. He could feel that the men respected him, but his reserve was a barrier that prevented any warmth or affection. At the end of every day Lewes retired to his tent and read or wrote long intense letters to Mirren, who was by now his fiancée. 'Let's get married right away, before I'm a Captain or a Colonel,' he wrote on 1 October. 'Just say yes, you'll marry me when I'm a proper Captain … or else I might die and then they would say poor dear.'[12]

David Stirling was hardly seen at Kabrit in September and October. He was in Cairo most of the time, either at his brother's flat or in his little office in GHQ. There were briefings and conferences to attend in the company of Bill, and he was putting his charm to good use, procuring equipment and supplies for the unit.

David preferred Cairo to Kabrit; it was a more comfortable environment. He needed the emotional and spiritual support of his two brothers, especially Bill, and in the Egyptian capital he mixed with his own social class. On the rare occasions that Stirling did visit Kabrit he saw that Mayne 'was emerging as the natural leader'. He sensed, too, he was 'growing apart from the men he commanded'.[13]

Mayne, who was known now within L Detachment as 'Paddy', had no trouble winning the respect of the men; he did that by his physical feats, whether in battle, in training or on the makeshift rugby pitch. But he had also earned their affection for the interest he took in them as men. In October Jim Almonds received word from home that his baby son was very ill; he soon recovered but in the interim Mayne had been 'particularly solicitous'.[14]

There was one way that Stirling could claw back some authority from Mayne: on the end of a parachute. Admittedly, Stirling's inaugural jump had not been a glorious moment in his military career but nonetheless he had jumped from the aircraft, which was more than Mayne had done. Stirling therefore took a more hands-on role in the parachute instruction than in any other aspect of L Detachment's training. He instructed Jim Almonds to put his carpentry skills to good use by building some jumping stands, which were hexagonal in shape 'with sides which increased in height as the trainee worked his way round it from 4 to 12 feet'. From these stands, the men progressed to jumping from a trolley, which had been stolen from a local quarry along with about eighty yards of rails. Once L Detachment had mastered leaping from the trolley, they boarded a truck for the next stage of their training. 'Afternoon spent jumping backwards from a lorry at twenty-five miles per hour,' wrote Almonds in his diary on 6 October. 'Three broken arms and a number of other casualties.'[15] Lt Bill Fraser was one of those who broke an arm, and Maggie McGinn and John Byrne were also injured.

Ten days later, L Detachment trooped mournfully towards a Bristol Bombay aircraft on the RAF aerodrome opposite their camp. 'I looked about me at the faces of my colleagues and their expressions told me that they were feeling just as bad as I was,' recorded Jeff Du Vivier in his diary.[16]

Du Vivier was to jump third in the first 'stick' of ten parachutists. He was trembling as the aircraft left the ground. He tried to whistle 'Roll Out the Barrel' to lift his spirits but his mouth was so dry the tune died on his lips. At 900ft the first pair jumped. 'There was a "swoosh, swoosh" as the two men disappeared into space leaving their static lines flapping at the side of the plane,' wrote Du Vivier. 'My hair stood on end.'

The sergeant despatcher signalled to Du Vivier and his jump partner. 'Like lambs going to the slaughter we stood up. My knees began to beat a tattoo on one another as I stretched up to adjust my static line. We moved towards the door and I glanced down. Mother Earth looked miles away and I wished I'd never been born.'

The despatcher yelled 'Ready' and a moment later slapped Du Vivier on the shoulder with a yell of 'Go!' Out he went. 'What happened next I can only faintly remember,' he told his diary. Terror, hopelessness, confusion … and then exhilaration. 'Everything steadied itself and I found myself sitting comfortably in my harness. I began to sing and shout.'

The Bombay took off with a second contingent, among them two men Du Vivier knew from No. 11 Commando, Ken Warburton and Joe Duffy. Warburton jumped first. Duffy followed, but not before he had hesitated at the despatch door. He had sensed something wasn't right, had looked up at the static-line fixtures. His reticence had elicited a scream from the despatcher and so out Duffy went.

Neither his nor Warburton's parachute opened. When they jumped into the slipstream the pressure buckled the clip and disengaged the static line ring from the rail.

No one else jumped that day. That evening David Stirling assembled the men and commiserated with them at the loss of their two comrades. However, he said, the reason for the malfunction had been identified and rectified, and parachuting would continue in the morning. He'd jump first and then Jock Lewes.

Few men slept well that night, including Stirling, who 'hated parachuting',[17] but the next day he led them out of the Bombay and there were no further casualties. Stirling had repaired the unit's collective morale by his courageous leadership and underlined that he was their commander.

11

In his office at GHQ, David Stirling discovered that he couldn't always get what he wanted. It was a novel experience. Hitherto he had done what he'd pleased. If he did encounter difficulties his instinct was to walk away rather than strive to overcome them. Cambridge, Edinburgh architects, the Scots Guards: there was a pattern.

He had even to an extent retreated from L Detachment, spending most of his time in Cairo rather than in Kabrit, where Lewes and Mayne ran the show. At least at GHQ he could rely on his brother for support. Furthermore Bill, with his influence, was able to open doors and initiate introductions that otherwise would have been denied David. For despite Gen Auchinleck's determination to slim down the number of staff officers at GHQ there were still a great many, among whom were a number who regarded irregular warfare as antithetical to the British army. David Stirling called them 'fossilised shits' and 'freemasons of mediocrity'.[1]

These staff officers made it their mission to obstruct or inconvenience anyone attempting to raise an irregular force, regardless of their name. 'I am afraid I carry damn little weight,' complained Maj Geoffrey Keyes in a letter to his father, the Director of Combined Operations.

'Most elderly majors in various HQs view me with extreme distrust, disgust and general Colonel Blimp outlook.'*[2]

Another officer who chafed at the bloody-minded short-sightedness of some staff officers was Capt Roger Courtney. A famous explorer and adventurer in Africa in the 1930s, Courtney had raised a small canoe unit in the summer of 1940 called the Folboat Section (the forerunner of the Special Boat Service) after their folding canoes made of wood and canvas. This section had been attached to No. 8 Commando and had carried out a handful of raids during the summer. They had experienced success and failure, said Courtney in a letter to Col Bob Laycock on 18 September 1941, from which they had learned much. 'Now that the Germans are entangled in the depth of Russia, the initiative on all enemy coastlines has passed into our hands,' he wrote. He wanted Laycock's support in taking his idea for a canoe reconnaissance force to GHQ because thus far he had met only indifference. 'I genuinely believe that careful reconnaissance of the Litanie [*sic*] River would have facilitated and lessened the dangers of the operation that C Battalion (No. 11 Commando) undertook.'[3]

Laycock, who was now in charge of all special service units in Egypt, duly wrote to Gen Auchinleck outlining his concerns that GHQ had lost interest in irregular warfare. On 30 October he received a reply from the Chief of the General Staff on behalf of Auchinleck. 'He wishes me to assure you that he is personally interested in the SS [special service] Troops,' wrote Lt-Gen Smith. 'The real difficulty about SS troops is that we simply have not got the men and we are now thousands of men short of our requirements in ordinary infantry battalions in the Middle East.'[4]

* Keyes eventually led a commando operation in November 1941 against Rommel's Libyan HQ. But Rommel was elsewhere and during the attack Keyes was killed. He was awarded a posthumous VC. Tommy Macpherson, who was involved in the raid, said, 'Keyes's death, sad as it was, was actually the sort of thing he had been looking for all his life.'

Courtney, Keyes and Laycock could only look on with envy at what David Stirling had achieved in a matter of weeks. Laycock, of course, knew how he had managed it. But neither Keyes nor Courtney would have been aware of Bill Stirling's influence within GHQ.

At SOE headquarters in London, however, there was growing puzzlement as to the whereabouts of Bill Stirling. He had sailed to the Middle East as part of the Yak Mission at the start of the year, and then vanished. In September SOE contacted Peter Fleming, who informed them that Bill had been transferred from his command to GHQ on 13 March, 'but cannot give any further information'.[5] That wasn't true; Fleming had seen Bill in Cairo in May, but he may have wanted to protect his friend at his request.

On 16 October 1941 SOE Cairo cabled the London office: 'Stirling is not repeat not employed by SO2 [the sabotage branch]. He is employed by Middle East Forces. We will have to telegraph details as soon as we can obtain them. This has so far proved difficult.'

It was an embarrassing situation for SOE, tasked with clandestine warfare yet at a loss to explain what had happened to one of their own. The puzzle was eventually solved when it went to the very top of the organisation.

Stirling, explained a cable sent on 28 October, 'was transferred from SO2 on the 18th March, since when, with short intervals, he has been in personal service of CGS. The telegram giving the above information states that the nature of this service is known to CD.'

'CD' was the codename for the head of SOE, Sir Frank Nelson.

Unfortunately for Bill Stirling, SOE London had also contacted the War Office in their attempt to unravel the mystery. The War Office in turn cabled the Brigade of Guards. On 3 November Maj A. G. Howe at Wellington Barracks informed the War Office that Stirling was working for the Chief of the General Staff and that GHQ had told him 'arrangements have been made to have him posted to GHQ retrospectively from the date he left us'.

Maj Howe added that he hoped 'that this matter will now be cleared up without any further trouble'.

It wasn't. Indignant that Stirling and GHQ had collaborated without its knowledge, the War Office ordered him to return to Britain. 'Posted to Home Establishment on completion of Special Employment under CGS' was the entry on Stirling's service record, dated 3 November 1941.

Bill had departed Cairo by the time David wrote one of his infrequent letters to his mother on 15 November, his twenty-sixth birthday. To her there was no pretence. He admitted his turmoil, writing that 'I hate Egypt and I have never been so homesick since the Lower 2nd at Ampleforth.'[6]

It was a frank admission to make. Having listed his physical frailties in his July letter, Stirling now described his mental anguish. Nonetheless, he wanted her to know that he achieved something of which she could be proud: his parachute unit was about to embark on its first operation and he promised her it would be more exciting than dangerous.

He ended his letter with a regret. 'It is very sad Bill has gone,' he wrote.

Jock Lewes also wrote home around this time. On 12 November he composed a long, eloquent and ardent letter to the woman he loved. 'My darling best loved Mirren, how I wish now that I could relax with you and just be together instead of having to write surrounded by reminders of all that thrusts between us!' he said. 'You and I, when we meet again will be different from when we parted, but this is the glory of it; we shall still be Mirren and Jock and whatever happens will be able to laugh in each other's eyes and love what we see.'[7]

To his father, the following day, Lewes spoke of the present: 'Now we want to prove ourselves. This unit cannot now die as Layforce died. It is alive and will live gloriously, renewing itself by its creative power in the imagination of men.'[8]

Lewes described a visit to Kabrit from Gen Auchinleck, who had found time in his schedule to watch an L Detachment exercise. Afterwards he talked to each of the men, 'and when he went he thanked us not for a good show but for a good unit whom he trusts'.

Lewes told his father: 'David has perforce been absent from the unit more often than not, and I have been in command this while. We have worked splendidly together ... we have fashioned this unit. He has established it without, and I think I may say I have established it within.'

On 15 November David Stirling paid a call on Peter Oldfield of the Air Reconnaissance Unit. He had requested some photographs of their targets and Oldfield 'show[ed] him how to get thro' Gazala defences to shoot up aircraft'.[9]

Later that day Stirling assembled L Detachment and divulged their operation, codenamed 'Squatter'. 'The plans and maps were unsealed, explained and studied until each man knew his job by heart,' Jeff Du Vivier recorded in his diary that evening.

The operation was to coincide with the launch of Auchinleck's long-waited offensive, Operation Crusader, the objective of which was to retake Cyrenaica and seize the Libyan airfields from the enemy, thereby enabling the Royal Air Force to increase their supplies to the besieged island of Malta. XIII Corps would advance against the Axis forces holding the front line, while XXX Corps would swing round the flanks and destroy Gen Rommel's armoured force of 174 tanks. Meanwhile the besieged garrison at Tobruk, seventy miles behind the German front line, would break out and meet the units of XXX Corps as they advanced west.

L Detachment's task was to parachute into Cyrenaica on the night of 16/17 November, between the two armies, and attack a string of Axis airfields at Gazala and Tmimi. They would then trek fifty miles inland to a rendezvous, where a motorised patrol of the LRDG, under the command of Capt Jake Easonsmith, would be waiting.

The LRDG were informed of their role in an operational order issued on 11 November. It was not well received. Their commanding officer, Lt-Col Guy Prendergast, regarded it as an affront to his men. On 21 October Prendergast had written to Maj Rupert Harding-Newman, a G2 (responsible for intelligence and security) at Eighth Army HQ at Bagoush. They were old friends, and had explored the Libyan desert together with Ralph Bagnold between the wars; Harding-Newman had also been a great help to Bagnold when he raised the LRDG in June 1940. Prendergast told Harding-Newman that he envisaged seven possible tasks for the unit during the impending offensive:

a) Topographical recce.
b) Dropping agents.
c) Traffic census.
d) Traffic census linked by W/T to ground strafing aircraft.
e) Laying ambushes on roads and shooting up convoys in order to encourage the enemy to escort them with amd. [armoured] cars withdrawn from the front.
f) Approaching aerodromes on foot at night with the object of damaging aircraft.
g) Observing enemy reactions to our main advance.

In Prendergast's view, 'the most useful role for all patrols in the period just before the advance would be that of trying to destroy aircraft on aerodromes'. As the only commitment the LRDG had at this time was to transport fifteen Libyan SOE agents to a coastal area and collect them later, he would have four patrols available to undertake raiding operations.

Prendergast proposed that each patrol – comprising five or six trucks, but occasionally four – be assigned an area in which to operate. 'These areas would contain two or three prospective targets, i.e. aerodromes which might not be in use at that time,' he outlined to Harding-Newman. 'On about D minus 4 the patrols would arrive in the neighbourhood of their areas and begin reconnoitring approaches to aerodromes.'[10]

Once the patrol had conducted a thorough reconnaissance, the raid 'would be carried out by small parties on foot who would hope to rejoin their vehicles after planting the bombs'. He ended by listing potential targets and telling Harding-Newman that the LRDG had started experimenting with a 'mills bomb [hand grenade] on top of an A/Tk [anti-tank] mine under the belly of the aircraft'. If planted under the belly of the aircraft 'it should do considerable damage'.

Prendergast had no idea that Jock Lewes had already invented his ingenious bomb and he was probably only vaguely aware of a unit called L Detachment. It was an unwelcome surprise, therefore, when he received his operational order on 11 November. The LRDG had not been allocated any airfields to attack, but they had been instructed to provide a taxi service for David Stirling and his men. Prendergast was annoyed and perplexed; the LRDG had been raiding enemy targets for over a year, including an Italian airfield at Murzak, which they'd attacked in their vehicles, machine guns blazing.

Prendergast had been commissioned into the Royal Tank Corps in 1925, aged twenty, and two years later, while stationed in Egypt, he had embarked with Ralph Bagnold and four others on an exploration of the Libyan desert in three Model T Fords. It had been an epic adventure, and a successful one, taking them four hundred miles west of Cairo to the oasis of Siwa, where Alexander the Great had stood in 332 BC.

There was a link, albeit a tenuous one, between the Prendergasts and the Stirlings. Prendergast lived in the Highland village of Fort Augustus, on land that had been once owned by the Lovats. The family had given the land to the Benedictine order in the nineteenth century, and an abbey was built, at which two of David Stirling's maternal uncles had been monks.

Prendergast and Stirling met for the first time by accident, shortly before the commencement of the November offensive. The commanding officer of the LRDG was dining at Shepheard's with Lt Alastair Timpson, who had just joined his unit. Stirling appeared and, Timpson recalled, 'sat at our table and told us of his operational plans for his newly formed parachute unit which he intended to use in the forthcoming offensive, which would require LRDG cooperation'.[11]

To blurt out such information in Shepheard's was a dreadful breach of security. Paddy Mayne would never have been so careless. He and all the men of No. 11 Commando had been issued with a special order by Lt-Col Pedder when they arrived in North Africa eight months earlier, one which cautioned them against any loose talk while in the presence of civilians, particularly those working in bars and brothels.

But Stirling had to show off, particularly as Timpson was an old friend. Educated at Eton and Trinity College, Cambridge, he had been commissioned into the Scots Guards and no doubt knew some of Stirling's reputation, if not all of it.

Prendergast disliked Stirling from the start, and, remembered Timpson, as time wore on he became increasingly bitter at his slovenly standards.

Early on the morning of 16 November David Stirling and his fifty-four men were flown from El Khanka airfield at Kabrit to Bagush, three hundred miles west. The RAF had put their officers' mess at the disposal of L Detachment, recalled Jeff Du Vivier, 'and we kicked off with a first-rate meal after which there were books, games, wireless and a bottle of beer each'.[12] Stirling was not with his men here, but wasn't too far away, at Eighth Army HQ, where he was presented with the meteorological reports for the next twenty-four hours; they were dire. A storm was on its way, and strong winds and heavy rain were forecast. Brig Sandy Galloway, Brigadier General Staff of Eighth Army, warned that a parachute operation would almost certainly end in disaster, especially as it was a moonless night. In addition, the drop zone was what the locals called *hammada*, a hard, stony surface. He advised Stirling to cancel the operation but left the decision in his hands.

What David Stirling would have given to have Bill at his side at this excruciating moment. His counsel would have been priceless. He might have used his own frustrated experience on Operation Knife eighteen months earlier to convince his brother to heed the advice of the brigadier. Live to fight another day.

Stirling returned to Bagush airbase and, he claimed, consulted the officers of L Detachment. In one account, written in 1958, he said that Jock Lewes was the first to assent, followed by Bill Fraser. But Fraser wasn't on the operation. The last officer to voice his opinion was Mayne, who, according to Stirling, declared: 'I joined this unit to fight; and if I don't get a crack at the enemy soon I may have to indulge in a few practice rounds with some of the chaps at Headquarters.'[13]

In his biography, however, Stirling's memory was that Lewes and Mayne immediately agreed that the operation must go ahead, and the other officers then also reacted positively.

Stirling's own instinct was to press ahead. A gambler by nature, he said that they should continue with the operation and to hell with the risk. The men had trained hard and were eager to go into action. After the countless aborted raids with Layforce, another cancellation would be damaging for morale. It would reflect badly on him, too, and he was desperate to prove the doubters in GHQ wrong.

At 6.30 p.m. the fifty-five men boarded some trucks and were driven the short distance to where the five Bristol Bombay aircraft were waiting. As Jeff Du Vivier's aircraft began taxiing down the runway he 'muttered a silent prayer and put myself in God's hands'.[14]

12

When Jeff Du Vivier hit the ground, he was seized by the wind and hurled across the desert floor, rolling and tumbling through the darkness as he frantically fumbled with the quick-release box of his harness. When he eventually freed himself from his parachute, he lay panting and disorientated. 'I was bruised and bleeding and there was a sharp pain in my right leg,' he wrote later. 'When I saw the rocky ground I'd travelled over, I thanked my lucky stars that I was alive.'[1]

Du Vivier rose gingerly to his feet, stripped off his tattered boiler suit to his khaki battledress underneath, and set off into the 'inky blackness' to find the rest of his eleven-man stick. He encountered Jimmy Storie, 'black and blue from the rocks' and nursing a stiff back but otherwise in one piece. Johnny Cooper also emerged from the darkness, his roller-coaster ride across the desert curtailed when his parachute snagged on a camel thorn bush. They began walking back along the bearing given by the RAF navigator and within an hour all of the men were accounted for, including the officer in charge, Jock Lewes. At half past midnight on 17 November, Du Vivier led them north towards their objective.

David Stirling's aircraft had arrived late over the drop zone. The flight had been a fraught one for the men inside the Bristol Bombay, as the wind and anti-aircraft fire buffeted the plane. The men were relieved when told to prepare to jump. That was until they felt the full force of the wind. 'I estimated this about thirty miles per hour,' wrote Cpl Bob Tait in his report of the operation. 'We all made very bad landings. I myself being the only one uninjured.'[2]

One man, Stanley Bolland, could not be found. Apart from Tait, the other seven were all carrying wounds of varying degrees, including Stirling, who had 'sustained injuries about the arms and legs'.

At approximately 1 a.m. the party struck out for the rendezvous with the other sticks assigned to attack two airfields in the Gazala area: those commanded by Jock Lewes and Eoin McGonigal. 'We should have reached this wadi before daylight, but the delay in dropping and assembling and the fact that we were dropped slightly out of position, threw the time schedule out and by daylight we were still in the open and had to lie up,' wrote Tait.

Stirling and his men spent the day sheltering from the torrential rain that had started around midday. Somewhere in the vicinity were Jock Lewes and his ten men, enduring the same atrocious conditions. 'The lightning was terrific,' noted Jeff Du Vivier. 'It continued to pour in buckets for about thirty minutes and by the end of this time we were sitting waist deep in a swirling tide of water.'[3]

At nightfall, Stirling announced that he was splitting the party. He and Bob Tait would continue to the target, while CSM George Yates and five men, including Sgt Len Colquhuon and Cpl Johnny Orton, would head to the rendezvous with the LRDG, which was approximately seventy miles to the south-west.

Yates had an interesting background. He had been a regular officer in the 1930s, but was cashiered; on the outbreak of war he enlisted in the ranks of the Guards, and had been promoted in the field by Stirling, just before Operation Squatter. After the war he would be court-martialled for a second time; he was not a docile character.

Yates was not alone in considering Stirling's decision unsound. Forcefully, he and others expressed opposition to the idea of splitting the party.[4] Surely they should stick together? What could two men hope to achieve – one of whom, Stirling, was injured – if they were unable to locate the other two raiding parties at the rendezvous overlooking Gazala? Given their own experiences, the chances that Lewes's stick and McGonigal's would arrive unscathed were slim.

Stirling was adamant, pointing to the fact that they were low on explosives and arms as they had lost much of their equipment during the landing. At around 7 p.m., Yates and his weary, sullen, injured men began the long trek towards the rendezvous with the LRDG* and Stirling and Tait started to climb an escarpment. As they neared its summit 'a terrific electric storm broke with hail and rain [and] we were unable to see more than a few yards in front and within fifteen minutes the whole area was under water'.[5]

The pair crawled and scrambled their way to the top and sought a way down the other side. But the wind and the rain were too powerful, and the visibility too poor, so Stirling 'abandoned the attempt and we turned away and marched south. The fact that the desert, except for the top of the ground folds, was flooded, made our march very difficult, also the cold and lack of food slowed us considerably'.

Lt-Col Guy Prendergast had entrusted the collection of L Detachment to one of his most talented and experienced officers, Capt Jake Easonsmith of R1 Patrol. An unorthodox and innovative officer, Easonsmith was remembered by one of his peers as 'a natural leader of men because he understood men in the kind of way which few others have done … he was also a master at the art of craft and guile'.[6] The previous month his LRDG patrol had ambushed an Italian convoy, killing an estimated six men and wounding twelve more while suffering no casualties themselves.

* They were eventually picked up by an Italian patrol driving captured British trucks.

Easonsmith and R1 patrol departed the LRDG base at Siwa Oasis at dawn on 17 November in six 30-cwt trucks. They also had with them two 15-cwt Bedford trucks belonging to L Detachment, one of which was driven by Lt Bill Fraser, whose broken arm had nearly healed. At 8 a.m. on 19 November they reached the secondary rendezvous in the Wadi-el-Mra and left the two Bedford trucks. They continued north-north-east to the principal rendezvous at Garet Meriem, 'a low hill at the point where the Trigh Capuzzo crosses the 23rd meridian east'.[7] En route Easonsmith encountered another LRDG patrol, Y2, commanded by David Lloyd Owen, whose instructions were to observe and report on enemy troop movements in the Bir Tengeder area.

Easonsmith and his six trucks arrived at Garet Meriem in the early evening. A few hours later, at 10 p.m., Jock Lewes's stick arrived. 'We had a meal of bully [beef] and biscuits and tea, which was undoubtedly in my opinion the best meal I have ever had in my life,' said Jeff Du Vivier.[8]

That they had reached the rendezvous, Du Vivier wrote in his diary, was due to one man, to whom he 'shall always be indebted'.

The rain had been so relentless, the wind so strong, the temperature so cold that one by one the men had started to weaken physically and mentally. Even Lewes had succumbed. Only one man remained upright and indomitable: Pat Riley. 'I'm sure he was for the most part responsible for our return,' wrote Du Vivier. Lewes eventually handed over command to Riley, requesting that he lead them home, and he did. 'He was the one who kept us going because we just wanted to fall out and die,' said Du Vivier. 'We were demoralised.'

As Lewes and his men wrapped themselves in LRDG blankets and went to sleep, David Stirling and Bob Tait appeared in the early hours of 20 November, two more grateful recipients of Jake Easonsmith's hospitality. No other men appeared during the night, and when dawn broke Easonsmith moved his men and Stirling's to cover, leaving a smoking fire on the low hill. Shortly afterwards nine more exhausted figures appeared.

The tale that Paddy Mayne told was similar to the others. An appalling drop, horrendous weather and a failed attempt to reach the target at Tmimi. He had left two wounded men on the drop zone with instructions to head to a rendezvous fifteen miles away the next morning. He had no further news of either, and nor had he any knowledge about the fate of Charles Bonington's stick, which had also been tasked with attacking Tmimi.*

Despite the ordeal, Mayne was in good spirits, and so were his men who, he wrote in his subsequent report, had all 'behaved extremely well and although lacerated and bruised in varying degrees by their landing, and wet and numb and cold, remained cheerful'.[9]

Easonsmith loitered at the rendezvous until the late afternoon of 20 November, eight hours longer than instructed. It was probably at the insistence of Stirling, who scanned the horizon, willing figures to emerge into the lens of his binoculars. But none did. The only friendly faces they encountered were those of Lloyd Owen's patrol, who informed Stirling that they had seen none of his men.

Eventually Easonsmith ordered Stirling and his twenty men into the LRDG trucks and they withdrew to the secondary rendezvous at Wadi-el-Mra, where Bill Fraser had nothing to report. They remained in the wadi for all of the following day, but 'no more men came in though trucks were spread over an 8-mile front to look for them'.[10]

On 22 November a wireless signal was received by Easonsmith, ordering Stirling and his men to be handed over to another LRDG patrol, R2, commanded by Lt Tony Browne, who would ferry them to Siwa. The handover was delayed because of marauding enemy aircraft, which forced Easonsmith to shelter throughout 23 November. Three days later Stirling and his men reached Siwa.

* In fact, Mayne and his men had been dropped far from their original drop zone and the rendezvous was not that close. The pair were captured, as were Bonington and his men.

Jim Almonds ran to greet the trucks as they approached. He had been stood down from the raid because of the worrying news from home about his baby, and he had endured an anxious few days waiting for the return of his comrades and friends. He stared in disbelief as only twenty-one men climbed wearily out of the trucks. 'From their appearance on arrival back at camp,' he wrote in his diary, 'the last ten days in the desert must have been hell.'[11]

Almonds had lost two of his best pals, Ernie Bond and Jim Blakeney (both captured), and Paddy Mayne was without Eoin McGonigal, whom he later learned had been killed during the operation. What Mayne hadn't lost, however, was his standing. On the contrary, he was now indubitably L Detachment's leader after the physical collapse of Lewes and the questionable decisions made by Stirling.

Significantly, the composition of the unit had also shifted away from Stirling and Lewes. The senior NCOs had been recruited from No. 8 Commando, men loyal to the Guards and by extension to Stirling and Lewes. But CSM Yates and Sgts Bond, Stone, Colquhoun and Lazenby had not returned, while several of No. 11 Commando's NCOs had made it back, including Sgt Edward McDonald and Cpls Du Vivier and Tait, who were both subsequently awarded a third stripe.

On 26 November, the day that David Stirling arrived at Siwa with the remnants of L Detachment, the Eighth Army had a new commander. Gen Sir Alan Cunningham had started to lose the confidence of Gen Auchinleck three days earlier with his gloomy reports from HQ. Operation Crusader had not gone according to plan.

The offensive had opened on 18 November over a sixty-five-mile front from Sollum to Jarabub. Armoured troops had made good advances, reaching the escarpment at Sidi Eezegh (thirty-two miles south-east of Tobruk) and capturing its airfield on the 19th. The next day Rommel seized the initiative with a bold counter-thrust that surprised his enemy. There were a series of long and confused tank battles before Rommel again caught the Allies off guard with a strike to the south-east, at Sidi Omar. Cunningham requested Auchinleck's presence in his HQ at Bagoush to decide 'whether it was necessary to break off battle to adopt a defensive attitude or whether to continue the offensive'.[12]

On 23 November Auchinleck flew to Eighth Army HQ and ordered Cunningham to remain on the offensive. The next day he decided to relieve him of his command and, on the 25th, sent Cunningham two letters announcing his decision, one as his superior officer and the other as a friend, in which he expressed his 'sense of pain' in replacing him with Lt-Gen Neil Ritchie.[13]

Stirling claimed that, following his return to Siwa, he had an audience with Cunningham at Bagoush. That would not have been possible, even if he had leapt in a vehicle and raced more than two hundred miles north to Bagoush, for Ritchie had by now assumed command and Cunningham was on his way to hospital to receive treatment for nervous exhaustion.

Stirling may have had a brief audience with Lt-Gen Ritchie – as he also claimed – but the new commander of the Eighth Army had far more pressing matters than the fate of twenty-one parachutists. Ritchie's orders from Auchinleck were a précis of those from Winston Churchill, sent by cipher message on 25 November: 'Fight out the battle to the last inch.'[14]

In making their bold thrust east, the Axis forces had extended their supply lines to such an extent they were now perilously exposed; Ritchie despatched two flying columns – E Force, commanded by Brig Denys Reid, and A Force, under Brig John Marriott* – to attack Rommel in the rear. Marriott – whose American wife had hosted some of No. 8 Commando's 'smart set' at Cairo house parties in the summer – had orders to 'move across the desert to Antelat to cut off

* Included in A Force was Second Battalion, Scots Guards, commanded by Lt-Col Bryan Mayfield, who was wounded in action in late December.

Rommel's retreat down the Benghazi–Agedabia road'.[15] Rommel's retreat, so the Eighth Army hoped, would be caused by their secondary offensive west along the coast.

Stirling said that he encountered Marriott at Eighth Army HQ. He listened attentively to his dilemma, and then suggested he attach himself to Denys Reid's E Force, based in Jalo Oasis. 'Sounds perfect,' replied Stirling. 'I'll push off to Jalo in the morning.'[16]

Marriott didn't mention this encounter in his privately published war memoir; he didn't mention Stirling at all. In fact, it wasn't John Marriott who came to Stirling's rescue, but Lt-Col Guy Prendergast.

One of Gen Cunningham's final acts as commander of the Eighth Army was to issue fresh instructions to the LRDG at Siwa. These were received on 24 November – as Easonsmith was bringing Stirling back – and must have roused mixed emotions in Prendergast: a combination of irritation and satisfaction. The LRDG were to 'act with the utmost vigour offensively against any enemy targets or communications within reach'.[17] Isn't that what Prendergast had envisaged the previous month in his memo to Maj Rupert Harding-Newman? Now the LRDG had the opportunity to demonstrate to GHQ that they were a unit of many talents: reconnoitring, surveying, transporting and raiding.

Prendergast ordered his patrols to 'attack transport and any other targets within reach', concentrating on Mekili, Gadd-el-Ahmar and the coastal road in the vicinity of Jedabia. On 28 November Prendergast sent a signal to Eighth Army HQ: 'As LRDG not trained for demolitions, suggest pct [parachutists] used for blowing dromes.'[18]

It was a magnanimous gesture, and it was readily accepted by GHQ. The idea of cooperation between the LRDG and L Detachment had first been raised at a conference held at Eighth Army HQ on 29 September, when it was decided 'that it would be necessary to attach a detachment of SAS to the LRDG to assist in future operations'.[19]

But following the failure of the inaugural raid, Prendergast's suggestion was born of sound military judgement. L Detachment's morale was shattered and they urgently required a mission if they weren't to wither and die. Prendergast had also been introduced to the Lewes bomb and recognised that it was far more effective than his idea of a device consisting of a hand grenade strapped to an anti-tank mine.

As for how L Detachment would reach their target aerodromes, that solution had been proposed by Jake Easonsmith during the journey from the rendezvous to Siwa: the LRDG would drive them to within a few miles of the target and the raiders could go in on foot. Far less risky than parachuting.

On 8 December an LRDG patrol commanded by Capt Gus Holliman set out from Jalo and headed north-west towards the aerodrome of Sirte, approximately 350 miles distant. There were twenty LRDG men in total, and eleven members of L Detachment, including Stirling and Mayne.

Much depended on the outcome of this raid, and probably the future of L Detachment. Another failure, and the loss of more men, would render the unit non-functional. They would be disbanded, the survivors returned to their unit and David Stirling – if still alive – would be humiliated in the eyes of his mother and brother. They had to succeed.

13

It had not been an easy run to the target. At times the terrain was so rocky and broken it took an hour to cover six miles. On the morning of 11 December the patrol was spotted by an Italian Ghibli reconnaissance aircraft, which strafed them with its light armament. There were no casualties, but when two more enemy aircraft appeared it was evident that they had been alerted to the presence of hostile vehicles; probably the Italians had intercepted a wireless signal sent by the LRDG patrol to their base in Siwa.

Stirling decided to improvise a plan. He and Sgt Jimmy Brough, a man he knew well from the Scots Guards and No. 8 Commando, would press ahead with the attack on Sirte; Mayne would lead the rest of the party in an attack on an aerodrome they had only recently detected, five miles west at the end of Wadi Tamet. It was agreed the two parties would penetrate their respective targets at 11 p.m., return to their LRDG escorts and eventually rendezvous at a point eighty miles south.

Stirling's thinking in splitting the party nine to two was curious; he believed that Sirte airfield was now on alert and so two men would have a better chance of slipping undetected onto the target than three or four or five. On the other hand two men, if challenged, would find it harder to make a fighting withdrawal. Mayne recognised the potential danger of taking nine men onto an airfield at night: it was too many; there was the risk they could become separated in the dark and blunder into a sentry.

Mayne therefore detailed three men to remain with the LRDG – one of whom was Johnny Cooper – and chose Ed McDonald, Reg Seekings, Harry White, Tom Chesworth and a soldier called Hawkins to accompany him to Tamet. They wore their khaki battledress under boiler suits that had been bleached in the sun until they were sandy in colour.

Unlike Stirling, who chose men from No. 8 Commando in his raiding parties, Mayne had a different approach: he had seen at Litani River how his fellow No. 11 commandos, men like Bob Tait, Cornelius McGinn and Jeff Du Vuvier, had reacted under fire. They could be relied upon. An L Detachment raid was, for Mayne, an opportunity to observe the mettle of soldiers from Nos 7 and 8 Commando.

The LRDG dropped Mayne's party at 6.30 p.m., around three miles from the target, and seven hours later they welcomed them in. One. Two. Three. Four. Five. Six. All safely back. The LRDG didn't need to ask what had happened. 'It was like a firework display,' said Cecil 'Jacko' Jackson, a Rhodesian member of the patrol. They had watched the pyrotechnics from a rise, 'a ringside seat',[1] according to Jackson, who ushered Mayne and his men onto the trucks and set off to the rendezvous.

The raiders had too much adrenalin coursing through their bodies to curl up and sleep so they regaled the LRDG with an account of the raid: at first they hadn't been able to locate any aircraft in the charcoal night. Then they spotted a thin strip of light that, on closer inspection, turned out to be the bottom of a door to a house. Inside they heard the hubbub of conversation. Mayne's boot opened the door. For a second that seemed to linger for minutes he said and did nothing, and the enemy aircrew sitting in the mess said and did nothing.

'Good evening.' Mayne's quiet voice shattered the silence. Then he squeezed the trigger of his Tommy gun. Two of his men stepped into the doorway and added more firepower. Someone planted a Lewes bomb by the door and then they withdrew. The bomb exploded, illuminating the aircraft and a petrol dump that were soon festooned with bombs.

When they arrived at the rendezvous, said Jackson, 'Mayne handed his score to Stirling: about thirty men killed in the officers' mess, twenty-four planes and a fuel dump destroyed, no casualties on his side.' It must have been an uncomfortable moment for Stirling, his delight at Mayne's success tempered by the admission of his own failure. He and Brough had infiltrated the airfield at Sirte with ease, the latter carrying the heavy haversack containing the explosives. There was no fence and the odd sentry they saw was easily avoided. Once on the aerodrome they could make out the shapes of many enemy aircraft; bombers, by the size of them. And then disaster. Stirling failed to see a slit trench containing two sleeping Italians. He stumbled into their den and they screamed like startled beasts. Stirling and Brough withdrew amid a cacophony of shouts and shots.

Mayne and Stirling returned to Tamet and Sirte at the end of the month. Same targets and same personnel, at least for Mayne. Only Reg Seekings wasn't with him from the first raid on Tamet. He had been loaned to Stirling and in his place was Guardsman Bob Bennett, formerly of No. 8 Commando

The Italians had beefed up the sentry detail in the wake of the first raid, but it presented no great problem to Mayne and his party. 'It was just as easy the second time, even though the enemy was on the lookout and had greatly increased the guard, placing them in batches of seven, about 30 feet apart,' said the Irishman. 'I had five men with me and on arriving at the drome we simply slipped in between the Italian guards. They were chattering gaily.'[2]

Mayne and his five men set the fuses on the Lewes bombs to thirty minutes. But one exploded prematurely. The sentries began shouting and running. One appeared before Mayne. '*Chi va là?*' he asked. 'It was the first time I'd ever been challenged,' said Mayne. 'So I replied "*Freund*" in German. Then they began firing but they didn't hit us, and we just slipped through them in the dark. We got twenty-seven planes.'

A report on the attack was written by Italian engineers. They had traced wheel tracks a mile south of the aerodrome and it was clear the raiders had penetrated the airfield on foot. Then, stated the report, 'The attack consisted in applying explosive charges to the aircraft, which the saboteurs managed to reach, eluding the vigilance of the guards. From investigations on the spot, it appears that the charges were applied to the wing root, on which they were simply rested.'

On the same evening, a few miles east, Stirling, Seekings, Brough, Johnny Rose, Charlie Cattell and Johnny Cooper had been halted by a newly erected wire fence around the aerodrome at Sirte. They edged round the fence, and away from two sentries manning a road block, looking for a way in. 'Suddenly Jimmy Brough froze and dropped to the ground,' recalled Cooper. 'He whispered loud enough for us all to hear: "For God's sake, stop the boss, we're in a minefield."'[3]

Cooper hissed a warning to Stirling up ahead. 'Instead of turning back,' said Cooper, 'he yelled out "What the bloody hell's the matter?" The reaction to this was that both sentries on the road block became noisy.'

Stirling and his men withdrew towards the rendezvous, where the LRDG were waiting. Stirling was at the head, dejected at another failure, so wrapped up in his own thoughts that he was almost shot by an LRDG sentry whose demand for the password had elicited no response.

Stirling had seen the 'pink glow' westwards and understood that Mayne had met with more success. He had to accomplish something to salvage some credibility. Stirling pressured Gus Holliman, the LRDG patrol commander, 'to drive down the road and let his men put bombs on any trucks they found parked'.[4] Off they set, recalled Jacko Jackson, but at 4.50 a.m. Holliman 'decided this was taking too long'.

An Italian report on Stirling's sabotage attempts remarked that explosive charges had been attached to a Fiat 634 lorry and also the base of a telegraph pole five metres away, both of which were destroyed.

The two raiding parties rendezvoused south of the coast. They exchanged familiar tales. Success for one and failure for the other. Tamet was now rechristened 'Paddy's Own'. The men were in awe of him. Seekings described in wonderment to the rest of the men how, on the first Tamet raid, Mayne had climbed onto the wing of one aircraft and ripped out the instrument panel with his bare hands. 'How he did it I shall never know,' he said.[5]

Stirling, on the other hand, was gaining a reputation for ineptitude: separating his men on the inaugural raid, literally bumping into a sentry on the second and shouting his presence to a guard on the third.

Underlining this inefficacy, Bill Fraser and four of his former commandos from No. 11 returned from a raid on Agedabia airfield having destroyed thirty-seven aircraft. Jock Lewes's disappointing raid on Aghyala had saved Stirling some face, but that only served to sharpen the division within L Detachment: the Guardsmen of No. 8 Commando didn't appear to be much good at irregular warfare.

On Christmas Day, Jock Lewes set out to raid an airfield at Nofilia. He had with him Jim Almonds, Jim Storie, Bob Lilley and Fred 'Chalky' White. They got to within sight of the aerodrome without a hitch and counted forty-three aircraft lined up invitingly. They marked eighteen for destruction on the following night, but in the interim most of the aircraft flew off.

Absorbing their misfortune they returned to the LRDG rendezvous and then set off for home. On 31 December they were spotted by a

Messerschmitt 110. It was not a fair contest and all the men abandoned their vehicles and sought cover among the rocks and scrub. Except Lewes. He remained in his truck's cab. 'Dear God,' thought Almonds. 'He's fiddling about with some papers.'[6] The German fighter came in low and opened fire with its cannons and machine guns. Lewes was hit in the back. Storie was the first to reach him. 'His back was shattered and he was saying something, the first letter ... but I couldn't make out the full name.'[7]

They buried Lewes in the desert. It was a hurried operation because they feared the return of the enemy in greater force. 'We never took anything off him – rings, watches – we just buried him,' said Storie. Almonds later confessed to his diary that he felt guilty about having put Lewes into the ground without even leaving a marker. 'No one will ever stop by his grave or pay homage to a brave heart that has ceased to beat.'[8]

Stirling was at once furious and devastated when he learned of Lewes's death. 'When we arrived at the oasis Stirling was there, and a few others, and he kicked up hell because we didn't bring his body back,' said Storie. He described Stirling as 'rocked by Lewes's death ... because he was the brains'. David, in contrast, 'had the pull that Jock never ... as the Stirling family was a well-known landowning family. He was born a gentleman.'

The death of Lewes removed a vital prop from the carefully constructed edifice of L Detachment. His presence as the unit's second-in-command had allowed Stirling to spend most of his time in Cairo; sometimes planning and other times gallivanting.

Stirling later wrote to Lewes's father, Arthur, to offer his condolences. 'Jock could far more genuinely claim to be the founder of L Detachment and the SAS Regiment than I,' he said, which was gracious, if untrue. Some of what followed was not. 'There is no doubt that any success this unit has achieved up to the time of Jock's death, and after it, was, and is, almost wholly due to Jock's work,' he wrote.[9] In fact, Lewes, like Stirling, was not one for filing notes carefully, and among his papers in his tent at Kabrit was virtually nothing pertaining to recruitment or instruction.

As many a commanding officer has done, Stirling embellished the deeds of the deceased to comfort a grieving parent or spouse; but in Stirling's case he was also undermining Paddy Mayne. From the outset he had been intimidated by the Irishman, and now coupled to this fear was a visceral envy. Stirling's outward confidence masked an acute insecurity. Mayne was a constant reminder of his own shortcomings as a man.

Several of the men were awarded medals for their feats on the December raids, among them Mayne, Bill Fraser, Jeff Du Vivier, Reg Seekings, Bob Tait and Jimmy Brough. On all but one citation the name of the recommending officer was David Stirling. Mayne, however, was awarded the DSO for the first Tamet raid on the recommendation of Brig Denys Reid, who praised his outstanding leadership and the manner in which he had accounted for so many of the enemy. Jimmy Brough's citation flirted with the truth. Stirling awarded Brough the Military Medal for his actions in the failed raid at Sirte on 11 December, writing: 'The activities of this NCO and an officer [Stirling himself] caused the mayor of Sirte to send to Tripoli for reinforcements. On this occasion he showed the utmost determination in the face of what appeared to be most formidable odds.'[10]

If the mayor of Sirte had indeed sent for reinforcements, it would have been because of Mayne's raiding party at Tamet, a few miles west of the Sirte aerodrome. They had destroyed twenty-four aircraft and shot dead thirty aircrew while Stirling and Brough were beating a hasty retreat from their target having tripped over a sleeping sentry.

14

The disaster of L Detachment's inaugural operation had not dissuaded David Stirling from his dream of leading a parachute force. It was his signature idea, one that would make his name. The LRDG had rescued L Detachment from oblivion (the LRDG nicknamed L Detachment 'Parashits'[1]) but Stirling didn't appreciate being reliant on the skill of others. He wanted the dominant role, and the same applied to any putative airborne unit.

In late December 1941 he contacted Peter Oldfield at the Air Reconnaissance Unit with a view to launching another parachute operation. He would require photos, but also an aircraft, and he had his eye on modifying a Wellington bomber held by Rear 205 Group.

Word of Stirling's plans were leaked to GHQ, prompting a flurry of angry messages. On 30 December Lt-Col M. B. Jennings sent a message to Col Roy Thurburn at Eighth Army HQ in Bagush. 'We have been in great difficulty during the last thirty-six hours over an alleged parachute operation which you have in view,' said Jennings, who added that it had caused a ruckus within GHQ.[2] He continued:

'Sterling [*sic*] appears to have told someone in RAF Ops about it, but of course not the right man. Sterling never breathed a word of it to anybody on the Ops side here. Sterling's RAF confidant [Oldfield] made arrangements for converting the aircraft but did nothing about telling any of his colleagues or about planning the operation. The result was that yesterday they turned on us for information as to the number of men to be dropped, the weight of the stores, the mileage and so on ... we all know Sterling's weakness for laying on his plans by the queerest methods. His ideas of organisation are elementary to say the least of it.'

Jennings ended his letter by telling Eighth Army HQ that he was 'arranging with RAF that they will not deal with Sterling direct unless he is armed with a written request from G (Ops) GHQ'.

The next day Col Thurburn sent an apologetic reply. 'I am sorry you had all this bother,' he told Jennings. 'I entirely agree with you ... and I have sent for Stirling to report here on his return, when I shall make the new procedure clear to him. I hope it will work, but I have found that his natural impetuousness and importunity make it difficult for him to stick to any procedure.'

The result of the brouhaha caused by Stirling's attempt to launch a parachute operation on the quiet was a combined army and RAF memorandum dated 25 February 1942, which laid out the procedure for planning minor operations involving parachute droppings.

By then, however, Stirling had a new toy to play with: canoes.

At the start of 1942 Col Bob Laycock was in command of a new entity called Middle East Commando, a disparate force that included L Detachment, some remnants of No. 11 Commando and Roger Courtney's Folboat Section, which had been renamed the Special Boat Section. Only the LRDG among the private armies fell outside Laycock's remit, as their myriad skills set them apart from mere commandos.

Courtney had returned to Britain at the end of 1941 to recruit and train more men as canoeists with a view to raising a 'Folboat Corps'. His men were sorry to see him go. 'He was a very tough sort of man,'

Keir House at the turn of the twentieth century. As a child David enjoyed its grandeur but as an adult it was a reminder of his shortcomings. *(© Look and Learn/Bridgeman Images)*

Bill's twenty-first birthday party brought together the Lovats and the Stirlings. Bill's in the centre in the grey three-piece suit. Behind him in the dark suit is David. Peter is second from left in the front row, with Hugh to his left. The boys' sister Margaret is in the middle row in the hat and dark polka-dot dress. In the front row are the Hon Mrs Stirling (far left) and Lord Lovat (far right). *(© Illustrated London News/Mary Evans)*

David was not keen on team sports at Ampleforth but he played cricket a few times for the Prep School 2nd XI in 1927. He is second from right in the middle row and to his left is Miles Fitzalan-Howard, the 17th Duke of Norfolk. *(Ampleforth Abbey Trustees)*

The Stirling brothers attended Ampleforth College, but whereas Bill, Peter and Hugh thrived academically, artistically and athletically, David was homesick and unhappy.
(Pixel Youth movement/Alamy Stock Photo)

The Gleneagles Ball was always one of the highlights of the Scottish social season. Here in the back row in 1929 are Simon Fraser, Lord Lovat (second from left) and Bill Stirling (far right). The Hon Mrs Stirling is second from right in the middle row. *(© Illustrated London News/Mary Evans)*

This photo, which appeared on the front page of the *Dundee Evening Telegraph* in 1932, was taken at Bill's twenty-first birthday party. Sandwiched between Bill and Lord Lovat is Mrs Bridget McEwan of Marchmont and Bardrochat.
(© D. C. Thomson & Co. Ltd)

In May 1940 Inverailort House became the HQ of the Commando Special Training Centre at Lochailort. In the ensuing months Bill Stirling and his staff schooled hundreds of students in the art of irregular warfare. *(Wikimedia Commons)*

Simon Fraser, 15th Lord Lovat, the Stirlings' cousin (seen here after the commando raid on Dieppe in 1942) learned to stalk on the Scottish moors as an adolescent in the company of Bill. *(© IWM H 22583)*

Bill and David in the uniform of the Scots Guards, possibly in December 1940 on the day of Bill's marriage to Susan Bligh at St Mary's Church, Cadogan Gardens, London. *(Jonathan Pittaway)*

Blair Mayne, back row, third from right, was part of the British army XV that thrashed their French counterparts in February 1940 in Paris. Also in the team were two friends from the Lions tour to South Africa of 1938 – Welsh-men Vivian Jenkins and Bunner Travers. *(Rugby Relics)*

David Stirling (left) and his cousin Andrew Maxwell volunteered for the 5th Battalion Scots Guards, nick-named the 'Snowballers', in February 1940, but saw no action. Stirling later invited Maxwell to join the SAS on their ill-fated raid to Benghazi in September 1942. *(Jonathan Pittaway)*

Believed to have been taken in the summer of 1940, this photograph shows Bill Stirling (seated) teaching some men – possibly some of the staff at Keir – how to strip and clean their rifles.
(Archie Stirling)

Wearing the uniform of the Scots Guards, Bill married Susan Bligh in December 1940. The next month he sailed to Egypt on a secretive SOE mission, and returned to his wife at the end of 1941.
(© Illustrated London News/Mary Evans)

Blair Mayne loved outdoor pursuits, whether it was rugby, cricket, hunting or fishing. He was a noted marksman and is seen here in the late 1930s with his rifle. David Stirling, on the other hand, was remembered by Lord Lovat as a danger with a shotgun in his hands. *(Stewart Maclean)*

Members of L Detachment and the LRDG in December 1941. Blair Mayne stands on the very far left, David Stirling is third from left and Reg Seekings is standing eighth from the left. *(Jonathan Pittaway)*

said one of the SBS, James Sherwood. 'And very likeable as a person. Not a blustering, swaggering sort of pistol-stuck-in-his-belt type of bloke, but a straightforward man with an adventurous spirit that he wanted to put to full use.'[3]

With Courtney in Britain, the SBS were without a leader and, said Sherwood, 'in a sort of limbo', whiling away their time in training while based on HMS *Medway*, the depot submarine ship in Alexandria. In January 1942 they came to the attention of David Stirling, who persuaded Bob Laycock to attach the SBS to L Detachment at Kabrit. 'He had very much more pull [than Courtney] because he had very high family connections with the powers that be in Cairo,' said Sherwood of Stirling. 'The SAS was established down at Kabrit and we soon learned that they aspired to take over the SBS … we didn't want to join the SAS, we didn't want to have anything to do with them, we wanted to remain our own independent force.'

The objections fell on deaf ears and the SBS were ordered to Kabrit where, to the fury of Sherwood and the rest of the unit, they were ordered to undergo parachute training. They refused to think of themselves as the SAS, however, and continued to take pride in being skilled canoeists of the SBS.

Two of their fifteen officers (and forty-five men) were Capts David Sutherland and George Duncan. Educated at Eton, Sutherland was commissioned from Sandhurst into the Black Watch and from there he volunteered for No. 8 Commando, acquiring the nickname 'Dinky' on account of his debonair attire.

Sutherland was unusual among the upper-class officers who joined L Detachment in that he preferred Mayne to Stirling. He found the latter convivial but recognised his limitations as a combat officer. Mayne was the opposite. He exuded menace, purposely, to men of Sutherland's class, but 'beneath this fearsome exterior lay a brilliant operational brain'.[4]

George Duncan, a sheep farmer from Dumfries in the Scottish borders, knew about Mayne's strengths and weaknesses. He had taken part in the Litani River action, and then witnessed the Irishman's rough handling of Geoffrey Keyes in the officers' mess.

Stirling had been promoted to major in January 1942 (and Mayne to captain) and authorised by Gen Auchinleck to recruit a further six officers and as many as forty men. The secondary offensive of Operation Crusader, launched by Gen Ritchie after the dismissal of Gen Cunningham, had been a success and Rommel had withdrawn to a new defensive position at El Agheila, four hundred miles west of the Egyptian frontier. Stirling had also won from Auchinleck approval for an idea to raid the port of Bouerat, just over two hundred miles behind the Germans' front line, and blow up enemy shipping, drawing on the expertise of the SBS.

While in Cairo David stayed as ever at his brother's flat. On 5 January Hermione Ranfurly came for dinner. He gave her an account of L Detachment's recent exploits, a tale that was fictitious and egocentric. 'As usual he and his men were dropped by parachute and after destroying enemy planes on the ground they were picked up by the Long Range Desert Group,' she noted in her diary. 'His score of enemy planes destroyed in this way behind enemy lines is now fantastic. David hates talking about his nocturnal raids so I felt honoured to hear a detailed account.'[5]

One of Stirling's talents was to confide in people, to give the impression these were details to which only they were privy. It made people feel they were special, and they fell under his spell.

When Stirling returned to Kabrit he informed Mayne that he was now in charge of training. His role was to whip the new recruits into shape; Stirling, meanwhile, would lead the Bouerat raid. Stirling claimed that he had no choice: Bill Fraser was missing (he returned a few days later after an aborted raid on Arae Philaenorum, with four men after an epic eight-day march across nearly two hundred miles of desert) and there was no other suitable candidate.

There were many, of course: Stirling could have made one of his senior sergeants training instructor. Pat Riley, for example, an ex-policeman and boxing champion, had the natural authority to perform the role. But Stirling wanted Riley by his side at Bouerat, along with his other precious guardsmen, Jimmy Brough, Johnny Cooper and Bob Bennett.

Stirling appointed Mayne out of spite. The sulky and irritable child of Keir had become the sulky and irritable man of Kabrit. By confining Mayne to base camp the Irishman would not steal his thunder once more. It was a decision that also revealed Stirling's inability to read a man and understand his strengths and weaknesses. Genius comes in many shapes and forms: scientific, artistic, political, architectural and sporting. Mayne's genius was for war. The speed of mind and body that had made Mayne a brilliant sportsman also made him a superb guerrilla fighter; so too his physical strength and freakish endurance. These were gifts from the gods, not skills that could be imparted on a training ground like a course in demolitions or close combat. Stirling should have recognised this, but envy got the better of him.

Mayne took the news stoically. When he wrote to his sister on 8 February he made no mention of his demotion, remarking only that he had been recently promoted to captain, which meant a pay rise.

Among the men Mayne had been detailed to train was a squadron of Free French parachutists under the command of Capt Georges Bergé, who had arrived in Syria from England in the summer of 1941 only to kick their heels for the next six months. When Bob Laycock heard of their availability he organised their transportation to Egypt and in early January they were sent to Kabrit, where they were welcomed by Mayne. 'Mayne was a huge man,' recalled one of the Frenchmen, Roger Boutinot, a baker's assistant from St Malo before the war. 'We called him "*l'armoire*" [the wardrobe].'[6]

Each day began at Kabrit with an eight-mile run, led by the PT sergeant, Gus Glaze. Mayne went too, and in the early evenings he would join in the games of rugby and basketball organised by the men. 'He would come in to see us some nights, drinking with us and talking,' said Boutinot. 'We used to go to the sergeants' mess and all mixed together.'

Bergé's second-in-command was a slim intellectual called Lt Augustin Jordan. He was a little unnerved by Mayne, and in time he came to nickname him *le grand tuer* (the great killer). Stirling, meanwhile, made Jordan feel good about himself because of his 'incredible human warmth that gave you wings'.[7] As a private, Boutinot had little personal contact with Stirling but on the occasions he observed him he was struck by the contrast: 'He was tall and slim, about half the size of Paddy Mayne, and when you saw him walking around he looked clumsy.'

David Stirling flew from Cairo to Jalo on 11 January. Among the dozen men with him were his coterie of trusted guardsmen and Flt Lt Derek Rawnsley, a friend of Peter Oldfield. Stirling had invited Oldfield to join L Detachment as one of his new officers, but the offer had been rejected and Oldfield suggested Rawnsley instead. He had no commando training to speak of, but on the other hand he was a product of Eton and Oxford.

When Stirling's party left Jalo six days later in an LRDG patrol commanded by Capt Tony Hunter, it had been augmented by the addition of Capt George Duncan and Cpl Edward Barr, like his officer a No. 11 Commando who had subsequently joined the SBS.

The journey to the target was long and arduous, over rough, broken country, but Stirling would have expected heavy going as Bouerat lay sixty miles west of Sirte, an area he knew well from the previous month. They also came under aerial attack but eventually, on 23 January, reached the first rendezvous point; here all but one of the LRDG vehicles would wait. Stirling and his men climbed into the other LRDG truck and set off for Bouerat. At the second rendezvous, on the outskirts of the port, Stirling began to organise the raiders into four parties, led by himself, RSM Pat Riley, Sgt Dave Kershaw and Capt Duncan. As he did so, Duncan and Barr were examining what little remained of their folboat. It was broken beyond repair. Neither was surprised and both were exasperated. If they had been briefed on the exact nature of the terrain they could have told Stirling that folboats were 'hardly suitable for lengthy overland transport'.[8]

The operation's *raison d'être* had been smashed to bits in the back of a truck. With no possibility of destroying enemy shipping, Stirling drew on his memory of the reconnaissance photos and detailed Duncan and Barr to attack a wireless station two miles out of town; the rest of the men would enter the port and sabotage what they could.

L Detachment slipped into the port undetected and planted bombs in a food dump, a workshop and among a fleet of petrol tankers. Nonetheless, it was a meagre haul in comparison to the fifty-one aircraft destroyed by Paddy Mayne, and made all the more so by the return of Duncan and Barr.* They had wrecked the wireless station, its mast now a heap of tangled metal in the sand.

The destruction of a wireless station was a boon, but Stirling was greedy for more triumphs that he could take back to Kabrit. 'David Stirling decided to motor on down the road to look for some more targets,' said Johnny Cooper.[9] Behind the wheel of the LRDG truck was Archie Gibson, the same Scots Guardsman who, two years earlier, had collected a languorous Stirling from a Hampshire railway station and then tried unsuccessfully to reunite him with his battalion who were on manoeuvres. 'I spotted a tanker, a dark shape at the side of the road,' remembered Gibson. 'David Stirling said: "I'll give a little lesson to the LRDG in how to blow up tankers" … so he got this

* Some reports state that Sgt Johnny Rose of the SAS accompanied them but the LRDG war diary said it was the 'Folboat officer and one man'.

Lewes bomb and put it on the tanker, but it went off with a crack but no bomb. The time pencil may have fallen onto the road.'[10]

Stirling tried again, and this time the bomb detonated. They continued down the coast road, like holidaymakers enjoying the sea air, stopping now and again to plant bombs on parked lorries or telegraph poles. In their insouciance it didn't occur to them that they may have alerted the Italians to their whereabouts. 'We were driving along and suddenly got a hail of fire,' said Gibson.

'David shouted "get off the track" but this ambush was beautifully placed and I thought the best thing to do was to stay on the track. Johnny [Cooper] got his Tommy gun jammed but moved into the back where there was a .5 Browning swinging on its mounting [it was actually a Vickers K] and Johnny started firing at the enemy over my head and hot shells dropped all around me. We just managed to get through … I had tremendous regard for Johnny.'

Had it not been for the Vickers, a new weapon that had come from the obsolete Gloster Gladiator aircraft, and had a rate of fire of a thousand rounds per minute comprising armour-piercing, tracer and ball ammunition, the ambush would have probably been successful; the post-operational report stated that at the moment of the ambush their Tommy guns had 'jammed as a result of a dust storm earlier'.[11]

Cooper was awarded a Distinguished Conduct Medal on the recommendation of Stirling and Gibson was rewarded by Lt-Col Guy Prendergast with a Military Medal. 'It was largely due to his coolness,' ran the citation, 'that no casualties were sustained by the party.'[12]

15

On 10 March 1942 Lt-Gen Neil Ritchie wrote to Maj Gen Arthur Smith to ask to whom David Stirling answered. Smith (at the demand of Winston Churchill) had just been sacked as Auchinleck's Chief of General Staff, his place taken by Lt-Gen Thomas Corbett, and Ritchie wanted to catch him before he left to take up his new appointment as major general commanding the Brigade of Guards. Smith informed Ritchie that L Detachment were under his command 'but revert to GHQ on completion of current operations'. He then warned the commander of the Eighth Army that he'd heard a rumour 'Stirling is planning an operation against shipping in Benghazi'. He was opposed to the operation, and others like it, such as Bouerat, because that was not why L Detachment had been raised. 'Stirling's chief value is that of commanding a parachute force,' explained Smith. 'We are, therefore, anxious that he should not be thrown away in some other role and I hope that any plan he has made will be carefully examined so as to ensure, as far as possible, that he does not do something foolhardy.'[1]

Interestingly, this view of L Detachment contrasted with the one expressed by John Whiteley, Brigadier, General Staff, of the Eighth Army, when he sent a top-secret memo to Prendergast on 3 January 1942. It concerned Stirling's recent attempt to obtain an aircraft behind the back of the RAF for a parachute operation. Whiteley told Prendergast that GHQ was opposed to such a scheme because Gen Ritchie 'considers that at present more valuable results are obtained by using the SAS Det. with your patrols and he is not in favour of the parachutists being employed as such'.[2]

Smith obviously disagreed with this view, and still believed L Detachment had a future as a parachute unit. There was something else, said Smith in a postscript to Ritchie, and that was that Stirling 'needs restraining, and we can't afford to throw him away'.[3]

Smith's warning came too late for Ritchie to rein in Stirling before he set out from Siwa Oasis in the company of the LRDG on 16 March. Siwa was the new base for the LRDG and L Detachment, a relocation forced on them by Erwin Rommel. On 21 January the Afrika Korps had launched a counter-attack against the Eighth Army, driving them back 350 miles east across Libya to the Gazala Line, which stretched for fifty-miles from the coast south-west to Bir Hakeim.

This reversal nonetheless created new targets for L Detachment, and in March they planned a series of raids in and around the port of Benghazi, four hundred miles west. Stirling remained convinced that a canoe could be transported across the desert and then employed to sabotage enemy shipping in the harbour. Capt George Duncan and Cpl Edward Barr didn't share this belief and consequently weren't among the six SBS personnel who travelled to Benghazi with eight SAS soldiers, including Mayne and Stirling. In Duncan's place was Capt Richard 'Tramp' Allott, a vastly experienced SBS officer who had taken part in Geoffrey Keyes's 'Rommel Raid' the previous November.

Mayne's inclusion – Jeff Du Vivier replaced him as training instructor – was an indication of the pressure Stirling was under. It was three months since L Detachment had enjoyed any significant success and the doubts expressed by Gen Smith to Gen Ritchie had been transmitted to Stirling in recent weeks.

Other raids were also under way with the objective of destroying the aircraft that were causing such damage to Allied convoys on the way across the Mediterranean to Malta: Bill Fraser was leading a team to Barce airfield, north of Benghazi; Lt Gordon Alston, a former officer in No. 8 Commando, was on his first L Detachment operation, taking a small party to attack Berca airfield; and another new officer, Lt Roy Dodd, had been tasked with raiding Slonta airfield, approximately fifty miles north-east of Benghazi.

Although escorted by the LRDG, Stirling was driving his newest toy – what he called his 'Blitz Buggy', purloined from a base workshop in Cairo, where it was being repaired after incurring damage during its unloading at the docks. The vehicle was a stripped-down Ford C11ADF station wagon, which Stirling had painted grey with a broad white stripe across the bonnet, the German air-recognition mark. For a final flourish he stencilled the SAS insignia – the flaming sword of Excalibur (not, as is often erroneously stated, a winged dagger) – onto both doors.

Stirling claimed it would be easier to penetrate Axis-held ports and towns in the Blitz Buggy, although why then decorate it with the SAS insignia? It was a vanity vehicle, which may have swelled Stirling's ego, but was a liability in rough country, particularly its fragile track rods. It was also more vulnerable to enemy mines, unlike the LRDG's tough and durable Chevrolet 1533s trucks.

There was also an authentic German staff car in the convoy, which Stirling intended to take into the heart of Benghazi, but this too was not made for four hundred miles of desert travel. It didn't get even half that distance before it went over a mine and wounded the driver, David Sutherland. The LRDG patrol commander decided that Sutherland's arm required immediate attention so he ordered one of his men, 'Jacko' Jackson, to return to Siwa with the casualty.

Sutherland recalled that on the journey south Jackson was 'kind, considerate and helpful to a tee';[4] the Rhodesian for his part was 'very glad to get rid of him'[5] on arriving at their destination. The problem with Sutherland, which applied to a great many of the young, privileged British officers in North Africa, was that they thought they knew best. 'He was new to the desert,' said Jackson, 'and inclined to query my navigation and other actions.'

Nevertheless, Jackson's reward for enduring Sutherland's back-seat driving was a few days lounging around Siwa, eating dates and swimming in the oasis's salt pools. When the LRDG patrol returned he received a full report from his friends about the raid on the Benghazi. 'The operation had not been a success. Stirling and his party had driven around Benghazi all night but they could not get the boat together [it was again broken], making it impossible to place any bombs or limpet mines on the ships in the harbour.'

Stirling had then tried to attack Benina airfield, but the Blitz Buggy got stuck on an escarpment and had to be 'helped down'[6] by the LRDG. Once on the airfield they found no aircraft. Nor had Alston or Dodd met with any success, though Bill Fraser had blown up the one aircraft he came across on Barce, as well as sabotaging four workshop trucks.

Fortunately, Jackson was told, 'Mayne was more successful getting fifteen aircraft on Berca airfield.' He'd taken just three men: Bob Bennett, Johnny Rose (christened Graham, Rose preferred his nickname 'Johnny') and Jack Byrne. Mayne knew about Bennett's capabilities under pressure, but he wanted to observe Rose and Byrne in action. One of the men who'd accompanied Mayne on his two raids on Tamet, Hawkins, had been RTU'd because, upon reflection, Mayne didn't believe he was L Detachment material.

Mayne's tally of destroyed aircraft brought up the century for the unit; he had sixty-six to his name and Fraser thirty-eight. Stirling had yet to get off the mark.

Capt Richard Allott had been dismayed by the amateurism of Stirling's Benghazi raid, particularly in light of what had happened to

George Duncan's folboat two months earlier. 'LESSON LEARNT,' he concluded in capital letters in his operational report: 'It would seem from this that a folboat is not suitable for use with LRDG unless a special container is devised, owing to the very severe conditions of the journey.'[7]

It was a conclusion Stirling should have drawn after the debacle at Bouerat.

L Detachment went on leave in April. Paddy Mayne contrived a way to visit the Gazala Line, five hundred miles west of Alexandria. His purpose was to obtain information on the fate of Eoin McGonigal, possibly even locate his burial place, but he returned to Kabrit unsuccessful. He wrote to McGonigal's parents to inform them of his pilgrimage and they in due course replied, thanking him for his kindness.

A wag had erected a sign at Kabrit on which was scrawled 'Stirling's Rest Camp', but L Detachment's commanding officer was rarely at home. In April he moved out of GHQ and installed his office in his brother's flat. Maps and aerial photographs were spread out on the dining room table, and the air was stale with nicotine. Peter Stirling's housekeeper, Mo, appeared with refreshments on demand.

Paddy Mayne attended when requested but he preferred Kabrit to Cairo. Sometimes he would drink in the officers' mess, at other times the sergeants' mess. The purpose was to unwind but also to observe, sizing up the new recruits by how they behaved. He noted the ostentatious, for in his view men who talked the most usually had the least to offer. In the sergeants' mess Mayne asked the men to address him as Paddy. 'The session would go on until Paddy would look at his watch and say, "Call me 'sir'. It is now Reveille,"' said Bob Bennett.[8]

In Cairo, Stirling recruited several new officers to the unit, all from the upper class; his class, the only class in which he felt at ease. Some were more suited to guerrilla raiding than others. Capt George

Jellicoe was the son of the 1st Earl Jellicoe and had risen as one would expect: Winchester, Cambridge (Trinity, naturally) and a commission in the Coldstream Guards. A Snowballer and an officer in No. 8 Commando, Jellicoe had wit, warmth and an interest in humanity in all its forms. The transformation of Jellicoe into a more unorthodox soldier had occurred at Bill Stirling's training centre in Lochailort in September 1940, which he remembered as 'extremely hard physically'.

Jellicoe was recuperating from a shoulder wound when by chance he encountered David Stirling at Shepheard's Hotel, 'where everybody met everybody'.[9] Stirling 'was in between raids by then, planning raids … staying with his brother Peter at their lovely flat'. David extended an invitation to Jellicoe, which was accepted, although Stirling had first to winkle his man from the Coldstream Guards.

Jellicoe was impressed by the change in Stirling, now a 'very different animal' from the 'Giant Sloth' he had known on board the *Glenroy* with No. 8 Commando, when he 'lay in his cabin the whole way out there and we hardly ever saw him'. According to Capt John Lodwick, who came to the Middle East via SOE, the commandos and then the SBS, Jellicoe 'was one of the few people, apart from Maj Paddy Mayne, who could cope with that diverse and volcanic personality [of Stirling]'.[10]

David Stirling's name now carried weight, particularly on the terrace at Shepheard's, where his entrance would cause the murmur of polite conversation to increase a decibel. Hail the leader of that mysterious and glamorous commando unit with their sand-coloured berets, their flaming-sword insignia and the dramatic 'Who Dares Wins' motto.

It was a masquerade that fooled even those in high command. They heard of the raids on Tamet, Agedabia and Berca and attributed the dozens of destroyed aircraft to the genius of Stirling, as opposed to the aggressive initiative of Mayne and Fraser and the men with them. In a memo to Auchinleck dated 22 April 1942, Gen Neil

Ritchie raised the issue of what to do with Middle East Commando. In his opinion Stirling should take over their command because 'as a leader of saboteurs and irregular operations he is a master'.[11] David's swashbuckling persona captivated the flamboyant society photographer Cecil Beaton, who spent several weeks in Cairo during a three-month tour of the Middle East in early 1942. The tour was the idea of the Ministry of Information and it produced in 1943 a propaganda book of photographs entitled *Near East*. Beaton's contact in Cairo was Randolph Churchill, the Prime Minister's son, who was working at GHQ. Beaton, 'a dandified aesthete', was a rapacious bisexual who'd slept with a number of actresses during his time working in America in the 1930s but who harboured a particular 'affinity for homosexual hedonists from a similar or higher social class than his own'.[12]

Through Churchill, he was introduced to Stirling and was 'fascinated' by him, a man he described as 'one of the most romantic figures of the war'. Beaton was invited to Kabrit to photograph a batch of new L Detachment recruits undergoing basic parachute training. 'This corps of commandos … is doing a preliminary training before the real course starts in three weeks,' he wrote. 'We watched some of the men fall from heights of eighteen feet in various ways: on one foot, on both feet, sideways, backwards. They jumped through a hole in the rostrum in quick succession.'[13]

But it was in Cairo where Beaton spent the most time in Stirling's company: photographing, observing and worshipping. He dined with him and a group of his friends, among whom was David's brother-in-law, Simon Ramsay, 16th Earl of Dalhousie, serving with the Black Watch. 'Stirling, Ramsay and the other officers seemed to be a serious sophisticated lot – like members of an Olympian club,' wrote Beaton. 'The easy laughter and childlike ragging that whiles away the time in many messes was absent … a most impressive group, too dedicated for small talk, they plot and carry out a primitive and savage form of warfare with a buccaneer's courage and philosopher's mental refinement.'[14]

Stirling appointed Jellicoe second-in-command of L Detachment. 'He wanted me to try and get a little bit more organization and administration into the outfit, which it rather lacked,' he said.*[15]

Stirling wasn't interested in administration; it bored him. It wasn't what a commando leader should be doing. It hadn't been Lewes's forte either, and nor was it Mayne's, but of the three Mayne was the one who wrote reports of their early raids. It was a residue of his legal background when, as a junior solicitor, he had spent many a tedious hour on administrative tasks such as case preparation and research. Gradually Mayne stopped the practice; if Stirling and Lewes didn't bother, why should he?

Mayne wasn't appointed second-in-command because Stirling felt threatened by the Irishman. Jellicoe was three years younger than Mayne and had graduated from Cambridge in the summer of 1939. In terms of life experience he was a stripling. But he was a friend and, more to the point, one who admitted he was under Stirling's spell. In that regard Jellicoe was not alone. Stirling's magnetism was irresistible to many, particularly among the ranks of the middle and upper-middle class where social climbers are often shameless in their sycophancy.

Capt David Lloyd Owen, a contemporary of Jellicoe at Winchester, said Stirling possessed 'a power over men which I had never seen before ... where that power of his lay is hard to define. I came under its spell because I was carried away by his enthusiasm, by his energy, by his oratory – for he would convince any man that black was white!'[16]

Carol Mather, who had served with Stirling in Layforce, said he was 'brilliant at charming people into doing something they did not want to do ... David had a penchant for big idealistic ideas'.[17] Within

* There was initially an administrative officer in L Detachment in the summer of 1941, Capt Thomas, but he soon faded from the scene.

No. 8 Commando, there was even an expression to describe those who had succumbed to Stirling's persuasive charm: they had been 'hotted'.

So intoxicating was Stirling's allure that it deranged men who, in terms of achievements, were far superior. One was Fitzroy Maclean, who had been educated at Eton and Cambridge, and who subsequently joined the diplomatic service in 1934. He was posted first to Paris and then to the Soviet Union, where he spent more than two years travelling around the country and chronicling the brutality of life under Stalin. In late 1941 he arrived in Cairo, having become the Conservative MP for Lancaster a few months earlier; Maclean, then an officer in the Queen's Own Cameron Highlanders, looked up an old friend from his days in the diplomatic service, Peter Stirling, and was introduced to David, who suggested, 'Why not join the SAS?' 'It sounded promising,' said Maclean. 'I said I should be delighted to join.'[18]

Maclean later likened Stirling to Lawrence of Arabia, the pair invested with 'a never-failing audacity, a gift of daring improvisation, which invariably took the enemy by surprise'.*[19]

* Maclean subsequently joined the SBS, commanding M Squadron, but he was not popular, being considered too regimental. There was a sense of relief among the soldiers when he left after a few months to become Churchill's representative in Yugoslavia. Jellicoe, in contrast, was universally admired and respected.

16

On 18 March 1942 the director of Combined Operations, Louis Mountbatten, was promoted to the acting rank of vice admiral and appointed to the Chiefs of Staff Committee. The following day he wrote to 'my dear Randolph' in response to a request from the Prime Minister's son that he would like to 'come back to the commandos'.[1]

In recent months Maj (acting) Randolph Churchill had been in charge of Army Information in Cairo, an appointment he had wangled after his brief stint with No. 8 Commando ended with his expulsion from Lochailort.

By early 1942, he was 'running a new propaganda and censorship branch at GHQ'. The American journalist Allan Michie liked the 'explosive, tireless, imaginative' Churchill, who recognised the importance of the media in the war effort. Having worked for a time on Lord Beaverbrook's *Evening Standard*, Churchill 'was smart enough to realize that a cooperative press could be one of Britain's most effective weapons'.[2] It was a struggle, however, to win over a military staff composed predominantly of men born in the Victorian age, dismissive of most of the popular press and its readership.

Churchill wanted a new challenge in the spring of 1942, likely inspired by the time he had spent with David Stirling in the company of Cecil Beaton; he pictured himself a paratrooper and Stirling was happy to help him realise his dream. Not even the commander of L Detachment, however, had the pull to extract Churchill from GHQ without first going to the top.

Mountbatten was only too happy to oblige, and after a brief word with Col Bob Laycock Churchill was transferred to L Detachment. Stirling was delighted. 'It was, of course, useful having Randolph in the commando as it meant we were received at a very high level,' said George Jellicoe.[3]

In effect, believed Stirling, Randolph's presence would ensure that he answered only to the Prime Minister. At the time of Randolph's posting to L Detachment, his father was ignorant of their role. 'I spoke to him on the telephone, which as you know is always difficult,' wrote Randolph's wife, Pamela, to her husband on 12 April. 'He had never heard of what David did, which made any explaining difficult – anyway I asked him not to send any cables about it, or interfere.' Evidently, the Prime Minister was a little perturbed to learn that his son had joined a commando unit, for Pamela asked him to 'write to Papa cos [*sic*] I think he will worry till he hears from you personally'.[4]

Randolph duly wrote home often, feeding his father's appetite for tales of gung-ho bravado. In a letter dated 28 April he described Stirling as 'a very great friend of mine' and continued:

> He is only 25 and recently got a DSO for his attacks on enemy airfields. At the moment the unit has 121 enemy aircraft [*sic*] to their credit. Apart from Bob Laycock, he is the most original and enterprising soldier I have come across. Not being a regular soldier he is more interested in war than in the army. He is one of the few people who think of the war in three dimensional terms.[5]

Randolph also informed his father that 'there are two or three other officers from No. 8 Commando, including George Jellicoe, who is coming as 2 i/c. My exact function is not settled yet and the whole establishment is under review. But there is no hurry as I have first got to do the course which takes about eight weeks.'

A few days later Randolph told his father about his parachute training. 'My first jump went off very well,' he said. 'I am much lighter than when you last saw me.'[6]

The soldiers at Kabrit had a different opinion of how he was shaping up. 'Churchill was a big blustering fat useless no-good,' said Arthur Thompson, who had recently joined L Detachment.[7] Roger Boutinot, the Frenchman, recalled that Churchill had – even by British standards – a considerable thirst: 'He was drunk all the time. One day I met him just outside my tent and he was there, completely nude, and the sun was beating down and he was fast asleep. How he came to us I don't know.'[8] Paddy Mayne dismissed Churchill as plucky but unathletic, and not endowed with any manners.

David Stirling's recruitment of Churchill, and Jellicoe and Maclean, was a protective barrier to keep Mayne at bay. The four of them spent more time in Peter Stirling's flat in Cairo than they did their tents at Kabrit.

'I nearly always stayed there when in Cairo at odd times between December 1941 and December 1943,' recalled Maclean. 'Not only was Peter immensely hospitable and very good company, but he was quite happy to let us use his flat as a dump for arms, ammunition, rations, operation orders, maps and plans. As can be imagined, it was also the scene of a number of very good parties.'[9]

David Stirling had also a small Praetorian Guard formed from the original members of L Detachment: Pat Riley, Johnny Cooper and Reg Seekings. Riley was unquestionably an ally, but Cooper and Seekings refused to take sides. Cooper had just turned nineteen when he joined L Detachment, the youngest member of the unit, and Stirling had assumed he was impressionable and obedient. But Cooper was very much his own man, mature beyond his years, and a sharp judge of character. In time he would become one of Britain's most respected and accomplished special forces soldiers, still fighting with the SAS in 1959, in the mountains of Oman, but even as a teenager he could see that Stirling was a willing guerrilla soldier but not a very able one.

By May 1942 Cooper and Seekings were spending more and more of their time at the flat, taking some of the logistical load off Stirling's shoulders by organising rations, ammunition, fuel and the routes for their operations.

Cooper was troubled by the physical deterioration of David. 'It was at this time we realised that [he] was pushing himself terribly hard,' he said. 'He suffered from migraines which meant wearing dark glasses and was often sick with desert sores which refused to heal.'[10]

Paddy Mayne also suffered desert sores, and Bill Fraser. Rare was the desert soldier who didn't. The sores were skin lesions on limbs exposed to sand and dust, which often ulcerated and formed ecthyma. The official Eighth Army treatment was to scrub the infected sore with a brush. This caused much pain and little healing. Various ointments were tried, and an antiseptic called flavine became popular. In L Detachment, Sgt Harry Bunfield considered the best treatment was 'to simply stick a piece of adhesive strapping over it and leave it there till it fell off, when it could be replaced with a fresh piece'.[11] After much experimentation, Capt Richard Lawson, the LRDG's medical officer, produced a remedy that cured most sores in six to nine days, and consisted of bathing the scabs, removing the dead skin and then applying sulphonamide powder in Vaseline.

Other than desert sores, Mayne was in prime physical shape. When he wasn't training with the men at Kabrit, he was haring around the rugby pitch or the basketball court. Stirling's fitness was poor by comparison. In Cairo he rarely exercised, spending his time smoking in his brother's flat or drinking at the Turf Club or Shepheard's.

Nonetheless, these moments were an opportunity for Stirling to exercise his imagination and in late April a plan began to form in his head for another raid on Benghazi. It was the principal supply port for the Afrika Korps, expected soon to launch an offensive against the British defences at Gazala.

The RAF had bombed Benghazi often, but Stirling pitched the idea of a daring raid on the port to GHQ. 'The plan,' said Fitzroy Maclean, 'was a small party should enter the town surreptitiously and make a stealthy tour of the harbour. If they found suitable targets – shipping in particular – they were to attack them.'[12]

The plan accepted, Stirling assembled his team, in fact his clique: Maclean, Alston, Seekings, Cooper, Johnny Rose and Randolph Churchill. None of his most experienced operators were included: no Mayne, Fraser, McDonald, Tait or Du Vivier. In Stirling's eyes they were No. 11 Commandos more than his own L Detachment.

The inclusion of Churchill was extraordinary; as he himself admitted to his father in a letter dated 28 April, he had eight weeks of training in front of him before he would be ready for any commando activity; unfit and overweight, kicked out of Lochailort for insubordination, there were few soldiers more patently unqualified for such a dangerous enterprise than Randolph. But his father was the Prime Minister.

Stirling had finally accepted that folboats were too fragile to be transported hundreds of miles across the desert, so he tasked Maclean with devising a new method of attacking the shipping in the harbour. First, he procured some rubber dinghies from the RAF base at Kabrit but they were orange, oddly shaped and noisy to inflate. L Detachment's demolitions officer, Capt Bill Cumper, suggested the small black manoeuvrable boats the Royal Engineers used, which were inflated with a pair of small bellows.

Over several nights they practised on the Great Bitter Lake, one of the party acting the Italian sentry while the others were the raiders, inflating the boats and paddling out to an imaginary vessel. The instruction to the sentry was to shout when he heard or saw something. 'This was generally very soon,' said Maclean. 'The bellows made a noise; our paddles made a noise.' They were also illuminated by the moon on the surface of the lake, clear as daylight. Maclean's doubt as to the wisdom of their mission were dismissed by Stirling, who declared that the sentries in Benghazi would not be as alert as the ones of the Great Bitter Lake.

To prove his theory, Stirling took his men to the port of Suez. They were challenged immediately by a British guard, who was told to fuck off. He did. Dummy limpet mines were successfully placed on two vessels at anchor and the next morning Stirling rang the port authorities to crow about his exploits. They were incandescent. Yes, they stood accused of lax security, but the raiders had endangered themselves; Royal Navy orders were that if anything suspicious was spotted in the water they were to shoot first and ask questions later. The men under Stirling's command were also unimpressed with his casual methods. 'Reg [Seekings] and I were most vitriolic about the risk to which we had been exposed,' remembered Johnny Cooper.[13]

The raiders rendezvoused at Siwa Oasis with the LRDG. Their patrol commander for the journey to Benghazi was Lt the Honourable Robin Gurdon, son of the second Baron Cranworth, a man who was more to Stirling's liking than a plain-talking Rhodesian or New Zealand officer.

In Stirling's initial plan Randolph Churchill would proceed no further than Siwa as he was too raw to go on the raid itself; Maclean said that the Prime Minister's son 'grudgingly accepted this arrangement but it was clear from the start that he would not be happy until he got his own way'.

On the eve of their departure from Siwa on 15 May Reg Seekings damaged his hand when a detonator exploded. It was cruel luck for him but a stroke of good fortune for Churchill, who took his place in the party. When Johnny Rose recounted the story of the raid upon his return to Kabrit he made no mention of Seekings's unfortunate injury, which was a curious accident to befall a seasoned commando.

In all probability he had actually been ordered by Stirling to make way for Churchill. In return, Randolph was requested to write to his father with an account of the daring raid on Benghazi.

'I found it extremely exciting,' he duly told the Prime Minister. 'Our object was to sink two enemy ships in Benghazi in such a way as to block the channel to the harbour.'[14]

Alas, said Randolph, the expedition, 'owing to a number of accidents proved fruitless, but it had a certain reconnaissance value'. Randolph may have invented an alternative version of the raid to mask its failing; Lt-Colonel Tony Simonds of SOE, Cairo, heard that Churchill, Maclean and Stirling had 'swum out and put timed explosives on several ships in the harbour'. Then, on driving out of Benghazi 'they were stopped by a German sentry who asked them for a light. Randolph, with a remark in German, told him to keep the box. When they got about a mile outside the German defences Randolph said, "For God's Sake run, just remembered I've given the sentry a box of Swan Vestas!"'.

Capt Malcolm Pleydell, L Detachment's new medical officer, got the warts-and-all story of the raid from Johnny Rose in the sergeants' mess, where he, like Paddy Mayne, preferred to drink of an evening. Rose told him how the LRDG had navigated them flawlessly over four hundred miles to the drop-off point south-east of Benghazi, and then waved off Stirling and his five men in the Blitz Buggy.

The operation went to plan, initially, explained Rose, but then the Buggy's wheels 'started to make a dreadful screaming sound'.[15] Rose and Cooper were ordered underneath the vehicle and discovered that the front wheels and axle had been damaged during the drive across the desert.

Outside Benghazi they encountered a road block manned by Italian colonial troops. By nature deferential to Europeans, these soldiers lacked training and motivation and they raised the barrier when Maclean, who was fluent in Italian and German, barked '*militaire*'.

The Blitz Buggy drove on, shrieking like a stuck pig, until it entered the town. There was little traffic on the road but the one vehicle they passed then turned and got on their tail. Moments later an air-raid siren went off. Stirling panicked and put his foot on the accelerator. 'We crammed on our full speed, getting up to 80 mph … and shot round a corner into a narrow street and drove on about 500 yards into the native part of the town,' wrote Churchill.

In a side street Stirling stopped; the men sat anxiously 'and awaited developments'. They heard police whistles and several heavy vehicles, and agreed that they appeared to have been rumbled. 'David gave an order for a half-hour time pencil to be put in the car which, as it was chock-full of thermite and plastic, would go off with a pretty detonation,' Churchill told his father.

They then 'legged it' through the side streets and took refuge in a bomb-damaged house. Someone suggested it might be an idea to change the half-hour fuse to a two-hour one, to give them more time to make good their escape. Stirling delegated the task to Rose and Cooper and the pair removed the detonator from the vehicle and threw it over a wall, whereupon it exploded.

By the time Rose and Cooper had rejoined their officers, the commotion had stopped. Maclean ventured out onto the street and asked a sentry what the fuss was about. It was a false air-raid alarm.

'In retrospect,' wrote Churchill, 'we were perhaps foolish to assume we were the cause of it, but so many circumstances taken together … all conspired to mislead us.'

They returned to the Blitz Buggy and Stirling ordered Rose to repair the vehicle while Churchill acted as his lookout. Already well behind schedule, Stirling decided they hadn't the time to carry out a thorough reconnaissance. Nor had they the time to inflate both boats; one would have to suffice.

Carrying the boat in its large kit bag, as well as the explosives, the four men set off for the docks five hundred yards away, guided by

Alston, who had been stationed in Benghazi for several months when it was in British hands. 'No sooner had they got down to the harbour,' Rose recounted, 'than they found they hadn't got the igniter, so Maj Stirling started off back to the car to get it.'

As Alston set off on a brief reconnoitre, Cooper and Maclean began inflating the boat. They pumped and they pumped, but it wouldn't inflate. Eventually they agreed it was punctured. Muttering imprecations, they returned to the car for the second boat.

Cooper and Maclean took a different route from the one trod by Stirling, so when he arrived at the harbour with the igniter he found himself alone. Stirling scuttled back to the car. On arriving, Rose told him he had just missed the other two, who had collected the second boat and were hurrying back to the harbour. 'You should have seen Major Stirling's face when I told him they had only just left,' remarked Rose. 'Well it was funny ... playing hide and seek round Benghazi in the middle of the night.'

By the time they were reunited on the quayside, a small but curious crowd had gathered, among whom were some sentries. Had they been Italian troops they would have seen there was something amiss about the four individuals claiming to be German troops on a night exercise. But the colonial soldiers were easily intimidated by the brisk authority of Maclean and Stirling. Maclean admonished the sentries and told them they were in Benghazi to probe their level of alertness, and they had failed the test. A report would be filed. With that the four British soldiers picked up the kit bag and marched back to the car.

Dawn was nearly upon them, so they hid in an abandoned house until nightfall, and in the early hours of 23 May they slipped out of Benghazi. They'd hoped no one would have noticed their withdrawal, but the moment they got on the main road the Blitz Buggy began its familiar caterwaul. Once more Rose was ordered under the vehicle and there he remained for the next hour and a half trying in vain to repair the axle. 'It was now about 3 o'clock and we had to get going,'

Randolph wrote. Stirling wanted to use their explosives in an attack on Benina aerodrome, but his comrades talked him out of it. 'The noise our car made might have made escape impossible and would have revealed the fact that we had been inside,' reported Churchill. 'It was very disappointing that we failed to achieve anything. On the other hand, it has filled us with confidence for future operations.'

Rose summarised the operation as 'a jolly game of hide and seek', one that resulted in his earning one of the more unusual Military Medals. 'The car broke down on two occasions, whilst in the town of Benghazi,' wrote Stirling in his citation. 'Sgt Rose displayed the greatest coolness in overcoming these breakdowns, although working under very trying conditions.'[16]

And yet, Rose added in his account to Malcolm Pleydell, the 'jolly game' ended in tragedy. Once back in Siwa, there was a rapid turnaround and then, said Maclean, Stirling departed 'in a hurry to get back to Cairo to report and make plans for the future. In such a hurry that, halfway between Alexandria and Cairo, the battle-waggon left the road and turned over.'[17]

Roaring along the coastal road at night, Stirling didn't spot the lightless truck at the back of the convoy until it was too late. In a letter to his father, Randolph described how Stirling swerved to avoid smashing into the back of the truck, only to clip its rear wheel and flip over. Maclean fractured his skull, arm and collarbone; Churchill suffered two broken lower ribs and dislocated a vertebra, Rose broke an arm and Alston and Cooper required hospital treatment. Stirling escaped without a scratch, or so he thought at the time. The only occupant who wasn't thrown clear was the veteran reporter Arthur Merton, employed by the *Daily Telegraph*, who had cadged a lift in Alexandria. 'He was pinned in the car,' said Randolph. 'He had a number of fractures in the head and unfortunately died before he got to hospital.'

The death of Merton was keenly felt by the British press. A man of great integrity and wide intellect, he was respected throughout the world. 'The death of Mr Arthur Sidney Merton ... brings to an abrupt close a varied journalistic career devoted to the peoples and politics of the Middle East,' stated *The Times* in its obituary. 'For the last 40 years Merton had been known throughout Egypt and the Arab countries as an indefatigable student of, and writer upon, the international relations of the States in all that region.'[18]

Stirling returned alone to Kabrit, where he was introduced for the first time to Capt Malcolm Pleydell. He asked him to examine his wrist and Pleydell diagnosed a scaphoid fracture. He advised Stirling to have it X-rayed. Stirling already had, on his return to Cairo following the crash. And the nurses had put his wrist in plaster. Stirling found the plaster a 'nuisance' and after a few days cut it off.

'I can't afford the time, Malcolm,' he explained. 'You can't do anything with your arm encased in one of those plasters.'[19]

Stirling was right. Time was against him. No matter how he or Randolph Churchill tried to dress it up, the Benghazi raid had been a fiasco. To make matters worse, his reckless driving had been responsible for the death of a respected journalist and severe injuries to the Prime Minister's son and Member of Parliament for Lancaster.

Stirling could feel GHQ breathing down his neck. He needed success; he needed Paddy Mayne.

17

Lt-Col Guy Prendergast could barely believe his ears when he heard of Stirling's nocturnal gallivant around Benghazi. The commander of the LRDG described the excursion as 'Gilbertian';[1] in other words, high farce in the best tradition of the nineteenth-century dramatist W. S. Gilbert, who with the composer Arthur Sullivan created many comic operas.

As an erstwhile explorer, Prendergast was familiar with the maxim that 'adventure is a sign of incompetence'; every time Stirling sallied forth across the sand he became entangled in high adventure. For some time Prendergast and the LRDG had been growing ever more exasperated with L Detachment, or more specifically its commander. In February Prendergast had written to Eighth Army HQ to complain at what he regarded as SAS intrusion on the operational area of the LRDG. 'I consider that it would be most unwise for Capt. Stirling's party to operate anywhere along the road for the present,' he said. The inevitable consequence of an L Detachment raid was an increase in enemy activity in the area, which jeopardised the LRDG, who were engaged on the surveillance of enemy traffic – what they called 'road watches', radioing back important intelligence on the strength and whereabouts of enemy forces.

In early 1942 the LRDG had replaced their ageing and unreliable Ford trucks with the latest Chevrolet model, and Stirling had petitioned Eighth Army to acquire the old vehicles for his unit. Prendergast intervened, writing to the Eighth Army that 'the old LRDG Fords which Capt. Stirling is proposing to take are in very bad order. I consider that Capt. Stirling is taking a big risk in using these vehicles for such a long journey in their present condition.'

Stirling was denied the lorries and continued using the LRDG, known by L Detachment as the 'Libyan Taxi Service'. Nevertheless, Stirling craved more independence for his unit, and to that end he approached one of their top navigators, L/Cpl Mike 'Lofty' Carr, a West Countryman who had been with the LRDG since January 1941. Would he like to join his unit? Carr turned down the invitation. He regarded L Detachment as distinctly second rate. But he did suggest another navigator, a recent arrival called Mike Sadler.

Prendergast agreed to release Sadler. While he'd objected to Stirling's appropriation of his old trucks, it was only out of concern for L Detachment; in principle he was eager to end the taxi-service arrangement as soon as there were some suitable vehicles, and the transfer of a navigator might also reduce Stirling's reliance on the LRDG.

By May 1942 Prendergast's patience with the LRDG playing 'universal aunt' to L Detachment had worn thin. He made a note in the war diary that 'these demands have usually been met, but not without straining the unit's own resources and personnel'.

To one of his officers, Lt Alastair Timpson, he expressed his displeasure in more forceful terms. Prendergast knew Timpson and David Stirling were old friends, and on one occasion Timpson returned to the LRDG HQ at Fayoum, near Cairo, and found a sullen Prendergast. 'One cannot blame Prendergast for being a little sour about the episodes when he had to cope with what went wrong in the administration of Stirling's glamorous sorties,' said Timpson.[2]

Prendergast was irritated at Stirling's poor communications; he might not respond to his signals about the organisation of LRDG patrols or at other times he changed his plans without consulting the LRDG. 'Why have I not been informed previously that landing operation no longer considered practicable?' he signalled on one occasion. 'I was invited to regard it as 100 per cent feasible and therefore planned on the certainty of supplies being available.'[3]

Prendergast was not alone in his frustration at Stirling's casual indifference to the logistics of war.

Peter Upcher was a quartermaster officer responsible for supplying the LRDG and L Detachment. 'The LRDG were absolutely magnificent,' he remembered. 'They appreciated the whole of the responsibilities regards supply and they realised how long it was to build up all these things. Guy Prendergast used to tell me exactly what was required ... but David [Stirling] wasn't interested in Q [quartermasters]. There were times when he said:

"I want so much."

I said, "You can't have it."

"Why not? I know you've got it."

"That's for the LRDG."

"I want it."

"My orders are the LRDG can have it, and there it is."'[4]

Randolph Churchill hadn't been well enough to write his account of the Benghazi debacle for several weeks because of the injuries he sustained in the traffic accident, what he described in a cable to his wife as 'severe and painful bruises'.[5] On 24 June he finally put pen to paper, and two days later he added a postscript:

> David has just got back safe and sound. He burnt down 3 hangars at Benina aerodrome, destroying about 14 aero engines, 4 aircraft, and all the aero-engine workshops. He waited till the first delayed-action charge went up and then opened

> the door of the guard-house. Inside, facing him, was a German officer seated at a table with about 15 German soldiers drawn up in front of him. David opened his hand and showed the Hun officer a hand grenade. The Hun wailed 'No – no – no! 'Yes – yes – yes!' replied David, lobbing it in and closing the door![6]

In fact, Stirling had been accompanied on the raid by Johnny Cooper and Reg Seekings, the latter having made a rapid recovery from his inopportune hand wound that forced him to relinquish his place on the Benghazi raid. Cooper's recollection was that most of the Germans in the guard-house were asleep in bunks when Stirling rolled a grenade across the floor.

For Stirling it was his first successful raid, one he knew would be regarded back at Kabrit as 'Paddyesque' in its ruthless audacity. But the excitement and stress proved too much as he climbed an escarpment to reach the LRDG rendezvous. He collapsed with what Cooper described as a migraine attack. 'Reg and I each took one of hands and we led him, staggering and half-blind, to the top of the ridge.'[7]

Cooper was concerned with Stirling's physical and emotional state. 'He rarely slept properly and his desert sores had been left untreated.' There was also his wrist, and the lingering pain from the back injury sustained in the first parachute jump twelve months earlier, which was also responsible for his migraine attacks. Nevertheless, said Cooper, he was his old self by the time they reached Siwa, 'extremely elated that we had finally emulated Paddy Mayne on our own'.

Randolph Churchill was an immature man and his letter to his father read like the hero worship a schoolboy has for the head prefect. 'David then hid for three days and then returned and shot up a lot of enemy transport about 4 miles outside Benghazi,' he wrote. 'He had twin mounted Vickers K. guns on a big truck and destroyed about 15 large lorries, killing about another 10 Huns. He then drove off and made good his escape.'[8]

In reality, Paddy Mayne was at the wheel and Reg Seekings was behind the Vickers, and only Mayne's skilful driving prevented them falling into enemy hands as they were pursued across the desert. But Churchill's role, as it had been when he was in charge of propaganda at GHQ, was to spin a yarn, embellish the truth, create an idol. It worked, particularly with his father. 'I lunched with Papa yesterday,' wrote Pamela Churchill to her husband on 10 July. 'He was very pleased with your letter to him and terribly proud; in fact, I have rarely seen him so excited. Having told me that I was not to mention it to a soul, he then said why hadn't I shown it to your friends and would I take a copy, which I did. He wanted it shown to Max [Lord Beaverbrook, the newspaper baron, and former Minister of Supply in Churchill's War Cabinet].'[9]

There was a PPS to Randolph Churchill's letter home: 'In your last letter, for which I thank you very much, you said you thought David Stirling would be returning to England. I gather Dickie Mountbatten asked for him but Middle East didn't want to let him go. ME offered him a much bigger job with promotion but he preferred to stay with L Detachment.'

Stirling wanted to remain because he preferred to be the big fish in the small pond. He now had celebrity; people looked admiringly at him when he walked into Shepheard's or strolled around the Gezireh Sporting Club or ordered ice cream at Groppi's, Cairo's famous café. He didn't want the mundanity of a staff job at GHQ. On 2 June he received an order from GHQ:

> 1. It has been decided that Major Stirling, L Det., S.A.S Bde., will not take part in active operations with his unit until further notice.
>
> 2. The reason for this decision is to enable Major Stirling to train other officers who will be available to take his place should be become a casualty.[10]

Stirling had no intention of obeying the instruction.

★ ★ ★

The injuries to Fitzroy Maclean, Gordon Alston and Randolph Churchill had deprived Stirling of three of his loyal followers. He had nearly lost a fourth, George Jellicoe, who had sailed to Crete in a Greek submarine on 12 June with Commander Georges Bergé and three of his French soldiers. Their objective had been an airfield at Heraklion, one of a series of raids launched on the island as part of an operation to destroy as many German aircraft as possible before a vital convoy left Alexandria for Malta.

The SBS had expected to carry out all of the raids but Stirling persuaded GHQ to allocate to L Detachment the most prestigious. Capt Mike Kealy, the SBS commander, was not pleased with the decision but, as one of his fellow officers commented, 'opposing Stirling was like trying to stop a steam-roller with a banana'.[11]

Jellicoe and his party ran into difficulty the moment they came ashore on the Cretan coast. Unprepared for the length of time it would take them to paddle from the submarine to the beach, they then wasted two valuable hours disposing of their two rubber boats. By the time they reached Heraklion they were nearly a day behind schedule. Nevertheless, they destroyed eighteen aircraft but on their trek to the rendezvous beach a Cretan betrayed the presence of the party to the Germans, and in the ensuing firefight one Frenchman was killed and Bergé and two others captured.

The three SBS raiding parties suffered no casualties but one of their airfields was devoid of aircraft and another too well-guarded. At Kastelli, however, Capt George Duncan and Cpl Barr accounted for eight aircraft, six trucks, four bomb dumps and nine oil and petrol dumps.

In the same period, Bergé's second-in-command, Augustin Jordan, was the only one of fifteen Frenchmen to escape from an ambush during a raid on airfields at Derna and Martuba.

Paddy Mayne had also had a narrow escape in June, while raiding Berca satellite airfield; a French raiding party unconnected to Jordan's team had attacked the main aerodrome a mile away ahead of schedule. Mayne had with him Jimmy Storie, Bob Lilley and Arthur Warburton, three men he had yet to observe in action. The Frenchmen's bombs began exploding just as Mayne and his men crept onto their target airfield. The quartet managed to extricate themselves but there was no question that the enemy had become more vigilant.

It had taken the destruction of 143 aircraft in six months, but Axis forces were starting to realise that the defence of their airfields left a lot to be desired. The Luftwaffe promulgated a memorandum in the wake of the June raids in North Africa and Crete entitled 'Proposals for the Improvement of Defence Measures against Enemy Commando'. According to the German air force, the commando units responsible for the raids 'consist chiefly of personnel especially suitable by reason of their profession – acrobats, boxers, etc. – specially equipped and with an extensive and thorough special training for sabotage and offensive raids'.

Among the suggested measures for implementation were:

- Every man must be equipped with pocket torch and signal pistol.
- Provision should be made for the equipment of guard-rooms with pistols for distribution to sentries and patrols.
- Watchdogs with trained men in charge are of value on all exposed airfields, as also are bloodhounds.[12]

Paddy Mayne had also been evaluating the defence of airfields. L Detachment had started to find sentries under aircraft, asleep more often than not, but nonetheless it was now more of a challenge to slip unseen onto airfields. According to George Jellicoe, Mayne's solution was to propose to David Stirling in June 1942 'that in future operations it would be useful if a jeep could be provided to transport the elements of the Special Air Service to the scene of operations. This would save, he thought, a lot of walking.'[13]

Stirling seized on the suggestion. Here was the opportunity to become independent of the LRDG and also gain greater autonomy from GHQ by establishing a base deep in the desert. Whether Mayne also envisaged using the jeeps to attack enemy airfields wasn't covered in Jellicoe's summary. He may have had that in mind, or it might have been Stirling's suggestion, or it could equally have been an LRDG proposition. They had pioneered the vehicle attack eighteen months earlier when they raided an Italian fort and landing strip at Murzak in one of the most remarkable guerrilla operations of the war. Murzak was a thousand miles west of Cairo as the crow flies and the LRDG knew the raid would be of little material significance; but that wasn't the point. The effect on the already fragile morale of Italian troops was immeasurable: they no longer felt safe anywhere.

The idea to procure jeeps was timely. On 26 May Rommel went on the offensive and by 14 June the Eighth Army was in retreat from the Gazala Line. The Royal Navy vacated their base at Alexandria and in Cairo the sky turned black as British staff officers in GHQ burned papers in anticipation of the German arrival. But the Eighth Army stopped its withdrawal at a small railway station called El Alamein, sixty-five miles west from Alexandria, and dug in across a thirty-five-mile-wide front.

Nevertheless, Siwa Oasis was now in German territory and the LRDG and L Detachment were forced to relocate; some of the LRDG went to Kufra, 350 miles south, while others returned to the Nile Valley. Stirling sent L Detachment to Kabrit while he went to Cairo to GHQ. There had been changes as a consequence of the Allied retreat, what was dubbed the 'Gazala Gallop', to El Alamein. Gen Auchinleck had sacked Neil Ritchie on 25 June, and taken command of the Eighth Army himself.

In the company of his Brigadier, General Staff, John Whiteley, Auchinleck informed Stirling that in the coming weeks he should focus on attacking transport on roads to the west, although he was also instructed to raid airstrips if the opportunity arose.

Stirling secured authorisation to procure a fleet of American Willys jeeps, each armed with two Vickers K guns, and a number of three-ton lorries. Two airfields, Fuka and Bagush, were attacked, the first by a combined party led by Bill Fraser and Augustin Jordan, and the second a joint attack by Mayne and Stirling. More than fifty aircraft were destroyed in total.

During this period L Detachment were based at a remote spot called Qaret Tartura; among the party was the medical officer Malcolm Pleydell. A healer and not a killer, he nonetheless got a vicarious thrill from being in the company of men whose job it was to take life. He observed but didn't judge, dissecting his comrades' character as if they were patients under his surgeon's knife. He enjoyed the ribald banter of the men, their intelligence and sensitivity that they concealed under their coarse exterior. He liked Jellicoe, honest and big-hearted, and Fraser, who looked too young for this way of life. Stirling he found to be a generous and warm commander. Pleydell noted his 'seemingly airy and casual way of referring to operations' but he suspected it might be a carefully constructed façade. 'His conversation would be, in part, a guardee manner of speaking,' he wrote. 'For Guards officers, as I had come to know, took great pains to conceal their true emotions by adopting an especially flowery form of expression.'[14]

The man who most intrigued him was Paddy Mayne. Pity the poor Italian sentry who looked up into that face on a dark desert night. There was no doubt Mayne enjoyed the war, at least this type of warfare; he had told Pleydell that raiding was an opportunity for 'some good killing'.

Guerrilla warfare required initiative and boldness and courage. For Mayne it was an extension of the boxing ring. The difference was that defeat on the battlefield often meant death. Mayne had evidently addressed the question in his mind and concluded that he would not pull his punches. He would be cold-blooded in the pursuit of victory but nonetheless he would respect the ethics of war. 'There was no give or take about his method of warfare,' wrote Pleydell. 'He was out to kill when the opportunity presented itself. There was no question of sparing an enemy – this was war, and war meant killing.'[15]

Yet what made the deepest impression on Pleydell was the quasi-maternal concern that Mayne displayed for his men. He was older than most by four or five years; he knew they looked up to him because of his status as a sportsman and soldier. He in turn felt protective towards men whom he knew felt a level of fear and anxiety he didn't experience – provided they weren't barrack-room braggarts. Pleydell described Mayne as a shrewd judge of character, and that '"Shooting a line" cut absolutely no ice at all with him and he could detect it straightaway.'

Like all natural leaders, Mayne formed a bond with those under his command who lived up to his standards. He asked a lot of himself and expected the same of his men. They respected him because they recognised Mayne was motivated not by personal ambition but by an iron will to succeed.

Being popular with his soldiers was of no interest to Mayne; they were his men not his friends.

Stirling, on the other hand, was charming on first acquaintance, but there was a superficiality to his bonhomie that the intuitive quickly perceived. Personal ambition burned through his false modesty. Stirling kept his men at arm's length in case they should see through his 'guardee manner of speaking' to the true emotions beneath.

Back at their hideout at Qaret Tartura after the raids on Fuka and Bagush, L Detachment threw a party to celebrate their success. Malcolm Pleydell's account of the shindig was revealing. In the darkness the men clustered together, smoking and joking and singing.

David Stirling and his clique of upper-class officers were further down the slope, out of range of the jar of rum that was passed from mouth to mouth. Mayne and Pleydell each had a swig and then listened as the men around them began to sing. Pleydell suggested to Mayne at one moment that the songs being sung were too sentimental. 'Och, Malcolm,' replied Mayne, 'there's nothing to worry about. They're happy, that's the main thing.'[16]

18

David Stirling returned reluctantly to Cairo at the start of August. On the night of 26–27 July L Detachment had used jeeps to launch a brilliant hit-and-run raid on the Axis aerodrome at Sidi Haneish. On his report on the attack, George Jellicoe estimated that eighteen aircraft had been destroyed and many more damaged, at the cost of two dead and three wounded.

Stirling had wanted to remain in the desert indefinitely, striking at more targets and being resupplied by the RAF; GHQ had other ideas, which led to 'a difference of opinion'.[1] Drawing on intelligence harvested by the LRDG, GHQ informed Stirling that his position was increasingly insecure because the Italians were now in possession of Siwa. He was therefore instructed to bring in his detachment.

Stirling found a gloom pervading the warren of rooms at GHQ. On 28 July Auchinleck had called a halt to his offensive, the First Battle of El Alamein, because he had run out of fresh troops. The previous day he had received a cable from Winston Churchill, whose interference the Auk was finding intolerable.

The Prime Minister's confidence in Auchinleck was running perilously low. He railed against the 'inexplicable inertia' of his command, particularly the failure to prevent Tobruk falling into German hands the previous month. The siege had become a symbol of defiance for the British people – in much the same way the siege of Mafeking had in the South African War at the turn of the century. Its loss, coming in a year that had also witnessed the humiliating fall of Singapore and Burma, threatened Churchill's prestige. In July, in the House of Commons, he had survived a vote of no confidence; he'd won easily – 475 to 25 – but nonetheless it was a deep embarrassment on a personal level and suggested to Britain's Russian and American allies that there were cracks in the country's leadership.

At the start of August Churchill flew from England bound for Cairo, the first leg of a tour that would also include Persia and Moscow, where it was his unenviable task to inform Joseph Stalin that the Western Allies' priority in 1942 was victory in North Africa and not an Anglo-American second front in Europe.

David Stirling met Winston Churchill briefly when he was in Cairo. On 9 August he wrote a memo to the Prime Minister, titled 'Proposals for Reorganising Special Services in the Middle East'.[2] Churchill had been urged by his son to meet the man who was – if Randolph's letters were anything to go by – single-handedly winning the war in North Africa. Randolph himself had spent part of his rehabilitation after the car crash in New York, but he was back in London by the end of July and wrote to his father on the eve of his departure for Cairo, briefing him on some of the characters he would meet. For instance, Air Chief Marshal Arthur Tedder, Air Officer Commanding in Chief, Middle East Command, was first rate; Richard Casey, the Minister of State in the Middle East, had a shaky grasp on military matters; and Lt-Gen Thomas Corbett, Chief of the General Staff, was 'a blockhead'. Randolph also remarked, 'It would be nice if you had time to see David Stirling.'[3]

According to Stirling, the Prime Minister found time to dine with him on two consecutive evenings at the British Embassy in the company of Gen Jan Smuts, the prime minister of South Africa, and Gen Harold Alexander, who had been nominated to command the British First Army in Operation Torch, the upcoming Anglo-American invasion of French North Africa. So well did they get on, claimed Stirling, that Churchill invited him for a post-prandial stroll in the Embassy garden, where, among other things, Stirling told the premier about L Detachment's role in an imminent raid on Benghazi. In the course of the conversation Stirling described Sicily and Italy as the 'soft underbelly of Europe'.[4] Churchill loved the image, and asked if he could adopt it as his own.

Stirling said he was invited back the following night and the evening finished with Churchill offering 'him a higher command if he would return to Britain and pass along his experience'.

Churchill had arrived in Egypt on the morning of 4 August, not long after his top military advisor, Gen Sir Alan Brooke, the Chief of the Imperial General Staff, had landed. At lunchtime, Jan Smuts arrived from Pretoria. Brooke had a nap in the afternoon, preparation for what he knew would be a fraught few days with many crucial top-level decisions to be made. At 5.30 p.m. Brooke and Auchinleck had a long interview with Churchill. They were then joined by Smuts, Vice Admiral Henry Harwood, Commander-in-Chief, Mediterranean Fleet, Richard Casey, Air Chief Marshal Arthur Tedder and Gen Archibald Wavell, Commander-in-Chief, India.

The conference lasted three hours and for much of the time an impatient Churchill interrogated Auchinleck about the inertia of his command. They ate dinner late, wrote Brooke in his diary, and he then spent three hours in the Prime Minister's room discussing the situation in North Africa.

The next day, 5 August, was another whirlwind of interviews and conferences. Churchill wanted a change in the command structure in North Africa and it was a question of finding the right people. At 5.45 p.m. he hosted a conference at the Embassy at which, noted

Brooke, were 'Smuts, Auchinleck, Wavell, the admiral [Harwood], Tedder, Casey, [Brig Ian] Jacob and self'. To Brooke's dismay, the Prime Minister kept talking for nearly three hours. Then dinner, and afterwards, the exhausted Brooke was 'dragged off into the garden by PM to report the results of my day's work … he kept me arguing till 1:00 a.m.!!'[5] The 6th was another frenetic day of conferences, what Brooke described as 'one of the most difficult days of my life'. Churchill took a series of momentous decisions and at 8.15 p.m. he cabled the deputy prime minister, Clement Attlee, in London to inform him: 'As a result of such enquiry as I have made here, and after prolonged consultations with Field-Marshal Smuts and C.I.G.S. [Brooke] and Minister of State [Casey] I have come to the conclusion that a drastic and immediate change is needed in the High Command.'[6]

Foremost among the changes was the division of Middle East Command into two separate commands: (a) 'Near East Command', comprising Egypt, Palestine, and Syria, commanded by Gen Alexander; and (b) 'Middle East Command', comprising Persia and Iraq, commanded by Auchinleck. Gen Montgomery would succeed Alexander in planning for Operation Torch, and Lt-Gen William Gott would command the Eighth Army. The following day was another full of 'high-level discussions', according to Brooke, and it ended with the terrible news that Gott had been killed en route to taking up his new post when his aircraft was shot down. 'After dinner PM, Smuts and I had conference as to how the matter should be settled.' In *The Hinge of Fate*, the fourth volume of his history of the Second World War, Churchill wrote that Gen Alexander arrived on the morning of 9 August, to be given his brief in person by Churchill: 'Your prime and main duty will be to take or destroy at the earliest opportunity the German Italian army commanded by Field Marshal Rommel.'

The aggrandisement of Stirling's exploits by Randolph didn't stem solely from starry-eyed devotion; in embellishing the truth to his father he saw an opportunity for himself to become a dashing war hero. No doubt encouraged by Stirling, Randolph wrote to Bob Laycock in August 1942 with his idea for a 'long-range sabotage unit', one that drew inspiration from the 'extraordinary success achieved by L Detachment SAS Brigade under the command of Major David Stirling, DSO'.[7] Churchill's idea was for a hand-picked force of highly trained men to parachute into Europe and embark on a campaign of guerrilla warfare. 'Their orders should be to remain in Europe for the duration,' he stressed. 'They will thus be able to operate for a period of many months instead of for only a few hours.'

Laycock replied on 18 August. It was an interesting proposal, he said. Did Churchill envisage his force wearing civilian clothes, as 'they would not last long in uniform'? Also, had he by any chance heard of SOE, who had been performing similar work for the past two years?

Fortunately for Laycock, Randolph soon lost interest in raising a band of desperadoes and focused his imagination once more on David Stirling. He dined with Evelyn Waugh and his wife Laura, and the novelist's diary makes it clear that Churchill had lionised his hero during the course of the evening. 'David's prodigies of courage become more legendary every day,' wrote Waugh. 'Randolph had a run with him to Benghazi.'[8] Waugh's sardonic observation was understandable, and he evidently found it hard to match Churchill's depiction of Stirling with the profligate loafer he'd seen in No. 8 Commando.

In lauding Stirling, Randolph had the approval of his father, who had returned to London on 21 August. He was soon under pressure once more about events in North Africa; the American Chiefs of Staff wished to postpone Operation Torch but in early September Churchill convinced Roosevelt to stick with the schedule.

A significant source of frustration for the Prime Minister was the respect – occasionally bordering on reverence – for Rommel. His defeat of the Allied forces in June had elicited much praise in Britain.

The *Yorkshire Post* attributed the Axis victory to 'Rommel's brilliant generalship, his boldness and resilience, his tactical cunning'.

What was required therefore, in Churchill's mind, was a counter to the adulation of Rommel, a soldier who was not just his match, but who was his superior in guile and courage. A warrior of whom the British could be proud.

The Prime Minister knew how to capture the imagination of the people: the bulldog spirit, the dauntless 'Few', the V for Victory. He was, after all, a journalist by trade. So too was his son. In the late thirties Randolph had edited the *Evening Standard* diary page (Winston had guest edited on a dozen occasions) and it was to that paper he gave the scoop of 'The Phantom Major'.*

The *Standard* ran the piece on 3 September. There was no byline but it was evidently the prose of Randolph, some of which he had first polished in the letter to his father in late June. He once more described the attack on Benina aerodrome, and again he omitted the presence of Reg Seekings and Johnny Cooper alongside Stirling.

'He sent all his men away and waited alone for the first explosion,' ran the report. 'The moment it came he opened the door of the German guard house. In front of him he saw a startled Hun officer sitting at a desk. Around the walls in bunks were about eighteen Nazi soldiers. Stirling had a grenade in his hand. "Nein, nein, nein!" said the Nazi, groping for his revolver. "Yes, yes, yes," said the British major, and he lobbed the grenade and slammed the door.' Randolph repeated the anecdote about Stirling hiding for three days and then 'descend[ing] on the enemy again to destroy 15 large lorries and wipe out about 10 more Germans'.

But above all, he fleshed out the 'Phantom Major' for his readers, a task to which he was eminently suited, being such a close confidant of Stirling's:

* The 'Phantom Major' was the tabloids' name for Maj Norman Bailey, a veteran of the First World War who killed his wife in Hove in December 1923 and then vanished. A huge manhunt ensued, but his body was eventually recovered from the Thames in May 1924 and an inquest concluded that he had shot himself.

> Major David Stirling, first cousin of Lord Lovat, the Commando leader, was taking horses from Alberta to Texas when he learned of the outbreak of war. He heard the news at Montana, sold the horses, and set off back to England. In the supplementary reserve of officers, he went to the Scots Guards. Months went by without any exciting action coming his way. He joined the Commandos, but again, although often on the starting line, action still passed him. This Scots Catholic, dark, handsome, 6 feet 4 inches in height, but with nothing of the 'tough' about him, decided that he would have to find his own way to the fighting.

The 'Phantom' had recently met Jan Smuts, a profound experience for the South African prime minister, who was moved to compare him to Lord Byron's Don Juan: 'The mildest mannered man who ever scuttled ship or cut a throat.'

The *Evening Standard*'s story was seized on with glee by the Scottish newspapers. The following day, the *Scotsman* published an almost verbatim reprise of their profile of the Phantom Major. As a footnote it ran a potted biography of the man who had struck terror into the hearts of Erwin Rommel and his men:

> Major Archibald David Stirling is the third son of the Hon Mrs Stirling of Keir, Dunblane, and the late Brigadier-General Stirling. He was born on November 15, 1915 and was educated at Ampleforth and at Cambridge. Major Stirling spent the winter before the outbreak of war ranching in British Columbia. His favourite sport is mountaineering, and he has climbed many of the Alpine peaks as well as many of the mountains in Scotland. Last year he was awarded the DSO, to which has been added a bar.

Such precise information could only have come from David Stirling, via Randolph Churchill. It was mostly accurate, except Stirling had been awarded just the one DSO.

Other newspapers and magazines began to print more fanciful accounts of the Phantom Major, or as the weekly magazine *John Bull* described him, 'the newest terror of the desert', who, 'towering 6ft 4in, is as lithe as a panther, a former boxing champion, one of the finest horsemen in the Army'.

Stirling was by now not only a champion pugilist, he was also fluent in German, and capable of fooling his way through enemy checkpoints and saving the lives of his 'merry men'. But what would one expect from this 'Robin Hood in battledress'?

In a couple of paragraphs, Stirling had appropriated Fitzroy Maclean's linguistic skills and Paddy Mayne's sporting prowess.

There were other embellishments. 'Just before the war he was breeding horses in Canada,' said *John Bull*. 'When Hitler broke loose he sold his stock and returned to England by fast passenger plane.'

They weren't Stirling's horses to sell and he returned home by ship.

The misrepresentation continued in the *People*. The Phantom got a whole page to himself on 11 October. 'He chose and created this hazardous assignment for himself, hand picked with great care and deliberation the men to follow him,' stated the newspaper. No mention of his brother Bill or Jock Lewes, and in describing how Stirling's 'wolves of the desert' had destroyed twenty-four aircraft in one raid and thirty-seven in another there was no acknowledgement of Paddy Mayne or Bill Fraser, the officers who had led the raids on Tamet and Agedabia. 'Over the far-flung wastes of the great Western Desert no name strikes more fear in the heart of the enemy than that of the Phantom Major,' trumpeted the *People*. 'Only the set of his shoulders and the glint in his eyes tells you that here is a man out of the common rut.'

The Phantom's fame reached as far as Australia. 'The major leads a band of men who have become known as super-commandos,' reported the *Sydney Sun*. 'Sometimes he goes out alone, on other occasions with a handful of his super-fighters. The "Phantom" disappears before the guards can recover. Even the Eighth Army chiefs do not all know the major by sight, but his name is a legend in every unit throughout the desert.'

Among the recruits 'hand picked' by David Stirling for his next attempt to lay waste to Benghazi was Capt Andrew Maxwell of the Second Battalion, Scots Guards. He was a cousin who had attended some of Mrs Stirling's balls, and while on leave in Cairo he lodged with Peter Stirling. David invited Maxwell to join him for the raid on Benghazi, a sort of busman's holiday.

Also recruited at Peter's flat was Brian Dillon, a motor contact officer with Headquarters, 1st Armoured Division. He described his first encounter with Stirling as 'strange'. 'He was sitting in a bath with a waiter with a silver salver with a whisky decanter on it,' he said. '"Have a drink, old boy." It was like something out of a play.'[9]

Stirling told Dillon to appear at GHQ the following day for a briefing on the operation he was planning, and provided him with an hour and the room number. Being a regular officer, Dillon arrived ahead of schedule, keen to make a good impression. 'I walked up to the number of this room, walked in there and lying on the table was a file labelled "top secret" saying operation whatever it was. And I read it. Then David Stirling appeared and they all came in and we started being briefed. And I said, "I know all about this." He said, "What do you mean?" And I said, "Well, the bloody thing was lying on the table, didn't anybody know?"' Stirling gave a sheepish grin and said it must have been left on the table by mistake when they went to lunch.

A couple of days later at Mary's House, 'a decorous officers' brothel' not far from the pyramids, Dillon ran into a good friend called Geoffrey Gordon-Creed, an officer in the Royal Gloucestershire Hussars, an armoured regiment, who had been awarded an MC in

1941. Dillon knew that Stirling was taking a couple of Honey tanks on the Benghazi raid and suggested to Gordon-Creed that there might be a job for him. Gordon-Creed was duly accepted and informed that the raiding party was rendezvousing at Kufra Oasis. When he arrived he was delighted to find two old friends, Carol Mather and Stephen Hastings. Of less satisfaction to Gordon-Creed were the two tanks he was supposed to lead to Benghazi, eight hundred miles north.

'The first one slid off a raised track within the oasis and immediately sank in a bottomless black ooze.' The second had covered only ninety miles when its engine blew. 'With my small command gone I was now a supernumerary,' said Gordon-Creed. 'David Stirling, however, was kind enough to allow me to tag along.'[10]

19

Lt Mike Sadler, the L Detachment navigator, described the Benghazi raid as 'a nonsense' and Cpl James Sherwood of the SBS said it was 'a complete fiasco'.[1] The initial idea, proposed by David Stirling after his game of hide and seek in the port in May, was 'to occupy the town for twenty-four hours and be relieved by a seaborne force from Malta'. According to Carol Mather, however, Stirling's scheme had 'unfortunately been talked about so that now the modified scheme was adopted'.[2]

There was another factor in play: Gen Bernard Montgomery. Appointed commander of the Eighth Army on 12 August following the death of Lt-Gen Gott, Monty was resistant to Churchill's back-seat generalship. He was patiently planning a big offensive for late October, to start from the Alamein line, and he had a task for the assorted 'private armies' under his command. Montgomery's concern was that Rommel's Afrika Korps were being greatly strengthened by regular supply convoys arriving at Tobruk, Barce and Benghazi.

The LRDG were to attack Barce (and also the fort at Jalo, in tandem with the Sudan Defence Force), a composite force of LRDG and commandos would target Tobruk and Stirling's objective was Benghazi. 'We were to enter the town, a force of two hundred strong, towards midnight and destroy ships in the harbour, port installations, the electricity and water supplies – in fact to cause as much alarm and despondency as possible,' said Mather. 'The conception of the whole operation had been David's and had been a direct outcome of his successful clandestine visits to Benghazi harbour earlier in the year.'[3]

Stirling's sorties had been anything but successful, although he had managed to slip in and out of the port without being apprehended. But stealing into an occupied town in an enemy staff car – even one whose axle screeched – was one thing; leading a force of 214 officers and men in a fleet of trucks and two tanks across eight hundred miles of desert was at best injudicious and at worst foolhardy.

Furthermore, so many people had been recruited – or in some cases invited – to join the raiding party that security had been compromised. 'In the lead-up to Benghazi rumours had been buzzing around Cairo that something was up,' said Mike Sadler.

Cecil 'Jacko' Jackson was part of the LRDG contingent attached to Stirling's force. Comprising S1 and S2 patrols, under John Olivey, the LRDG were to attack the airstrip at Benina, east of Benghazi, while the main raid was in process. Jackson shared Sadler's misgivings. 'We were not happy about this job,' said the Rhodesian. 'There were too many people involved and there had obviously been talk before the newcomers left Cairo.'[4]

More intimately involved in the planning was Maj Vladimir Peniakoff, commander of a small unit called No. 1 Demolition Squad, composed of five British officers and forty British and Arab soldiers. For several weeks they had been operating behind enemy lines in a similar fashion to L Detachment; the difference was in the leadership. Peniakoff, nicknamed Popski, was a forty-five-year-old Russian who had been born in Belgium and educated at Cambridge. David Hunt, who in August 1942 had been posted to the intelligence staff of GHQ Cairo, described Popski's Private Army, as it was dubbed, as 'a serious organisation, at any rate in its early days. While it was small it was good.'[5]

Peniakoff was dismayed at what he saw at GHQ in August 1942. 'My sense of propriety was shocked at the light-hearted manner in which the problems were tackled,' he said. 'Ten per cent planning, ninety per cent wishful thinking.'[6]

Peniakoff exempted the LRDG from his criticism; they were masters of the desert. He was thinking more of David Stirling, who 'pranced' while he and the LRDG 'plodded'. He couldn't fault his 'boyish enthusiasm' but his scheme to invest Benghazi was 'mad ... with little more than pea-shooters they were going to capture the whole of Cyrenaica from Benghazi to Tobruk'.

On 6 September David Stirling flew from Cairo to Kufra with Andrew Maxwell and Fitzroy Maclean; the latter was operational for the first time following the car accident on the way back from Benghazi four months earlier. He felt a sense of foreboding ahead of his return to the port. 'There were signs that too many people knew too much,' said Maclean. 'There were indications that the enemy was expecting the raids and was taking counter-measures.'[7]

While Stirling travelled in comfort, his men endured a gruelling nine-hundred-mile journey in their jeeps and Chevrolet trucks. They left Cairo in three convoys – one led by Paddy Mayne, the second by Capt Bill Cumper and the third by Capt Sandy Scratchley – on 20 August, with orders to be in Kufra no later than 3 September. Scratchley, a noted jockey before the war, was a phlegmatic and competent officer but he was inexperienced in desert travel and his convoy soon encountered problems; vehicles became separated, petrol ran short and trucks got stuck. All the time David Stirling was signalling Scratchley to hurry up. Eventually, Scratchley's patience snapped. 'He made a signal to David,' wrote Carol Mather, a member of Scratchley's column, 'saying that by these repeated demands for speed our party was spread over five hundred miles of desert, that half of them were lost, some of them probably dying of thirst and that he was going to call a halt for three days at Wadi Sura, and that he was quite prepared to resign his position in the SAS if told to do anything otherwise.'[8]

Stirling was suffering the cost of his cavalier attitude towards the logistical side of operations. On 23 August, for example, a conference was held at GHQ, hosted by Brig George Davy, Director of Military Operations. Its purpose was to agree upon the most effective way of coordinating the enterprises of the various organisations during the upcoming raids. Lt-Col Guy Prendergast, CO of the LRDG was present, but L Detachment was represented by a Maj John Freeland, a general staff officer within GHQ.

Where was Stirling? He should have been present for such a crucial meeting, or at the very least he should have deputised Paddy Mayne, Bill Fraser or Fitzroy Maclean. His failure to do so did not surprise Davy, who had grown accustomed to Stirling's methods. 'He was quite fearless,' he wrote later. 'Unfortunately he was too persuasive and he used to go direct to the C-in-C (Auchinleck) and I was often confronted with a fait accompli.'

One repercussion of Stirling's absence was keenly felt by Carol Mather as he tried to contact Cairo on the LRDG wireless truck. He couldn't because he was using the wrong signal procedure. 'Later I found out that David had left Cairo some time since and that this was the work of some sheltered GHQ major – John Freeland; may God rain curses on his head for ever more.'[9]

Mather should have directed his wrath at Stirling. Signals had been discussed at the planning meeting on 23 August, and Freeland pointed out that 'until L Detachment had its own signals it would have to rely on the LRDG for intercommunication'.[10]

Why didn't L Detachment have signallers of their own, a year after their formation? The LRDG had two signallers from the start, and within six months it boasted its own signals section commanded by Capt Tim Heywood.

The convoy eventually reached Kufra, tired, irritable and despondent. Stirling was as fresh as a daisy. He had even had a scale model made of Benghazi and he invited his men to gather around his handiwork as he explained how the attack would unfold. Peter Upcher, Kufra's quartermaster officer, was aghast. 'Right in the middle of Kufra so that any spy could see them,' he said. 'The LRDG weren't quite like that.'[11]

On 12 September Stirling and his raiding group, codenamed 'Force X', rendezvoused just south of Benghazi with a local man who had been recruited by British intelligence in Cairo into the Libyan Arab Force. He had just returned from the port and reported that thousands of additional troops had arrived to reinforce the garrison. Furthermore an anti-tank ditch protected by mines had been dug around the whole city. That evening Stirling sent a signal to GHQ, 'repeating what they had been told and asking whether it could be confirmed'.[12] The signal surprised David Hunt and the rest of the intelligence staff in Cairo. Three days earlier the RAF had conducted an extensive air reconnaissance of Benghazi and the photographs revealed no trace of an anti-tank ditch, mines or wiring. One couldn't have been dug since because GHQ intelligence knew the enemy lacked the materials and the manpower.

Stirling was ordered to ignore the 'bazaar gossip'.*

He didn't. 'Unfortunately the wonders of science, if I may so describe photographic reconnaissance, made less impression on David Stirling's party than the supposed evidence of an eyewitness,' said David Hunt. Fearful of encountering the enemy's defences, Stirling and Maclean concocted a new plan of attack, which the latter explained in his subsequent report: 'We could not go in unobtrusively from the east because we could not get across the anti-tank ditch, so we decided we should have to attack up the main road to the south.'[13]

* Stirling claimed this was the wording of the signal he received from GHQ but both David Hunt and Brig George Davy, then Director of Military Operations at GHQ, had no knowledge of such a signal.

Hunt was incredulous when he read Maclean's report. 'Whether or not there were any defences elsewhere, there were bound to be some on the main road,' he commented.

Many of the men in the column thought the same thing. James Sherwood said he and the rest of the SBS were 'thoroughly out of sorts with one another, and irritable and grumbling' as they approached the target. Their instructions from Stirling were to paddle out to the harbour and sink enemy shipping with limpet mines. 'Nobody was enthusiastic about this,' said Sherwood, quite apart from the 'fact that we didn't want to be with the SAS anyway'.[14]

To reach the plain leading to Benghazi entailed a tricky descent from the hilly jebel overlooking the port. 'The route was so tortuous we had to switch lights on, which was not a very clever thing to do,' recalled naval officer Brian Scott-Garrett, attached to the raiding party with a handful of other sailors in order to seize ships and sink them to block the harbour.[15] 'No doubt the lights must have been seen from the enemy's side descending the hill.'

The LRDG decided it was madness to continue. The route, John Olivey told Stirling, was impassable. They would try to locate another track down. 'With great difficulty we got the trucks back to the starting point, and realised it was too late to look for another route in the dark,' said Cecil Jackson. 'We drove into a deep wadi [Wadi Gamra] and camouflaged the trucks.'[16]

John Olivey had had no hesitation in aborting his mission, recognising that to continue was to court tragedy.

When Stirling and his forty-vehicle convoy reached the plain they picked up the main road and headed towards the southern end of the town. 'We should have been approaching Benghazi when the RAF departed [after an air raid timed to coincide with Stirling's assault] around midnight,' said Scott-Garrett.[17] 'As it was it was getting on towards four in the morning. Finally we came up to a bar across the road, a toll gate.'

James Sherwood watched as the Phantom Major got out of his vehicle, 'quite casually, all the headlights beamed away behind him', and with Bill Cumper walked up to the barrier.[18] Stirling instructed Cumper to raise the barrier. He did, and with a theatrical flourish declared: 'Let battle commence!' In the next instant the enemy troops began firing.

The still of the jebel in which the LRDG were camped was shattered by a 'great commotion'. Jackson and the rest of the men ran to a vantage point where they could see the southern perimeter. 'It was obvious that Stirling had been expected,' he said.[19]

According to Jim Almonds, who was subsequently captured, the order to withdraw came from Paddy Mayne. That the men were able to get away with only six dead, eighteen wounded and five captured or missing, was largely due to the courage of Cornelius McGinn, who, from the twin Vickers in the lead jeep, poured a withering fire into the enemy's positions on either side of the road.

Daylight arrived soon after the ambush and the British endured a hellish few hours as they withdrew up the escarpment. 'The SAS were badly mauled because they kept exposing themselves,' said Jackson. 'This was mainly due to their having taken on many new inexperienced men for this job.'[20]

One of those men, Capt Andrew Maxwell, wrote to his mother upon his return to Cairo on 20 September. 'We had a certain number of casualties, but no one you knew and eventually got home safely,' he told her. 'To put your mind at rest, I have been forbidden to join David and I don't think I shall be allowed out with him again.'[21]

Despite his ordeal, Maxwell told his mother he was very 'impressed' by David and he was going to write to Margaret Stirling to tell her what he thought of her brother. In the meantime, 'I am staying with Peter in Cairo. We had a ball in the flat last night, which was very successful.'

20

The fact that Stirling and his men escaped from Benghazi with relatively light casualties was because the enemy had not prepared a large-scale ambush. The troops on the other side of the barrier were a regular sentry detail, perhaps augmented by a few more additional soldiers, who had spotted the convoy's headlamps from afar. They had only light weapons. Had they been properly prepared, with anti-tank weapons and heavy machine guns, the SAS would have suffered far more casualties.

Of paramount importance to Winston Churchill, however, was the fate of Stirling. On 27 September Gen Alexander received a message from London: 'Personal from Prime Minister to Commander-in-Chief, Middle East. Have you heard rumours that David Stirling is missing? Can you give me any news?'

A day later Alexander replied: 'David Stirling safe and well in Cairo.'[1]

Like Randolph, like so many others, Winston had fallen under David Stirling's spell. He even distributed a copy of his son's letter about the first farcical raid on Benghazi to members of the Imperial General Staff. Churchill was old and unhealthy, his vigorous youth a distant memory, but Stirling was a reminder of the cavalier he had once been.

GHQ considered the Benghazi operation 'ill organised', and in a memo to the Director of Military Operations it was proposed that 'before further operations are undertaken it is most advisable to reform the squadron'.[2] On 19 September a meeting in GHQ had examined the signal arrangements during the various unsuccessful raids. Communication with Stirling's force 'had been unsuccessful over a period of forty-eight hours, both via LRDG channels and by the direct link, from which it appeared that the commander of Force X [Stirling] had ordered wireless silence ... it was agreed that while the full facts were at present unavailable, such a silence was undesirable and dangerous'.

That comment demonstrated the ignorance in GHQ as to how Stirling ran his unit. It wasn't so much a squadron as a set of cliques: Stirling and his upper-class friends; Mayne and the men he considered most effective operators; Bill Fraser and his Scottish commandos; and what remained of the French detachment.

Nonetheless, a reformation of L Detachment was urgently required. The problem was its commander. He may have been the Phantom Major to the British tabloids, the terror of the Hun, but to his soldiers, increasingly, he was a liability. Stirling had shown himself repeatedly willing to gamble with their lives in his pursuit of glory.

When word reached Cairo of the Phantom Major moniker it must have sparked a mix of hilarity and indignation. All the falsehoods and fabrications would have been harmless enough had Stirling not stolen the valour of his comrades. The LRDG was particularly affronted. There was no mention of their role in any of the press clippings sent to Egypt. They had vanished into thin air. When GHQ asked the LRDG in late 1942 for a potted history of the unit for its records, Bill Kennedy Shaw, the intelligence officer, corrected this oversight when he wrote of their role in transporting L Detachment to Axis airfields in the winter of 1941/42: 'In these sorties more than eighty aircraft were destroyed, and though the actual destruction was the work of the SAS, to whom every credit is due, it was the months of desert experience behind LRDG which placed them in a position to do their work.'[3]

GHQ's problem was to how to manage Stirling, a conundrum with which they had been wrestling since July, when they bemoaned his habit of being 'imperfectly connected with other operations of Eighth Army'. Lt-Gen Thomas Corbett, Chief of the General Staff, wrote a memo on 17 July in which he said of Stirling: 'It is considered that his present and future operations should be more carefully co-ordinated and controlled, both in planning and operations, by HQ Eighth Army with whom he should have a direct point to point wireless link.' Corbett concluded by stating that Stirling had been given instructions to this effect.[4]

But he had artfully won the ear of the Prime Minister and had even sent him a personal memo after their meeting in Cairo in which he outlined his vision for the future with himself at the epicentre. In effect, Stirling had made a pitch to take command of all Special Service Units in the Middle East; here was GHQ's chance to shackle him to a desk. In late September Gen McCreery, Alexander's Chief of Staff, wrote to his boss proposing that L Detachment, the SBS and 1 Special Service (a commando force) should merge under the command of David Stirling, who would be promoted to lieutenant-colonel.

Alexander sanctioned the restructure and it was also decided to award L Detachment regimental status. The SAS regiment would comprise an HQ squadron and four combat squadrons with a total strength of twenty-nine officers and 572 other ranks. It wasn't quite the elevation it first appeared; Lt-Col Stirling was informed that he must start behaving like a regimental officer, reporting to the Director of Military Operations. He was no longer permitted to beg, borrow or steal from the general staff at GHQ, the navy or the air force. Furthermore, in a memo dated 28 September GHQ stated that 'it was agreed that Lt-Col Stirling would not go out on raids himself owing to the information which he possesses'.[5]

At the start of September a proposition had been put to the Director of Military Operations that the SAS and LRDG should be combined and 'armour, artillery and infantry the size of a regiment should be added for seaborne operations'.[6] It would be commanded by Lt-Col Henry Cator, a decorated veteran of the First World War who, as well as being a brother-in-law to Queen Elizabeth, had raised a commando troop in Palestine in 1940. In the course of the month Cator's name was replaced by David Stirling's. How the LRDG reacted to the idea has been lost to history, but ultimately Stirling never got his brigade.

The SBS were however placed under Stirling's command, as they had been in the Benghazi raid the previous month. That decision led to the departure of Mike Kealy, who returned to the UK. Kealy didn't believe Stirling understood how to use this small but highly skilled amphibious unit; he simply wanted it under his control. Certainly, in the autumn of 1942, the SBS were left to languish at Kabrit despite representations from David Sutherland to participate in raids with the SAS.

Nonetheless, in the space of fifteen months Lt David Stirling, the Giant Sloth, had become a Lt-Col with a DSO and a nickname known throughout the free world. But his rapid rise had far outstripped his capabilities and in his success lay the seeds of his destruction.

There was a shock in store for some of the SAS's officers now that Paddy Mayne had been invested with some authority. Promoted to major as part of L Detachment's expansion, Mayne was appointed commander of A Squadron and instructed to select approximately eighty men from the existing personnel, as well as the new recruits who had been sent to Kabrit from Middle East Commando with no say in the matter.

Competency not class was the criterion by which Mayne selected his squadron. He chose Capt Bill Fraser as his second-in-command, and he also called on Capt Bill Cumper who, like Fraser, had risen through the ranks. So had Lt Johnny Wiseman, who had enlisted as a trooper in the North Somerset Yeomanry and fought the Vichy French in Syria. He had joined L Detachment in September, when he presented himself at the Stirlings' flat in the hope of employment. Like Brian Dillon, Wiseman's interview took place in the bathroom. 'David was in his bath and I asked if I could join the regiment,' he recalled. 'He looked me up and down and said, "Well, I've got a draft going out to some Egyptian name tomorrow. If you're in one of the trucks, yes, if not, no."'[7]

Mayne gave Wiseman a more thorough grilling, enquiring about the fighting he had experienced in Syria, before inviting him to join A Squadron. Wiseman fought in the SAS for the next three years, often by Mayne's side. 'I admired him enormously. I was very proud to be taken on by him,' he said. 'He was an exceptional man, particularly in action; the calmest, quietest man you ever saw, no matter how many shots were going around.' Wiseman was small, chatty and pugnacious, and he had a tendency in the mess to irritate Mayne as a fly does a horse. 'He could be quite frightening,' said Wiseman. 'Not a man to get on the wrong side of.'[8] Mayne selected none of Stirling's friends. They didn't like him, and he didn't respect them. Carol Mather and Stephen Hastings got a taste of this antipathy in early August when they returned to Kabrit from the jeep raids inside Libya. When they were roused from their lie-in, having skipped physical training, and ordered to see the adjutant they presumed it was a joke. 'At Kabrit one never knew who was adjutant from one day to the next,' said Mather. Under Stirling, maybe, but he was at his brother's flat and Mayne was in command. 'We were confronted by Paddy occupying the adjutant's chair and demanding why we were not on PT at six o'clock this morning with our men,' said Mather. 'We produced in reply an impressive total of hours of sleep which we had not had during the last month.'[9]

Mayne gazed impassively at Mather and Hastings. Then he reminded the pair that he and the rest of the men had been similarly deprived of sleep. Yet they had still appeared at 6 a.m. 'We apologised with bad grace and walked out annoyed and puzzled, determined to leave Kabrit without delay,' admitted Mather. 'We left for Cairo that afternoon and reported ourselves to David.'

In a subsequent letter to his father Loris, a good friend of Gen Montgomery, Mather described Peter Stirling's flat as 'really our HQ'.

Hastings and Mather were brave and determined soldiers, but in Mayne's eyes they were Guards officers not guerrilla fighters. When A Squadron departed Kabrit for the Libyan desert on 7 October with instructions to attack Rommel's lines of communication and ambush his motorised columns, Mayne had rinsed his force of Stirling's influence. Shortly before he left he wrote to his sister Barbara, replying to a letter in which she had asked if it was true he had been awarded a Military Cross. He told her that he had been promised a decoration but he would believe it when he saw it, explaining: 'My CO [Stirling] is very apt to promise things that don't happen. He has promised me leave at home, sort of present for a good boy, but it keeps being postponed.'[10]

For the next two months, recorded the LRDG's intelligence officer, Bill Kennedy Shaw, the activities of Mayne and his men 'reminded one of [Sir Henry] Morgan or [Capt William] Kidd and the pirates of the seventeenth century, secure in the palm-fringed creek of some West Indian island, thrusting forth to raid the fleets of Spain'. Mayne operated entirely independently from the LRDG, a unit he respected and valued in a way Stirling didn't. The LRDG reciprocated this esteem. Kennedy Shaw recognised that Mayne was an audacious privateer and not a playboy soldier. 'Stories of their operations used to reach us at Kufra,' he said. 'Tales of trains mined, railway stations wrecked, road traffic shot up and aircraft burned on their landing grounds.'[11]

* * *

While Paddy Mayne and his men were committing piracy against the Axis forces, the Phantom Major was in hospital suffering, as he told his mother in a letter, from painful desert sores. It was unusual for a soldier to be admitted to hospital with the ailment, particularly as Stirling had been back in Cairo for several weeks, away from the dust and the sand. He may have been hospitalised not with desert sores but with ulcerative diphtheria of the skin, which was often exacerbated by poor nutrition and exhaustion.

These factors accumulated to decay a soldier's spirit as well as his skin. At the same time as Stirling was taken to hospital one of Mayne's officers, Capt Jim Chambers, was being treated by Malcolm Pleydell for his sores. The medical officer was worried that they weren't responding to treatment; of equal concern was Chambers's mental health. He lacked his usual ebullience. Chambers was despatched to Cairo at the first available opportunity, but he died on 4 December of a diphtheritic infection.

Stirling was also suffering from solar conjunctivitis, a common affliction in the Desert War caused by dust being whipped into the eyes and exacerbated by the glare of the sun on the white sand.

Mentally, Stirling was shattered, and a hospital bed was a respite from the rising pressure of commanding a regiment. From the outset his friends had wondered how he would cope with the new role; did he even realise what it entailed? David Lloyd Owen feared he didn't. Stirling was like the actor who enjoyed being on stage in front of an audience but who abhorred the drudgery of rehearsal. That L Detachment had been born was largely down to Bill Stirling; that it had then survived and expanded into a regiment was thanks to the LRDG and Paddy Mayne; remove his supporting cast and Stirling was lost on his stage.

In becoming independent of the LRDG, said Lloyd Owen, Stirling 'began to lose his effectiveness because he necessarily had to concern himself with the mechanics of administration ... the tedious business of worrying where the food, the ammunition, the communications, the fuel and water were to come from was something with which he did not want concern himself. Up until then the LRDG had done all that for him.'[12]

A regimental war diary was started at Kabrit in October 1942, but it wasn't until 12 November that the diarist remarked that Lt-Col Stirling had arrived from Cairo. Stirling had been released from hospital only a few days earlier. While recuperating at his brother's flat, he set about recruiting new officers for B Squadron. The background of the intake was predictable: Maj Andrew Bonham-Carter, son of an air commodore; Maj Vivian Street, son of Harold, aide-de-camp to King George VI; Capt the Hon Pat Hore-Ruthven, son of Lord and Lady Gowrie; Capt Denis Murray, son of Sir Stephen, a High Court judge in Bombay. Stirling also invited his brother's flatmate Charles Johnston to join the SAS, 'as soon as I could get myself out of the Embassy',[13] regardless of the fact that Johnston was a career diplomat with no military experience. Johnston never took up the offer.

Another recruit was Douglas St Aubyn Webster Berneville-Claye, the son of Lord Charlesworth – or at least that was what he told Stirling in his interview. In fact, his father ran a pub in Harrogate. The twenty-four-year-old Berneville-Claye was a fantasist, a bigamist and a confidence trickster. Very little that came out of his mouth was true, such as his assertion he had been educated at Charterhouse and Oxford, and had been a barrister before he was commissioned in 1941 into the West Yorkshire Regiment, having passed through the Royal Military Academy Sandhurst. In reality, Berneville-Claye had that year been bound over for two years for stealing eleven bankers' cheques from army officers recovering at a convalescent home and six instances of obtaining money under false pretences while posing as an RAF officer. He had a long list of lady friends, some of whom he married simultaneously and others who bore him children, and among his actual jobs prior to the war were freelance journalist, riding instructor and barman. But he cut a striking figure, muscular, with a dapper moustache and boyish good looks. Above all, he had a gift for pulling the wool over the eyes of gullible upper-class types. One of whom was Stirling.

The choice of Pat Hore-Ruthven was also unwise. Paddy Mayne would not have accepted him into the regiment. He was an aristocrat and the best friend of the late Geoffrey Keyes, Mayne's bête noire. Hore-Ruthven was idealistic, chivalrous and naive; not psychologically equipped for guerrilla fighting. After the death of Keyes in the poorly planned Rommel Raid, he had written an elegy, one verse of which ran:

> He died as other brave men died
> But for valiant quenched vitality
> Deeds sprint; to immortality
> A young man lingers lightly
> Where he dies.

Hore-Ruthven was a married man two years Stirling's senior, who had accomplished much in his life, but so deeply did he fall under his spell that he gushed like a schoolboy when he dined with Hermione Ranfurly, whose husband had chosen Hore-Ruthven as his best man at their wedding in 1939. Stirling, he declared, was the greatest soldier he had ever met, and he reeled off a list of his exploits behind enemy lines. 'If I had not known Pat well I would not have believed them,' Ranfurly told her diary.[14]

Stirling's method for selecting the other ranks was flippant, as Bob Lowson remembered. He had first seen action with the Independent Companies in Norway in April 1940 and was a veteran of several battles by the time he was wounded in the summer of 1942 fighting with Middle East Commando. After a stay in hospital he rejoined his troop, only to learn that they were being disbanded. Stirling soon arrived to pick over the carcass of Lowson's commando. 'Stirling came round in the morning and just by looking at people he chose who he wanted. He said, "I don't like your face" and that was that.'[15] Lowson's face did fit.

On 23 October Montgomery launched his great offensive at El Alamein, the beginning of the end of the Axis forces in North Africa. A threat remained, however, that of a German push through the Caucasus into Persia, a country described by Fitzroy Maclean as 'the gate to India … the source of immensely important oil supplies'.[16] There was a modest Anglo-Russian presence already in Persia but Gen Henry Wilson, the Commander-in-Chief Persia and Iraq Command, believed it needed augmenting. In October Stirling – at the request of Gen Harold Alexander – sent Maclean north to assess the feasibility of 'raising a small force on SAS lines to operate on enemy-occupied territory in Persia in the event of a German break through'.[17]

On 16 November Maclean wrote to Stirling from Tehran to inform him of the latest developments, namely the authorisation from the 10th Army of 'our raising up to a squadron here'. He would finalise arrangements the following day and then begin recruiting: 'All volunteers will, of course, come to Kabrit for training and will be available for use anywhere.'

Maclean was staying at the British Legation and among the other guests was Duncan Sandys, Financial Secretary to the War Office and Winston Churchill's son-in-law, 'who tells me he saw you quite recently, which is reassuring, as John Hamilton, who is also staying has a story of your having been badly smashed up, somehow. I hope that in fact you are flourishing.'[18]

Had Stirling suffered an accident of some sort or was Hamilton's description of his being 'smashed up' a reference to his accumulation of maladies?

Something was up. On 30 October Col Bob Laycock, now in Britain, received a signal from Dickie Mountbatten, Chief of

Combined Operations, requesting the presence of George Jellicoe and David Stirling in London. Five days later Stirling replied from a hospital bed:

'Impossible leave now. Sending Jellicoe. Ready to leave immediately direct contact you. Urgent.'[19]

Not many subordinates flatly refused an order from Mountbatten.

Jellicoe flew from Cairo on 7 November. The previous day Laycock had written to Charles Forbes, Admiral of the Fleet, during the course of which he said that 'David [Stirling] is being flown back to this country for a short time as soon as he can be spared from the present battle'.

That was also the message in the letter that Stirling had given Jellicoe to post to his mother on arrival in England. Sorry for the short missive, he told her 'I shall be home myself in about a fortnight's time. I am tremendously looking forward to it.'

But the days passed and there was no word from Stirling as to his likely day of arrival. He didn't respond to cables from London. In desperation, Laycock sent a telegram to Peter Stirling on 19 November: 'Please exert your influence to get David back to United Kingdom if only for a short period.' The next day David Stirling wrote a long letter to Arthur Lewes, father of Jock, and concluded: 'In six week's [*sic*] time I hope to be returning to England for a five week's [*sic*] visit. If I may get in touch with you on my arrival, I will be able to give you a much more complete account of Jock.'[20]

Leaving aside the incongruity of writing a letter of condolence eleven months after the event, Stirling appeared not to have communicated this timetable to Laycock.

His excuse for not returning immediately to England was that he could not be 'spared from the present battle'.[21] His poor health was the real reason; he didn't want anyone in London to see just how worn down he was, physically and emotionally. Stirling's wilful refusal to obey an order from Mountbatten and Laycock was not only insubordinate, it was also irresponsible, a dereliction of his duty as commander of the SAS. The reason Stirling had been summoned to London was to participate in some high-level discussions concerning the future of his regiment. Mountbatten, having broached the subject with Gen Dwight Eisenhower, Supreme Commander Allied Expeditionary Force of the North African Theater of Operations, envisaged the establishment of a new force to operate in the Western Mediterranean, as a complement to the SAS in the Eastern Mediterranean. One name put forward to lead the force was Lord Lovat and would consist of his No. 4 Commando and a number of American personnel. The two entities would be under the administration of Combined Operations HQ.

There was only one escape route for Stirling from Mountbatten, Laycock and his brother, and that was west, or 'up the blue', as the Long Range Desert Group called the desert hinterland. On 20 November B Squadron, under Maj Vivian Street – a man who had been awarded a Military Cross in 1938 for his courage fighting Arab insurgents in Palestine and was one of the few eminently qualified officers recruited by Stirling – had set out on the long overland journey to western Libya. Once there they would establish a forward base and attack the Axis forces as they withdrew west in the area between Sirte and Tripoli.

On 21 November Street's second-in-command, Peter Oldfield, followed with the remainder of the squadron, a contingent of Free French and some vehicles for A Squadron. On the same day the SAS war diary recorded the arrival of another new officer, Maj Wilfred Thesiger, DSO. The thirty-two-year-old had been decorated the previous year for his courageous leadership in fighting the Italians in Abyssinia under the command of Orde Wingate. Thesiger, a product of Eton and Oxford, was at a loose end in Cairo when he heard about the SAS and their impending operation in Libya. He knocked on the well-worn door of Peter Stirling's flat and introduced himself to David as someone who had been with Wingate in Abyssinia, spoke Arabic and was at home with desert life (he had served in the Sudan Political Service from 1935 to 1940). Thesiger asked Stirling if he could join his mob. Stirling enquired how he knew they were about to go raiding. 'I don't really know, but these things get about,' replied Thesiger. Stirling picked up the phone and asked to speak to Thesiger's brigadier at GHQ. 'I've got a Major Thesiger with me,' he said. 'I'm taking him on a forthcoming operation. So please release him at once.'[22]

The next day Thesiger was in Stirling's patrol when they left for the desert, to the chagrin of Col John Hackett, who 'protested as loudly as I could'.[23] Since September, Hackett had been the commander of G Raiding Force, a new branch established by GHQ in order to keep Stirling on a tighter leash, which included prohibiting him from participating in raids himself because of the information he possessed.

Though he liked Stirling, Hackett understood why others in Egypt didn't. 'The SAS were very careless,' he said. 'They would leave a lot of stuff around, and they would stir the thing up no end, and out would come the Axis forces to see what had stirred it up, and they would find the LRDG … this had to be prevented so I drew a line down the map [on 22 September 1942] … saying "west of this, LRDG only, east of this, SAS only" and that kept them more or less out of each other's hair.'

Stirling subsequently claimed that he had placated Hackett by telling George Jellicoe to remain behind as his second-in-command, but Jellicoe was by this time in England enjoying some leave and also discussing the future of special forces operations post-North Africa.

Days after Stirling had fled Cairo, Fitzroy Maclean's letter from Tehran arrived, but that, like Mountbatten, would have to wait. Hackett wasn't so easily outmanoeuvred, however, and he flew west to Eighth Army HQ, where he knew Stirling would pass through en route to western Libya. Having intercepted Stirling on 26 November, Hackett had him agree that he would begin raiding enemy targets no earlier than 4 December and no later than the sixth of that month.

On 29 November B Squadron rendezvoused with A Squadron at Bir Zalten, a remote spot about eighty miles south of the coastal town of El Agheila. Wilfred Thesiger noted that Paddy Mayne's men had a 'quiet self-confidence that was impressive'.[24]

Malcolm Pleydell was disturbed when he saw Stirling. 'He was not looking too fit, I thought, for he had only just been discharged from hospital,' he wrote.[25] As well as the desert sores, which were still causing him discomfort, Stirling was obliged to wear dark glasses because of his conjunctivitis.

Mayne and his men, in contrast, radiated a ferocious vitality, and they bombarded B Squadron with tales of their piracy in the last couple of months. It was decided that A Squadron would harry the Germans in the Sirte area, while B Squadron would attack the enemy further west, around Tripoli.

The two squadrons departed the next day, and on 1 December Stirling sent a signal to Hackett to say that 'he had decided to delay his attack until the night of 10th/11th December but he gave no reasons'.

Perplexed, Hackett demanded an explanation and was informed that Stirling was waiting for the 'road covering parties' to move into position. Hackett was puzzled by what Stirling meant so he asked for a repeat signal, which, 'when it arrived did not clear the matter up'. Hackett asked again, but there was no further communication from Stirling.

The postponement 'raised administrative difficulties' and it was feared that B Squadron may now not have adequate supplies to enable them to execute their orders. Stirling remained incommunicado for several days.

Then on 14 December he signalled GHQ 'to the effect that owing to casualties to vehicles he could not operate West of Tripoli until later'.[26] The message caused considerable inconvenience within GHQ and Eighth Army HQ; discussions began as to whether the Libyan Arab Force should be deployed to the target area instead of B Squadron SAS.

December went well for A Squadron, remarked Malcolm Pleydell, with the raiders achieving a lot of success at the cost of few casualties. They celebrated Christmas at the Bir Zelten rendezvous, sleeping in caves hollowed out of the chalk and sandstone cliffs. It was always the most melancholic day of the year for the fighting soldier, when thoughts inevitably drifted to home.

They had a party in the evening. There was rum and singing and merriment. The bond between the bearded and unkempt men was intense. Mayne joined in the songs and recited some poetry, but despite the encouragement of his men he declined to sing a solo. None of the men persisted.

Pleydell saw that Mayne was a born leader. He had a way with the men under his command that both inspired and reassured them. He exuded a steely confidence that was infectious. He could on occasion be abrupt and irascible, and yet, reflected Pleydell, 'despite, or together with, these characteristics, he would be the first man to come up and try to discover why you were depressed at Christmas time. Such were a few of the qualities that made him so successful as a commander.'[27]

David Stirling was back in Cairo by Christmas. In contrast to the successful raids carried out by A Squadron, B Squadron had met with a series of disasters; the terrain in their operational had been less conducive to guerrilla war but the underlying reason for their failure was inexperience. Pat Hore-Ruthven had been killed* (a fate that befell Capt Denis Murray in January), and Vivian Street, Peter Oldfield, Carol Mather, and several other officers had been captured.

* SAS veteran Reg Seekings was with Hore-Ruthven when he was killed on 20 December. In the account he gave in person to Gen Henry Wilson on 18 March 1943, Seekings described the death of a brave but reckless man, who charged the enemy as if a cavalry officer in the Crimean War.

On Christmas Day Stirling paid a rare visit to Kabrit, where a new batch of recruits was undergoing their training, one of whom was Lt Peter Davis. 'Beyond the usual Christmas clichés he did not say much,' Davis recalled. 'But despite this his powerful personality made itself felt … such was his magnetic personality, that having conceived one of these hare-brained schemes, he was able to persuade very important people to give them their support.'[28]

In January 1943 Stirling came up with his most hare-brained scheme yet: he would lead a small raiding party west from Tripoli, attacking enemy lines of communication, reconnoitring the terrain for the Eighth Army preparatory to a fresh offensive and ultimately pushing into Tunisia to become the first unit from the Eighth Army to link with the First Army as it advanced east from Algeria.

What a coup it would be for the Phantom Major. A spectacular to silence his doubters, his critics and, above all, Paddy Mayne. Stirling had gambled on making B Squadron operational in November when, as subsequent events had proved, they were callow and ill-equipped for their task. Now he must gamble again in his ceaseless quest for glory.

21

Capt George Jellicoe arrived back in Kabrit on 12 January 1943 to report to David Stirling on his two months in England. There was much to tell. Stirling had absented himself from some crucial meetings about the future of special forces operations in the coming months. Fortunately Jellicoe had proved to be a more than able deputy. On 1 January he had written a paper in which he stated that in his opinion 'the Mediterranean Basin offers the fullest scope for small scale raiding that has existed in any theatre of war since September 1939'. In his view, the Eastern Mediterranean was especially suitable. 'The type of operation envisaged,' continued Jellicoe, 'would be the simultaneous "strike" of 100 small parties previously injected by all available methods into the Balkans or the Greek Islands' (which is what Jellicoe, as commander of the Special Boat Squadron, did in 1944 to great effect).[1]

The Eastern Mediterranean would be the preserve of 1SAS, 'with attached American personnel', and they as well as the force operating in the Western Med would come 'under the operational control of the local C in C.'

Jellicoe would have known that such a reorganisation would upset Stirling, who would view it as an affront to his authority. The SAS was his 'private army' and he wanted to keep it that way. Braced for a fraught encounter with Stirling, Jellicoe instead discovered that he was neither in camp nor in Cairo; he was more than a thousand miles away at Bir-el-Gheddafia, south of the Libyan capital of Tripoli.

There was a chaotic air about Kabrit, with comings and goings as new recruits arrived, including two American naval officers, the advance party of the US contingent expected to join the SAS, and a detachment of Greek soldiers, and trained men departed for operations in the desert. Gen Harold Alexander had been scheduled to visit Kabrit on 9 January to watch a demonstration of canoeing, jeep travel and demolitions; when it was realised there was no senior officer available to greet him the visit was rearranged for 14 January.

It rather underlined what Jellicoe had expounded to Lord Louis Mountbatten, Chief of Combined Operations, in a letter he wrote on the eve of his return to Egypt. Having thanked the CCO and his staff for their 'advice and considerable assistance' during his two-month sojourn, he continued: 'In general I feel that it would be most useful if, in the future, you could become our "Foster-father".'[2]

There were inadequacies in training and recruitment that required urgent addressing and Jellicoe expressed his hope that the CCO and 1st SAS could establish a system of loaning and interchanging personnel, because frankly in Kabrit 'we have one or two "tired business men" who could well profit from a short rest from operations'.

Of even greater concern to Jellicoe was the realisation that the SAS had not evolved since its formation in the summer of 1941. 'Our operational success depends, to my mind, largely upon technical proficiency,' he wrote. 'I was shocked when I returned here to discover that technically we were, in some ways, up to eighteen months out of date. This was because liaison between the United Kingdom and the Middle East became dilute as soon as it is not direct.'

The man who had opened Jellicoe's eyes to the deficiencies of Lt-Col David Stirling's 1SAS was Lt-Col Bill Stirling.

* * *

Bill Stirling had reached England on 10 January 1942 in a truculent mood, furious at being ordered home by the War Office when his work in Cairo was far from complete. He was still, officially, a member of SOE, but events in GHQ had soured the relationship. The War Office, for their part, were in a sulk at being kept in the dark about Stirling's role working for Lt-Gen Arthur Smith. On 11 January Stirling was ordered to report to the Scots Guards training battalion.

Five days later he was 'released from military service for four months' and attached to the Ministry of Supply.[3] Bill took a train from London to Scotland, where his good humour was restored the moment he walked over the threshold at Keir House into the arms of his wife and his baby son, Archie, born while he was in the Middle East.

Whatever Stirling's Ministry of Supply role entailed it was not a hindrance to resuming his life as laird of Keir; welcoming visitors to admire his narcissi and flowering shrubs for the twelfth annual Scotland's Gardens Scheme; opening school fêtes and hosting shooting and stalking parties on his estate.

Stirling spent much time at his office in Glasgow, overseeing his flourishing business interests. His secretary was Daphne Llewellyn, the youngster sister of Hermione Ranfurly, with whom Bill had connived to reveal the extent of the incompetency within SOE Cairo. 'He was at that moment half in SOE and half not,' recalled Llewellyn.[4] 'He was running the family estate, a huge estate, and had quarries and things like that.' Llewellyn, who had worked as a secretary for MI5 in 1941, spent much of her free time socialising with Bill and his wife at Keir. 'They were a mad family, the Stirlings, delightful, but totally mad. They were a wild lot,' she said. 'They had a wonderful mother … how she kept them all in order, I don't know, but she did in a sort of way. How can I describe them? They were quite unique. Enormously tall, all of them, and it was very unusual at that time for anybody to be over 6ft but they were all about 6ft 2 [*sic*]. David was very quiet.'

Hermione Ranfurly also commented on this facet of David's personality; of the brothers, when they were in each other's company, David was the quietest. In their presence his alter ego had to be concealed; it emerged outside the family circle.

Eventually a bright spark in the War Office suggested that Bill Stirling might have more to contribute to the war effort than shooting grouse and picking winners from the tombola.

On 29 September 1942 (the day after 1SAS came into existence) a confidential report was compiled on Bill Stirling with a view to promoting him to lieutenant-colonel and appointing him commander of the Small Scale Raiding Force (SSRF), a commando unit that had been operating from its base in southern England against Nazi targets along the French coast. Asked for his opinion of Bill Stirling, Brig Colin Gubbins of SOE remarked: 'A capable and efficient officer who has a quiet and determined way with him, a good initiative and pertinacity. A good disciplinarian. A very good knowledge of infantry weapons, tactics, etc., and an excellent trainer.'[5]

As to his suitability to lead a special forces unit, Gubbins commented: 'He appears to have all the necessary attributes of a commanding officer, i.e. firmness, power of command, drive, etc.'

Stirling was confirmed in his role as commanding officer SSRF on 17 October.

The unit had been formed in 1941 and was under the operational control of SOE. Its first CO was Maj Gus March-Phillipps, a contemporary of Bill's at Ampleforth; in its obituary the school magazine described him as undistinguished academically and athletically, 'although he did get a reputation for being rather hare-brained'.

March-Phillipps was killed in a raid on the Normandy coast in September 1942 and although command passed to his second-in-command, Geoffrey Appleyard, it was considered wise to bring in a man with more experience of special forces warfare: Bill Stirling.

He was instructed to submit ideas for raids direct to Mountbatten and Stirling had at his disposal a Royal Navy raiding flotilla composed of a variety of vessels. Among the men of SSRF was Peter Kemp, who had been involved in Operation Knife in April 1940. He was pleased to be reunited with Stirling who, he recalled, initiated a change in policy: 'In future, selected officers and NCOs from the commandos would be sent to us for a short period of training in the specialised technique of small-scale raiding, after which we should take them on a raid.'[6] Unlike David, who regarded training as irksome and incidental to guerrilla warfare, Bill knew it was imperative that any recruit first undergo a rigorous training period prior to operations.

The first SSRF raid under Stirling's authority was launched on the night of 11–12 November against a semaphore station fifteen miles north-west of Saint Brieuc on the Brittany coast. Kemp was among the raiders whose orders were to destroy the station and bring back a prisoner. They failed in both objectives, although in a fierce fight with the station's defenders they killed several Germans before withdrawing.

Stirling was on the quayside at Dartmouth when the commandos disembarked. Kemp felt a keen sense of disappointment as he described the raid. Stirling listened in silence and then told Kemp he was justified in withdrawing when he did in light of the situation. 'I will say so in my covering report … you must have given the enemy quite a shock, which is one of our objects.'[7]

Kemp wrote two reports about the raid, one a summary that Stirling handed in person to the Prime Minister. Churchill read it 'and made the simple comment, "Good!" and so I suppose that honour, at least, was satisfied'.

A fortnight after the raid, on 25 November, Bill Stirling chaired the first meeting of what, he informed those present at Combined Operations HQ in Whitehall, would be a weekly event. Listening to his words were several CCO staff officers (including Maj Ian Collins, late of No. 8 Commando, who had for a few weeks in August

1941 helped David Stirling with the administrative side of raising L Detachment) and George Jellicoe.

Stirling announced that in future SSRF would be known as No. 62 Commando, and he then explained it had been agreed that Combined Operations HQ 'should be responsible for the supply of equipment to the SSRF and 1st SAS Regt, Middle East'. They discussed the requirements for special forces: silent Sten guns, 'killer guns' [pistols with silencers], telescopic sights, mortars and spigot mortars, the latter capable of projecting a '2 to 4lb charge up to 200 yards'.[8]

Jellicoe requested that he be allowed to take five killer guns to Kabrit for trials, and he expressed an interest in flame-throwers and fifty folding motorcycles. He also submitted an order for 250 limpet mines, 200 wire cutters, 100 light telescopes, 500 magnetic compasses and 102 folboats, some three-seaters and others two-man canoes. As for clothing, Jellicoe produced a long list, including a superior quality of boot, sleeping bag and haversack.

Bill Stirling raised the question of the Lewes bomb; on his instruction tests had been conducted on its efficacy and the results showed that 'the type of Plastic and Thermite bomb used by 1st SAS Regiment to be uneconomical in weight'. Consequently it was recommended that replacing Thermite with powdered aluminium would 'produce a bomb more efficient both as an incendiary and as an explosive'. Stirling announced that a series of experiments would be run shortly to discover if indeed this innovation was superior to Jock Lewes's original.

There were further meetings throughout December, at which one of the central discussions was the suitability of canoes and catamarans for special forces operations; among those who attended were Maj Roger Courtney, commanding SBS, Lt-Commander William Luard of the Naval Intelligence Division and Capt Wykeham Martin of SOE.

In between meetings Jellicoe visited bases and depots to test out the boats, weapons and personal kit. When he wasn't working he let his hair down in a variety of ways, and more often than not in the company of Bill Stirling. He spent a weekend at Keir goose shooting at night with officers from No. 62 Commando, and he and Bill dined regularly at White's. On one occasion Evelyn Waugh joined them, and afterwards he and Jellicoe went to the Jamboree nightclub in Wardour Street. Waugh drank too much, danced with another man's woman and was punched in the face for his impertinence. Waugh's assailant was arrested but charges were later dropped, and Jellicoe assured the newspapers it was 'just a bit of a mix-up'.

Before Jellicoe had met Bill Stirling, however, he had reported to Brig Bob Laycock, commanding 1st Special Service Brigade. In a summary on the jeep raids of July, Jellicoe explained that it had been Paddy Mayne's suggestion to acquire some jeeps. He described how the vehicles had been used, including a brief account of the raid on Bagush the previous July when David Stirling and Paddy Mayne 'drove on to the aerodrome and destroyed by machine gun fire from their vehicles a further ten or fourteen aircraft'. They withdrew in the face of heavy enemy fire but Stirling 'was unable to resist the temptation to return, to Capt. Mayne's disgust, in order to despatch a few more aircraft!'[9] Mayne's 'disgust' with Stirling's bravado was understandable. He never took unnecessary risks. He possessed what Mike Sadler described as 'controlled recklessness';[10] not a gambler by nature, Mayne could nonetheless weigh up the odds in an instant and he had the self-control never to overplay his hand. Not so Stirling.

Jellicoe also briefed Laycock on the damage wrought by Paddy Mayne's A Squadron in October, when they had sabotaged the railway line used by the Germans to transport supplies east through Libya once every three days throughout the second half of the month.

In a reply dated 27 November, Laycock thanked Jellicoe for his diligence and said, 'I am sorry to hear that we are unlikely to see David before the New Year ... will you please tell Saunders [Hilary St George Saunders, the Combined Operations' recorder] all you know about David and his doings, as this should, without doubt, take higher precedence in the historical records of the war. I am convinced that Saunders will never be able to get anything out of David himself.'[11]

There was much to ponder as Jellicoe flew back to Cairo. As he admitted to Lord Mountbatten in a letter of 6 January, the SAS had not exploited the technical advances in weapons and equipment of the last year and a half. Throughout their partnership with the LRDG from December 1941 to June 1942, raiding parties comprising five men carried the same arms on each operation: each soldier was in possession of a .45 Colt handgun, two hand grenades and eight Lewes bombs, and one soldier had a Tommy gun.

David Stirling was an imaginative strategist; from his brother's flat he produced ambitious schemes, which he sold to GHQ with his grandiose patter, but he wasn't interested in the technicalities of raiding. He hadn't experimented with new weapons, such as the Sten gun or the lightweight American M1 carbine; nor had he investigated footwear in order to alleviate the high incidence of fungal infections suffered by his men. The only innovation had been the introduction of the jeep, which was Paddy Mayne's idea. Yet having taken stock of these vehicles in early July 1942, Stirling was still reliant on the LRDG on operations because, as the LRDG war diary noted, L Detachment 'were not yet fully proficient in wireless and navigation'. Why not? Both skills, particularly the latter, were crucial to an irregular unit in the desert, and Stirling had had nearly a year to school his men. His failure to do so exemplified his slipshod attitude.

Nor had Stirling shown any inclination to befriend the indigenous population, as the LRDG had done – what later came to be known as 'winning hearts and minds'. 'Ralph Bagnold had a lot of contacts with the Senussi headmen,' recalled Mike Carr, an LRDG first navigator. 'But he couldn't be seen to talk to them or as soon as he had left they would be bumped off. So I would drive Bagnold in a truck to a point in the desert where we would meet the headmen.'[12] They passed on information, perhaps the location of an enemy camp or topographical advice about a particular route, and in return the LRDG supplied the Senussi with food and basic medical aid.

When Jellicoe arrived back at Kabrit it was immediately evident that the regiment had 'got rather large, a little bit unwieldy'.[13] There was a message from David Stirling instructing him to lead a squadron of Greek soldiers to Tripoli in preparation for operations into Tunisia. On 25 January, 121 officers and men of the Greek Sacred Squadron and forty-one officers and men of D Squadron, SAS, left Kabrit under Jellicoe's command for the long drive across Libya.

By which time, David Stirling was a prisoner of the Germans.

On 12 January, the day Jellicoe arrived in Kabrit, Stirling was at Bir-el-Gheddafia, waiting for the arrival of two French contingents under the command of Lt François Martin and Capt Augustin Jordan. He was regretting his lackadaisical approach to logistics, fretful that he didn't have enough petrol to get him through Tunisia. He told Johnny Cooper to hunt down some more, which he did from the squadron's base at the oasis of El Djofra. One of the drivers despatched in a three-ton lorry from the base to Bir-el-Gheddafia was Bob Lowson, a newcomer to the SAS. Stirling had expected more petrol and expressed his disappointment in forceful terms, relaying a message to Lowson via Cooper that 'if he had time he would come and shoot you'.[14]

Stirling was under immense strain, physically and mentally, and consequently his judgement was askew. Furthermore, in deliberately isolating himself from GHQ and surrounding himself with inexperienced and obsequious officers there was no wise counsel to call on. He had in effect backed himself into a corner. To abandon his grand plan to drive through Tunisia to link up with the First Army would be a humiliation, a loss of face he could not countenance. He had to push on, regardless of the risk. And this risk had been spelt out by brigadier George Davy, Director of Military Operations in Cairo. 'He told me of the route he was going to take, close round the flank of the Mareth Line,' he recalled after the war. 'I said he was going into an area where the natives were known to be hostile and that he would be captured, I suggested he should take a wider sweep. However, he was obstinate as usual.'

Johnny Cooper, the most experienced SAS soldier in the patrol, considered the plan to drive north a 'risky business as we had no prior intelligence of enemy dispositions'.[15]

At dawn on 15 January the Anglo-French column of eight vehicles departed Bir-el-Gheddafia, and they crossed the Tunisian border north of Ghadames. Twenty-four hours later Capt Jordan followed in their tyre tracks. They rendezvoused on 21 January a few miles south of Bir Soltane and Stirling informed Jordan that he had received a signal from GHQ to the effect that the Eighth Army had taken Gafsa and Tripoli; therefore Stirling ordered Jordan and Martin to attack the enemy's lines of communications between Sfax and Gabes.*

Stirling and his fourteen men left twelve hours later, bound in their five jeeps for the Gabes Gap, eighty miles north, a geographical bottleneck between the Tunisian salt flats and the Mediterranean Sea. 'It was exhausting work,' said Cpl Reg Redington, one of the drivers, who remembered how thin Stirling was by this time: 'There wasn't much meat on him.'[16]

The terrain was good – hard-packed sand – but desert driving is a challenge at any time, and especially when deep inside enemy territory. Near dusk on 23 January a Storch reconnaissance plane passed overhead, but the patrol was soon through the Gabes Gap.

Early the next morning they drove through a German column of Panzergrenadiers that had camped overnight on either side of the road. Cooper could smell the brewing coffee as the soldiers sat around their vehicles. 'Many of them looked at us curiously but we just stared back and motored on,' he said.[17]

* Jordan and his men were soon captured, and Martin's smaller patrol was also attacked, forcing them to trek on foot for three days, until picked up by American troops.

The men were now dog-tired. They had driven through the night. It was hard to keep awake, said Mike Sadler, 'as they drove in bright sunlight across mainly farmers' dust fields'.[18]

As they approached the Jebel Tebaga the terrain became hillier, with wadis running from the fields into the rising ground. Stirling ordered the column into one of the wadis and they drove along the dry river bed for a few hundred metres before he called a halt. Get your heads down, he told his men, and they would continue at dusk. No sentries were posted. Such an oversight was incomprehensible unless, perhaps, Stirling was courting capture. Physically, he was a wreck, but he may also have been suffering an incipient nervous breakdown from the pressure of command.

'Our big mistake was that we weren't vigilant,' said Reg Redington. 'We'd been driving the whole night and were tired. We laid up in a wadi and I remember putting my Smith and Wesson by my side. We could see the Germans from the wadi.'

Mike Sadler and Johnny Cooper were further up the wadi from Redington, Stirling and the rest of the patrol. 'The wadi was bending so we weren't in their sights,' said Sadler. 'We turned in to our sleeping bags … it was an error of judgment in a way, but I don't think we could have got out in any circumstances having got in because I think we were in a trap.'

Cooper observed a German vehicle stop on the road below. Then it continued. Within him was a nagging unease; if he hadn't been so exhausted his wits would have been alive to the danger. 'After the previous forty-eight hours of hard slog none of us was in a position to be vigilant,' he said. 'This was to be our tragic mistake.'

The vehicle observed by Cooper contained men of the Fallschirmjaeger z.b.V 250, a paratroop force that hadn't been long in North Africa. Prior to their arrival in Libya they had received instruction in Germany in how to drive the Willys jeep, several of which had been captured in 1942. 'Professional racing drivers were used to show us how to drive and control the vehicles,' said Sgt

Heinrich Fugner, an experienced combat veteran who had joined the unit in the summer of 1942, 'but we later found out that desert driving is very different from racetrack driving.'[19]

For several days they had been hunting for enemy commandos under the command of Capt Scherer, with the help of a native scout who 'could follow the traces of a mouse over rocks'.

Scherer had split his company into two platoons and one, led by Lt Neumaan, had been pursuing Lt François Martin and his French patrol. Sgt Fugner was in Scherer's platoon, and they had been tailing Stirling's patrol since the previous day. Much of the Jebel Tebaga was 'not very suitable for hidden movement', he said. 'We dismounted and searched the wadi. Since it was the middle of the day, our search was easy.'

It was now in the early afternoon. The Germans advanced cautiously. Their prey were seasoned commandos; they expected fierce resistance. Onwards and upwards they crept.

Stirling had removed his boots before slipping into his sleeping bag. So too had Reg Redington, only a few yards away from his commanding officer. He was asleep in an instant. 'Next thing I knew someone was kicking my feet and shouting "Raus, Raus!"' he recalled. 'I looked up, saw a German standing over me and reached for my Smith and Wesson. But it was gone.'[20]

Sgt Fugner kicked one of the sleeping soldiers 'and pushed the muzzle of my machine pistol into his chest so he wouldn't think of doing something stupid'. The SAS soldier didn't. 'There was a pretty good turmoil going on with men running around, but surprisingly enough not too much shooting.'

In fact, the only shots fired were by the Germans, in the direction of Johnny Cooper, Mike Sadler and a French soldier called Freddie Taxis. They hadn't removed their boots, and they leapt out of their sleeping bags and sprinted out of the top of the wadi and further into the jebel. 'It was a hard run up the hillside,' said Sadler. 'But luckily we had managed to get into a little narrow gully among the bushes … I had a lot of telegrams which I buried under me during the afternoon. Then some goats came round us. There was a shepherd there but I don't know if he had seen us. We didn't make ourselves known, we just laid doggo and hoped they would go away. We stayed there till dark and in the meantime they took the rest away along with the jeeps.'[21]

The Phantom Major had been caught without having fired a shot in anger. 'They had not posted any sentries,' said Fugner. 'Maybe they felt so safe in their hideout.' He recalled that Stirling was dressed in similar attire to his men, although his bearing 'was clearly that of an officer and gentleman'. The other thing that struck Fugner was his 'tired and exhausted state'.

On 5 February the *Yorkshire Post* was one of several British newspapers to carry a pulsating report on the adventure of three soldiers under the headline 'EIGHTH ARMY MEN LINK UP IN TUNISIA'. The breathless copy had been filed by the American correspondent Noland Norgaard of the Associated Press: 'The vanguard of the British Eighth Army – three sunburned bewhiskered desert raiders – who, in an almost incredibly bold venture, disrupted Axis communications and shot up transport columns far in Rommel's rear, reached this outpost of United States and French troops in Southern Tunisia in the first junction of Allied forces converging from east to west,' he wrote. The soldiers were Lt Michael Sadler, Sgt John Cooper and Sgt A. F. Taxis of France. Sadler said their four-day trek to Tozeur, a Free French outpost, had been 'an interesting trip'. The report added that the trio were parachute troops 'under the command of a 6-foot-4 former Scots Guardsman who lived part of the time before the war on a New Mexico ranch'.

Sadler didn't mention the 'Phantom Major' in his conversation with Norgaard and his press colleague A. J. Liebling, and nor did Cooper; he referred to their commanding officer as 'Big Dave'.

22

There was, so David Stirling claimed, an additional factor that spurred him through the Gabes Gap: 'to consult my brother Bill, who had recently arrived on the First Army front, with the 2nd SAS Regiment'.[1]

He hadn't. The 2nd SAS Regiment was not in existence when Stirling was captured and his brother was thousands of miles away.

The first weeks of 1943 had been frenetic ones for Bill. The previous November, when the idea of a new raiding force to operate in the Western Mediterranean had been mooted, the man proposed to command it was Lord Lovat. It was an obvious choice, and his No. 4 Commando had a fine reputation. But in January Brig Anthony Head, a staff officer and Combined Operations HQ, flew to North Africa to discuss the putative organisation with Gen Eisenhower, Gen Alexander and Brig George Davy, the Director of Military Operations at GHQ. On 20 January 1943 he explained in a letter to Maj Gen Joseph Haydon, his superior, what had been agreed: 'The dispatch of a force to operate on the same lines as David Stirling with Gen Eisenhower; but it was felt, and I think rightly, that two hundred men would be sufficient to start with.'[2]

There was a potential fly in the ointment, however, namely who would have command of the new force. 'Another very important point is the personality of the commander,' wrote Head. 'Although they are cousins, I am told by Davy, the DMO to General Alexander, that [David] Stirling and Lovat do not always see eye to eye. It would mess up the whole thing if the commanders of these two forces fought and you may wish to reconsider the question of sending out Bill Stirling.'

Gen Haydon heeded the advice of Brig Head. Bill Stirling was appointed to command the new force on 2 February, its personnel coming from the ranks of his Small Scale Raiding Force,* and the following day he wrote to his friend and commanding officer, Brig Bob Laycock, begging his forgiveness for his 'scrawl' and blaming it on the jolting train he was on to Stranraer.

The letter was a thank you 'for all that you have done for 62 Commando and myself – I can only say that I hope we will justify your faith in us'. Stirling assured Laycock that he had tied up loose ends and asked him to keep an eye out for 'poor' Ian Collins, who was getting a hard time from one or two senior officers who considered that the former tennis star lacked military efficiency. He ended the letter by saying that the CCO, Lord Mountbatten, 'has taken a great deal of trouble over my party – explained the form in N Africa to me at length for which I was most grateful … I will send you a signal on arrival.'[3]

David Stirling was officially reported missing on 14 February, the SAS war diarist noting that he was 'believed prisoner of war'. On the same day Paddy Mayne arrived at Kabrit from the ski school at Cedars in Lebanon, where A Squadron had been undergoing ski training.

George Jellicoe had first heard a rumour of Stirling's fate ten days earlier. Immediately he turned his squadron round and headed back to Cairo, reaching the Egyptian capital on 15 February. Sending them on to Kabrit, Jellicoe paid a call to Peter Stirling to brief him on what

* Bill Stirling and his men never served under Eisenhower's command; although 'Ike' was enthusiastic, other senior American officers weren't, regarding Stirling's presence as an encroachment.

he knew of his brother's capture. The next day Peter wrote to his mother at Keir:

> He was on his way to join 1st Army and had practically got through when the disaster occurred ... David's capture is regarded as a great blow here as there is literally no one of the same prestige to replace him. It was particularly bad luck as the operation he was engaged on was of no particular importance in itself.[4]

Peter added that Bill had just arrived in Cairo for a few days. Bill stayed with his brother at his flat, where Charles Johnston, Third Secretary at the British Embassy, was also lodging. Peter's Egyptian housekeeper, Mo, described the dynamic of the Stirling brothers to Johnston prior to Bill's arrival: 'Colonel Bill got big flat in Scotland, plenty land, plenty money. My Peter and Major David no money at all, allwise [always] playing card, playing horse.'[5]

Johnston had of course already met David, but he was looking forward to Bill's arrival as between them they 'had acquired military fame in the Middle East as founders of the Special Air Service'. He described the Stirling brothers as 'operators ... they were tuned in to all the old-boy networks. Ministers and generals viewed them with indulgence.' Johnston had been in Japan in 1941 but he had heard how Bill and David had created a small irregular unit that summer, albeit only after they had been compelled to deploy 'all the weight of their private contacts to overcome the violent opposition of the military bureaucracy'.

What surprised Johnston on meeting Bill was that he was similar in character to David. Neither made a 'swashbuckling impression'.

When Jellicoe arrived at Kabrit it was, according to John Lodwick, a scene of 'chaos' with no one sure what to do. 'A great and powerful organisation had been built up, but it had been an organisation controlled and directed by a single man,' he said. 'Stirling alone knew where everybody was, what they were doing, and what he subsequently intended them to do.'[6]

It was true. While Paddy Mayne had a tight grip on A Squadron, he had no idea of B Squadron's movements and he was nonplussed by the Greeks, French and various other nationalities ambling around when he arrived. 'Stirling, alone, had known the whole story ... control by a powerful personality with a hundred different irons in a very cramped fire,' said Lodwick. Stirling had also known that a reorganisation of special forces in the Mediterranean was afoot, and it was more evidence of his immaturity and irresponsibility that he had allowed himself to be captured at such a crucial juncture for the SAS.

Nevertheless, thanks to the accomplishments of A Squadron the previous autumn, morale was strong. 'There was a general feeling that operations had become successful and even with Stirling's capture ... that it was still thought we were a going unit, ready to go,' said L/Cpl Duncan Ridler, a recent recruit to 1SAS.[7]

In order to untangle the logistical knot it was little use knocking on the door of Peter Stirling's flat to search for documents and instructions; Stirling had no time for administrative filing. His head was his cabinet.

On the last day of February Bill Stirling wrote to Bob Laycock from Algiers, where he was in the company of Randolph Churchill and the American war reporter Virginia Cowles; she would be taking the letter with her when she flew to London the next day. No. 1 SSRF had established their camp at Philippeville, under the command of Maj Geoff Appleyard, and Stirling was about to put them through a training programme similar to his one at Inverailort, which Appleyard told his parents in a letter was 'quite the toughest thing physically I have ever done'.[8]

Not for the first time Bill Stirling had been busy clearing up the mess created by his brother. He informed Laycock that he had spent three days in Cairo earlier in the month but hadn't found the time to see his secretary at GHQ, Lt-Commander I. G. Mason, 'as I got involved in the intrigue over David's successor, had to visit Kabrit and generally I did not have much time to spare'. He added, 'I hope you will have an opportunity to pay a visit to Kabrit. I think it would interest you.'[9]

Stirling continued:

> I have collected the private armies in this area which for the most part consist of David's representatives whom he has infiltrated ... there is no doubt that all SAS activities for the Mediterranean should be under one hand & it is a great pity that David has been bagged as a parochial outlook prevails which he could have dealt with.
>
> I am having a shot at it myself but I am handicapped by lack of status and the fact that SAS has asked that I be appointed to command them as well as the party here. Anthony* has I hope put the matter in hand and seems to have been doing useful work in Cairo.
>
> I do not think it matters in the least who commands SAS so long as it is someone who has this idea and who controls small raiding activities so far as personnel is concerned over the whole Mediterranean basin.
>
> So much for what is depressing and a bore. I have a section of my advance party operating on the open flank ... the rest of my party will either (a) operate with Geoffrey [Appleyard] by sea or (b) operate with instructions on land or (c) proceed to Kabrit by air for training. The whole of our existence depends on success, & I am determined that none of this party of mine shall operate until in my opinion they are fully trained. David's original success was due almost entirely to the training worked

* Col Anthony Head, chief military planner with Combined Operations. Head was not a man who tolerated young arrogant aristocrats; in September 1942 he had written to Bob Laycock to lodge an informal complaint against the Stirlings' cousin, the 15th Lord Lovat, describing him as a 'temperamental prima donna'.

> out by himself and carried out by Jock Lewis [*sic*] at Kabrit over a period of 8–10 weeks – which we unfortunately cannot allow ourselves.
>
> Randolph is a problem. I cannot allow him near men, and there is a coalition of all headquarters to obstruct him. I have put him up for an operation on his own, which may be the saving of him. It is by no means safe, but he is mad keen to do it and in my opinion would probably get away with it, secure a handsome decoration, richly deserved, have the laugh on headquarters generally whose hate is largely their inferiority complex, and gain for himself the respect of men who would I am sure follow him when he gains in confidence, loses his excitability and learns not to be clever at their expense.*

Bill Stirling's summary was concise, coherent and candid. He recognised his brother's talent for infiltrating and appropriating other units.

He also referenced David's 'original success', a tacit admission that the last twelve months had for the most part been a failure. But whatever success L Detachment had achieved it was only partly attributable to the training programme devised by his brother and based heavily on what he had endured at Lochailort in the summer of 1940 under the supervision of Bill and Lord Lovat.

The destruction of more than one hundred aircraft between December 1941 and March 1942 had been the work of Paddy Mayne and Bill Fraser with their (predominantly) No. 11 commandos. The pair had a natural flair for guerrilla fighting, but the training that had hardened them physically and temperamentally had been done on the Isle of Arran in the winter of 1940–1. Neither had learned anything

---

* Randolph didn't succeed in persuading Stirling to let him be operational. Instead, as Gen Sir Harold Alexander cabled to a relieved Winston on 4 July 1943, though his son 'is with Colonel Bill Stirling's second SAS regiment … he will be acting as a liaison officer between this unit and 51 Division and … will not actually be taking an active part in the forthcoming [invasion of Sicily]'.

from Jock Lewes or David Stirling in that regard, other than being schooled in explosives by the former.

Unquestionably, had Mayne been killed or captured on the first L Detachment operation in November 1941, the unit would not have survived into 1942. He had carried – aided by Fraser – L Detachment ever since, whereas David Stirling had attempted to turn the unit into the military equivalent of White's, an exclusive club for the rich and well-connected.

Bill Stirling might have lacked his brother's status in Cairo, having been absent for fifteen months, but he possessed an eye for dissecting a man's character that David lacked. In one sentence he had Randolph Churchill to a tee, and he had the measure of Paddy Mayne. By 15 February Mayne, George Jellicoe and Vivian Street had assembled at Kabrit. The latter had escaped from captivity, and on 18 February he wrote to his father from the SAS base. 'I was given a very difficult choice,' he explained: 'Either go to the [Rifle Brigade] or else to remain with 1SAS Regiment as second-in-command, possibly commanding it. I couldn't make up my mind which to do so told them at GHQ that they must decide for me. Although 1SAS is probably much more fun I suppose as I am a regular I ought to do the other, and I think that's why they decided I should.'[10]

Bill Stirling didn't mention Street to Laycock but it's probable he was a factor in GHQ's decision to return him to the Rifle Brigade. There was in Stirling's mind only one man who could command the SAS, and that was Paddy Mayne. A superb operator, he was also a natural leader of men; his only failing was a frustration and impatience with upper-class senior officers which occasionally manifested itself in a brusque and disrespectful demeanour in their presence.

Bill Stirling had a high regard for Mayne as a man and as a soldier. He didn't hold his grammar school education against him. In letters he addressed him as 'My dear Paddy', and the respect was reciprocated.[11] Bill talked to Mayne as he did both Lord Mountbatten and the parlour maid at Keir: without condescension. Social status meant nothing to him. It was the man not the rank that mattered. His cousin, Lord Lovat, was of the same opinion. 'The war meant a welcome freedom from class, money and position,' he reflected. 'The newcomer [to the commandos] was judged on his merits.'[12]

The same was true of Mayne. 'There was nothing stuck-up about him,' recalled Lt Peter Davis. 'He would talk for hours to anyone whether a man, NCO or officer, on terms of absolute equality.'[13]

As Bill Stirling had informed Bob Laycock, the SAS wanted him to take over from his brother, but unlike David he could control his conceit; his concern was No. 1 SSRF in Algeria and he had no wish to take over other regiments and units. He was confident Paddy Mayne could perform the role.

Nonetheless, as he stated to Laycock, while it was imperative that the various disparate forces – SAS, SBS and the Greek Sacred Squadron – should continue to operate independently, what was required was an overall commander, almost a chairman of the board: an experienced organiser and an administrator with a temperate character. Laycock agreed with Bill Stirling's analysis and advised GHQ as to its value. On 8 March Lt-Col Henry Cator was appointed commander of Raiding Forces. Six months earlier Cator had been mooted as a possible CO of a new HQ Raiding Force, only for Stirling's name to be pushed in front of his by some means. The raiding force hadn't come to pass on that occasion, but now it came to fruition.

Under Cator's command were:

a) New SAS Commando Squadron
b) New SAS Small-Scale Raiding Squadron
c) Greek Squadron (Sacred Heart)
d) Raiding Forces Signals
e) Light Repair Section
f) Any other forces that may from time to time be put under your command.

Listed in the memorandum sent to Cator were his responsibilities, which included:

General supervision to ensure that training is thorough and in accordance with GHQ policy.
Selection of training sites in conjunction with unit commands.
Responsibility for the administration of the units under your command.
Responsibility for ensuring adequate supplies of arms, fuel and equipment to raiding parties.

On 19 March the 1SAS war diary stated that the regiment had been 'reorganised'. Now there was: 'Special Boat Section* under Major Jellicoe and the Raiding Forces under Major Maine [*sic*]. Various officers and men who the new establishment is unable to cater for have been warned for other jobs or units.'[14]

Among the men returned to their units were those Mayne considered David Stirling's picks, the upper class and the incompetent. It was now his regiment, and in the weeks that followed he put his men through a training programme that tested them physically and mentally, and taught them myriad new skills such as cliff-climbing and close-quarter shooting.

Lt-Col Cator made the odd courtesy call but he understood that he was surplus to requirements. 'As far as Raiding Forces Headquarters were concerned, they might just as well have not existed for all the effect they had on our training or our control,' reflected Peter Davis. 'All decisions rested solely with Paddy.'[15]

* Soon changed to Special Boat Squadron, to avoid confusion with Roger Courtney's Special Boat Section, then back in Britain.

23

David Stirling claimed he was a truculent and troublesome prisoner from the start. Within hours of his capture he had escaped, bolting for freedom after being allowed outside his makeshift cell to stretch his legs. With a 'blood-curdling yell' Stirling dashed into the desert blackness as his two guards stood a couple of yards away, smoking.[1] He ran for six hundred yards and then dived into a clump of bushes. For a man who was exhausted, physically weakened by illness and not a natural athlete even when healthy, it was an astonishing feat to outrun two well-nourished adversaries who were, furthermore, armed.

The indefatigable Stirling was soon on the move again, marching fifteen miles that night, and spending the day holed up in a barn. He set off at dusk. Five miles later he came to an enemy landing strip. For two hours he reconnoitred the aerodrome, planning how he would return with the SAS to raid it.

With that done he pressed on, covering ten miles over rocky terrain. At dawn he chanced upon a small ravine and slept for the rest of the day. It had been over two days since his capture and he had eaten only a chunk of bread, some dates and a slice of cold meat given to him by a local. His luck ran out early that evening, when he was betrayed to some Italians. He didn't go without a fight, however, and it took several soldiers to subdue him.

The Germans confirmed that Stirling did escape not long after his initial capture, but he was soon back in their custody after he was betrayed by some Arabs to whom he had turned to help. They 'offered him to us for eleven pounds of tea'.[2]

Stirling maintained that he remained the scourge of Italians even when a prisoner in their own country. As he was being escorted ashore at an Italian port, 'he seized both his guards by the necks, bumped their heads together and flung them over both sides of the gangway into the water'.[3]

In fact, Stirling was flown to Sicily and then on to Rome.

He was incarcerated in the Caserma Castro Pretorio Interrogation Centre, along with the rest of the men captured in the wadi, one of whom was Reg Redington. The day after his arrival Redington was warned in the dining area by some of his fellow inmates to 'be careful what you say because we know for a fact that there are the enemy among us'.[4]

Stirling arrived on 15 February and underwent a routine interrogation at the hands of an Italian and a German officer. In the adjoining cell to Stirling's were an RAF officer and a captain in the Royal Army Service Corps called John Richards.

When Carol Mather had been captured the previous month, he had shared a cell with an RAF pilot who said that he had been shot down. Scrutinising the man, Mather saw that while he had a large rip in one leg of his flying uniform, the skin underneath was unblemished. The pilot was very chatty and, nudge-nudge, wink-wink, told Mather, 'There's no need for me to ask who you fellows are, I saw your crowd down at Kufra.'[5] He said he had once had the honour of flying Paddy Mayne back to Cairo in his transport plane. The pilot threw in a couple of other SAS names. Mather sensed something wasn't quite right about his companion and feigned ignorance.

Mather was correct in his assumption. Axis forces had obtained Mayne's name from one or more of his men in A Squadron who had been captured the previous October during operations in Libya. Befriended by Capt John Richards of the Royal Army Service Corps, the SAS soldiers had been tricked into gossiping a little too much about life under Paddy Mayne.

Richards's real name was Theodore Sherman Schurch, born in London in 1918, baptised at the city's Swiss Church and registered as a Swiss citizen by his father. He grew up in Wembley and worked with several firms in north-west London as a costing accountant. At the age of sixteen Schurch had joined Oswald Mosley's British Union of Fascists and 'rapidly assimilated their doctrines'.[6] On the instruction of the BUF, Schurch volunteered for the British army in 1939 and he was soon put in touch with the Italian intelligence service.

Described as 'an exhibitionist ... of a low mentality [and] poorly educated', Schurch discovered he had a flair for impersonating well-to-do British officers. Inhabiting their skin was an elaborate form of escapism from his own humdrum existence.

Over five days Richards, the RAF officer (almost certainly a stooge too) and Stirling were often in each other's company, 'at meal times and at exercise and had a number of conversations'.[7]

In February 1943 the Axis forces were ignorant of the structure of the 'private armies' operating in the desert; so too was most of the Allied press corps in North Africa. L Detachment and subsequently the SAS were believed to be an adjunct of the Long Range Desert Group, the most famous of the units. They had received publicity for their exploits, including a glowing tribute in *The Times* on 1 April 1942. The paper told of how the LRDG 'have been a constant thorn in the enemy's side and have sown chaos and confusion behind his lines'. Although *The Times* mentioned that the senior officers were experienced desert voyagers of pre-war days, it didn't name them or give any clue as to the identity of Bagnold, Prendergast or Bill Kennedy Shaw.

On the other hand, David Stirling courted celebrity and it was therefore mistakenly assumed that the Phantom Major commanded the LRDG.

When Rommel learned of Stirling's capture, he wrote that his men had surprised a 'British column of the Long Range Desert Group in Tunisia and captured the commander of the 1st SAS Regiment ... thus the British lost the very able and adaptable commander of the desert group which had caused us more damage than any other British unit of equal strength'.[8]

Even Alan Moorehead, the distinguished Australian war correspondent, made this error in reporting the feats of the LRDG. 'They were,' he wrote, 'the picked men who set out alone in half a dozen vehicles or more and disappeared for weeks or months at a time ... they steered for hundreds of miles by compass over a wilderness far south of Tripoli that had never been explored before. They swooped suddenly at night upon isolated German airfields and smashed up the grounded aircraft. They burst into Italian huts and mess rooms hundreds of miles behind the front and, like a gang of desperadoes in a Wild West thriller, shot up everyone and everything they could see. They laid ambushes along the coast roads and mined bridges.'[9] He had conflated the LRDG and SAS, and attributed their feats to the brilliant leadership of their CO, 'probably the most resourceful adventurer in the desert war', who was caught while trying to blow up a railway train. The pair had probably met on the terrace of Shepheard's, where Stirling was in the habit of talking too much, not something that could be said of the shy, stammering Ralph Bagnold, or the austere and discreet Guy Prendergast.

Stirling was vain and voluble in the company of John Richards. On 18 February, three days after Stirling's arrival at the Interrogation Centre, British codebreakers at Bletchley Park intercepted a message sent from Rome by the Italian intelligence service. It ran:

'Lt-Col Stirling, commander of the Long Range Desert Group, who was captured at Tunis, has explained that all groups of the LRDG

(28 patrols altogether) are operating at present in night actions in the Gabes-Sfax sector with a strength of six to eight men each.'[10]

This was indeed the area designated to Stirling in Eighth Army Operation Instruction No. 6, of 3 January 1943. It stated: 'From 13th January eight patrols under Lt-Col Stirling were to operate under command of First Army in the Area Gabes-Sousse.'[11]

Sousse is a Tunisian city a hundred miles north of Sfax, but as far as Stirling was aware the French detachments under Lt Martin and Capt Jordan were still operating somewhere around Sfax.

Stirling didn't only divulge the location of these patrols but he also told Richards their orders. In another cable intercepted by Bletchley Park, the German Luftwaffe Field Marshal Albert Kesselring, whose men had captured Stirling, reported: 'The task of these groups is to interrupt Axis road and railway traffic by mine-laying and by damaging or destroying bridges and concrete roads.'[12]

The Italians and Germans were surely surprised how easy it had been to fool the Phantom Major. He also gave them the name of the man he expected to replace him as commander: Paddy Mayne.

Eventually Stirling was taken from the Interrogation Centre for a long journey north to his new home.

One of the first letters the Hon Mrs Stirling received after David's capture was from George Jellicoe, who had met her only a few weeks earlier, when he visited Keir to enjoy some goose shooting with Bill Stirling. 'Bob Laycock will be informed, as will the PM when definite news of David is received,' he wrote. On a more personal level, he told Mrs Stirling, 'I think I am a fairly discriminating person – and a harsh judge – but I am quite unashamed in avowing my devotion to him. I am so sorry for you as I know how you will hate the idea of David in prison.'[13]

Another letter to arrive at Keir was from Peter Stirling, sent on 15 February from Cairo, and Bob Laycock also contacted Mrs Stirling with the latest news from Gen Alexander at GHQ. On 3 March, Mrs Stirling replied to Laycock, writing: 'Thank God David is alive – but it's impossible to think of him a prisoner & I hate to think of his inactivity and sense of frustration because there was so much for him to do.'[14]

Then a letter arrived from David himself. Mrs Stirling relayed some of its contents to Laycock. He was 'caught literally with my boots off', and then after his escape he was apprehended through 'the treachery of an Arab'. Stirling told his mother he had been flown to Italy and that news of his capture had been broadcast on Rome Radio. He declared his confidence that his 'exasperating situation' wouldn't last long, but he hoped he would be imprisoned in Italy 'because it is easier to escape in Italy than in Germany'.

Bill had also been in touch from Egypt. The three days he spent in Cairo and Kabrit had revealed much about his brother's strengths, and his weaknesses as the commanding officer of 1SAS. What he had learned hadn't surprised Bill; same old David – imaginative, immature, immoderate and ill-disciplined. His mother would have understood the implication in Bill's letter when he wrote, 'I really think that as David, by all the rules, should have been killed at least ten times over, a short stay in the bag is not a bad thing for him.'

Only Bill and his mother, and to a lesser extent Peter, knew the real David. Immune to the magnetism that had drawn in George Jellicoe, Fitzroy Maclean, Pat Hore-Ruthven, the Churchills and many other distinguished people, David's family didn't see him as a genius guerrilla leader but as a callow and restless young man.

While Bill expressed his relief that David's incaution had been curtailed by captivity, Laycock wrote again to Mrs Stirling: 'He has done more for his country than any single individual of his rank in the army,' he declared. 'If anyone ever deserves the VC, it is David. I am sure too that others feel this. I wish that he was still under my command so that I could take a more legitimate part in recommending him.'

There was of course another member of the Stirlings' secret club, a man who was no doubt relieved David was a prisoner and no longer in a position to endanger the lives of the men under his command: Paddy Mayne. There is no record of his ever having lauded Stirling's martial qualities. The only reference to Stirling that Mayne committed to print was in his diary in December 1945. He was on an expedition to Antarctica, and increasingly exasperated with the leadership qualities of the naval officer in command of the party. This man was skilled in 'making you think you are a most important person', wrote Mayne. 'Stirling was a master of that art and it got him good results.'[15]

24

At the end of February 1943 David Stirling was transferred to Campo 5 at Gavi, a prisoner-of-war camp opened by the Italians in June 1942 for Allied officers with a reputation for awkwardness: *pericolosi* in Italian. Word began to filter out to other POWs in Italy that Gavi was a 'hell camp', run by a brutal commandant.

When Stirling arrived he was greeted by several familiar faces, one of whom was Tommy Macpherson, formerly of Layforce Commando. Macpherson had been captured in November 1941 during the raid on Rommel's headquarters that had cost Geoffrey Keyes his life. He had been one of Gavi's first inmates and described it as 'a genuinely medieval fortress which didn't seem to have been improved much since. It looked a little bit like Stirling castle but in a much less good state of repair.'[1]

The fortress was a thousand years old, and the prisoners' quarters comprised two cramped and insanitary courtyards. One was at the top of the castle, joined to the lower courtyard by a narrow roadway cut out of the rock and known as the ramp. So steep was this roadway that it required a strong and purposeful stride to ascend it at a normal pace. The two hundred officers lived in cells in both courtyards while the fifty batmen were housed in the lower courtyard, as were the cookhouse, infirmary, mess and parcel store. Campo 5 Gavi, a 'bad boys' camp', according to Macpherson, was staffed by two colonels, twelve officers and 240 other ranks, many of whom were carabinieri.

Another who greeted Stirling was Jack Pringle, whom he had known before the war. 'We had a lot of mutual friends, I knew his family and he knew mine,' said Pringle. 'When I was at Sandhurst he had friends at Sandhurst, and sometimes he came down on the weekend and we would see each other.'[2]

The pair were from the same social class. Born in Chicago to an American mother, Pringle's paternal side was Scottish; his father was the eldest son of Sir John Pringle, who had made his fortune in the West Indies. Pringle was handsome, gifted (he spoke fluent Italian, French and German), athletic (he was a talented polo player) and courageous (he had been awarded a Military Cross while fighting in an armoured car regiment). Stirling's arrival gladdened Pringle; here was someone from a happier time. They had mutual acquaintances and experiences, which could be turned into reminiscences to help pass the tedium of captivity.

The arrival of any new prisoner was an event at Gavi, a break from the dreary routine that began at eight o'clock each morning with roll call and ended at half past eight in the evening when inmates were ordered into their quarters.

Jack Pringle had been captured in November 1941 during the battle of Sidi Rezegh and had acquired a reputation as an escaper. So, too, had Lt Alastair Cram, taken prisoner on the same day and in the same battle as Pringle. That his attempts had all failed did not dispirit Cram, a Scottish artillery officer, who was a lawyer and a noted mountaineer. For him, planning an escape, the physical and mental preparation it entailed, was both an act of resistance and a means of overcoming the apathy that settled on so many POWs.

Another Scot, Lt George Millar of the Rifle Brigade, agreed. Single-minded and ferociously self-disciplined, he was appalled to count in his first camp at Padula the number of prisoners who seemed content with their situation. Officers, in particular, unburdened by responsibility, were happy for others to give orders and slowly 'stifled and stagnated and sulked'. There were even some who resented escapers, especially Cram, who had made two attempts to flee Padula. 'No hero in the camp,' said Millar, 'he was regarded rather as a nuisance, as someone who interfered with the comfort of others.'[3]

Stirling was searched, registered and escorted to a cell in the lower courtyard, which was windowless and about ten feet square, with a door leading to the prison compound. Pringle was Stirling's first visitor. 'David had a very commanding personality,' he said. 'His eyes were penetrating but friendly … in the next year or so, I observed his eyes turning angry at times, and when they did, the look of anger was very like that of a raven as portrayed in bird books.'[4]

Pringle invited Stirling to the cell he shared with Alastair Cram and a Fleet Air Arm officer called Peter Medd. Cram's accomplishments were numerous: Scottish half-mile champion in 1933, the conqueror of most Alpine peaks, the co-founder of the Perth Mountaineering Club and a degree in law from Edinburgh University. He was also known to his fellow prisoners as 'The Baron', the most audacious and ingenious British soldier in captivity.* Cram was well equipped to resist Stirling's magnetism but he couldn't; its pull was so strong that it clouded his judgement. 'David was one of the most forceful men I have ever met,' he said. 'It was impossible to work contrary to David. One could rarely if ever shake him from schemes of the utmost hazard.'[5]

Cram's physique also left him at a disadvantage: he was 5ft 8in. Physically and temperamentally, he was oppressed by the new inmate.

Yet Cram had all the attributes of a natural escaper. Small, wiry, strong and supple, he was everything physically that Stirling was not.

* The inspiration for Cram's nickname was Baron Gottfried von Cramm, a brilliant German tennis player who won the French Open in 1934 and 1936, and lost to Fred Perry in the Wimbledon final in 1935 and 1936.

He was also the opposite of Stirling in temperament. The reason Pringle and Cram were escape partners was because they were both 'systematic, analytical, thorough, sceptical and forever optimistic'.[6]

Stirling shared only their optimism. He first bragged to Cram and Pringle of his exploits with the SAS before asking, 'Is there any way out of here?' He said he simply had to get out because the SAS were nothing without him. He also told them of his plan to 'form an SAS Brigade ready for the coming operations in Europe'.[7]

Pringle and Cram looked at one another. They were part of a ten-man team working on an extraordinary attempt to tunnel out of Gavi. The possible route out of the fortress had been discovered by accident, by a trooper in the 8th Hussars (Pringle's regiment) called Hedley, who was quartered in an orderlies' room just below the mess hall. Rolling over on his bunk one day in the autumn of 1942, Hedley's head banged the wall and he gave a murmur of surprise. Was that a hollow sound? With the curiosity of the habitually bored, he and a cellmate began probing the wall, chiselling a hole through which a head was eventually stuck. There appeared to be a shaft of some description. Hedley dropped a stone: one, two, three, four seconds later, he heard a splash.

Exactly how the discovery was transmitted to Gavi's official escape committee is disputed but the outcome was the establishment of a ten-man team comprising Hedley and his cellmate, Pringle, Cram and Peter Medd, a Royal Engineers officer and explosives expert called Jerry Daly, who had Cram's small and sinewy physique, and four South Africans: Allen Pole, Charles Wuth, Buck Palm and Bob Paterson.

George Millar described the key figure in the escape team as Buck Palm, 'a loose slouching man with a lined, rugged, heavy-jawed face and a mane of black hair as long as Samson's'.[8] Palm, like Paddy Mayne, was a man of action whose physical and mental strength made him a born leader. He had a deprived upbringing, suffering at the hands of a violent father, but had grown into a self-reliant and resourceful man who was a wrestler, miner and a prospector before becoming a fighter pilot on the outbreak of war.

A body-builder, Palm was likened by Cram to Tarzan, and he was just as fearless as the jungle-dweller. He made the first exploration of the shaft and returned to report that the water was in fact a huge cistern sixty feet below the orderlies' room. The cistern had been constructed when the fortress was enlarged in the seventeenth century; it measured 120ft by 60ft, and could hold two million litres of water.

Palm returned regularly to the cistern, along with Allen Pole, a trained mining surveyor, and together they examined the walls in the pitch black, drawing on their knowledge and experience to search for any weak points in the bricks and concrete. It was cold, tiring, challenging work but eventually they selected the spot at which the tunnelling would begin, just above the water line and into the eastern face.

Palm led the tunnelling work. 'Day after day, and in the icy water, Buck swam across the reservoir and tunnelled through sixteen feet of solid rock,' remembered George Millar. 'In order to split the rock he smuggled down quantities of wood and built large fires against the face. Then, when the stone was hot, he flung bucketfuls of cold water against it to crack it. Then he smashed into it with his great crowbar. What a man!'[9]

Millar was less enamoured of David Stirling. He found him 'strange' and overbearing.

There were setbacks. Six weeks into the tunnelling the incessant autumn rain flooded the cistern and all their backbreaking graft was submerged. A new tunnel was started, forty feet higher than the first, and going in a different direction, south, so that once they were through the wall the escapees would be directly above the carabinieri's quarters on the fortress's lowest bastion. From their mess window high up, the prisoners studied the escape route once they were out on to the roof of the carabinieri's quarters: drop onto another roof below, then onto a sloping parapet and finally jump silently to the ground. But that was only half the escape. They would then have to avoid observation from the guard tower, tiptoe past the guardroom to the eastern wall and, having tied a rope to an olive tree, abseil down to freedom. 'It was a grim-looking route,' conceded Cram. 'Exposed, chancy, but Gavi was a grim fortress and demanded desperate means and risks.' Exposure to risk was a hazard for any escaper. That was what made it so intoxicating; it was a drug. One of Gavi's inmates, Don Riddiford, said, 'Once an escaper, always an escaper ... it is a most exciting activity and I can honestly say that I have never found anything to pass it.'[10]

But the risks any skilled escaper made were calculated ones, which entailed rigorous planning and careful deliberation: what clothes to wear; forged identity papers; a cover story; the route to freedom. 'We spent hours studying our route from the mess-room windows,' said Cram. 'So that we knew every tile, every stone on the roof.' Cram was also responsible for preparing the men's escape haversack, a task to which he applied himself with customary diligence. He even calculated how many calories per day they would need as they headed to the Swiss border.

And then Cram did something extraordinary: he agreed to the suggestion that David Stirling should join their escape team. 'Jack and I were convinced that the most valuable service we could render would be to return David to England,' he said.[11]

From a practical point of view, there was no logic to their decision to bring Stirling into their team. He was not in good physical shape; he had no experience of escaping; he spoke no language other than English; he was naturally clumsy; and at a gangly 6ft 4½in he was hardly built for tunnelling, leaping and abseiling. Had he told them about his broken wrist? Had the joint fully healed? Would it be able to withstand a strenuous abseil?

Jack Pringle argued the case for Stirling to Col Ken Fraser, Gavi's Senior British Officer, and then in walked the Phantom Major, the friend of Churchill, to stress how important it was for King and Country that he rejoin the war effort. Fraser agreed to his joining the team.

To accommodate Stirling, Cram and Pringle were obliged to alter their plan for once they were out of the fortress. After abseiling down the wall, the pair had intended to split from the other eight members of the party and take a train to the Swiss border; but Stirling spoke no Italian and would stand out a mile on a provincial train. They would go on foot. After all, Stirling had told Cram that he was, like him, an experienced mountaineer.

Now that Stirling was on the team he attempted to take control, urging them to leave on the first stormy evening. One night towards the end of March the weather was rotten and so the eleven escapers wriggled through the hole and into the shaft in the order that they would emerge from the tunnel: it was agreed the South Africans would go first, with Buck Palm at the head; they drew lots for the other positions and Cram took fifth spot, followed by Stirling sixth and Pringle seventh.

The storm had abated, however, by the time they were in position to crawl through the tunnel. It was a clear moonlit evening. Palm took them back to their quarters, where the orderlies who had been deputised to sleep in their beds to fool the guards were awoken; they returned and removed the dummies from their own beds.

Three weeks of frustration passed before the weather was suitably bad for a second attempt. The same procedure was launched with the orderlies and dummies, only this time Palm squirmed through the tunnel and emerged onto the roof. He climbed silently to the ground without a hitch and heard music from the carabinieri's quarters. Allen Pole, Charles Wuth and Bob Paterson followed. Then came Cram. The quartet of South Africans then made their way across the terrace to the olive tree for the final stage of the escape while Cram waited for Stirling. The minutes passed and the rain poured. Still no sign of Stirling. Cram had watched the last of the South Africans abseil over the wall. He couldn't wait any longer. It was now or never.

Stirling finally squeezed his frame out of the tunnel after an exacting passage. As he negotiated the descent from the hole he became entangled in the coils of barbed wire above the carabinieri's roof. Further time was lost as he freed himself.

Once on the ground, Stirling saw Cram disappear over the wall on the end of the rope. Now was the time for caution, for stealing cat-like across the terrace to the olive tree. Instead, Pringle watched as Stirling went 'ahead striding rapidly towards the sapling and the rope'.[12] Some Italians, clearly the worse for wear, tumbled out of a hut but failed to see Stirling in their stupor and the driving rain. Stirling strode on, still making no attempt at stealth. More Italians emerged and this time spotted the tall figure walking purposefully towards the tree. Bedlam. There were shouts and cries, and Stirling made a dash for the wall. Cornered, he was soon overpowered. Pringle kept his head. As the guards subdued Stirling, he nipped across to the rope. To his dismay, it had snapped in two and he was only able to abseil halfway down the wall before leaping the rest of the distance. Unlike Cram, who had broken two ribs and suffered concussion when the rope cleaved in his hands, Pringle executed a parachute roll on landing and trotted off into the night.

Stirling and the other four men were taken back to their cells and a manhunt was launched for the six who had escaped. Five were soon apprehended. Only Pringle remained free. With his customary determination and resourcefulness, he covered 150 miles as he headed north to the Swiss border. It was within his sight when he was recaptured.

Stirling spent five more months in Gavi. There is no evidence that he used the time to prepare for another escape; Alastair Cram and George Millar, however, were fitness fanatics who worked out early each morning, and Buck Palm ran a daily fitness course. 'I was hardening my body every day for the ordeal that surely lay ahead,' said Millar.[13]

Stirling didn't strengthen himself physically; nor did he learn another language. The one activity in which he showed an interest was gambling. The casino, recalled Millar, was 'run by a syndicate of shrewd officers in one of the larger cells in the lower courtyard'. Officers frequently ran up large debts, which were paid with camp money or IOUs to be settled upon repatriation. Millar sometimes watched them play faro, baccarat or 'two more childish games called "Winnie" and "Cars"'.[14] On his first evening in Gavi, Stirling won £100 in the casino.

On 8 September Italy signed an Armistice with the Allies. For the sixty-eight thousand British and Commonwealth prisoners in Italy the celebration was swiftly superseded by uncertainty. What now? 'Stay put' was the official instruction, a controversial order that may have originated with MI9, which was working for the British Directorate of Military Intelligence, or it may have come from Gen Montgomery. He believed that an unstoppable momentum would gather behind the Allies as they advanced north through Italy. The Germans would withdraw and leave behind the Allied prisoners. It was a miscalculation. The Germans began taking control of Italian POW camps, and while thousands of prisoners disobeyed the instruction to stay put and successfully escaped, many didn't.

The Germans arrived at Gavi on 13 September. A lot of the prisoners, including Cram, Stirling and Pringle, concealed themselves in the fortresses' many nook and crannies. But they were all eventually winkled out and herded onto a train heading north. A few men leapt from the wagons before they reached the Austrian frontier; Alastair Cram concocted a more cunning plan and feigned acute appendicitis that required his removal on a stretcher at Bolzano, forty miles south of the Brenner Pass.

Stirling and Pringle continued on into Austria. When the train stopped at Innsbruck a guard opened the door to their wagon, did a head count and then ambled off, leaving the door unlocked. For Pringle and Stirling, it was too good an opportunity to pass up. Slipping out of the wagon, they threaded their way through Innsbruck and struck out west towards Switzerland across the foothills of the Tyrol. One hundred miles lay ahead of them, a distance Pringle estimated would take at least a week. They were recaptured on the third day and transported to Stalag XVIIIC in Markt Pongau, but the pair were soon on the run again, having surmounted the barbed-wire fence without too much difficulty, and they disappeared into the Alps. 'We walked all the next day and the day after, traversing a spine of mountains running east,' said Pringle. 'We had no plan … we were on a sure loser, but we were free and on our own.'[15]

Pringle might have stood a chance of reaching the Yugoslav border had he been unaccompanied. He spoke fluent German and was inconspicuous in stature. With Stirling in tow he must have known recapture was inevitable. On their second night the pair knocked at the door of a remote cottage and were invited in by the husband and wife. Pringle explained they were fascist Italians en route to Markt Pongau; soon they were eating soup and bread. To excuse Stirling's silence, Pringle explained he spoke only Italian. The Austrians weren't stupid. The husband finished his soup and said he was off to check on the cows; he returned with four soldiers.

25

In January 1944 David Stirling and Jack Pringle arrived at Mährisch-Trübau, about one hundred miles east of Prague in what was then the Sudetenland. They had spent a few weeks in a POW camp in Eichstatt in Bavaria before their transference to Oflag VIIIF, where they were reunited with several men who counted Gavi as an alma mater: Alastair Cram, Richard Carr, the one-time adjutant of the LRDG, and Maj Roy Wadeson, a popular figure who had fought in the First World War.

Cram had been sent to Mährisch-Trübau in late December and was agreeably surprised by what he found. Established in the First World War, the camp had been converted into a military academy during the 1930s before reverting to its original purpose after German occupation. Its greatest feature, to a veteran POW such as Cram, was the central heating. Compared to Gavi, Oflag VIIIF was luxurious; the majority of the prisoners were quartered in rooms on four floors that had once been occupied by academy officers. Some rooms held eight inmates, others sixteen, and a few contained twenty-five beds. The prisoners dubbed the grey stone building the 'biscuit factory'. Additionally, nearly 250 Indian officers were housed in bungalows at the top end of the camp, and between them and the biscuit factory was a single-storey building known as the theatre block, and an open-air swimming pool that in January 1944 was in use as an ice rink. In total there were fifteen acres inside the prison wire, with a cookhouse, two spacious dining rooms, a gymnasium, football pitch and an infirmary.

Jack Pringle soon discovered that a good friend was in the infirmary: John Comyn, with whom he had been commissioned into the 8th Hussars on the same day in 1935. Jack and John exchanged gossip and adventures, and then Pringle told Comyn about David Stirling, and 'said that as soon as I was better I must meet him'.[1]

Comyn fulfilled the engagement on his release from the infirmary. 'It was a memorable meeting,' he said. 'David Stirling had the most magnetic personality I have encountered. Six foot six [*sic*], of persuasive charm, his dark eyes had a compelling intensity. Many found themselves following his behests even against their better judgement.'

Having entranced Comyn, Stirling invited him 'to join the secret organization he and Jack Pringle had created in the camp'. Comyn felt honoured to be asked, and augmented a staff that included Stirling, Pringle, Anthony Simkins, a barrister before the war and an officer in the Rifle Brigade during it.* Comyn enjoyed his newfound status. 'This group controlled all intelligence, escaping and security activities in the camp, as well as a "news agency", and was supported by a cohort of watchers, tunnelling specialists, forgers of passes, tailors, map makers, wireless experts, carpenters and linguists,' he said. 'All working under David's inspiring leadership.'

Stirling had been inspired to form his organisation during his brief stay at Eichstatt, which had been the scene of a mass escape in June 1943, when sixty-five prisoners tunnelled their way to freedom. His ambition was to establish a new record.

Another recruit was Mark Ogilvie-Grant, one of the Bright Young People of the 1920s, enthusiastically and unashamedly homosexual,

---

* Simkins joined MI5 at the end of the war and served as its Deputy Director-General from 1965 until his retirement in 1971.

and the lover of Alastair Hugh Graham when they were honorary attachés in Athens. He was Stirling's general dogsbody, or as Pringle put, a 'backroom boy',[2] unfailingly cheerful and industrious, who enlivened their drab surroundings with his singing and paintings of gnomes and fairies.

Anthony Simkins had been a prisoner of the Italians since 1941, with the exception of six weeks in the autumn of 1943 when he had walked out of his camp following the armistice. He was recaptured by the Germans as he attempted to reach the Allies in the south of Italy. Simkins was not alone among British officers in adapting to the privations of a prison camp; he and most of his peers had boarded at British public schools and were therefore inured to spartan living.

For Stirling, however, captivity rekindled painful memories of his schooldays, when he was unhappy and homesick. He had been a wilful youth, who bridled at all authority, except his mother's, and adulthood had not matured him in this regard. He resented his guards with a schoolboy petulance, calling them names and making gestures behind their backs. An escape attempt was the ultimate act of rebellion.

When Stirling had told Pringle of his scheme he said the goal was to spring 'about 150 officers' from the camp. Pringle harboured doubts that the idea would be accepted, 'but David set out to sell the idea to the SBO'. The SBO – Senior British Officer – at Oflag VIIIF was Col Cyrus Waddilove, one of five old boys of Ampleforth College imprisoned with Stirling. This connection worked in Stirling's favour, as did the fact that he 'was a talented persuader who did not always convince by logic, rather by giving the strong impression that he was sorry for you if you were not up to grasping his point'.[3]

Stirling was adroit at manipulating people with passive aggression. Then, sensing that Waddilove was weakening, Stirling closed the deal with a promise that in return for the authorisation to establish his organisation he would obtain a wireless set for the camp. 'This was an attractive offer and the SBO agreed,' said Pringle. 'In fact, when David made these promises he had no idea how he would be able to keep them. David was not short of self-confidence.'[4]

Stirling aimed to have the 150 prisoners escape by June 1944, by which time he was sure the Allied invasion of Europe would be well under way.

As Pringle acknowledged, Stirling didn't lack for self-confidence. That can be a positive trait, if controlled and deployed with intelligence and guile. In a wayward character an excess of self-confidence is dangerous. When Stirling dreamed up his schemes he saw only a glorious climax. He was poor at assessing risk and identifying and eliminating potential obstacles. Stirling had been cavalier with the lives of the soldiers in the SAS, and in Oflag VIIIF he now embarked on a scheme where, once again, his ego imperilled the lives of those under his command.

Alastair Cram estimated there were about four hundred prisoners involved in some capacity in Stirling's organisation. Its committee was split into four sections: intelligence, security, news and information, and what was described by Pringle as a 'police force and manpower pool'.

One POW who didn't join was the Honourable Philip Kindersley, a thirty-seven-year-old Old Etonian and City stockbroker. He had been captured in North Africa while serving in the Coldstream Guards and referred to Stirling's committee as the 'cloak and dagger men'.[5]

Another critic was Capt G. C. Williams, a Cavalry officer, who had also been taken prisoner in the Desert War. He had little time for Stirling, and his 'fantastic scheme for a mass break from the camp', or Pringle, whom he described as 'David's Man Friday'. Williams regarded Stirling as an arrogant hot-head, and in a private memoir, written in 1946, he gave an example of his volatility. Ordered out of his hut onto the parade ground, 'Stirling picked up a German officer and shoved him against the wall thinking he was only a lieutenant . . .

unfortunately he had read his pips wrong as the German was also a lieutenant-colonel, the new second-in-command of the camp.'[6]

Increasingly, the bulk of the prisoners (estimates as to their exact number vary from 1850 (Philip Kindersley) to 3000 (Pringle)) came to resent the power and influence wielded by Stirling, the 'escape dictator', as some called him. He was the de facto SBO, with Waddilove the puppet leader. This state of affairs, said John Comyn, was to 'the dudgeon of the older colonels, who could not understand how and why David appeared to have acquired such influence'. One of the deepest sources of resentment was his commandeering of Red Cross parcels. From them were removed quantities of coffee and cigarettes, which were used to bribe the ageing reservists who made up most of the camp's guard detail.

Nonetheless, Stirling's organisation produced some brilliant craftsmanship, much of it under the direction of forty-eight-year-old Pat Clayton, a founding member of the LRDG. Indeed, it was Clayton who, in January 1941, had pioneered the tactic of attacking enemy targets in Libya using machine guns mounted on vehicles when they raided Murzak.

At Oflag VIIIF Clayton supervised the production of maps, ration cards, identity cards and all the paraphernalia required by an escaper. Anthony Simkins was in charge of security and it was his responsibility to prevent the Germans finding any of the forged documents; his greatest challenge in this respect was Stirling, who frequently left forged identity papers and travel permits where they could easily be discovered.

There were soon four tunnels being dug, but one by one they were discovered. The result of German thoroughness in their regular sweeps of the camp, or was there an informer within their ranks? Stirling was unperturbed and produced another plan. Having obtained from the Germans a quantity of plywood in order to construct a platform for Highland dancing, an activity that Stirling told the commandant was essential for the Scottish soldiers, he oversaw its construction in one of the dining rooms. He selected the building because of its proximity to the perimeter fence, and his ambition, of which John Comyn was a part, was to 'surmount the high wire fence that surrounded the camp, by night, the camp lights having been fused and diversions arranged to distract the sentries'.

This audacious scheme was to be achieved by fabricating ten bridges 'made from plywood, hollow structures twenty feet long by three feet in section, each to take fifteen men over the obstacle'. When asked what he intended to do about the guards in the watchtowers, Stirling explained they would be neutralised by hoses used as water cannon. The idea was absurd, 'suicidal' to some,[7] as was Stirling's imaginative plan for the next phase of the mass breakout. 'We escapers were to hide up in the houses of friendly Czechs as a "goodwill mission", to provide them and their compatriots with confidence that the Allies would stand by Czechoslovakia should the Russians attempt to impose a Communist regime,' said John Comyn.

This required a contact within the Czech resistance. How was that to be achieved?

Comyn and Jack Pringle thought that a charismatic South African medical officer called Gerald van Zouco could be the solution. He had won the trust of the Germans and, consequently, was sometimes escorted outside the camp to treat sick locals. Anthony Simkins suspected there was more to van Zouco than met the eye and expressed his concern that he could be a German stooge. Alistair Cram also harboured doubts about the doctor. He felt 'an instinctive distrust for van Zouco', whom he regarded as 'a clever opportunist ... glib and convincing in "selling himself" wherever he believed personal profit lay'.[8]

Pringle went to see van Zouco to sound him out. The South African said he was willing to help Stirling in any way he could. The pair conceded it was a 'definite risk' to work with van Zouco, but they were confident they could use him to the organisation's advantage without compromising its security.

Van Zouco wasn't the only officer in the camp who aroused suspicion; there was another suspected stooge, one who was personally acquainted with Stirling. He had recruited Douglas Berneville-Claye, aka the son of Lord Charlesworth, to the SAS in 1942. In December that year he had been taken prisoner in Libya (it might well have been Berneville-Claye who gave Paddy Mayne's name to the Germans), and once in captivity he became an informer. To his fellow prisoners, Berneville-Claye – who by now claimed he had inherited his dead father's title – was known as 'Lord Chuff' because of his braggadocio, and eventually the Germans removed him from the camp for his own protection.

Van Zouco was more discreet than Berneville-Claye, but Cram and Simkins were right to be suspicious; van Zouco was not his real name; it was Gerald Marcel Salinger, he was not South African and he was not a doctor. His father was a Berlin Jew and his mother hailed from the Baltic states; he had studied medicine in his father's home town for a brief period before working as an electrical appliance salesman and then a chiropodist. Imprisoned by the Gestapo prior to the war, van Zouco had escaped from captivity and enlisted as a medical officer in the French Foreign Legion. After a series of escapades, including service in the Waffen SS, he was recruited by the German intelligence service and planted as a spy.

On account of an administrative error when van Zouco arrived at Oflag VIIIF his credentials were not passed onto the camp commandant; he therefore assumed that van Zouco informed on his fellow prisoners out of treachery and not because he was a German agent.

Van Zouco arranged for Jack Pringle to leave the camp to visit a medical review board in the town of Zwittau, ten miles west of Mährisch-Trübau. He also organised a visit from someone purporting to be a member of the Czech underground; this man passed to Pringle the addresses of two safe houses in Prague where escaped POWs would be harboured.

On that same evening news reached Oflag VIIIF that the Nazis had executed a number of escapees from Stalag Luft III, what has been subsequently immortalised as the 'Great Escape'.* What the POWS didn't know was that on 4 March 1944 the Gestapo had promulgated an order that in future all recaptured POWs were to be executed.

The news of the mass execution of POWs didn't dampen Stirling's enthusiasm. On the contrary, said Pringle, we 'felt we must push on faster than ever',[9] and now that they had the safe houses in Prague it was time to launch the first escape attempt, christened the 'First Flight'. It was, said Philip Kindersley, 'a disaster', resulting in the death of Peter Griffiths, who was killed jumping from a train while being escorted with some other air force officers to a new camp.[10]

Next an officer attempted to smuggle himself out in the camp's laundry baskets in the hope of reaching Prague and establishing contact with the Czech underground. He was caught and sentenced to thirty days' solitary. Stirling remained undeterred, still fixated on his own 'great escape'. Cram considered the idea 'indefensible' and told Stirling that 'the whole scheme now seemed so phoney' that he wouldn't be part of it.[11]

Stirling continued to welcome ideas for escapes. One was presented by an infantry officer called Humphrey Moon, who had for some time observed the Russian work parties that were regular visitors to the camp. They entered through a side gate near the football pitch, where there was no checkpoint. Moon's plan was to disguise five POWs as Russians and a sixth as their German guard, and simply march out of the gate at the end of the day.

Stirling authorised the attempt and soon his organisation was working flat out to provide uniforms, keys, an escape route and all the relevant documents. Among the six men chosen for the escape were Maj Roy Wadeson, a fluent German speaker, and Lt Hugh Mackenzie.

* On the night of 24/25 March 1944, seventy-six prisoners escaped from Stalag Luft III in Lower Silesia. Three reached freedom but the rest were caught, and fifty were executed.

Their orders from Stirling were to go to the safe house in Prague and prepare the Czech resistance for the imminent arrival of 150 prisoners from Oflag VIII-F.

The plan worked to perfection on the night of 20 April, but within twenty-four hours two of the escapees had been apprehended and a third was returned to the camp a few days later. A fourth member, Leslie Hill, reached Prague only to find that the addresses of the safe houses didn't exist. Mackenzie and Wadeson were also caught, but how and when and where are a mystery. So too was the manner of their death. Their ashes were sent in unmarked urns to Oflag 79 with no explanation about their fate.

None of this was known to Stirling, who was getting ready to launch the mass breakout. Ten days before the escape attempt, the Germans announced they were transferring all the prisoners to a new camp, Oflag 79. Disturbed by the information supplied by van Zouco about the attempts to contact the Czech resistance, the Germans had decided to move the prisoners to Brunswick in Lower Saxony.

The overriding emotion at news of the relocation was one of relief. 'Saved by the gong!' in the words of Alan Hurst-Brown, who like many in Oflag VIIIF believed that Stirling's breakout would have been a massacre.[12] Even John Comyn recognised its flaws: 'So ended the great escape plan,' he wrote. 'Its scale and objectives were doubtless over-ambitious. It caused the death of three officers, and might have caused the deaths of many more.' On the other hand, he said, Stirling's 'inspiring ideas and example did a lot for our morale and undoubtedly his project gave the Germans considerable concern as to security in their "Protectorate" of Czechoslovakia'.

George Millar was less forgiving. He had successfully escaped during his transfer from Gavi – for which he was awarded a Military Cross – and reached Britain, where he joined SOE, earning a DSO for his clandestine work in France in 1944. After the war he wrote to Comyn, remarking: 'Jack [Pringle] was a great escaper. What a shame that at the end he came under the aegis of David Stirling with his crackpot, mass-escape, up-with-the-Stirling image. And he got dear old Waddie [Wadeson] killed.'[13]

Pringle, too, had started to lose patience with Stirling. He had selflessly incorporated him into the escape attempt at Gavi and had also taken Stirling with him when he escaped from the train at Innsbruck. On both occasions Stirling's flaws had resulted in their recapture. What exasperated Pringle was Stirling's inability to learn from his mistakes and his idleness, particularly his refusal to master even the basics of a language such as Italian or German. Paddy Mayne would have sympathised with Pringle; Stirling's trouble, as he had demonstrated as a student, soldier and a prisoner, was that he was an ideas man rather than an industrious man.*

* Nonetheless, Stirling was awarded an OBE in the autumn of 1946, on the recommendation of Col Cyrus Waddilove and seven unnamed colleagues at Oflag VIIIF, 'for his work in connection with escape activities'. In particular, the citation praised Stirling's organisation 'of a large mass break which resulted in the move of the whole camp to Brunswick'.

26

David Stirling's next camp was the most famous: Oflag IVC, better known as Colditz. He and Pringle were transferred to the notorious castle in Saxony in August 1944. Philip Kindersley recalled that Col Cyrus Waddilove was removed on the same day as Pringle and Stirling; the men, he said, were 'all sorry to see Waddilove go'.[1] He made no comment about the other two.

At Colditz there was no weak Waddilove figure to be manipulated by Stirling; the SBO was Col Willie Tod, Royal Scots Fusiliers, a fierce but fair man. Among those under his command was Douglas Bader, the RAF fighter ace with artificial legs, Charles Upham, VC and bar, and several 'Prominenten' – what the Germans called officers whose relatives held positions of power and prestige in Britain and the Commonwealth.

Tod evidently made a rapid assessment of Stirling's talents and gave him a task commensurate to his capabilities: coordinating the black market activities at Colditz. 'The most amazing results were obtained,' said Lt Jerry Wood, a Canadian inmate. 'To begin with, one would have thought it impossible to induce a camp of individualists such as ours to voluntarily co-operate on a matter like Black Marketing, when food was on the ragged edge and some individuals exclusively enjoyed lucrative sources of supply. Using his personality only, the Colonel [Stirling] got everybody to jump into the same boat. That meant what extras did come into the camp were evenly distributed.'[2]

The luxuries amassed by Stirling were then used by two POWs, Dick Jones and Cenek Chalupka, to bribe the guards into disclosing little nuggets of information that were pooled to provide an intelligence picture of the local area.

It was a smart move by Tod: he spotted Stirling's gift for salesmanship, his brilliance at persuading men to part with their judgement or, in this case, their food. But in appointing Stirling to this role, Tod also ensured he did not have the time to plan another escape.

Pringle remained faithful to Stirling throughout their years as POWs, Jeeves to Stirling's Wooster. He was a fine soldier and a brave man, intelligent, but too trusting of Stirling's proclamations. Towards the end of the war Stirling described to Pringle a plan 'as to how the SAS should be used in the Far East theatre'.[3] He made it sound like a formality, that as soon as he was back in England he would assume command of the SAS and lead them east to help defeat the Japanese.

The reality on being repatriated was bitter for Stirling to stomach. On returning to Britain on 15 April 1945 he and the other POWS were confined to a holding camp for two days. 'It was too ludicrous,' he recalled. 'We were put inside a camp that had a wide perimeter and there were all the official nannies there. We were told we had to be there for two days and they patronized us rotten.'[4]

Incarcerating men on their return to their native land after years of imprisonment was insensitive in the extreme. For Stirling it was excruciating. He was desperate to return to 'his' regiment. But on his liberation from the holding camp he received a nasty shock. He wasn't wanted. Whether he presented himself at SAS HQ at Chelmsford to be told in person he was a supernumerary isn't recorded. But he did arrive at Keir House on 22 April.

On announcing David Stirling's return to Keir after four and a half years' absence, the *Stirling Observer* credited him with a DSO and bar, an inaccuracy that had been in media circulation for three years.

A month earlier the *Belfast Telegraph* had congratulated Lt-Col Robert Blair Mayne on a second bar to his DSO. By the time Stirling was back in Scotland, Mayne was being recommended for a Victoria Cross, in recognition of his courage and leadership on 9 April, when he repeatedly exposed himself to enemy fire in order to rescue some of his men who were pinned down in a roadside ditch north-east of Oldenburg.

The legend of Paddy Mayne had been growing for some time. Two years earlier he had assumed command of the Special Raiding Squadron, one component of Raiding Forces under Lt-Col Henry Cator.

On 10 July 1943 the SRS were in the vanguard of the invasion of Sicily, fighting their way up the east coast of the island, and then across into southern Italy where they wrested from the Germans the coastal towns of Bagnara and Termoli, the latter a bloody engagement that left more than a score of SRS dead. Mayne was awarded a bar to his DSO for his 'courage, determination and superb leadership', and the squadron received a visit after the battle of Termoli from Gen Miles Dempsey, commander of XIII Corps. 'In all my military career – and in my time I have commanded many units – I have never yet met a unit in which I had such confidence as yours – and I mean that!' he said in an address to the squadron. He then listed the reasons for their success: they took their training seriously, they were well disciplined, physically fit, confident in their abilities, careful planners and, 'last of all, you have the right spirit'.[5]

Their reputation grew still further in 1944, by which time the SRS had reverted to 1SAS and were part of the SAS Brigade, 2500 men in total, comprising 2SAS, two French regiments, 3 and 4SAS and a Belgian company, under the command of Brig Roderick McLeod, whose role was not unlike that of Lt-Col Cator the previous year.

During operations in Occupied France in the summer of 1944 the SAS Brigade were estimated to have killed 7733 German soldiers (at a loss of 330 SAS killed or wounded), destroyed 740 motorised vehicles, seven trains, 89 wagons and 29 locomotives and sabotaged important railway lines carrying men and munitions towards Normandy on 164 occasions. SAS troops also trained and organised disparate Maquis groups, called in four hundred air strikes on German targets and carried out countless valuable reconnaissance patrols for the advancing Allied forces.

Gen Eisenhower, Supreme Allied Commander in Europe, sent his 'congratulations to all ranks of the Special Air Service Brigade on the contribution which they have made to the success of the Allied Expeditionary Force'.[6] Mayne was awarded a third DSO.

On 3 March 1945 the *Sphere*, a weekly magazine, ran an article headlined 'Britain's Guerrilla Chief', a precis of a brief talk given by Mayne about his regiment's achievements, 'exploits that read like a schoolboy thriller'. It continued:

> Lieut.-Colonel Mayne is Chief of the Special Air Service Operators, a phantom army which has been operating for the past three years behind enemy lines, ambushing road convoys and causing confusion and destruction. With only a mental map of the country, Lieut.-Colonel Mayne parachuted into France a month after D-Day, and with the help of the Maquis set up headquarters for his army of 200, whom he met in Normandy. This army of Special Air Service Operators piled into fifty jeeps, and Mayne led them through the German lines to Nièvre, south-east of Paris. From there he harassed enemy troop and supply columns en route to pressure-points in Normandy, and intercepted and disorganised the Germans when they retreated following the American break-through. He and his men wrecked more than 1,000 Nazi supply trucks

> during this operation. Lieut.-Colonel Mayne has conducted this type of guerrilla warfare since the North African campaign, when he and his men attacked airfields and destroyed enemy planes by planting time-bombs in the petrol-tanks. Lieut.-Colonel Mayne himself destroyed forty-seven [*sic*].*

It was unusual, practically unheard of, for Mayne to discuss operations with a correspondent. He may not have known his words would be published, or he may have been launching a pre-emptive strike against Stirling, whom he knew would soon be liberated from captivity.

The previous August there had been a flurry of newspaper articles about the SAS, most of them sensationalist and inaccurate, and many of them giving undue prominence to David Stirling. None more so than the *Sunday Express*, which devoted a whole page to the SAS and included a photograph of Stirling. The *Express* was a Lord Beaverbrook title, as was the *Evening Standard*; Mayne must have suspected the hand of Randolph Churchill.

Mayne believed that if David Stirling resumed command of the SAS he would in a matter of weeks undo all the good work he had done in transforming it into a force respected by friends and feared by foes.

Fortunately for Mayne, his view was shared by Mike Calvert, who had returned from fighting with the Chindits in Burma to replace Roderick McLeod as brigadier of the SAS Brigade on 23 March 1945, just prior to operations in Germany. He had worked closely with Mayne and Lt-Col Brian Franks, the CO of 2SAS, in planning the SAS role in spearheading the Anglo-Canadian armoured advance through western Germany. 'Mayne, he put in a lot of objections but he couldn't have given me greater loyalty and he was very careful of his men and so would do very good planning,' said Calvert. He

* Mayne had in fact parachuted into the Morvan, west of Dijon, on 8 August, following the Allied breakout from Normandy. He spent the next two months motoring across northern France between operational bases, issuing fresh instructions to his four squadrons, as the US Third Army advanced rapidly east towards Germany.

was less effusive about Franks. 'He was all right … he knew all the aristocracy, and so he could go and see General Dempsey and he'd complain that "this is not what we're cut out for".'[7]

Mayne learned of Stirling's liberation on 20 April as he led B and C Squadrons of 1SAS through the wooded countryside east of Oldenburg. A signal sent over the brigade's communication channel ran 'David Stirling reported released'. A second message was received the following day: 'David Stirling in great heart, sends many messages and congratulations to all, and hopes to come out and visit you soon.'[8]

Lt-Col Brian Franks, an Old Etonian who knew Stirling socially, replied early the next morning: 'Delighted at news of Stirling's safe return. All ranks presume he will resume command after period of leave.'

It was a presumptuous message from a relative newcomer to the brigade, and a provocative one too, intended to undermine Mayne. The Irishman's riposte was sent on 22 April: 'Pleased to hear of David's release. Hope he has long leave and rest he deserves.'

The Stirlings were not a demonstrative family but the return of David, her problem child, must have been a day of powerful emotion for Mrs Stirling. The war had taken one of her children, Hugh, and David had been gone for more than four years. He had returned thinner but famous, a war hero honoured by the locals as his father had been nearly half a century earlier when he came back to Keir from the South African War. Capt Archibald Stirling, however, had his future planned out: run the estate, find a wife and start a family. David Stirling's prospects were more uncertain.

It was a full house at Keir to welcome David. Peter was home, preparing for a new posting to Budapest, and so was Bill with his wife, Susan, and two children, three-year-old Archie and eleven-month-old Hannah.

On the surface, life for Bill hadn't changed much in six years. The previous week he and Susan had welcomed visitors to Keir as part of the annual Gardens Scheme in aid of the Queen's Institute of District Nursing, and Bill was scheduled to open the Cambusdrennie farm fête, where he would judge the children's fancy dress competition.

David didn't stay long at Keir; once his leave had expired he returned not to the SAS HQ in Chelmsford but to the training battalion of the Scots Guards. But he had been home long enough to learn from Bill exactly how the SAS had evolved in the two and a half years since his capture. No one was better placed to describe the bitter fight for the regiment's survival than Bill, for he had led the crusade and he had sacrificed himself in the pursuit of victory.

27

The spring of 1943 had been a challenging period for Bill Stirling, one that required his utmost tact, toughness and tenacity. Having visited Cairo and Kabrit to grasp the full extent of the chaos left by his brother after his capture, Bill flew to Algiers, where he was in command of No. 1 SSRF. He was soon in conflict with Lt-Col Young of SOE, who had arrived in Tunisia in November 1942 in command of Brandon Mission. His brief had been to launch sabotage attacks against enemy targets by boat, but these were largely ineffective and several operatives had been captured. Stirling didn't think much of Young either as a man or a soldier, and he openly exhibited his disdain, which included criticism of Young's treatment of Arabs. It boiled down to a territorial fight, and Stirling eventually triumphed because he 'is in very high favour with commander in chief Mediterranean [Admiral of the Fleet Andrew Cunningham, whose brother, General Alan, had commanded the Eighth Army when Bill had worked at GHQ in 1941] and with military and planning authorities in Algiers'.

Stirling now began to transform No. 1 SSRF into a much larger force, on similar lines to 1SAS, soon reaching four squadrons with a strength of 450 men. On 13 May 1943 it was officially designated 2nd Special Air Service Regiment.

One of the first recruits to 2SAS was a tank officer called Roy Farran, who remembered Bill Stirling as 'a mountainous man, who shook us warmly by the hand and asked us a few embarrassing questions. He radiated an encouraging aura of confidence.'[1] Stirling told Farran what he told every potential officer: he would be on a two-week probation and if he failed to measure up in that time he would be returned to his unit. Stirling then invited Farran to join him and George Jellicoe – training in Philippeville with the SBS – for lunch.

Bill Stirling was determined to recruit only the best officers for his unit, and to train them up before sending them on operations. He did not want what he termed 'café gangsters' as officers.[2] This may have been a rebuke to No. 8 Commando, who in 1940 were issued with melodramatic instructions by their commander, Bob Laycock, including an exhortation to demonstrate 'the lightning, destructive and ruthless methods of the gangster'.[3]

Similarly, Bill Stirling weeded out the weak and undisciplined. 'Cunning was far more important than macho toughness, he wanted people who could look after themselves and thus look after the operation itself,' recalled Sgt George Daniels. The men were also encouraged to try a variety of weapons and choose the one they felt most comfortable with. 'It might have been a Tommy gun, a [Colt] 45, but I favoured the 30-calibre carbine, one of the US ones, because it was light and fairly accurate and you could use it close quarters or at a distance,' said Daniels. 'I also tried the Sten and the [German MP40] Schmeisser, but ... they were both too mass-produced in my mind.'[4]

Geoffrey Appleyard had been with SSRF since the beginning and was Stirling's second-in-command, in charge of A Squadron, comprising twelve officers and 156 men. On 25 June he wrote to his parents, telling them 'Bill Stirling is still in command of the regiment and I think we are building up something that will do great things in the future'.[5]

Stirling had encountered a problem, however: Gen Bernard Montgomery. Now that the war in North Africa was over, he had turned all his attention to the imminent invasion of Sicily and the commander of the 15th Army Group was not as receptive to Stirling as Admiral of the Fleet Andrew Cunningham.

In August 1941 Bill had used another connection, to Lt-Gen Arthur Smith, to obtain on behalf of David the approval from GHQ for a parachute unit that would be deployed strategically, not tactically, in support of a larger army operation.

But, as Bill had discovered during his visit to Cairo and Kabrit in February, David had mishandled L Detachment after Bill's recall to the UK in November 1941. Only occasionally had he used L Detachment strategically, instead filling its ranks with his friends and embarking on hare-brained and pointless raids to Benghazi and elsewhere. Parachuting as a means of operating had been abandoned by David, despite enthusiasm within GHQ in 1942 to resume its use.

Bill was determined to deploy the SAS as had been the original intention in 1941 and so he wrote two memorandums. The first, undated, was headed 'Appreciation of 2SAS Regt' and its purpose was to explain to the 15th Army Group how his regiment could best assist in the invasion of Sicily by performing tasks not normally attributed to regular formations.

'SAS Regt,' wrote Stirling, 'after initial training by parachute, operates in such numbers as are most suitable for the task in hand, and is specially trained to gain access by any means available. A loose organisation by squadron, troop section and group [i.e. two to four to eight men] makes it possible to operate without notice or reorganisation in small or large numbers.'[6]

The second memorandum was written on 1 July and stressed the importance of establishing and maintaining a mutually beneficial relationship with senior command. 'An SAS regiment, unorthodox, fighting irregularly, depends upon the enthusiasm of the commander by whom it is employed. While the personality of a commander is positive, so the personality of a staff is invariably negative, and when the staff gets between the commander and the SAS regiment, the latter has little prospect of useful employment.'

Bill may have suffered in his ambitions for 2SAS from his brother's impertinence. In the autumn of 1942 David had angered Montgomery with his 'rude' behaviour in demanding authorisation to recruit men for the SAS from the Eighth Army.*

Bill Stirling had proposed inserting numerous small parachute teams into Sicily and Italy, but without success. In his memo of 1 July he tried again: '2nd SAS Regiment is prepared to accept rough, unreconnoitred landings which can easily be undertaken with imperceptible increases in dropping casualties and advantages too obvious to mention,' he wrote.

Looking further ahead, Stirling continued:

> After a few months, should requirements appear for the disruption of Italian communications via Albania to Greece, a force of 300 men could work over hundreds of miles in up to 140 parties with shattering effect. In Italy, jeep patrols brought in by gliders could fight their way to vital objectives with explosives by the ton. In concert with a major operation, mountainous areas could be infested with small parties, which if sufficiently numerous will completely saturate local defences and paralyse communications.

Roy Farran stated that Bill, in his deployment battle with 15th Army Group, 'won to some degree and we were used properly 50% of the time'.[7]

* Montgomery did not forget Stirling's impudence, reminding John Hackett, who had been present, of it when the pair met in February 1945.

On 12 July two sticks of ten men parachuted into Sicily to attack targets on the north-east coast of the island, but most of their equipment – including wireless sets – was damaged in the drop and they soon ran out of food. In addition, they were inserted too near towns and villages, and Axis troops were soon hunting them. Most of the SAS managed to evade capture and link up with the advancing Allied forces but it was a lesson learned for Stirling.

Two months later five two- and three-man parties of troops from 2SAS parachuted into northern Italy to blow up railway lines in order to reduce the flow of German traffic south to the landing beaches at Salerno – exactly what Stirling had envisaged in his memo of 1 July, only on a much bigger scale. One of the officers was Capt Tony Greville-Bell, who had joined the SAS from the 7th Armoured Division.

Between them Greville-Bell and his men destroyed five trains, blocked the La Spezia to Bologna line by collapsing a tunnel and cut the railway lines in numerous places. Stirling had lobbied HQ for permission to drop scores more SAS teams into Italy and he was bitter that his request was denied. He wrote an indignant memo, stating: 'Examination should be made into why, aircraft and personnel being available, an effective force was not sent against German L [ines] of C [communication] in northern Italy … I submit that this paper merits consideration by the General Staff in relation to all future major operations.'[8]

The bulk of 2SAS landed in the southern Italian port of Taranto on 7 September with orders to drive inland by jeep and reconnoitre the area prior to a large airborne invasion. Some of these patrols ranged fifty miles inland – good training for the role the SAS would play in the invasion of Germany.

Meanwhile, another 2SAS operation, codenamed Jonquil (Bill Stirling was in the habit of naming operations after his favourite flora: Narcissus, Jonquil, Begonia, Marigold and Snapdragon), involved parachuting into central Italy to round up stray POWs, like shepherds combing the hills for their flock. The SAS would then guide them to four muster points on the coast between Ancona and Pescara, where they would be collected by boat.

Operation Jonquil was not a success. Only fifty POWs were rescued and its failure left 2SAS despondent. Bill Stirling blamed its failure on staff officers in 15th Army Group who had not heeded his advice during the planning of the operation.

The disappointment of Jonquil, however, was offset by the success of Lt Alistair McGregor and his small party, who had dropped inland near Chieti, with orders to eliminate an SS unit that had moved into the area to track down escaped POWs. McGregor's men killed dozens of SS men in ambushes and remained behind enemy lines until January 1944, operating as guerrillas and causing considerable inconvenience to the Germans.

There was an ugly incident on the troopship that carried 2SAS back to Britain in March 1944. By now Roy Farran and Bill Stirling were friends. So, too, was Tony Greville-Bell, although he had been punished by Stirling shortly after his arrival in the regiment in 1943. Slipping out of barracks to pay a courtesy call on some nearby nurses one time too many, Greville-Bell was transferred temporarily to Popski's Private Army, an experience he did not enjoy.

It was a lesson well learned by Greville-Bell, who in future understood that while Stirling wasn't 'regimental' he expected his officers to show self-discipline and moderation. This included in the officers' mess, where card games were popular. Bill Stirling participated in the gambling but never let the stakes get out of hand and sometimes suggested to a younger, less wealthy officer that it might be an idea to call it a night.

Stirling's style of leadership, allied to his theories on the most effective use of the SAS, had started to alienate a small coterie of upper-class officers, one or two of whom were friends of David. They had joined 2SAS having heard of the exploits of the Phantom Major and they didn't consider Bill sufficiently gung-ho. 'Bill Stirling had a great concept for strategic use of his SAS troops operating in small groups behind the enemy lines in depth,' said Roy Farran.[9] 'But he found it very difficult to explain to regular soldiers brought up to believe that the first principle of war was to destroy the enemy. Bill didn't agree with that, and he had a lot of trouble convincing people that you should drop small parties behind the enemy lines to cut their lines of communication to cause panic and chaos.'

On the ship home there was 'a bit of a mutiny among SAS people', according to Farran, who named Maj Peter Miller Munday, Maj Esmond Baring, a member of the banking family, Maj Philip Yorke, the ninth Earl of Hardwicke, and Capt Ralph 'Toby' Milbanke as the agitators. 'All those who opposed Bill Stirling weren't real soldiers, weren't real fighting types,' said Farran, who together with another group of officers, including Greville-Bell and Alistair McGregor, rallied to Stirling's side.

'They had little meetings on the ship, talking about getting rid of Bill and complaining to higher command,' said Farran. 'They used some pretty unfair tactics, too, saying he had not taken part in operations himself, which is true, but then how could he have done it given the way we were operating in Italy? He had taken part in commando operations before the SAS was formed.'

The instigator was Milbanke, who had served with David Stirling in No. 8 Commando and, even in that louche company, was known as a singular rake. Ignorant of guerrilla warfare, and the worst sort of playboy soldier, Milbanke was measuring Bill by David's sloppy yardstick, an irony that was unlikely to have been lost on the elder Stirling.

When 2SAS arrived at their new home in Prestwick, Milbanke was RTU'd. The others remained in the regiment, with Hardwicke given a training role, but, said Farran, the 'incipient revolution' never completely dissipated.

On 21 March, five days after the arrival of 2SAS in Scotland, Bill Stirling wrote to a man he knew shared his philosophy on guerrilla fighting. Addressing the letter to 'My Dear Paddy', Stirling thanked Mayne for his help in establishing a base for 2SAS and he referenced a memo called the 'jeep paper',[10] which was discussed in greater detail when they met two days later.

On 4 April the SAS Brigade was issued with an operational order by 21st Army Group, responsible for planning the invasion of France. It stated that the primary task of the SAS would be 'attacks on suitable types of objectives in the concentration areas of hostile mobile strategic reserves behind the length of the French Channel coast'.[11] In effect, the SAS would parachute into 'an area inland from the coast to a depth of 40 miles' as and when German Panzer reserves were observed moving towards the beachhead. Lightly armed, the SAS's only advantage would be if they had the element of surprise on their side, but the chances of parachuting into enemy territory without being seen were very slim.

The SOE agent M. R. D. Foot, who was by now attached to the SAS Brigade, recalled that Brig Roderick McLeod 'knew nothing of SAS in a proposed semi-clandestine role; nor did his brigade major, the equally unflappable Esmond Baring, of the County of London Yeomanry'.[12]

Bill Stirling and Paddy Mayne, on the other hand, were incandescent at their orders, exasperated that once more the SAS was to be used tactically and not strategically, parachuted well behind the main battle area to establish bases from which they could attack enemy communications.

According to Foot, Bill Stirling 'had a memorable row with McLeod about what the brigade's strategy ought to be'. McLeod refused to accede to Stirling's demand that the SAS make an official protest about their orders. So Stirling went above McLeod's head. Supported by Mayne, he protested to Lt Gen Frederick Browning, the Commanding Officer of the Airborne Corps. 'Browning sided with Stirling, so McLeod had to appeal over Browning's head to Montgomery, who sided with him,' said Foot. 'Stirling went to Eisenhower, who took the opposite view. McLeod had to go to Downing Street and get Churchill to resolve the problem in his favour. Stirling went back to Keir in plain clothes.'

Bill's departure was not his decision. The writer Christopher Sykes, who had joined 2SAS as an officer at around the same time as his friend Evelyn Waugh, remarked after the war that Stirling had 'serious differences' with McLeod and consequently he 'had been asked to resign his command'.[13] The diary entry of Hermione Ranfurly on 14 June 1944 stated that she had dined with the Woodruffs and Evelyn Waugh, who informed her that like Bill Stirling he had received a 'bowler hat'; this was officers' slang for the sack.

Stirling left the regiment and was replaced by Brian Franks. But his actions had not been in vain. The initial operational order was cancelled, and the SAS were instructed that they would be used strategically, in central France hundreds of miles behind the beachhead, attacking enemy lines of communications and sabotaging their transport routes north. Exactly what Stirling and Mayne had advocated from the start.

Apart from the small band of upper-class mutineers in 2SAS, the officers and men were deeply upset to see Stirling depart. 'We were absolutely in agreement with Bill's resignation and in fact the senior officers, of whom I was one then, were inclined to resign as well, but Bill told us not to,' said Greville-Bell. 'Bill got all the officers together and said, "I won't forgive any one of you if you don't back up Brian."'[14]

Sgt George Daniels, who had been awarded a Military Medal in Italy in 1943 for blowing trains off tracks, could see how much it hurt Stirling to take his leave of his regiment. 'He came to the men and said why he had resigned,' said Daniels. 'It was a blow to morale. Bill could handle himself in any company, he certainly did with the men. They admired him enormously.'[15]

Stirling did leave Franks with one awkward problem, however: what to do with Evelyn Waugh. As one of the few men in Britain who could manage the novelist, Stirling had agreed to take him on as a staff officer in the autumn of 1943. Waugh was pathetically grateful, as he remarked to his diary in a series of entries in September. They also shed some fascinating light on Bill Stirling's lone fight to ensure the SAS remained a separate entity and was not swallowed up by the Airborne Corps. 'Bill Stirling arrived at White's before luncheon and I was able to get ten minutes alone with him,' wrote Waugh on 23 September. 'He promised to take me back when he went, but his own position is clearly precarious – so precarious that he is thinking of going straight to the Prime Minister over the Army's head.'

The next day the pair dined together and Waugh 'offered myself ... to help Bill Stirling in getting out his project for an expanded SAS. Accordingly I spent most of the day with him. He is vastly different from Bob [Laycock] – a romantic, more imaginative, more moral, less alert, less concrete. My chief value to Bill is to give him someone he can trust to discuss the project with.' Then, on 25 September, Waugh lunched with John Betjeman and in the evening he and Bill 'went to White's and kept the barman and underporter up till 2 playing slosh [a game with balls played on a billiard table] with them and drinking hard'.

On 29 September Waugh wrote, 'Bill has fixed luncheon with the Prime Minister to discuss the future of SAS. I hope to get appointed G2 [a major; he was G3, a captain], though, war weary, I dread the prospect of organization and training and a hundred new acquaintances.'[16]

Stirling eventually accepted Waugh in 2SAS in October. But on 9 November, as Waugh prepared to sail on a draft to North Africa, a cable arrived cancelling the departure. A despondent Waugh wrote in his diary four days later, 'We have no one in this country responsible for us and SAS is in process of absorption by Airborne Corps with, I think, the elimination of Bill.'[17]

Waugh's gloom was misplaced. He remained in 2SAS, who were to return to Britain in early 1944, and he was sent on a parachute course. He didn't last long, however, injuring his knee early on. During his convalescence Waugh began writing a novel, to be called *Brideshead Revisited*, but before he could complete the book the War Office instructed him to report for duty in London. Waugh appealed to Stirling, who contacted the War Office and told them he required Waugh for 'secret work of great importance'. Stirling then gave Waugh six weeks' sick leave so that he could finish his book.[18] 'With your permission I would like to have Bill Stirling as Catholic godfather as I am now deeply indebted to him,' Waugh wrote to his wife on 12 May 1944. With impressive foresight, he then told Laura about some of the goings-on in 2SAS in Scotland, including news of Philip Hardwicke. 'All the old gang is assembling round Bill,' he wrote. 'My chief fear is that he himself will fall and all of us be exposed.'[19]

28

David Stirling was in London at the beginning of May 1945, and there was a touch of déjà vu to his existence. It was as if it was 1940 again. He spent his days with the Scots Guards training battalion and his evenings disporting himself in London's restaurants and clubs. A frequent companion was Hermione Ranfurly, who for several months had been employed as the aide-de-camp to Air Marshal John Slessor, Commander-in-Chief RAF Mediterranean and Middle East. She and Stirling dined together on 5 May and they were joined later by his brother Peter and Fitzroy Maclean. David was his incorrigible self, telling all and sundry about his plan to go to 'the Far East war'. It was a fun evening, recorded Ranfurly in her diary, and everyone was in good heart.

Three days later Victory in Europe was declared. Paddy Mayne was in Brussels with B and C Squadrons, en route to a rendezvous with A and D squadrons at Poperinghe, seventy miles west. The next day the regiment was reunited, and it celebrated the end of the war in strong beer and good voice.

A week later 1SAS and 2SAS were in Norway, ostensibly to disarm three hundred thousand Germans but for the most part enjoying the weather and the affectionate hospitality of the locals. David Stirling was not with them. He was still in London, in the company of

Hermione Ranfurly, who was impatiently waiting for her husband to return from Rome, where he was on the Allied staff. Daniel Ranfurly knew he could trust David with his wife. They dined together at the exclusive Bagatelle restaurant in Mayfair, one of Princess Elizabeth's favourite venues, and their photograph appeared in the 23 May issue of *Tatler* above the caption 'At a table for two were Col. David Stirling and the Countess of Ranfurly. She was Miss Hermione Llewellyn before her marriage.'

Ranfurly found Stirling thinner than she remembered in Cairo, so dining in some of London's top restaurants was a good opportunity to fill out his tall frame. Of more importance to Stirling was the fact that the Countess of Ranfurly still believed in the myth of the Phantom Major. When he spoke, she listened, and that was increasingly rare for Stirling since his return to Britain the previous month.

He claimed, subsequently, that he still had the ear of the Prime Minister and on three occasions he met Winston Churchill to discuss the deployment of the SAS to China on what Stirling called his Chungking Project, a guerrilla campaign against Japanese forces. To expedite his plan, Stirling envisaged a new SAS Brigade comprising the existing 2SAS, an American regiment recruited from the ranks of the Office of Strategic Services (the US equivalent to SOE), and a regiment of recently released POWs. Oddly, there was no place for Paddy Mayne's 1SAS in Stirling's prospective brigade.

Brig Mike Calvert had no idea of what Stirling was plotting; on the contrary, as far as he was aware the SAS – including the two French regiments – would parachute into Thailand and coordinate guerrilla operations with local insurgents against one Japanese division. Their deployment to South East Asia Command had first been discussed in the autumn of 1944 in a memorandum written by Lt-Col Ian Collins, entitled 'Notes on future of SAS'. In the paper, submitted to Brig Roderick McLeod, Collins outlined the role the SAS Brigade could play in China, Indochina and Siam under SEAC.

Evidently, Calvert expanded the idea to Louis Mountbatten, the Supreme Allied Commander in South East Asia, not long after taking command of the SAS Brigade. On 11 May 1945 he received a reply from Mountbatten, thanking him for his 'most interesting description of SAS activities during the latter part of the campaign in Europe: I was especially interested to hear of the development and success of the armoured jeeps [but] after consideration, I am of the opinion that it is not feasible to raise, train and operate SAS formations in this theatre.'[1] However, by the end of May, Mountbatten had revised his opinion, having consulted Maj Gen Richard Gale, commander of I Airborne Corps. Gale had been impressed with what the SAS Brigade had achieved in France the previous year, as he made plain in a memo to Lt-Gen Lewis Brereton, commanding general, First Allied Airborne Army, in January 1945 when discussing future employment for the SAS. 'I am convinced that there is a place in the Allied army for SAS troops,' wrote Gale, 'that is troops who are trained to fight in small isolated parties behind the enemy lines. I do not regard these troops as saboteurs but as highly skilled, highly trained independent units.'

As a result of Gale's endorsement, it was proposed to send '2 British and 2 French Battalions' to the Far East to carry out jeep operations along the lines envisaged by Calvert.

Stirling dined with the Prime Minister on the last day of May, at the request of Randolph, who was bringing his son, four-year-old Winston, to see his grandfather. A few days later, on 4 June, he was at Claridge's with Hermione Ranfurly and Air Marshal and Lady Slessor. They talked about the war in the Far East, she noted in her diary, and Stirling had told her he was keen to participate.

Stirling was calling on all his contacts in an attempt to re-exert his influence on 'his' regiment. But on 5 July Churchill was swept out of power in the general election and Stirling lost his most important ally. But still he persisted, desperate to usurp Calvert. But to no avail. 'Stirling must obviously receive his instructions from SACSEA [Supreme Allied Commander, South East Asia (Mountbatten)],' stated a memo sent from the Far East to the War Office on 24 July, suggesting an irritation at Stirling's scheming. Another followed on the same day: 'Gale prepared [to] accept Stirling as Deputy to Calvert.'[2]

Dinner at Claridge's with his friends was far more agreeable than many of the engagements Stirling had to endure in the summer of 1945 as his indiscretions began to catch up with him. The British army had in their custody Douglas Berneville-Claye, still calling himself Lord Charlesworth, who had surrendered in north-east Germany wearing a black SS tank uniform bearing the insignia of Hauptsturmführer in the British Free Corps. His tale was a tangled one (which the British intelligence services were unable to unravel) but he claimed to have served in the SAS and to have also known Stirling while in Oflag VIIIF and Oflag 79. Col Cyrus Waddilove testified that Berneville-Claye received favourable treatment from the Germans while a POW and described him as 'an impatient and rather silly type'. One of the MI9 officers who interrogated Berneville-Claye in May 1945 remarked that he was 'a thoroughly nasty bit of work'.[3]

Stirling had recruited Berneville-Claye to the SAS in August 1942, but he told investigators that the man was foisted on him and had not been operational. This was a lie. Berneville-Claye had taken part in the Benghazi raid fiasco in September and subsequently operated with A Squadron in Libya from October to his capture in late December, commanding B Patrol of A Squadron under Paddy Mayne. Stirling had commanded B Squadron and Berneville-Claye's name (albeit spelt 'Clay') is listed in a memo of November 1942 entitled 'Intentions of Lt-Col Stirling, 1SAS Regt. up to 2 Dec 42'. When this was put to him by the investigating officer, 'Stirling denied that B-C was more than a nominal member of the SAS.' He said he had 'flatly rejected [Berneville-Claye] for operational duties but he was allowed to take charge of a transport convoy'.[4] The officer sensed Stirling's mendacity and concluded: 'The fact was Stirling had free choice of officers when he formed this Service in Mideast.'

The investigation into Berneville-Claye's activities as a prisoner of war threw up further embarrassment for Stirling. Another POW, a Lt Calthrop, raised suspicions among his fellow inmates in Oflag 79 and one, a Capt Micklethwaite, told MI5 on 31 May 1945 that Stirling, the camp's security officer, was not interested in probing Calthrop's credentials. It was only when Stirling was transferred to Colditz, and his position filled by Capt Jack White-Abbott, that 'a more detailed investigation' into Calthrop was initiated.[5]

Later in the summer Stirling was interviewed by a Capt G. Gray at the War Office ahead of the court martial of Theodore Schurch, aka Capt John Richards of the RASC, on nine charges of treachery and one of desertion.* What, Gray wanted to know, had Stirling told Schurch in the Rome Interrogation Centre in February 1943?

Stirling denied he had revealed any sensitive information. If he had, it was inaccurate and 'designed to deceive'.[6]

The response had been expected by the office of the Judge Advocate General, who had predicted Stirling would be 'very loth to say that he had discussed secret information even with a man whom he understood to be a fellow officer and prisoner of war … [but] it may be sufficient corroboration if they met and had a conversation'.[7] In any case, the prosecutors were in possession of Italian messages intercepted by Bletchley Park codebreakers, which revealed the extent of Stirling's careless talk. When Schurch's trial began in September it was covered extensively in the newspapers and Stirling's name was mentioned in many reports, as one of several who had been hoodwinked.

---

* Schurch was convicted on nine charges of treachery and one charge of desertion, and was hanged at Pentonville prison on 4 January 1946. Berneville-Claye was imprisoned for six months in 1946 for theft and subsequently immigrated to Australia. In 1964 the *Canberra Times* reported that Berneville-Claye was the city's new senior Scout leader and described him as 'one of the top five British agents of World War II'. Three years later he was unmasked as an imposter and received a fine for wearing medals to which he was not entitled. He died in 1975.

There was also the matter of Gerald van Zouco, aka Salinger, who was being held in London. Alastair Cram, The Baron, had returned to Britain after his twenty-one escape attempts during captivity, and joined the SAS. It was a decision that embodied his conflicted view of David Stirling. There was a part of him that he idolised and another part he abhorred. Cram had escaped from Oflag VIIIF and gone to Prague in search of Roy Wadeson and Hugh Mackenzie, only to be snared in a trap by the Gestapo. He was therefore certain that van Zouco was a German agent. Yet he was 'amazed' to learn that Stirling 'continued to believe in him' when van Zouco called on Stirling for help from a London detention centre.[8]

A thorough investigation was launched by the War Crimes Group of the office of the Judge Advocate General into the deaths of Wadeson and Mackenzie. While Jack Pringle cooperated to the best of his ability, answering a list of fourteen questions sent to him in January 1946, Stirling was less forthcoming in what he knew about van Zouco and the possibility he had been an enemy stooge. Perhaps he was embarrassed or perhaps he considered the matter closed now that the war was over. The War Crimes Group wrote to him in September 1946 to request an interview but received no reply; they tried again and received an assurance from Stirling that he would fulfil his obligation. But on 15 January 1947 the War Crimes Group reported that 'no statement has yet been received from Colonel Stirling. He promised to report to this office some weeks ago but has so far failed to do so.'[9] He still hadn't made an appearance by May that year. Eventually the War Crimes Group gave up and it was decided to close the investigation into the deaths of Wadeson and Mackenzie.

It was remarkable that Stirling had been duped three times, and on each occasion by a poorly educated working-class man: van Zouco, Schurch and Berneville-Claye. What weakness had they spotted in their victim? There were several: the arrogance of the entitled, the credulity of the aristocratic and Stirling's colossal vanity. Put together, these flaws were easily exploited by men who made up in cunning what they lacked in formal education.

Stirling received no official reprimand for his incaution. Yet unquestionably it had been noted by his superiors. He was a poor judge of character; in fact, his judgement in general was weak. Look at the manner of his capture. It was clear that he had been promoted beyond his ability in 1942. No official reprimand, maybe, but the army placed a black mark by his name.

The return to Britain was a crushing anti-climax for Stirling. That breezy message received by the SAS on 21 April had been sent with so much unbridled enthusiasm: 'David Stirling in great heart, sends many messages and congratulations to all, and hopes to come out and visit you soon.'

How disillusioned he must have felt, how bitter too, at being unable to resume where he had left off in January 1943. The war had, so Stirling imagined, been the making of him. Prior to its outbreak he had been a loafer, a loser, a lounge lizard. L Detachment had given him a new life and he had discovered his gift for casting a spell over soldiers and making them do things against their better judgement. Men looked at him in awe: the guerrilla leader and great escaper.

Surely he could expect such reverence upon his return to Britain. The thought had nourished him throughout his incarceration. What had he told Jack Pringle and Alastair Cram on his first day at Gavi? That he simply had to escape, because without him the SAS was nothing. Now he was confronted with the reality: the SAS had thrived in his absence.

Instead of garlands Stirling received questions from investigators and quizzical looks from SAS soldiers at Chelmsford who gazed for the first time upon the stringy lieutenant-colonel and made a mental comparison with Paddy Mayne. It was almost as if his magnetism only worked abroad, and within the confines of his native land his power waned; he was back to being David Stirling, fourth-born of the Honourable Mrs Stirling.

Nonetheless, on 10 July Stirling succeeded in getting himself posted from the training battalion of the Scots Guards to deputy commandant of SAS Headquarters. There wasn't much to do as 1 and 2SAS were in Norway and would remain there until the end of August. Stirling lasted a week in his new post. On 17 July his service record notes that he relinquished thc appointment. There must have been a serious rupture of some sort. Did it involve Paddy Mayne?

If the pair did meet in the summer of 1945 it wasn't for long and it would not have been a raucous reunion. According to Reg Seekings, 'after the war they weren't speaking to each other because there were certain people feeding stories to one another, deliberately building up trouble'.[10]

Who might those people have been? David still had friends within 2SAS, some of the officers who had conspired against his brother in 1944. There was still, incredibly, a faction within the SAS Brigade and the army in general that looked down on Paddy Mayne because he was Irish, middle class and the product of a grammar school. Not the sort of chap who should be commanding a regiment.

Brig Mike Calvert wasn't among their number. He had recommended Mayne for the Victoria Cross, and was supported by Lt-Gen Simmonds, General Officer Commanding II Canadian Corps, and by Major Gen Vokes, commander of the 4th Canadian Armoured Division, who commented: 'I observed the very marked respect and regard in which he was held by his officers and men'.[11] There were also statements from Lts Lockett, Scott and Surrey-Dane. Field Marshal Bernard Montgomery's signature is also on the citation of June 1945. But at some point in the weeks that followed it was decided that Mayne didn't deserve a VC and instead he was awarded a fourth DSO. His actions at Oldenburg on 9 April fulfilled the criteria for the bestowal of the VC, and no compelling case has ever been presented as to why the medal was not forthcoming.

The news of the third bar to Mayne's DSO appeared in the newspapers on 12 October 1945, four days after the SAS Brigade had been disbanded. 'Leader of Skymen wins fourth DSO' was the headline in the *Daily Mirror*, which then listed Mayne's remarkable war exploits, from the desert of North Africa to the beaches of Sicily and Italy to the forests of France and finally into Germany.

None of the newspapers mentioned David Stirling.

On the same day, Brig Calvert wrote a paper entitled 'Future of SAS Troops', and in the course of four pages raised and explored eight of the most common criticisms levelled at special forces by senior regular officers during the war. He was anxious to have input on how these criticisms could be powerfully overcome when he saw the Chief of the Imperial General Staff to discuss the regiment's future.

Calvert sent the memo to eleven of the most prominent figures in Britain's special forces. The first name on the list of recipients was Lt-Col William Stirling.

At the end of October Calvert was in Tarbes, in the south-west of France, the new HQ of 3 and 4SAS. In a ceremony to honour the French soldiers who had served in the SAS, Calvert presented to the French SAS the hats worn by Napoleon and the Duke of Wellington. The presentation was covered in the British newspapers, which must have been another painful reminder to Stirling of how far his star had fallen. Less than a month earlier he had relinquished his rank of temporary lieutenant-colonel, held since 1942. He reverted to the rank of major.

In March 1946 the inaugural Special Air Service Regimental Association newsletter was published; it was a rudimentary affair, just five typewritten pages, and concerned principally with news of former soldiers adjusting to life as civilians. However, on the front page were reproduced two letters: the first, addressed to 'My Dear Stirling', was from Winston Churchill, gladly accepting David's offer to be the Association's patron. The second was from the Association's president and was a congratulatory note on the first issue and a reminder of the dinner on 17 December 1946 at the Connaught Rooms. It was signed plain 'David Stirling'.

In fact, the dinner was held on 16 December with Air Marshal Sir Arthur Coningham the guest of honour. The *Observer* reported that many French members of the regiment had made the journey, as had Paddy Mayne, 'whose immense charm and cunning could only be compared to his mountainous physical proportions'.[12] Mayne had intended to fly over from Ireland, but bad weather led to the cancellation of his flight; so he took a boat, the *Ulster Monarch*. The last time he had been on the *Monarch* was in 1943, when she had ferried him and his men to operations in Italy.

Stirling also attended. The *Observer* described him as 'a sleepy imperturbable Scot'. It was probably the last time he and Mayne met.

On 24 July 1947 Stirling's rank on his service record was entered as Captain, Supplementary Reserve of Officers with the War Substantive of Major. In the same month the SAS was revived as a territorial unit – 21SAS (the numbering a reversal of the two wartime regiments) – under the command of Lt-Col Brian Franks and recruitment began in August. There was no post for Stirling other than his appointment in November as an honorary lieutenant-colonel. It was a meaningless promotion, a caress of Stirling's ego, but it was prudent to award him a sinecure rather than to give him any hands-on role.

PART III

29

For a decade after the war, David Stirling had little to do with the SAS, despite the fact that Brian Franks had raised a territorial regiment. An SAS squadron had been formed to fight in the Korean War, but it was instead posted to Malaya to help quell a communist insurgency. In Malaya they came under the command of Mike Calvert, who had recently established a force called the Malayan Scouts. One of their squadrons, C, was comprised of Rhodesians, and Calvert had personally overseen their recruitment in Salisbury. 'I saw a lot of Colonel Calvert when he was out here and [he] told me he was exceedingly pleased with his Rhodesian Squadron,' wrote Stirling in a letter dated 12 February 1952.[1] Despite the fact he was younger than both Franks and Calvert, Stirling had no inclination to rejoin the army. Or perhaps he wasn't wanted.

In the 1952 issue of the SAS Regimental Association newsletter it was revealed that the Scouts 'will shortly be renamed the 22nd SAS Regiment' and there was a notice inviting wartime NCOs and subalterns to re-enlist as they were short of experienced personnel.

Among the other items of interest in the 1952 newsletter was a notice that the annual reunion would be in Harrogate on 26 July that year. Lt-Col Paddy Mayne had already confirmed his presence. David Stirling did not attend.

In the immediate aftermath of the war Stirling had been the same feckless and aimless man as before. Much of his time was spent in London, drinking and gambling. 'Dined with David Stirling at White's,' wrote Evelyn Waugh in his diary on 22 March 1946. 'We drank three bottles of champagne.' On 8 August of the same year, Waugh remarked: 'The last three weeks in London passed like three months in lassitude. After 1st August White's was shut and I saw few friends. I had people to drink champagne with me at the Hyde Park Hotel most evenings, chiefly the same gang, David Stirling, Ran Antrim [Randal John McDonnell, 8th Earl of Antrim], Christopher Sykes, Bridget Parsons, etc.'[2]

In 1947 Stirling opened two fish and chip shops in partnership with the wife of George Jellicoe, employing ten ex-servicemen; neither appeared to have been successful. Then he emigrated to Rhodesia and by 1949 – almost certainly with the financial and moral support of Bill – he had formed Gemsbok Rhodesia Development Company Ltd. His secretary was Arthur 'Stuka' Stokes, a former officer in the LRDG, who was also the chairman of the Rhodesian branch of the wartime unit. There were annual reunions in Salisbury, but Stirling never showed.

Bill Stirling was a frequent visitor to Africa, sometimes accompanied by Bryan Mayfield, his wartime comrade and his partner in the Houston Quarry Company Ltd, which had been launched in 1940 and had grown into a firm of engineering surveyors and quarrymasters.

In July 1948 a newspaper reported that Stirling, together with some Italian engineers, was 'surveying and constructing roads for the Uganda Government in East Africa and the Congo hinterland, [and] more than £1,000,000 will spent on the preliminary work which will take a year'. He also hoped to oversee the construction of a 150-mile canal from Lake Victoria to Lake George. 'About forty of my old

Commandos are with me in the firm,'* Stirling told the reporter. 'The country in which they will operate is full of wild animals. Part of it is malarial, part scourged with the tsetse fly.'[3]

Another ambition was the construction of a railway between Kenya and Tanganyika, and for this project Bill enlisted David to scout some locations for a base. David suggested Salisbury, where he had set up home in the upmarket suburb of Highlands. It was an elegant house with a large garden and a swimming pool.

Nonetheless David was determined to step out from his brother's shadow and in 1949 he became involved in a scheme to conduct a comprehensive survey of the Upper Kalahari Lakes, and the Linyanti, Okavango, Chobe and Upper Zambesi river systems. An organisation was formed of representatives of Northern and Southern Rhodesia and the Union of South Africa to achieve this aim. Among the members was Roy Welensky, head of the Northern Rhodesian Labour Party, who wished for a union with Southern Rhodesia for greater economic prosperity, and Maj Gen Sir Francis de Guingand, Montgomery's former Chief of Staff, and an old boy of Ampleforth. On 4 January 1950 the *Scotsman* ran an article about the organisation, the Central Rhodesian Development Scheme, including a press release written by David Stirling in which he outlined their vision of 'powered irrigation', why it was important, and what it would cost to conduct an inter-territorial survey: £160,000 maximum though this 'could be further reduced if it were decided to invite Colonial Development Fund to contribute'.

It was his association with some of the members of the organisation – especially Welensky, who was subsequently described by *Time* magazine as the 'white supremacist Prime Minister of the Rhodesias and Nyasaland'[4] – that inspired Stirling to form the Capricorn Africa Society (CAS) in 1949 along with Neil Wilson, a Southern Rhodesian parliamentarian and journalist. Their objective was nebulous from the

* This was one of many examples of Bill Stirling's largesse. He also offered Pat Hore-Ruthven's widow, Pamela, a house on the Keir estate in which to live with her children, but she declined.

start. Stirling said he had 'sounded out the opinions of many men from Governors to native chiefs in the Rhodesias, Kenya and Tanganyika',[5] and his dream was to lead southern Africa into a brave new world where white and black coexisted in blissful harmony. Yet in October 1950 Wilson had written an article for *New Rhodesia* magazine that stated that native Africans would be accepted as equals only if they 'obtained' a standard of civilisation acceptable to Europeans.

This was similar in tone to a letter sent to the Right Honourable Oliver Lyttelton, MP, the newly appointed Secretary of State for the Colonies following the victory of Winston Churchill's Conservative Party in the general election of October 1951. The correspondent was Raymond Byrne, who described himself as 'one of forty to fifty Old Etonians settled in Southern Rhodesia'.[6] Lyttelton had been educated at Eton and Trinity College, Cambridge, and Byrne wanted to express his delight at the return to power of the Tories after six years of socialist governance. He also wished to state, on behalf of the Capricorn Africa Society, of which he was a member, that he was sure Lyttelton shared their desire to ensure that the British Colonies in Africa survived as a 'bastion of Western Civilisation'[7] in the face of growing African nationalism and the rise in Egypt of communism.

Wilson and Stirling soon fell out and Stirling led CAS into the new decade. Unfortunately he failed to take the people with him on his transformative journey.

On the eve of CAS's Salisbury Declaration in July 1952, that there would arise 'a single self-governing Federation under the British Crown wherein all men shall live side by side in concord, sufficiency and freedom', the *Daily Express* reported that in Rhodesia there was 'between 60 and 80 per cent opposition to federation among the white population and an almost total opposition among Africans'.[8] Stirling had proposed a referendum on federation but, confronted with this overwhelming resistance, that objective was put on hold, and in fact the declaration was delayed until December.

The prime mover in the postponement was the British government. On 10 June, Hugh Parry, a colonial administrator in Southern Rhodesia, sent a memo to J. E. Marnham, Assistant Secretary of State, British Colonial Office, in which he complained that 'that wild man Stirling is proving most obstinate about not publishing his panacea for East and Central African ailments'.[9] It wasn't the first time that the Colonial Office had impugned Stirling's character: 'unreliable' and 'wildly indiscreet' had also been deployed in earlier correspondence that year.

In July Lord Salisbury, the Leader of the House of Lords, described Stirling's Declaration as 'a real danger' and pressure was brought to bear on CAS to postpone its promulgation because it was feared it would 'do a great deal of harm to the cause of Central African Federation, particularly if it took place in the context of a "Settlers'" convention in Salisbury'.[10] Stirling agreed to redraft the Declaration and publish it at the end of the year without any signatories.

To coincide with the declaration, Stirling outlined his objectives in an interview with the *Daily Herald* on 8 December: namely, to merge six British territories: North and South Rhodesia, Nyasaland, Kenya, Uganda and Tanganyika, a two-thousand-mile chain stretching from the Equator to the Tropic of Capricorn, from Ethiopia to South Africa, in which lived a quarter of a million whites, two hundred thousand Asians and twenty-five million Africans, speaking 170 different languages. The Capricorn Declarations proposed the establishment of African 'Crown States' which in time would form units in the federation governed by Africans.

There were sceptics, among them the *Daily Worker.* The socialist newspaper suspected Stirling's self-governing federation was simply an attempt to maintain the empire beneath the veneer of greater autonomy for Africa. As evidence they pointed to Stirling's idea for the creation of 'Open Areas', where the land would be controlled by Europeans and standards of European civilisation would be maintained.

On 12 December 1952 the *Western Mail* ran a piece on CAS based on an interview with the 'Phantom Major', the first time that moniker had been used since the war. 'Colonel Stirling is not going to be pleased with me about this reference,' said the paper. 'In fact, he would much prefer to be known as plain "Mr. Stirling", for he believes that his project is more important than himself. But we think it is right to say who he is because we are so often told that Elizabethans do not exist today … [but] it is appropriate that in the new Elizabethan Age an essentially Elizabethan figure should come forward with what is one of the most ambitious Empire-building projects of the 20th century.'

In describing CAS as an 'Empire-building project', the *Western Mail* appeared to confirm the suspicion that Stirling did not have the Africans' best interests at heart. The paper added that the project would create a 'vast new British nation of 25,500,000 people covering an area in Africa rather less than half the size of the United States'.

The Times's correspondent visited Northern Rhodesia to investigate how CAS had been received by the Africans. Poorly, he reported on 7 February 1953, and there was much cynicism. Why? 'Fear that they will be deprived of their land; fear that the Southern Rhodesian attitude on Native government will reduce the power of the chiefs; and fear of the Southern Rhodesian attitude to race relations, particularly as manifested in the pass laws. The chief of the Bemba tribe, Chitimukulu, pledged his allegiance to the anti-Federationist African Congress.' This congress, added the reporter, which was closely aligned with the African mine-workers' union, was well organised and 'a remarkable feature [was] the cooperation of the traditional authorities, the chiefs and the now educated class'.

The educated wing of the African Congress had started to exploit the superstition of some tribes. 'The old banyana, or vampire, scare is also recurring, and in some quarters it is held that Colonel David Stirling's Capricorn Africa Society are banyana,' said the *Times* correspondent.

To counter this criticism CAS opened six branches across southern Africa and employed an African agent on a handsome salary with orders to diminish the influence of the African Congress.

Stirling was also arousing the hostility of white Africans, particularly the business community in Salisbury, who were worried he was involving himself in matters he didn't fully understand and 'might enflame settler hostility'.[11]

Among those who had an astringent view of Stirling was Sir Edward Twining, the Governor of Tanganyika for much of the 1950s. Erika Johnston, who farmed on the northern face of Mount Kilimanjaro, recalled that Twining 'went out of his way to avoid David though his door was always open to David's eldest brother, Bill, who was more concerned with economic development in Tanganyika'.[12] Johnston, of Swedish stock, drew an interesting comparison between the Stirling brothers in her 1971 memoir, *The Other Side of Kilimanjaro*. David, she wrote, was a 'tall, dark, gaunt soft-spoken Highlander … who had no scruples about beating on anyone's door [on behalf of CAS]'.[13]

In contrast, Bill, who had bought a farm at Ol Molog, a few miles north of Kilimanjaro, one of several parcels of land he owned in Tangayika, was described thus: 'This tall, heavily-built man was a stimulating addition to Ol Molog on his brief visits. He is always surrounded by an air of mystery, big-time business deals, and a restlessness which is disconcerting for he is always on the move … if we thought David could not keep his seat out of an aeroplane, we found him a novice compared with his brother.'

David Stirling continued to beat on doors and chase prospective donors, but the responsibility began to take a physical and emotional toll, as it had in the autumn of 1942 when he struggled to cope with the pressure of commanding 1SAS. Now, as then, he was confined to his bed for several weeks. Once recovered, Stirling began to change his position. In 1954 he published CAS's manifesto, in which he declared himself no longer in favour of African federation. *Truth*, a British periodical, described it as 'a very curious ideological somersault ... in view of Stirling's about face on the federation issue it is difficult to see what useful purpose his ambitious venture can possibly serve now. There are far too many organizations treading on each other's heels in British Africa today.'[14]

Truth questioned Stirling's claim that his society 'has the unqualified support of many church leaders of all denominations in Africa'. It listed some of them and wondered if they agreed that CAS, 'deprived of its main plank, can usefully go forward on a programme of vague spiritual uplift, emotion and undefined ideals of "human relations"'.

There was a wave of resignations in the wake of the manifesto, including that of J. G. M. Bernard, a former secretary of South Africa's United Party, who accused Stirling of attempting to cultivate a 'small elite at the expense of the raw uncivilised Bantu'.[15]

In a desperate attempt to keep alive his dream, Stirling made frequent trips to the USA and London in search of investment, drawing on old acquaintances and appealing to their conscience to put their hand in their pocket. Among those who pledged their support were Dudley Clarke, Sir John Slessor and Daniel Ranfurly. In America he struck up a friendship with the influential financier Bernard Baruch, who had been a confidant of Woodrow Wilson and Franklin Roosevelt, and counted Winston Churchill among his close friends. It was probably the Prime Minister who made the introduction to Baruch on Stirling's behalf.

There was one man, however, who never fell prey to David's persuasive powers.

On 22 December 1954 Bill Stirling convened a meeting of Capricorn's London Committee and learned that David had run up debts of £3200 (approximately £85,000 today), although he believed the sum was likely to be considerably higher. Consequently, Bill cabled his brother and scolded him for not being wholly truthful about his overdraft position. Warning David that the future of Capricorn was at stake, Bill reminded him that his financial contribution was dependent on him raising the balance of £8000. If he didn't, then the position would be 'very serious'.[16]

Bill was himself under pressure because of his business interests and also his sponsorship of his siblings' various projects. Peter had left the diplomatic service in 1949 to go into business with Bill, and he was now in Iran establishing an oil drilling business. To raise funds Bill had started to sell some of Keir's art collection, amassed by his grandfather a century earlier. In 1953 the Victoria and Albert Museum bought five paintings by William Blake, and Bill was also looking for a buyer for El Greco's *The Dream of Philip II*. After protracted negotiations it was bought by the National Gallery for £55,000 (approximately £1.4 million today).

Such were his commitments that Bill regretfully resigned as North Lanark's Unionist candidate for the 1955 general election.

Despite his impecuniosity, David Stirling still had some powerful and influential friends in Rhodesia. None carried more cachet than Laurens van der Post. They had met for the first time in the winter of 1952–3 and for once it was Stirling who was bewitched, describing how van der Post's 'enthusiasm and knowledge of the African people propped up our morale'.[17]

Like Stirling, van der Post was one of many siblings (thirteen in his case) born to an elderly and distant father and an assertive mother. As a result both exhibited a lifelong penchant for invention and inflation. It's not hard to understand why van der Post was receptive to Stirling. One of his many concoctions was that during the war 'he served in early Commandos and Special Forces'.[18] He had in fact enlisted in the Military Police before joining the Intelligence Corps.

Van der Post became CAS's spiritual advisor, and with Stirling made two tours of the six territories.

In one hostile venue, van der Post faced down the crowd with a compelling speech, which Stirling described as 'courageous ...

so typical of Laurens'.[19] In return, van der Post dedicated *The Dark Eye in Africa*, published in 1955, to Stirling, and described him in characteristically florid and imprecise prose: 'He … formed the long range Desert Reconnaissance Group, and became one of the most formidable thorns in the Germans' flesh,' wrote van der Post. 'He was captured by them much later in the war during a raid which suddenly descended from out of the Sahara Desert, hundreds of miles behind the front lines.'

Van der Post also stated that he and Stirling had both pondered 'deeply about the problems of Africa' while prisoners of war, the fruit of their thoughts being the Capricorn Society (van der Post in later years described himself as a co-founder).[20] There is no evidence that either man gave Africa much consideration during their years as POWs.

They also appeared on the wireless together, in May 1956, each giving a talk on the 'lure of the desert'.[21]

What Stirling (and many others) didn't know was that Laurens van der Post was a fantasist. He was also a control freak, a bully and a sexual deviant, who around the time he befriended Stirling seduced and impregnated the fourteen-year-old daughter of a friend who had been entrusted to his care during a sea voyage. What he wasn't, however, was homosexual, despite the fact many of his friends were; this led to speculation, which prompted van der Post at the end of his life to 'leave a memorandum attesting that he himself had never been homosexual'.[22]

Stirling's desire to meet van der Post stemmed from his reading of *Venture to the Interior*, his 1952 bestselling account of his travels in Nyasaland. But swathes of the book were either made up, deliberately vague or exaggerated; his war record, for example, and how he came to be captured by the Japanese, and the mystery surrounding his sudden promotion from captain to lieutenant-colonel. Van der Post also liked to boast of his associations with, among others, Lord Louis Mountbatten, Carl Jung and D. H. Lawrence, even if in most cases

bove) Bill Fraser, photographed in France in 944, was a superb special forces officer who ever received from David Stirling the credit e deserved for his contribution to the SAS. *lex Prochiantz)*

ight) The loss of Jock Lewes in December 941 was a huge blow for David Stirling, een here in the desert, and left him isolated. o compensate he began to surround imself in 1942 with an upper-class clique of uestionable competency. *(Courtesy of John Kane)*

ohnny Wiseman (far right), and next to him Malcolm Pleydell, behind the lines with Blair Mayne's Squadron in December 1942. The pair were great admirers of the Irishman. *(Courtesy of John Wiseman)*

Randolph Churchill, seen here on the day he married Pamela Digby in 1939, was invited to join th
SAS by Stirling in April 1942. He was not a success. *(TopFoto)*

Some of the soldiers from Fallschirmjaeger z.b.v 250, shortly after they had captured Stirling as he slept unguarded in a wadi on 24 January 1943. His jeep is visible on the right. *(Jonathan Pittaway)*

AS officers await an inspection from Crown Prince Olaf in Norway, 28 July 1945. Right to left: ılex Muirhead, Blair Mayne, Harry Poat and Brian Franks. Mike Calvert is ninth from the right. Mayne refused to wear the maroon beret, introduced in 1944, preferring the sand-coloured beret of North Africa days. *(Trinity Mirror/Mirrorpix/Alamy Stock Photo)*

Blair Mayne instructs some of his men on the technicalities of scrummaging during an informal rugby match at Darvel, Scotland, home of 1SAS in the spring of 1944. *(Courtesy of John Kane)*

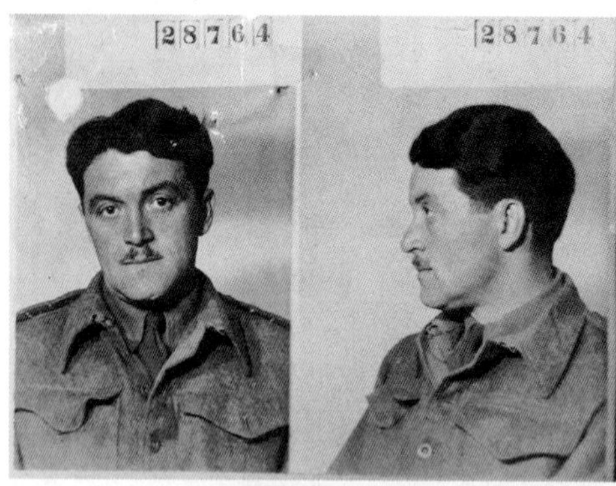

The German informant Gerald van Zouco, photographed shortly after his arrest in 1945, was one of the several imposters who fooled David Stirling during the war. *(The National Archives)*

(above) Taken in the garden of the British Embassy during Churchill's visit to Cairo in 1942, this photo shows the prime minister and his confidants: Tedder, Brooke, Harwood and Casey at the back, and Smuts, Auchinleck and Wavell in front. But no David Stirling. *(Photo by Express/Getty Images)*

(left) David Stirling and Hermione Ranfurly at Mirabelle's restaurant in Mayfair in May 1945. The photo, taken by the famous society snapper A.V. Swaebe, appeared in *Tatler*. *(© Barry Swaebe Archive)*

When David Stirling returned to the UK in
1945 he came under the command of Brigadier
Mike Calvert, seen here consoling the widow
of a fallen French SAS officer. It was not a
satisfactory arrangement for Stirling.

(Courtesy of John Wiseman)

David Stirling's house in the affluent Highlands suburb of Salisbury, Rhodesia. During this period he had little to do with the SAS or LRDG, channelling his efforts instead into the Capricorn Africa Society. *(Jonathan Pittaway)*

avid Stirling and
vo delegates at the
alima Conference in
956. Organised by the
apricorn Africa Society,
ne multi-racial convention
eceived much publicity
ut suffered when the
eynote speaker, Laurens
an der Post, failed to turn
p. *(Jonathan Pittaway)*

(above) David Stirling in his Mayfair office in August 1974, shortly after his role in GB75 had been exposed. Some tabloids labelled Stirling a 'Colonel Blimp' but he denied his organisation was a 'private army', although he admitted his concern about the influence of the far left. *(Keystone Press/Alamy Stock Photo)*

(left) Sir Fitzroy Maclean in the presence of Prince Charles in 1978. Maclean served for a brief period in the SAS and played a large in mythologising David Stirling post-war. *(PA Images/Alamy Stock Photo)*

'avid Stirling, in the car, Mike Calvert (bowler hat) and the Very Reverend Fraser McLuskey at memorial service in France in 1989. Stirling was generous in his support of Calvert after his fall om grace. *(Terry Fincher Photo Int/Alamy Stock Photo)*

'lair Mayne's statue was inaugurated in his native Newtownards in 1997, in the presence of four of is former comrades. Left to right: Jim Almonds, Jimmy Storie, Reg Seekings and Johnny Cooper. *Courtesy of Jimmy Storie)*

David Stirling's statue was unveiled in 2002 on the Hill of Row near the ancestral home at Keir. *(Be Cleuch/Alamy Stock Photo)*

David and his youngest sister, Irene, chose not to be buried with the rest of the family in Lecropt Old Churchyard, in the grounds of Keir, but instead they were laid to rest a hundred miles north in Beoraid Cemetery in Morar. *(© Leighton Thomas)*

they were grossly exaggerated. Stirling was taken in and believed his friendship with van der Post would open doors.

Not even van der Post's influence, however, could save CAS from its slow death. The fundamental problem was Stirling himself. Roy Welensky mocked him for 'head-in-the-clouds' approach, and many found his ideas risible.[23] Stirling's visceral opposition to the idea of African nationalism also led some to drift away.

Above all, however, it was his prickly character that caused an 'allergic' reaction among many who supported greater freedom for Africans but did not consider Stirling to be the right man to achieve that aim. He was headstrong, bombastic and conceited, and he could not help taking 'delight in antagonising local white opinion'.

In a debate with the far-right activist A. K. Chesterton, of the League of Empire Loyalists, he interrupted his opponent with a yell of 'fascist!', causing an outcry among the audience.* In his closing argument, Chesterton – who won the debate by 278 votes to 191 – belittled what he called Stirling's slander. 'People who descend to those tactics haven't got an answer to your argument.'

In June 1956 Stirling organised the first multi-racial convention of CAS members at Salima, on the western shore of Lake Nyasa, in a self-contained village dubbed 'Capricorntown'. The keynote speaker was van der Post, but he didn't turn up.†

Another notable absentee was Lt-Col Sir Stewart Gore-Browne, DSO, who since 1935 had been on the Northern Rhodesia's legislative council. Though he could be paternalistic in his attitude to

* The debate took place in Salisbury in July 1957 and the motion – put forward by the League of Empire Loyalists – that the ideas or the Capricorn Africa Society, if adopted, would mean the ruination of British Africa. A. K. Chesterton and Leslie Greene spoke on behalf of a League of Empire Loyalists; Col David Stirling and Leopold Takawira represented the Capricorn Africa Society. The League of Empire Loyalists carried the motion 278 to 191. A recording of this fascinating encounter is housed in the British Library sound archive entitled 'In Defence of the British Empire!'

† Despite van der Post's no show at Salima, he and Stirling remained good friends and, after the latter's death in 1990, van der Post described his life as 'noble, complex and significant'.

the black population he had far more faith in their ability to govern themselves than Stirling. He had resisted Stirling's overtures to align himself with CAS because he believed it was an 'attempt to forge an alliance between responsive whites and "the right kind" of blacks … a common front composed of superior figures of both colours'. He also 'distrusted Stirling's authoritarian personality' and the charade of a committee that ratified the decisions he alone took.[24]

Although Gore-Browne didn't attend the conference in Salima, a friend from Kenya called Clarence Buxton was among the two hundred attendees and reported that 'usually the "Fuhrer", as David was nicknamed, could be seen giving someone a caning for some ill-judged amendments during the day's debates or a brain-wash about future policy and activities, but all interspersed with the amazing personal touch which has drawn so many diverse men and women to him'.[25]

Time magazine also sent a reporter to the conference, which was chaired by 'David Stirling, 40, a hard-driving bachelor who led a commando unit in daring raids against Rommel behind German lines in the western desert'.[26]

The reporter was unconvinced by what it saw, including Stirling, who 'strolled about, arguing, urging, explaining'. 'Blacks have criticized the Capricorn Society because they feel that its multiple vote is merely a device to preserve white supremacy,' they continued. 'Whites who think Capricorn's sponsors are dilettantes out of touch with reality bitterly refer to it as the "Leprechaun Africa Society".'

Not all Africans were critical of CAS. One, Lawrence Vambe, believed that Stirling's vision of the sharing of economic and political power between white and black people 'made a lot of sense … but Stirling's ideas did not take root, because the majority of Europeans did not wish to face the truth'.[27]

The *Time* report put CAS's membership at five thousand, some way short of the twenty thousand that Stirling predicted by 1957; in fact, membership dropped to 2566 a few months after the conference. By June that year Stirling was tired, emotional and disillusioned, conscious that CAS was in its death throes. Matters came to a head during a meeting with J. C. Morgan, the chief secretary at the office of the High Commissioner in Salisbury. Morgan told Stirling that if CAS continued to oppose Federation it 'would be embarrassing to Government'. The chief secretary recorded what happened next in a memo to the Colonial Office: 'Col. Stirling then became rather hot under the collar (he is known to be somewhat excitable) and nearly walked out! I calmed him down … Stirling then apologised for his display of temper and we proceed [*sic*] on an even keel.' Morgan reported that they parted amicably, 'but I must confess, having regard to Col. Stirling's excitability, that I have some doubts as to whether he will not let his enthusiasm run away with him with possible embarrassing results for us'.[28] One young liberal Briton who was sceptical of Stirling's movement was John Reed, a student at the University College of Rhodesia and Nyasaland, and a committed supporter of African nationalism. 'It is impossible to appraise whether Capricorn is … a good or bad thing because the whole thing is so utterly unrealistic,' he wrote in his diary on 23 May 1957. 'It is obvious the Africans are not behind Capricorn … Capricorn offers the Africans nothing – it merely asks them to be good.'[29]

Another who left was Peter Mackay, a former Scottish soldier who had helped organise the Salima conference. He resigned a few weeks later because in his view CAS had become paternalistic, 'a well-meaning but inevitably implausible instrument for political improvement in the colony'.

David Stirling had taken a shine to Peter Mackay, who was uncomfortable in his presence, telling his mother in a letter that Stirling's subsequent pursuit of him in 1958 was a 'stalk'.[30] Specifically, Stirling wanted Mackay to be bursar of the Capricorn Society's College of Citizenship, Ranche House, in Salisbury. 'Although flattering to the ego, [it] has its irritant value also,' Mackay wrote. 'Yesterday Stirling told me that I had said NO so firmly that he felt I was at least halfway to accepting the job.'

On this occasion Stirling failed to get his man and Mackay launched an anti-federation magazine.

30

The timing of Paddy Mayne's death could not have been better for David Stirling. The Capricorn Africa Society was clearly not going to change the world in the way he had envisaged on its formation in 1949.

By early 1956 Laurens van der Post understood that the project was doomed because African nations were now finding their voice. When this realisation dawned on Stirling, wrote van der Post in his 1982 autobiography *Yet Being Someone Other*, he became 'dangerously infected with defeat for the first time in his life'. Stirling needed to forge a new identity once more. Now he saw an opportunity. Mayne was dead, Jock Lewes was dead and Bill Fraser was disgraced, reduced to the ranks of the Gordon Highlanders in 1946 for drunkenness and then drummed out of the army. A similar fate had befallen another potential obstacle, Mike Calvert, convicted in 1952 of gross indecency with a sixteen-year-old German youth.*

In the decade since the end of the war there had been several books about Britain's private armies, none particularly flattering to David Stirling. The first had been published in 1945 by Bill Kennedy Shaw, erstwhile intelligence officer of the LRDG. He named the book after his unit and was complimentary about the SAS although he never

* Stirling never shunned Calvert, unlike many military men, despite his fall from grace.

once referenced the Phantom Major and rectified a mistake – probably the fault of Randolph Churchill – in the Ministry of Information's pamphlet 'The Eighth Army', which claimed Stirling had commanded the LRDG. 'This is incorrect,' wrote Kennedy Shaw. 'Stirling was never in the LRDG. These raids were the work of his men (SAS troops, not commandos) who were carried to the scene of action by an LRDG patrol.'[1]

A year later Malcolm Pleydell published *Born of the Desert* under the nom de plume Malcolm James, an account of his seven months in L Detachment, in which the reader was left in no doubt that Paddy Mayne was the spiritual leader of the unit and not the fragile, unhealthy David Stirling.

Two years after *Born of the Desert*, Roy Farran produced *Winged Dagger*, which had as its hero Bill Stirling, who was 'with his brother David the pioneer of the SAS idea'.

Vladimir Peniakoff was next in print, in March 1950, with a memoir about Popski's Private Army in which he was effusive about the LRDG and sceptical about the 'prancing' David Stirling. 'I see this book as immeasurably the best personal account of war in the Middle East, North Africa and Italy yet written,' opined *Tatler*. 'There has been nothing like it and (unless David Stirling of the SAS or Prendergast of the LRDG comes forward) it is unlikely that it will be equalled in the future.'

Lt-Col Guy Prendergast had no intention of publishing his war memoirs. But *Tatler* had given Stirling an idea. In May 1950 he contacted his old friend from SAS days, Vivian Street, and suggested he might like to write a history of the regiment. Street then approached Maj L. E. O. (Pat) Hart, a wartime member of the SAS who was second-in-command of 21SAS in 1950. He thought such a book would be wonderful and in a letter to Brian Franks on 26 May 1950 wrote, 'I suggest Ian Collins is the obvious chap to print the book … I imagine that Bill Stirling, Paddy Mayne etc. would have no objection.'[2] Franks endorsed the project, and in the next issue of the SAS Regimental Newsletter Hart placed a notice asking for veterans' recollections. In October Hart wrote again to Street informing him that the response to the notice had been disappointing, except for a contribution from David Stirling. He had submitted a lengthy memorandum entitled 'The Origins of the Special Air Service' that he had written two years earlier at the prompting of Roderick McLeod, then Assistant Commandant at the Camberley Staff College.

Hart replied to Stirling on 12 October, writing: 'I hope you will not mind my having copies made of your memorandum on the SAS as, of course, it is tremendously interesting to us and I should very much like your permission to use it in connection with the various papers which I am continually having to write about the Regiment.' In the next paragraph, Hart told Stirling that he had recently seen his brother Bill. 'It is of course tremendously useful to me to get views of the real experts as often as I can,' he wrote. 'Apart from the pleasure of doing so, I hope it will prevent me talking too much nonsense.'[3] Within a few weeks, however, Street had abandoned the project. He had left the Staff College in the summer for an appointment at the Ministry of Defence and, what with the war in Korea, he no longer had time to write a book.

Hart wrote to Franks on 1 December to break the news and propose three options: get someone else within the regiment to write the book, approach Hilary Saunders, who the previous year had published a history of the Commandos, *The Green Beret*, or 'drop it for the moment'.[4] Hart preferred the latter course of action.

But David Stirling didn't. He contacted another of his former officers, Carol Mather, who sent a two-page letter along with a possible outline to a number of L Detachment officers. 'The book has David's blessing and he will write the introductory chapter and possibly one other,' explained Mather, adding that the Hon Mrs Stirling had agreed to act as editor for the time being. Her son's vision for the book was:

Chapter 1: Genesis – David Stirling
Chapter 2: Early trips with the LRDG – Paddy Mayne
Chapter 3: Crete – George Jellicoe
Chapter 4: The Benghazi Weekends – David Stirling or Gordon Alston
Chapter 5: The Fuka Landing Grounds – Carol Mather*
Chapter 6: Benghazi Revisited – Carol Mather
Chapter 7: Autumn at Howard Cairn – Sandy Scratchley
Chapter 8: The Movement West – Gordon Alston
Chapter 9: Link Up – French [SAS] or Mike Sadler.

The working title was 'Rendezvous' and the instruction to the contributors was that it should be 'written spontaneously with emotions' so as not to be 'too conventional and colourless' like Kennedy Shaw's book on the LRDG.[5]

The idea came to naught for reasons undisclosed. One suspects that Paddy Mayne would not have been enthusiastic, recognising straight away that it was simply an exercise in self-promotion by Stirling with the help of his friends. Without Mayne's involvement the book had no credibility.

So Stirling decided to go it alone. He wrote a war memoir and sent it to the publisher John Murray in the autumn of 1951. On returning to Africa Stirling asked his friend the Conservative MP Julian Amery to act as his agent in his absence. Amery wrote to John Murray on 31 October to enquire if he would publish Stirling's memoir. No, was the response, from Sir John Murray himself. 'I am so sorry that we could not feel the necessary confidence in its prospects to make an offer of publication, but we found it rather disappointing,' he wrote on 2 November. 'Colonel Stirling has tried many things, but always just

---

* Mather had already drafted several chapters of his wartime memoir, which was eventually published in 1997 under the title *When the Grass Stops Growing*.

before we get to exciting results he seems to switch on to something else, and this does not altogether satisfy the reader.'[6]

Stirling's memoir was evidently an accurate account of his wartime deeds. It had to be. He dared not embellish or fabricate the facts for fear of Paddy Mayne's reaction. But Mayne's death in 1955 removed that anxiety. Now Stirling could be as extravagant with his prose, and the truth, as he wished.

Stirling had given his story to journalists before, quite apart from Randolph Churchill in 1942. On his return to Britain from captivity in 1945 he had collaborated with Allan Michie – whom he had first met in Cairo – on a book entitled *Honour for All*, a collection of stirring wartime stories. Chapter Two, 'Phantoms of the Desert', concerned the SAS and there were several incidences of Stirling tampering with facts he felt confident couldn't be contradicted by Paddy Mayne. Readers were told that during a visit to Cairo Winston Churchill had met Stirling and 'offered him a higher command if he would return to Britain, and pass along his experience but Stirling … pleaded to be allowed to remain with his men, among whom a rare feeling of comradeship had developed'.[7]

Stirling said that he had opposed an increase in L Detachment's size, telling GHQ, 'Just give me five good men and I'll guarantee to get in anywhere, regardless of how many sentries the enemy has.'

He claimed he had escaped from captivity in Austria when he 'successfully jumped from the train near Innsbruck'. He and Jack Pringle had slipped out of an unlocked wagon door when the train was stationary at Innsbruck. Stirling also took credit for the design of the SAS badge, the flaming sword of Excalibur, when in fact it was the idea of Bob Tait.

A more recent encounter with a journalist had occurred at White's in the spring of 1954, when Stirling dined with the foreign editor of the *Daily Express*, Charles Foley. He was researching a book, *Commando Extraordinary*, about the German commando leader Otto Skorzeny. They discussed France's recent defeat at the Battle of Dien Bien Phu in Vietnam, and Stirling outlined why he believed the communist threat was now so grave that the War Office should establish a 'directorship of strategic assault personnel'. In addition to some trenchant views on this subject, he also discussed the war years. 'I have been assured,' wrote Foley, 'that Stirling, when war came, was so unwarlike that the outbreak found him thousands of miles from home, riding down the Rocky Mountains on horseback.' That was true. What wasn't was Stirling's assertion that he left 'his German prison camp in time to lead the [SAS] brigade on what would have been their biggest operation … to have loosened Japan's hold on her empire by severing all communications between China and Malaya'.[8]

Perhaps Stirling might have asked Foley to write his biography had he not in 1955 moved to Cyprus to become editor of the *Cyprus Times*; more likely, however, Stirling knew from the start the right author for the job: the glamorous and talented American Virginia Cowles.

Described by the *Illustrated London News* as 'an ardent globetrotter', Cowles was a veteran war correspondent who had covered the civil war in Spain and the Second World War, during the course of which she met both Bill and David Stirling in North Africa. Cowles was a prolific author. She was a close friend of the Churchill family and her 1953 biography of Winston, *The Era and the Man*, might also have influenced Stirling in his choice of biographer. In its review of the book, the *Sphere* said: 'This biography is shapely, lively and often provocative. Miss Cowles writes with partiality, it is true, but she has succeeded in giving a very clear rendering of a pro-Churchill view of Churchill.' On receiving his complimentary copy, Churchill sent a letter of gratitude to Cowles.

Cowles's next book was *Edward VII and His Circle*, which appeared in 1956. Evidently, she went straight from that project into writing

Stirling's memoir, which was published two years later. There would have been little time for in-depth research, but of course Stirling's unpublished autobiography would have provided her with much information. He informed Cowles that he 'did not keep detailed records' of L Detachment operations, but he could provide her with several 'eye-witness accounts'.[9]

His own, obviously, and also those of Sandy Scratchley, Gordon Alston, Stephen Hastings, Vivian Street, Fitzroy Maclean, Peter Oldfield, Carol Mather, Johnny Cooper, David Lloyd Owen, David Sutherland, Pat Riley, Alastair Timpson, Reg Seekings, Bob Lilley, Bob Bennett and Michel Sadler.

In other words, it was Stirling's gang; no big brother or Bill Fraser or Bob Tait or Charles Bonington, and certainly no Malcolm Pleydell, *persona non grata* after the publication of *Born of the Desert*.

Surprisingly, there was no contribution from George Jellicoe. Admittedly, he was working for the Foreign Service in Baghdad in the mid-1950s, although he returned frequently to London for meetings. Had he and Stirling fallen out? Cowles was generous in describing his character, except for a sly aside that his courage came from the amphetamine Benzedrine, 'which he took liberally', and forced some upon Georges Bergé when they raided Crete in June 1942. Benzedrine was taken by the British army towards the end of the war in North Africa; it was Montgomery who popularised its use when he was appointed commander of the Eighth Army in August 1942. Brian Dillon recalled that Benzedrine was issued during the Benghazi raid the following month. Stirling was in command of this operation and Jellicoe was not involved as he was recovering from an operation on his knee.

There was an additional noteworthy paragraph in Cowles's acknowledgments:

'It may be interesting to the reader to know that many of the private reports were written not long after the war ended, at Colonel

Stirling's request, for his own files. Others were written to give me the necessary information in compiling this book.'

As for the title, that was obvious.

The Phantom Major was published on 5 May 1958. It was a book that Britain needed, a timely boost for morale, as well as a tonic for Stirling, who that March had looked 'far from well', according to Evelyn Waugh.[10]

The previous eighteen months had shaken the nation's confidence. The Suez Crisis had been a political disaster and a military humiliation. Britain now answered to the United States as the sun set on its empire; India declared independence in 1947, Sudan in 1956, Malaya and Ghana in 1957. More countries were lining up to wave goodbye to their colonial master.

Britain wanted a hero, a reminder of its glorious past, and Virginia Cowles offered them David Stirling. Prior to the book's release, the publishers ran a publicity campaign in the national and regional press. 'One of the great personal adventure stories of the war,' ran the blurb. 'The daring exploits of David Stirling and the SAS, who operated continuously behind the German lines. Churchill, quoting Byron, called him the "mildest mannered man who ever scuttled a ship or cut a throat".'

When the articles about the Phantom Major first appeared in 1942, that Byron line had been attributed to Jan Smuts, the South African prime minister. No matter: it captured the essence of David Stirling.*

The reviews were ecstatic. *The Phantom Major,* gushed the *Sphere,* 'is the story of David Stirling's war told with tremendous spirit by Miss Virginia Cowles. Her book is more exciting than any fictional work of adventure and a splendid record of a man who added a new and permanent regiment to the British Army'.

* The Byron comparison did come from Churchill, in a letter to his wife from Cairo dated 9 August 1942. See page 391.

The *Daily Express* hailed Stirling as the man 'who mucked up enemy troops in the Western Desert and so shortened the war for us'.

The *Birmingham Post* said Stirling was 'a genius' and wondered 'how many Stirlings could even a British Army hope to discover?'

Very few, according to Brig Bernard Fergusson, who had enjoyed a distinguished war fighting with Orde Wingate's Chindits. His family knew the Stirlings socially – his father was the 7th Baronet of Kilkerran – and Fergusson couldn't speak highly enough of the book or the subject in a review for a Singapore newspaper. Plus, he confided to his readers, 'I have also heard [Stirling] described by a former FBI agent as being the "perfect killer: without fear, pity or remorse"; but only the first and third attributes are true.'[11]

The reviewer in *Tatler* said that 'Miss Cowles's book fills me with enthusiasm, not least because her picture of the alarming hero has depth and is not merely the conventional eccentric Englishman at war being incredibly brave and recklessly original'.

The *Belfast Telegraph* said the book 'abounds with anecdotes of almost incredibly audacious sabotage', which, the paper respectfully pointed out, were also the work of 'the late R. Blair Mayne'.

The *Long Eaton Advertiser* described Stirling 'as heroic, original, fiercely individual, humorous and highly effective. He deserves to be a myth.' Furthermore, '*The Phantom Major* can be read as an exciting story of adventure in war but unlike most such stories it has a chance of being read and believed fifty years hence.'

There were one or two curmudgeons among the reviewers. The *Western Mail* was critical of the book's abrupt conclusion after the capture of Stirling in January 1943. 'Here the book ends, and that is its principal fault; it is never sure whether it is a history of the SAS or a biography of David Stirling. As a result it is unsatisfactory as either.'

It was *The Times*, however, that displayed most courage in confronting *The Phantom Major*. It was, it admitted, 'an inspiring adventure story, told with competence by an accomplished journalist, though containing some minor inaccuracies'. It also scoffed at the idea, propounded by the author and the subject, that Stirling was an outsider like T. E. Lawrence and Orde Wingate. No, said *The Times*, 'Stirling belongs to the Establishment'. Another gripe was that the book centred too much on the Phantom Major and Cowles had failed to 'reproduce the tang of the sharply individualistic characters that went to form the SAS'.

The *Times Literary Supplement* headlined its review 'Pimpernel of the Desert' and enjoyed the daredevil narrative but wondered if a purist might not 'accuse Miss Cowles of "writing up" her subject for the sake of the narrative'. The *TLS* reviewed *The Phantom Major* alongside another recently published war memoir, *G Patrol* by Stirling's old friend Michael Crichton-Stuart, formerly of the LRDG. The book's title was as prosaic as the prose, said the reviewer, although to the student of military history, Crichton-Stuart's memoir was 'incomparably more valuable' than *The Phantom Major*. 'Though the LRDG never fired the public imagination in the same way as other private armies that came into being in the last war, it was in fact the forerunner of all of them.'

The journal of the Royal United Services Institution agreed, describing *The Phantom Major* as 'a companion piece to *G Patrol* since, after his initial failure by parachute, Major Stirling abandoned the air and relied on wheels and the LRDG to transport his small raiding parties'.[12]

Someone who read the *TLS* review was the eminent military historian Basil Liddell Hart. He was an original and unorthodox theorist when it came to waging war, a man who saw how mobile mechanised warfare would revolutionise the next conflict before anyone else in Britain. An acquaintance of the Rommel family, Liddell Hart edited *The Rommel Papers* in 1953, a collection of the dead general's notes and letters.

Liddell Hart should have appreciated an 'innovator' like David Stirling, but he did not. Cutting out the *TLS* review for his file,

Liddell Hart underlined with a red pencil several words including 'absolutely authentic', and in the margin next to the sentence declaring that Stirling had 'revolutionised the whole conception of warfare' he put a large exclamation mark. What, he must have spluttered, was revolutionary about the Phantom Major? As Crichton-Stuart had written in *G Patrol*, after the calamitous first raid there were no more parachute operations, and the LRDG taxied the SAS to their targets.

Liddell Hart continued his red-pencilled analysis of *The Phantom Major* when it was serialised in four editions of the *Sunday Times*. Stirling, said the paper, was the 'bugbear' of Rommel, who had mentioned him 'frequently' in his diary; '2' annotated Liddell Hart in the margin, referring to the actual number of times the general had referenced Stirling, erroneously believing him to be the commander of the LRDG. Also flagged as dubious was the story of how Stirling had obtained approval for the raising of L Detachment.[13]

David Stirling had but one objective when he first met Virginia Cowles to discuss his biography: to diminish Paddy Mayne and glorify himself. In Cowles, an American obsessed with British high society, he had a toady with a gift for purple prose. Her pen sketched a portrait of Stirling which, to veterans of L Detachment, reminded them of a certain Irishman. 'Stirling became a legend to the men who served him,' wrote Cowles. 'There was no trap from which he could not fight his way, no occasion on which he could not outwit the enemy … a blackbearded giant with inexhaustible energy … the dark, shrewd eyes shone with a cold determination.'

This set the tone for what followed. The Phantom Major was fearless, swashbuckling, audacious and irreverent, a man admired by prime ministers, cherished by generals and feared by his enemies.

It was a Hollywood fantasy in which the truth was sacrificed for titillation. The only way Stirling could pitch his idea for a parachute unit to Gen Auchinleck, wrote Cowles, was to break into GHQ. In *The Phantom Major* he spotted a gap in the perimeter fence and squeezed through; in the version he gave to Charles Foley for *Commando Extraordinary*, he hoisted himself over the fence. Neither was true. Bill had handed the memo to Gen Smith.

Also fictitious was Stirling's assertion that he had flunked university because of the time he spent gambling at Newmarket; his three terms at Cambridge had not coincided with the course's racing calendar.

It was then, wrote Cowles, that the young Stirling had a dream: to become the first man to climb Mount Everest. It would require five years of training; as part of his preparation he went to the USA in the winter of 1938–9 to hone his climbing skills. This revelation must have been a surprise to his mother, who had arranged for David to spend a year ranching. Another inaccuracy she probably noted was the description of David as standing 6ft 6in, when in fact, as he recorded in filling out the immigration form at New York in 1938, he was 6ft 4½in. But by adding an inch and a half David surpassed the 6ft 5in Bill. Such minor details mattered to him.

Paddy Mayne was introduced to readers while under 'close detention' for knocking an officer unconscious. He wasn't. As Stirling had told Charles Foley a year or so earlier, Mayne had been 'rescued from an infantry base'[14] in Egypt as he waited to hear if he might be posted to the Far East. Throughout the book Mayne was depicted as a wild, monosyllabic, truculent, barely controllable Irishman. In describing the hours before the inaugural raid in November 1941, Cowles quoted Mayne saying that the operation must go ahead regardless of the deteriorating weather, because 'if I don't get a crack at the enemy soon I may have to indulge in a few practice rounds with some of the chaps at Headquarters'.

Indeed the only man with the power to bring him to heel was the Phantom Major, who was 'some years younger than Mayne'. He was ten months Mayne's junior.

Also vindictively belittled was the LRDG, dismissed as 'a reconnaissance and a ferry service ... not supposed to take part in raids', and in particular their commander Prendergast (Cowles didn't even mention his Christian name). Without his support in the winter of 1941–2, L Detachment could not have survived. But Prendergast had made no secret of his disdain for Stirling's leadership and so his vital role in resuscitating L Detachment was reduced to a single sentence in which Cowles described him as an 'able' officer and the second-in-command of LRDG. In fact, Prendergast assumed command of the unit from Ralph Bagnold in the summer of 1941, before the formation of L Detachment.

Another sloppy error was the spelling of Jock Lewes's surname as 'Lewis', while Bill Fraser was credited as having taken part in the inaugural parachute operation, when he had been with the LRDG at one of the two rendezvouses.

Stirling's blunders – such as his shouting in the middle of a minefield at Sirte and his failure to post sentries prior to his capture – were omitted, as was the deterioration of his health; the death of the journalist Arthur Merton was blamed on the careless driving of the convoy with no mention of Stirling's excessive and reckless speed; it wasn't Mayne who spotted the potential of the jeep but Stirling, 'who immediately recognised it as the ideal vehicle'; there was no reference to Douglas Berneville-Claye or Theodore Schurch, but there was of a series of high-ranking officers, all enraptured by the Phantom Major. None more so than Brig John Marriott, commander of the 22nd Guards Brigade, who was portrayed as a confidant of Stirling's throughout L Detachment's existence. Not long after the publication of *The Phantom Major*, Marriott wrote his own war memoir but there was no mention of David Stirling.

Similarly, Bernard Montgomery didn't find space to talk about Stirling or the SAS in his memoir, published in 1958, although the impression conveyed in *The Phantom Major* is that he was a great admirer after being won over by Stirling's boldness. In reality Montgomery regarded Stirling as impertinent.

Stirling once again denied Bob Tait the credit for designing the SAS insignia. But Tait was mentioned in Cowles's description of the first raid in November 1941. In this account, Tait and Stirling split from the rest of the party and valiantly trekked for miles to make a reconnaissance of enemy positions. Stirling subsequently reported this intelligence in person to Gen Cunningham, claiming that for half an hour he watched the road from the escarpment and saw no armour but some supply trucks.

Not only had Cunningham been removed from command by the time Stirling had returned from the operation, but Bob Tait's version of events was markedly different in the report he wrote just a few days later.

Tait said that as he and Stirling climbed the high ground 'a terrific electric storm broke with hail and rain [and] we were unable to see more than a few yards in front and within fifteen minutes the whole area was under water … [we] abandoned the attempt and we turned away and marched south'.[15]

The Phantom Major was as much fiction as fact and, even by Cowles's standards, so oleaginous as to border on the absurd. She saved her best to last, describing Stirling in the epilogue as a 'well-established legend' and declaring that his 'admirers found it highly amusing that he should end the war with a DSO and nothing else'.

Bill Stirling must have found much of *The Phantom Major* amusing. The man portrayed bore little resemblance to the brother he had known and nurtured through the war. He must also have struggled to recognise himself. Bill had four entries in the index. He had been depreciated by David and his crucial role in establishing the SAS all but erased from the regiment's history.

There was nothing about the pivotal part he had played in establishing at Inverailort what was essentially the first special forces training school, where David had undergone instruction before his appointment as his brother's adjutant.

Readers were informed that Bill Stirling was an officer in the Scots Guards. No mention of Operation Knife, the Yak Mission or working for the Chief of Staff Lt-Gen Arthur Smith. But how could there be? Because David's daring break-in to GHQ to push his memo into the hands of Lt-Gen Neil Ritchie was far more entertaining than the reality: that Bill gave the memo to Smith, who gave it to Ritchie, his deputy, who read it and three days later summoned David to GHQ for a meeting.

Also fallacious was David's account of 2SAS. He made out that it was formed by Bill in the autumn of 1942. That was the reason he had risked the drive through Tunisia, to link up to the First Army, 'to consult my brother ... who had recently arrived on the First Army front with the 2nd SAS Regiment'.[16]

Bill was in Britain in January 1943, commanding the 1st SSRF; 2SAS was officially formed on 13 May 1943.

Bill made no comment about *The Phantom Major*, publicly, or, it's believed, even privately to his brother. He was a secure man, equable and content, and one who appreciated his good fortune. He had a beautiful wife and four healthy children. He had suffered grief, the loss of a brother and the death in infancy of two children, in 1943 and 1952, but he accepted their deaths as part of life. One suffered, one celebrated, one carried on; 'gang forward', to quote the family motto.

In contrast, David was still the problem child, insecure and unfulfilled and unhappy. After the failure of the Capricorn Society he had become aimless and dejected, but the publication of *The Phantom Major* had resurrected his wartime alter ego. Bill was happy to play along with the charade if it gave his brother meaning to his life.

There was a further reason why Bill stood aside in the retelling of the SAS history: primogeniture. As the first born he had inherited land, titles and status. His siblings had had to make their own way. Bill was generous in his financial support of his siblings, but nonetheless they had grown up in his shadow. Peter Stirling good-naturedly formed the Younger Brothers' Society with Richard Stanley, the younger brother of 18th Earl of Derby, and once a year they dined out at the most expensive restaurant they could find, beginning the meal with grace: 'For what they have and what we ought to have had may the Lord make them truly thankful'. The meal was charged to their brothers' accounts.[17]

Peter had Bill's character, but David was a narcissist, resentful of his lowly position in the Stirling family, the 'notorious sulker', as he was known in his youth.[18] So Bill bequeathed him the glory of the SAS.

31

The Phantom Major sold well and, more importantly, restored David Stirling's reputation. After a decade and a half of self-imposed exile in southern Africa, he returned to Britain to exploit the success of the book. He had left Rhodesia on business after the Salima conference in the summer of 1956, the business being to secure a publishing deal and to introduce Virginia Cowles to the people who could vouch for his brilliance. He had promised the Capricorn Society he would return, and he did, briefly, but in September 1958 he left for good, owing, as a Colonial Office memo noted, to ill health.*

Stirling had boasted that by the end of 1957 Capricorn would have twenty thousand members but by the start of 1960 it had just 123, forty-nine of them black. A visiting official from London described the society as 'moribund',[1] and yet it limped on for five more years thanks to the dedication of a few hardy souls. There was one success from all the dreams laid out by Stirling: Ranche House College, a multi-racial 'college of citizenship' that he had proposed in 1958.

---

* Stirling claimed in his biography he remained active in CAS until 1962, but his entry in *Who's Who* stated it was 1959. The historian Ian Hancock dated his departure to 1958 in *White Liberal Moderates and Radicals in Rhodesia*. In November of that year Evelyn Waugh wrote a letter to Daphne, Lady Acton, in which he expressed his dismay in learning from Stirling his intention 'to introduce Television into Rhodesia'.

It was launched in Salisbury two years later and offered students of all races a technical and literary education, much to the displeasure of the Rhodesian right wing.

Had Stirling been less hubristic in his governance of Capricorn Africa Society he might have achieved much more to promote racial cohesion in southern Africa; as it was the college was a modest achievement for a society that a decade earlier had promised such a grandiose vision.

Back in Britain, Stirling was in demand, his name a byword for courage and daring. He was invited to compile an entry for inclusion in *Who's Who*, an honour that had never been accorded his eldest brother.

The Second World War general Sir Richard Gale referenced him in a series of articles that he wrote for a newspaper in the autumn of 1958, called 'Bible Battles'. As Stirling had raided the Nazis, he wrote, so Jonathan attacked the Philistines.

On 16 March 1959 the celebrated gossip columnist of the *Daily Express*, William Hickey, reported that Stirling had 'spent the weekend in a small private house party with the Queen'.

The house in Devon belonged to Denys Rhodes and his wife Margaret, who was a cousin of the Queen. 'This is the first time I have spent a weekend in a party with the Queen,' Stirling told the *Express* before pre-lunch cocktails on the Sunday. 'Although I have met her before.'*

Stirling was by then something of a television celebrity. The previous month he had been the subject of the first episode of a new BBC series hosted by Sir Brian Horrocks entitled *Men of Action*. He described Stirling and his men as 'eighteenth-century pirates', who were 'the toughest body of men on operations in the Middle East'.

---

* At the Coronation in 1953, Stirling had been one of four hundred Gold Staff Officers, ushering the eight thousand guests to their seats. In his biography he said he was a 'Gold Stick Officer'. Perhaps he was confused; Gold Stick in Waiting was a far more important role and was performed by Maj Gen Howard-Vyse.

The *Daily Mirror* approved: 'Using an amazing model of jeeps and blazing aircraft, Sir Brian showed how Stirling got his reputation as "The Phantom Major". The last war is old stuff now – but underneath Sir Brian's enthusiasm is the implication that there's plenty of guts and courage in the nation yet – if put to the test.'

The Special Air Service had been tested for much of the 1950s, first in Malaya and since the autumn of 1958 in the Arabian Peninsula, supporting the Sultan of Oman Sayid bin Taimur, a reactionary despot, as he was challenged by three rebel leaders who had the support of Saudi Arabia. The rebels had established a stronghold at the top of the Jebel Akhdar, the Green Mountain. In January 1959 D Squadron arrived to help clear the jebel of insurgents, and among the officers was Johnny Cooper, still with the regiment eighteen years after he had taken part in the inaugural L Detachment raid. A less experienced officer was Peter de la Billière, who had joined the SAS three years earlier, 'entranced by David Stirling's visionary concept'.[2] The jebel was taken after a short but fierce fight which, said Cooper, proved that a small force could defeat the enemy and the terrain if they had the requisite determination.

In 1963 Johnny Cooper and Peter de la Billière were in action together once more, this time in the Yemen, and all thanks to David Stirling.[3]

The previous year de la Billière had been loaned to the Federal Regular Army in Aden, a British possession since 1839. The High Commissioner was Sir Charles Johnston, who twenty years earlier had worked with Peter Stirling at the Embassy in Cairo. One April day in 1963, David Stirling arrived at Government House and in the presence of Tony Boyle of the RAF, the High Commissioner's private secretary, discussed 'his idea for sending support to the royalist forces who were waging a guerrilla war of resistance against the [Egyptian-backed] republicans in the Yemen'. Stirling asked Boyle if he wouldn't mind assisting people as they came through Aden. It was, said de la Billière, the start of 'an extraordinary covert operation which lasted for five years', and had a profound impact on the politics of the Middle East.

The Phantom Major had returned, as arrogant and intemperate as ever. This time, however, it wasn't GHQ that was exasperated by his unruliness but the British government. Harold Macmillan, the Conservative Prime Minister, wished to support the Yemen's royalist forces but in an unofficial capacity so as not to upset Washington, concerned that British involvement would imperil the stability of Saudi Arabia. Neil 'Billy' Maclean, a Scottish Tory MP, had visited the Yemen and Aden on a fact-finding trip in March 1963 and upon his return reported to Julian Amery, the Minister for Aviation, David Stirling and Brian Franks (now involved with MI6) at White's. Asked to recommend a reliable figure to lead a mercenary operation to the Yemen, Franks suggested Col Jim Johnson, a commodities broker at Lloyd's who had recently retired from command of 21SAS.

They were soon introduced by Amery to the royalist foreign minister Ahmed al-Shami, who handed Franks, the managing director of the Hyde Park Hotel, a cheque for £5000 to fund the operation. Franks cashed the cheque and kept the money in one of the hotel's safety deposit boxes.

Johnson started to recruit mercenaries in Britain and France, all of whom spoke Arabic, and who were employed fictitiously by David Stirling's Television International Enterprises company, based in his office in Sloane Street. TIE had been established in 1961 and Stirling signed his first contract to supply educational television programmes to Kenya the following year. The company also provided Stirling with useful camouflage for his shadier activities.

The plan was to fly the mercenaries to Aden, then on to Beihan and smuggle them over the border into the Yemen, where they would blow up the Egyptian aircraft at Sana'a aerodrome and wage a guerrilla campaign.

That took Stirling to Aden in April 1963, to ensure his 'people' could pass through, and with that permission obtained he contacted Johnny Cooper – then second-in-command of the Muscat Regiment – and persuaded him to lead the sabotage operation. Cooper flew to London, met John Woodhouse, commanding officer of 22SAS, and secured the release of three soldiers – a mortar expert, a medic and a firearms expert – so they could take part. All were granted one month's leave by Woodhouse. (In his authorised biography, Stirling describes the three men as ex-SAS soldiers.)

On the eve of their planned departure the Profumo Affair broke, throwing the Tories into disarray. The Colonial Secretary, Duncan Sandys, phoned Stirling and told him to abort the operation for fear the party could be dragged into more controversy. Stirling procrastinated long enough for Cooper and his team to fly out of London. A couple of weeks later they were successfully inserted into the Yemen, where they killed scores of Egyptians in several engagements.

Later in 1963 Peter de la Billière was working as an undercover agent as part of the covert operation, receiving intelligence reports from Cooper, who had returned to the Yemen for a second time. In November Stirling visited and at last de la Billière met his hero. 'I found him extremely exhilarating,' he wrote. 'His personality was so strong that he had a magnetic effect on other people.' He enjoyed Stirling's company; the evenings were always entertaining as he held court with memories of the past and visions for the future. 'He put over his own ideas with such force that it was difficult to argue with him,' recalled de la Billière. 'Even if some of the ideas did not seem very sound, he had a knack of making them appear brilliant.'

Stirling told de la Billière that 'he had rather lost interest in the SAS' after the war but his involvement in the Yemen had 'rekindled his enthusiasm for irregular warfare'.

The covert involvement in the Yemen continued uninterrupted for six months, and so successful did Stirling consider it that in

February 1964 he wrote to Duncan Sandys with an idea to create in Kenya 'some form of Special Force with functions which are clearly outlined in the paper which I enclose'. The three-page document had been written with the input of John Woodhouse and Bob Laycock. Stirling sent it to Sandys on the eve of his visit to the country without informing Laycock. So he wrote to his old colonel: 'Although, as you will know, I do not give a damn about normal procedures, I would never allow this attitude, at any time, to lead to embarrassing you as Colonel Commandant of the SAS.'[4]

The Kenyan special force never materialised because in May 1964 the Egyptian newspaper *Al-Ahram* published a series of letters between Tony Boyle and Johnny Cooper, which included references to the latter's experience of 'demolition and small arms and the dropping of weapons by parachute'.[5] The *Sunday Times* reproduced the correspondence in July, although only after a tussle between the editor Denis Hamilton and the owner Roy Thomson, 1st Baron Thomson of Fleet, who had 'interests' in Stirling's Television International Enterprises. Other papers swooped on the story, among them the *Daily Express*, which ran the story under a 'Gun Running Storm' headline in its edition of 6 July, naming Boyle and Cooper, and describing Stirling as deeply involved.[6]

The scandal was raised in Parliament when the Labour MP Richard Marsh asked the Prime Minister, Alec Douglas-Home, to clarify Britain's role in the Yemen. Marsh mentioned the trafficking of arms by former British army officers and said he found it hard to believe that Stirling, Cooper and Boyle 'could, in an area as dangerous as this, engage in activities on this scale without anyone noticing'. To which Douglas-Home replied, 'I must take their word for it – and I do.'[7]

The revelations were deeply embarrassing to the government and to the SAS. As John Woodhouse said in an interview years later, the 'British public was not aware of the existence of the SAS … this lack of publicity over the SAS in the 50s and early 60s was a considerable military advantage'.[8] It allowed the regiment to operate anonymously, as they had with such effectiveness in the Jebel Akhdar in 1959; this was a benefit politically as well as militarily. But, thanks to Stirling, the SAS were caught in the harsh glare of a media spotlight in the summer of 1964.

Despite the adverse publicity Stirling and his mercenaries continued their involvement with the royalist forces, organising resupplies by air and land via Saudi Arabia. According to the MI6 historian Stephen Dorril, 'in order to ease his relations with the Saudi government, Stirling worked closely with Kemel Adham, the chief of the Saudi intelligence service and brother-in-law of Faisal, who was regarded as the King's *éminence grise.* Stirling also cooperated with the well-connected Jersey arms dealer Geoffrey Edwards, who was trying to clinch a multi-million-pound arms deal.'[9]

The Arab historian Said Aburish characterised the relationship thus: 'The Saudis' use of Stirling was nothing but an expression of need; they needed his services, they didn't have anybody with his expertise, they didn't have anybody of his stature ... to say that he was a mercenary is to sell him short. He was a mercenary and simultaneously he was an extension of British policy. He wasn't doing anything illegal, his government knew about it and approved.'[10]

Nonetheless Stirling did on occasion embarrass the government with his high-handed meddling. On 3 March 1966 the front page of the *Daily Mirror* screamed '"Royal Snub" row may kill arms deal'; the ensuing story detailed how a £100,000 deal hung by a thread after Princess Margaret and her husband, the Earl of Snowdon, had taken over the whole of the first-class section of a flight to Hong Kong. In itself nothing out of the ordinary, said the paper, except it meant that the Emir Sultan, brother of King Faisal of Saudi Arabia, and the man who had signed the arms deal, 'was bundled into an economy seat at the back' leaving his entourage 'stunned and angered', particularly when there was no invitation to meet Her Royal Highness.

The story, which was taken up by the *Daily Express* and the *Financial Times* (as well as several foreign papers), caused panic within the Foreign Office, and embarrassment for the British and Saudi royals. The Saudi Embassy in London issued a statement in which they rejected the *Mirror*'s story:

> His Royal Highness knew before the flight began that he was going to have a second-class seat in the aeroplane. He knew that the first-class part was fully booked. When his booking was made, he agreed to take a second-class seat because he could not put off his journey. He was not aware at the time that Princess Margaret would be travelling in the aircraft and did not learn of this until he was on his way to the airport.

Princess Margaret asked officials to tell the Sultan that she had no idea he was on the flight, but had she, she would have been 'delighted to meet him'.

The Saudi Embassy had told the truth in its statement: the Sultan had indeed changed his seat at the last moment and accepted a second-class seat accordingly. Neither he, nor the Foreign Office, were aware that Princess Margaret was now on the same flight.

The Foreign Office then tracked down the source of the story. A cable from London to Jedda revealed that, at the airport, 'Colonel David Stirling (perhaps prompted by Geoffrey Edwards) complained to BOAC demanding a letter of apology from their Chairman to the Sultan because of their failure to find a first-class seat'. When no such letter was forthcoming, a petulant Stirling 'let the Press have the story'.[11]

The hoo-ha didn't damage Stirling's standing with the Saudis. In 2007 the *Guardian* ran a series of investigative reports into British arms deals with the Saudis in the 1960s and 1970s. The first major deal was concluded in 1967 – the year Stirling set up Watchguard International, the world's first private security company – and involved the sale of forty-two Lightning fighter planes plus an AEI radar contract. Foreign Office papers reveal that Stirling was involved in the deal; so too was his business partner Geoffrey Edwards, who according to the *Guardian*'s investigation 'pocketed £2 million of the commissions as his own reward'.[12] Stirling's reward was a Saudi contract to run a radio station in Aden.

The singles chart of 1966 was an illustration of how the tectonic plates of British culture were shifting. Frank Sinatra, Val Doonican and Petula Clark were selling a lot of records but music of a different kind was starting to dominate the music scene: louder, brasher, bolder. The Rolling Stones had two hit songs in 1966: 'Paint It, Black', about the grief and depression of losing a partner, and 'Have You Seen Your Mother, Baby, Standing in the Shadow?', a title that might have resonated with David Stirling.

The 'Swinging Sixties' has become a cliché but nevertheless it was a decade in which deference for the upper classes began to be usurped by disdain. One of the early casualties was Harold Macmillan. A Victorian, educated at Eton and Oxford, a decorated veteran of the First World War, the son-in-law of the 9th Duke of Devonshire, Macmillan was in 1963 prime minister of a country that had little in common with the one into which he had been born in 1894. Mocked by the acidic young satirists in programmes such as *That Was The Week That Was*, Macmillan's premiership was dealt a fatal blow by the resignation of John Profumo, his Secretary of State for War.

Previous generations of politicians, such as David Lloyd George, had been able to lead private lives that were far removed from the image they projected to the public without fear of being exposed. No longer. Newspapers lasciviously reported the sex lives of the Establishment and for the first time the public understood that while they had more money than them, the great and the good had fewer morals.

* * *

It was a shock for David Stirling when he found himself in the firing line of the iconoclasts. For his entire life he had more or less done as he'd pleased, and to hell with the consequences. But on 17 September 1967 the *Sunday Times* colour supplement published a long article by the thriller writer Len Deighton entitled 'The Private Armies'. It was a chapter from a recently published book, *Alamein and the Desert War*, which was a collection of essays written by historians and veterans of the North African campaign. Deighton contributed two chapters, one of which was 'The Private Armies', describing to readers some of the activities of the LRDG, the SAS and Popski's Private Army. 'The LRDG threw bombs into car parks, shot up tented camps and roared down main roads with headlights on and guns blazing, but these activities were extracurricular,' he wrote. 'These bearded brigands with their improvised equipment and informal discipline probably had the highest IQ of any unit in the army. They well knew their most important function was the constant collection of intelligence.' Deighton described some of L Detachment's failures, but without the bravado of *The Phantom Major.* After the first raid, he wrote, 'the SAS gave up the idea of parachuting to war and became in effect a raiding force of the LRDG, sharing their bases and using the LRDG as a "taxi-service" for raids'.

Once Stirling had finished reading Deighton's article he called his lawyer. In a subsequent letter to Bob Laycock, which he copied to Brian Franks, George Jellicoe, Sandy Scratchley and Anthony Head, Stirling explained why he had launched a libel action against the *Sunday Times* and Sphere Books Ltd, Deighton's publisher. It concerned what Deighton had written about the Benghazi raid of September 1942, when the SAS was ambushed on the road into the port. Stirling reproduced the offending sentence:

'For weeks rumours of it had been going around the Cairo bars. Stirling himself had insisted upon talking about the raid during two social gatherings at the British Embassy in Cairo although warned not to do so.'[13]

Stirling told Laycock that the two social gatherings were in fact 'dinner parties on two consecutive nights at the Embassy to meet the Prime Minister (W.S.C)'. He listed the other guests, including Gen Smuts, Alan Brooke and Alexander, and then explained that his purpose in attending was to enlighten Churchill about 'what the SAS was doing'. Stirling continued: 'The phrase "insisted on talking ... although warned not to do so" refers to a particularly idiotic staff officer in GHQ who had the temerity when he heard I was going to meet the PM to say that I must not talk to him about the Tobruk and Benghazi raids because to do so would be a security risk.'

Stirling told Laycock that clearly the author 'had it in' for the SAS and he WAS taking legal action to protect the good name of the regiment, particularly those men who had participated in the Benghazi raid.

Stirling also reproduced for Laycock's benefit a letter he had just received:

> Dear David
> I have recently read an article in the Sunday Times. As one who played a very small part in the Benghazi Raid, I can only say that if you were so irresponsible as is suggested, you and the men you selected, trained and led, would have not earned the place they hold, not only in British, but also German military history.
> Yours sincerely
> Joseph Slattery
> (Late Capt. 1st SAS Regiment)

There was no Capt Slattery in the SAS. Stirling might have received a letter sent by a fantasist, but more likely he invented Capt Slattery to underline his point to Laycock.*

* I have the nominal rolls for 1SAS from 1942 to 1945 and a Capt Slattery does not appear on any. The SAS Regimental Association archivist has no record of such a name. Nor does a Slattery appear in the list of officers credited in *The Phantom Major* as having participated in the Benghazi raid of September 1942.

Stirling listed other grievances with Deighton's article, including his reference to the recruitment of commando officers in the bar of White's and the implication that the SAS were 'in effect a raiding force of the LRDG'. This, he claimed, 'is entirely untrue'.

He explained that he had launched his legal action not just for the honour of the SAS, but because 'the article has already done a great deal of damage to my commercial activities ... and this slander, which suggests that I am a loose-tongued chatterbox, disastrously damages the prospects I have of gaining contracts'.

Stirling concluded by saying that his counsel's opinion 'is that I shall succeed in getting substantial damages for the slanderous references to me in the article'.

Stirling also wrote to Brig George Davy, who in 1942 had been the Director of Military Operations at GHQ during the planning of the Benghazi raid. Unlike Laycock, who was firmly on Stirling's side, Davy was more objective in his reply and said he was not in a position to advise how far to take the matter. On the subject of 'leakage of information', however, he told Stirling: 'I heard afterwards of cases of leakage being attributed to soldiers of SAS. But I never knew of the Embassy VIP dinners until you told me this week and I read VC's [Virginia Cowles's] book.'

In fact, Laycock harboured doubts about the wisdom of Stirling taking the case to court, telling Davy in a letter dated 22 November 1967 that 'there is always the possibility of his having to fork out a tidy sum if he loses'.

Privately, Stirling knew that it was a gamble. In the witness box, would he be prepared to lie about twice dining with the Prime Minister at the British Embassy in Cairo? Would he have confirmed under oath that he discussed the Benghazi raid with Churchill while strolling across the Embassy garden? And if the *Sunday Times* called as witnesses, say, Claude Auchinleck, Harold Alexander, Charles Wilson, Ian Jacob and Richard Casey, what might they say about Stirling's presence at the Embassy dinners?

But Stirling had no choice. He had recently launched Watchguard International, and the depiction of him in the *Sunday Times* as indiscreet would be detrimental to his business.

In the end, Stirling's self-confidence won the day. His bluff elicited an out-of-court settlement of £7000 and a grovelling apology in the *Sunday Times*, which included:

> We have been informed by Colonel Stirling and fully accept the following position. In fact, Colonel Stirling was invited by the British Ambassador at Cairo to attend two dinners on successive evenings in honour of Winston Churchill; that the other guests at those dinners were of the very highest rank and importance and included – as they were then – Field Marshal Smuts, General Sir Alan Brooke, General Sir Claude Auchinleck and General Alexander; and that the only occasion that Colonel Stirling discussed the raid was after dinner on the first evening when Winston Churchill called him into the garden where they had a private discussion about the SAS and about the forthcoming raid on Benghazi.

Despite the victory, Stirling continued to protest his innocence – a little too much. On 22 May 1968 he wrote a statement for publication in *Mars and Minerva*, the regimental journal of the SAS. It was an undignified whine, and not completely rooted in reality. 'Those early SAS operations were painstakingly planned and executed,' he wrote. Some were – the ones involving Mayne and Fraser – but many of Stirling's raids, such his excursion to Benghazi harbour with Randolph Churchill and Fitzroy Maclean, were more redolent of a French farce than a special forces operation.

Stirling excoriated Len Deighton with words that to a few readers of the statement would have been deeply ironic: 'In his article to which I object the author allowed his imaginative mind to rove without any inhibition of being obliged by his own conscience or by terms of reference.'

That Stirling could write such a sentence revealed the depth of his shamelessness. Not only had he fabricated much of what he told Virginia Cowles but in the years since his deceit had metastasised.

The French soldiers, for example, who arrived at L Detachment in January 1942 from Syria; in *The Phantom Major* he said only that he 'finally got permission for these men to join'. When Stirling was invited to address a French marine parachute regiment in Bayonne in the 1960s he had a far more colourful recollection of the incident. Gen de Gaulle had categorically refused to countenance the idea of releasing the men to serve in the British army, Stirling told his audience. 'I ignored this advice and proceeded, as fast as possible, to a location where this formidable man, Charles de Gaulle, would only be for a few hours.'[14]

The French general asked Stirling his business and he explained the purpose of his visit.

'No, positively not … goodbye sir,' snapped de Gaulle.

'"Hell," I said under my breath, but so that he could just hear me. "He is as pigheaded as those bloody English at MEHQ."'

At which moment, said Stirling, 'a tiny grin transformed his expression and he commented, "Well, it appears as though you are not English."'

'Wholly not, mon general,' retorted Stirling. 'I am Scottish and was brought up in the tradition of the Auld Alliance.'

So charmed was de Gaulle by Stirling's audacity that they sat down 'and began what turned out to be a series of very exacting and precise questions. It took only half an hour for my proposal to be agreed.'

It was a lively tale, and a pack of lies. De Gaulle never met Stirling; he wasn't even in the Middle East in the winter of 1941–2.*

---

* In an essay of 1974, published in the *Ampleforth Journal* as part of Stirling's obituary in 1990, Stirling repeated this claim, stating: 'I well remember going to Beirut to see General Charles de Gaulle to get his consent for the Free French to join the SAS. Before granting it, he asked many searching questions about our unit's role and about our operational methods.'

The reality was that Stirling the narcissist was increasingly living in a fantasy world. He was a habitué of London's most exclusive casinos, clubs and restaurants. He liked to gamble at John Aspinall's Clermont Club with other members of the British aristocracy. 'He was quiet, but menacing in a quiet sort of way,' said Aspinall of Stirling. 'With David you always knew he had strangled forty-one men and therefore it gave the man an aura. One wondered how many throats he had slit.'[15]

None. And as for strangling forty-one men, who had told Aspinall that? Probably the Phantom Major, one of the most lethal men in Britain. In his own mind. When Sir Iain Moncreiffe wrote the introduction to Lord Lovat's memoir, *March Past*, in 1978, he claimed that Lovat and David Stirling had been categorised by Adolf Hitler as 'dangerous terrorists' and at his 'personal directive' a reward of 100,000 marks had been offered for their capture. Once in captivity they were to be 'exterminated'.

That obviously didn't happen to Stirling. Perhaps Hitler had found him too charming.

Stirling added to his own lustre with anecdotes of his indomitability, such as the evening in 1954 when he and Dr Michael Wood, chairman of the Kenya Branch of the Capricorn Africa Society, were attacked by two men as they left a dinner party in Nairobi. The middle-aged pair not only fought off their assailants but killed them in self-defence. Wood never endorsed this story, and at the time that the incident was alleged to have occurred he was in England on a Marks Plastic Surgery Fellowship with Sir Archibald McIndoe.

Then there was the occasion in London when Stirling, in his sixty-fifth year, gave a hiding to a pair of would-be muggers as he strolled across Green Park one May evening in 1980; by an extraordinary coincidence it was the same evening that the SAS stormed the Iranian Embassy.

In his statement to *Mars and Minerva* in 1968, Stirling lamented the decline of respect in modern Britain, embodied in a media 'which now appear too often hell bent on eroding away the remaining vestiges of our country's basic moral discipline and principles by snide mockery of traditional institutions and the people honourably serving them'.

Stirling's hypocrisy was as breathtaking as his mendacity. He had spent a decade dishonouring the name of the regiment he helped found in 1941. The Special Air Service had once fought Nazis and Italian fascists, but when Stirling returned to Britain he immersed it in grubby mercenary operations in the Middle East, creating political tensions in a region that at the time was a proxy cold war.

In 1970 Stirling was at the centre of more intrigue. With the backing of rich Libyan exiles, he concocted a plan to overthrow President Muammar Gaddafi, who the previous year had staged a successful *coup d'état* against King Idris, a friend of the West.

In May 1970 Stirling began to plan a mercenary operation to depose Gaddafi, a scheme that had the covert support of MI6 and the CIA. The Americans soon withdrew, having concluded that Gaddafi was as hostile to the Soviets as he was to the West, and therefore in their view an acceptable if disagreeable leader. Britain turned instead to France and recruited a number of mercenaries with the tacit approval of Paris.

Throughout the summer of 1970 a team of mercenaries was assembled, one of whom was Peter McAleese, who had served two spells with 22SAS in the 1960s before leaving the army in 1969 to work in the oil industry in his native Scotland. McAleese received a telegram from a former sergeant-major in 22SAS offering him some work. He was told to report to a flat in Montpelier Street, Knightsbridge, where there were about twenty other young men, 'and lo and behold David Stirling was there … and the next thing he opens this case, one of these ones with a combination lock, and out comes this envelope and "bit of expenses for you chaps".'[16]

Each of the envelopes contained £200 – just the hors d'oeuvre. McAleese had been told he would receive £5000 (£60,000 in today's valuation) once the 'work' was completed. But the plot fell apart. For three years it was hushed up, until the *Observer* revealed its details on 13 May 1973 in a front-page splash that included photographs of Stirling and Keir House.

The original intention had been a clandestine seaborne landing on the Libyan coast from Malta, and then an assault on a Tripoli prison, known as the 'Hilton', to release 150 political prisoners who would foment revolution.

The men recruited had been 'predominantly ex-SAS', reported the *Observer*, and when they were assembled at Stirling's 'command post' in Knightsbridge, 'a special morale-boosting briefing was given by Colonel Stirling in the handsome drawing room of the flat opposite Harrods'. The plan 'came within a hair's breadth of upsetting the balance of power in the Mediterranean and the Arab world'. The operation was scheduled initially for November 1970 but had been postponed (and revised) to early 1971 after warnings from America not to proceed. The utmost discretion was now required. But Stirling 'was telling all and sundry at White's about the progress of the operation'.[17]

MI6 expressed their disquiet at the lax security, as did Mossad, the Israeli intelligence service, and eventually on 29 December 1970 Stirling was ordered to cancel the mission. He ignored the instruction, however, and went ahead with the operation but someone – probably MI6 – tipped off the Italians and in March 1971 the mercenaries' assault craft was seized by the Italian authorities as it was about to leave Trieste.

The 1970s was not a propitious decade for David Stirling. Shortly before he began to plan his Libya coup, he suffered a serious car crash in Scotland as he drove home to Keir after attending the wedding of his niece, Lady Elizabeth Ramsay, the elder daughter of his sister Margaret, the Countess Dalhousie, at Brechin Castle. He was taken to Stirling Royal Infirmary, where he remained for more than a month recovering from a punctured lung and several broken ribs.

His fortunes, his reputation, declined in parallel with the country's, which was beset by economic turmoil for much of the decade. But it was a time of strife and conflict and unrest around the world, the backwash from the 'Swinging Sixties' when it was all supposedly peace and love. A new generation had a voice and they were demanding greater justice, economically and socially. There was a coup in Chile, a regime change in Cambodia and a desperate humiliation for the Americans in Vietnam. Irish terrorists exploded bombs in London, Palestinian ones executed Israeli athletes in Munich and far-left extremists kidnapped and murdered their opponents in Italy. There was an oil crisis in the Middle East and a revolution in Iran.

When the Honourable Margaret Stirling died in August 1973 she took her leave of a world utterly unrecognisable from the one she had known as a young woman. She had once been a celebrity; her evening gowns described in fawning detail in newspapers and the movements of her family chronicled in *Tatler.* She had thrown balls, hosted garden parties and danced with Europe's aristocracy. But there were new celebrities now: football players, racing drivers and pop singers.

'A lady of outstanding personality in her work for charity, the Hon Mrs Margaret Stirling of Keir, OBE, died at Moral Mailing Inverness-shire on Saturday aged 92,' reported the *Strathearn Herald* on 11 August. 'She was the widow of Brigadier-General Archibald Stirling of Keir, Dunblane, who died in 1931 and a daughter of Lord Lovat.'

The *Herald* was the newspaper that, in 1918, had described her husband as a 'pervert' and 'papist' on account of his religion.

An anonymous tribute was published in *The Times* on 14 August: 'She was keenly interested both in farming and the estates of Keir and in local administration, while the breadth of her interests made her the kind of reader whom serious authors and publishers most hope for, always eager to buy good new books as well as to lend them, and to borrow (and return),' it said of Mrs Stirling. 'Immensely warm-hearted and sociable, alive to the arts … she carried her public work lightly with zest and a great sense of fun. She was a stayer.'

The death of his mother left Stirling conflicted. Relief, on the one hand. Summoned by Bill to Scotland in her final days, David was petrified at the thought of the encounter. He stopped at a pub for a drink, for a drop of Dutch courage but also, he confessed, in the hope that if he dawdled she might die before he arrived. She didn't. Stirling loved his mother dearly but he never earned her respect, and right up to the end 'she was always asking what I was going to do with my life'.[18]

Nonetheless, he grieved for his mother, a woman of virtue and nobility, who as a widow dedicated her life to charitable works and raising money for those less fortunate than herself. He had inherited one trait from his mother, a social conservatism, and when he looked at what Britain had become in the 1970s he mourned not just her passing but the death of what he considered his country's greatness.

Something had to be done, and it was, by Gen Sir Walter Walker, who began to tour the country warning that socialists were only months away from seizing control of Britain. He gained a growing support base, among whom were members of Unison, established in 1973 by George Kennedy Young, former deputy director of MI6. He saw his organisation as a new SOE, ready to wage a clandestine war in the event of a communist takeover of Britain. Young's imagination was as fertile as Stirling's and claims that he had the support of many prominent politicians, businessmen and police chiefs were not taken too seriously.

In 1974 Walker launched Civil Assistance, in order, he told reporters initially, to step in 'if there was a collapse of law and order',[19] a concern that had grown following the election victory of Harold Wilson's Labour Party in March that year. But as his membership grew so Walker became more pugnacious. He refused to rule out a military coup during an interview with the *London Evening News*. 'Perhaps the country might choose rule by the gun in preference to anarchy,' he said, adding: 'I think it is the duty of all of us who care about Britain [to] try to waken the country from this awful sleeping sickness.'

Stirling shared Walker's concerns. In an interview with *The Times* on 29 July he explained that he had written a discussion paper about the maintenance of vital services in the event of a general strike. 'There are many people in Britain now who think some kind of crunch is coming,' he said. 'The exchange of ideas and of papers about what to do if it takes place is happening all the time, but the main problems that people wanting to take action have come across are the legal difficulties. Moving into installations owned by the Government is a very delicate business, and that is one reason for the secrecy surrounding those people who have already made positive plans.'

Stirling concealed from *The Times* that he had plans of his own to deal with what he viewed as the pernicious spread of socialism within Britain. On 31 July he wrote to Lord Hailsham, who had resigned as Lord Chancellor earlier that year. He sought an audience. Why exactly, he didn't elaborate, but he believed His Lordship would offer wise counsel. 'If there is to be an effective challenge to the left-wing Union extremists, it is surely of the gravest importance that this should be mounted by the centre and not the right-wing extremists,' wrote Stirling. He also complained of intrusive newspaper coverage, and accused *The Times* of misquoting him in an attempt to 'distort' his 'sound undertakings'.[20]

But a few days later a small journal called *Peace News* scooped Fleet Street with the revelation that Stirling was in fact head of an organisation called GB75, 'a private army' ready to implement the measures that he vaguely outlined to *The Times*.*[21]

Unlike Walker's group, which relied on public donations, GB75 was financed by businessmen, one of the most generous being Geoffrey

* *Peace News* won the 1975 Scoop of the Year award at the What the Papers Say dinner. According to Stirling, they were tipped off by the secretary of one of his associates, who had 'left-wing inclinations'.

Edwards, the arms dealer with whom Stirling had collaborated in Saudi Arabia nearly a decade earlier.

Stirling's plan was to have in place by November 1974 a regional network of volunteers trained for any eventuality, but the disclosure of his intentions caused uproar. Stirling's name was by then well known for its nefarious links to mercenary-led coups in African and Middle Eastern nations, and the left-wing politicians and newspapers seized on the news. Labour's Defence Secretary, Roy Mason, described Stirling's organisation as 'near-fascist'.

The *Birmingham Post* columnist Clive Wilson wrote that 'there is something rather pathetic about the sight of retired Army officers sallying forth, sabres rattling, waving Orders of the Day intended to save the country from a fate worse than World War III'.[22] Several newspapers derided Walker and Stirling as a pair of doddery 'Colonel Blimps'.

Much was made of the fact Stirling's office was in Mayfair, at 22 South Audley Street (it may just have been a coincidence that this could be abbreviated to 22 SAS) and there were insinuations he was aligned with the Conservative Party.

Stirling was not prepared for the furore that erupted in light of the revelations about GB75. Perhaps years of meddling in the politics of Middle Eastern and African countries had induced in him a complacency that he could tamper with British democracy as he saw fit, and without repercussions.

Intriguingly, at around this time Stirling was in communication with the notorious French far-right agitator Pierre Sergent, a veteran of the Indochina War, who, in 1961, had been a member of the vicious terrorist Secret Army Organization (OAS) that sought to overthrow President de Gaulle and continue a French presence in Algeria. (He would later become an MP in Jean-Marie Le Pen's National Front party.)

Stirling wrote a long essay which, he stated, was in response to 'Pierre Sergent's invitation to provide an analysis of our SAS philosophy and briefly to chronicle our operational performance'.[23]

Stirling rebutted Mason's accusations of neofascism, declaring: 'Our motivation is to reinforce parliamentary authority in the country whereas Mr Mason is associated with a political party, the left-wing of which can be genuinely stated to be thoroughly undemocratic.'

In an attempt to quell the rising indignation, Stirling gave a series of interviews in which he requested he be referred to as plain Mr Stirling and not Col Stirling. 'I was never a regular soldier and haven't been in the army at all for thirty bloody years,' he said.[24] To *The Times*, he described GB75 as an organisation of 'apprehensive patriots' with one or two paid executive officers.[25] There were no more than a few thousand members and he stressed that 'GB75 was not a private army and so far as he knew none of the members was a former SAS man'. It was, he said, an 'apolitical' organisation but one that was raised to counter the 'chaos' caused by left-wing activists.

At Stirling's request, the *Daily Express* sent its top correspondent, Chapman Pincher, to Mayfair, where he found 'a big craggy Scot with a face that beams with honesty [who] lit a large cigar with a Churchillian gesture'. Chapman Pincher had met Stirling a decade earlier in Kenya, when he had been advising the politician Bruce Mackenzie 'to set up an SAS-type unit, which scored some notable successes against terrorists', and was a fan. 'If ever a man was born for battle,' he wrote, 'it was the former wartime hero now aiming to become the champion for the silent majority.'[26]

Stirling told Chapman Pincher that GB75 would be 'a well-drilled middle-of-the-road movement truly representative of the moderate majority', whom he believed were fearful of the growing influence of the far left in British society.

Stirling was delighted with Chapman Pincher's article, boasting to members of GB75 in a letter (which was subsequently leaked to the *Guardian*) that his old friend had done 'his very best to diminish the damage' caused by the *Peace News* exclusive with a 'friendly' article.[27]

Another journalist granted an interview was Gavin Young of the *Observer.* Apart from their age (the interviewer was thirteen years younger than his subject), the pair had much in common: Young, the grandson of a baronet and the son of a lieutenant-colonel in the Welsh Guards, had been educated at Rugby and Oxford. Also a lifelong bachelor, Young had served briefly in his father's regiment before spending two years wandering among the Marsh Arabs. He had also worked briefly for MI6. Young and Stirling had several mutual acquaintances, including the Fleming family and Wilfred Thesiger. Tall and handsome, described as resembling a 'successful young brigadier', Young was at home among the members of White's, where the interview took place.[28] He charmed some interesting observations from Stirling's friends, which he included in a front-page feature on 25 August 1974. 'When you ask about him, those who have known him well immediately start using adjectives like "high minded" and "sly",' wrote Young of Stirling. 'One old chum says quite fondly that in politics David Stirling's ideas are quite unreal. A fellow member of White's ... says that Stirling has a sense of humour and it's "always rather fun" to meet him in there ... but even he, liking him, thinks of him as someone who believes you can get around any kind of obstacle with courage and a bit of luck.'

In Young's estimation, Stirling did 'seem to be a bit dotty'. He was also alive to his subject's false modesty, and his habit of prefacing sentences with 'no swankers ...' or 'it seems so like swanking, but ...', before launching into yet another bout of braggadocio.

There were a couple of interesting asides in the article, the main focus of which was GB75. Perhaps disarmed by his debonair interviewer, Stirling admitted that his decade in Rhodesia had achieved nothing. 'Capricorn was Utopian. Almost Walter Mitty,' he said of his society. 'We were a total failure.'*

* The fantasist Walter Mitty is a fictional character created by novelist James Thurber in his 1939 short story 'The Secret Life of Walter Mitty', which was made into a film in 1947.

They also discussed the war, which according to Young was Stirling's 'high spot', when 'he and his brother Bill invented the Special Air Service, an almost freelance affair officered mainly by well-born officers'.

The Conservative Party was quick to distance itself from GB75; Airey Neave, MP for Abingdon, warned of the 'great dangers' of an unofficial force.[29] One of the few Tories to stand by Stirling was his former L Detachment friend Carol Mather, who defended him against charges of raising a private army and described Stirling as 'the most unorthodox of a long line of brilliant and unorthodox British military leaders, to be rated alongside Lawrence and Wingate'.[30]

But when it was clear to Stirling that he was becoming increasingly isolated politically, he announced he would step down from GB75 as soon as a suitable replacement was found. A new director was appointed, but in April 1975 the organisation was disbanded. Stirling wrote to members explaining why, and urging patriots to join a new organisation which would be an anti-extremist reaction force within the trade union. This was TRUEMID, the Movement for True Industrial Democracy, but this too was short-lived, as was the Better Britain Society. Stirling wrote once again to Lord Hailsham at the end of May 1975, 'about the need for a new Constitutional Settlement'.[31] He enclosed a precis of the Better Britain Society, in which he outlined its three major objectives: a) A new Constitutional Settlement. b) The enactment of a new Education Bill drastically revising the schooling methods. c) To back TRUEMID in its reform of the Trade Union movement.

Lord Hailsham showed scant interest in the Better Britain Society and Stirling remained chairman until its nebulous aims defeated even him – although not before he had threatened legal action against the *Times Educational Supplement* in 1976 for their coverage of his society.

In 1976, the SAS were officially deployed to Northern Ireland (by Harold Wilson, the Labour Prime Minister), though they had been working in the Province for three years, often in small teams attached to regular infantry units. Initially the SAS had been engaged in surveillance and intelligence-gathering, but in 1978 they killed several IRA men in ambushes. Then in July that year the SAS mistook an inquisitive teenage boy, John Boyle, who had stumbled across an IRA weapons cache, for a terrorist and shot him dead. It was a propaganda coup for Sinn Fein, the political wing of the IRA, who, in alliance with elements of the British far left, accused the SAS of being little short of government assassins.

One of the most radical left-wing publications in Britain in the late 1970s was *Time Out*, now a listings magazine but at the time staffed by some journalists who were sympathetic to Irish Republicanism, the Soviet Bloc, Iranian Marxists and the Red Brigade of Italy.

Time Out became a ferocious critic of the SAS. An article in its issue of 21–27 July 1978, entitled 'The Pedigree Dogs of War', purported to be an exposé of what it dubbed the mercenary 24SAS (21 and 23SAS were territorial regiments and 22 the regular) and known officially as KMS Ltd, a 'highly organised network for the employment of former SAS members – a network that many in the SAS itself fear is transforming the regiment into a training ground for other people's private armies'.

They printed a photo of Stirling, captioning him the founder of the SAS and GB75. But *Time Out* was more concerned with his mercenary contacts, depicting him as a Fagin figure who, through Watchguard International – or 'Plan-a-War' as they called it – controlled a gang of former SAS officers, including Jim Johnson, who would 'roll up to the conflicts of the world's uglier conflicts like flies to a corpse': Zaire, Angola, Lebanon, Oman, Rhodesia and East Africa. The *Time Out* journalist who wrote the article, Duncan Campbell, said that Johnson and his men went by the motto 'Who Pays, Wins'.

It was a damning indictment of how Stirling had corrupted the SAS. There was an element of journalistic licence in the report, but a lot of the article was true. The magazine also reported that Stirling had tried to suppress their story in the days before publication, as was his habit with any adverse publicity.

In 1970, a few days before the publication of a *Sunday Times* Insight feature about Stirling's links to Saudis in the Yemen, the paper contacted him for comment. Stirling and his legal team stalled the publication of the article for a week and in the interim Jim Johnson produced an alternative version for the *Daily Telegraph*, creating a cover story for the issues raised in the unpublished article.

As a result, the *Sunday Times*, 'under severe pressure',[32] didn't run with its scoop that claimed Stirling had told King Faisal of Saudi Arabia he could raise a 'task force' to invade the Yemen and destabilise the government through sabotage operations. Stirling had promised the Saudis that his 'access to the Special Air Service Regiment of the British Army' would be beneficial in forming such a task force. Roy Thomson, the owner of the *Sunday Times*, accused Stirling of having 'infringed a basic code of integrity' in his behaviour; Stirling rejected the charge in a letter dated 9 February 1970, stating that he had not misled him at any stage, and that he had sabotaged the article because the *Sunday Times* was intent on 'publicly claiming that the Israelis supplied, by aircraft, war materials to the Royalist Yemen'. This, he claimed, was contrary to a request Stirling had made to Thomson. 'The story of the British participation in the Yemen which all concerned would have far preferred to remain under wraps, had to be paraded in three articles in the *Daily Telegraph* in order to avoid the infinitely worse evil of allowing your Insight team to make its claim of Arab-Israeli collusion,' wrote Stirling. He concluded the letter by expressing the wish that their spat would not impair their personal relationship.

Four days letter a triumphant Stirling wrote to his friend Julian Amery, recounting his tussle with Thomson and his 'scavengers' at the *Sunday Times*. 'When it became clear that they were determined to publish,' stated Stirling, '... there was only one course left open; to pre-empt the *Sunday Times* by publishing the facts from a sympathetic and reliable angle in the *Daily Telegraph* ... hopefully the Insight team is left biting its grubby fingernails up to the elbow.'

Time Out reported that Stirling had employed similar tactics against them. This time, Stirling co-opted the *Daily Mail*, which published a story it described as a 'worldwide exclusive'. The paper revealed that a company based in the Channel Islands provided former SAS men to act as bodyguards for British ambassadors and other diplomatic staff as part of a 'secret' contract.

The Foreign Office issued a swift riposte to the *Mail*'s story, denying most of what had been written and stating that it employed no armed bodyguards from private companies. The only 'secret' contract was an arrangement with a specialist British company to send teams to a select number of embassies to train local staff in security measures.

Time Out ran another piece about the SAS in December 1978, headlined 'What Makes the Special Air Services [*sic*] Special'. The peg on which the article was hung was the trial of the SAS soldiers who had shot dead sixteen-year-old John Boyle in the summer, in the mistaken belief he was an IRA terrorist.

As the title indicated, it was a sloppy article, a history of the regiment based on hearsay and published sources, specifically Philip Warner's 1971 history of the SAS, the foreword of which was written by Stirling. *Time Out* described the wartime regiment as 'Café Society Gangsters', but it confused No. 11 Special Air Service Battalion, commanded by Maj Trevor Pritchard, with L Detachment, SAS when the two were in fact separate entities. It also claimed that the SAS, on the orders of Winston Churchill, 'turned their guns on the left-wing ELAS resistance movement in Greece'. The SAS did not deploy to Greece during the war, and while the SBS and the LRDG were in the country in 1944, they were there as garrison troops:

glorified policemen, in effect, caught in the crossfire of an incipient civil war.

A paragraph was devoted to Stirling. In the context of the article it was largely innocuous; it described his capture 'by a German army dentist' and his subsequent escape, only to be 'recaptured by an Arab shepherd'.

Stirling would have been best advised to ignore *Time Out*'s hatchet job. The magazine couldn't even get the regiment's name right and the article was littered with inaccuracies. Instead he sued, winning substantial damages when the case was heard in the High Court in April 1979.[33] In the libel action Stirling's counsel, Richard Walker, told the judge his client objected to its 'highly condensed and selective account of his capture and recapture in North Africa in 1943. The article referred to his being captured by a dentist, ignoring the fact that there were some five hundred Germans nearby.'

Stirling also challenged *Time Out*'s claim that he had been recaptured by an Arab shepherd; in fact, the shepherd had betrayed him to an Italian search party.

Richard Walker added that Stirling considered the article 'implied incompetence, inefficiency and cowardice on his part and that he had been a party to, or had connived at, the publication of an untrue account of the SAS's history'.

Virginia Cowles had described Stirling's capture by a dentist in *The Phantom Major*, so there was nothing overtly defamatory in the *Time Out* article. Had the magazine hired a more diligent lawyer they would have been able to subject Stirling to an uncomfortable grilling on the stand. He claimed that the dentist was one of five hundred Germans who captured the SAS patrol in January 1943, yet in the interview that Johnny Cooper and Mike Sadler gave to American correspondent Noland Norgaard after their escape from the wadi they said they had been 'ambushed by a German patrol'.[34] This patrol, as Cooper described in his memoirs, was part of an elite group of paratroopers from Fallschirmjaeger z.b.V 250, on a mission to track down enemy commandos. A patrol would not have comprised five hundred soldiers.

One of the Germans, Sgt Heinrich Fugner, mentioned nothing of Stirling's capture by a dentist in his post-war account, but recalled that some of the SAS were examined by a 'doctor and his medics who were with the Panzergrenadiers'.[35] This was the motorised column that the SAS had passed on the road a short while before they turned off into the wadi to camp.

Furthermore, Stirling might have evaded capture had he posted a guard. The fact he hadn't might well have 'implied' incompetence and inefficiency on his part. This penchant for litigation was telling. A warrior who had faith in the veracity of his exploits would not have rushed to court at the smallest slight to his reputation. Stirling, however, had the sensitivity of the charlatan, the ardent defensiveness of a man with something to hide.

When he had written his statement for *Mars and Minerva* in May 1968, he added a late footnote prior to publication, explaining that he had triumphed in his libel case against the *Sunday Times* and Sphere Books Ltd, who had disparaged him and the SAS in publishing Len Deighton's 'The Private Armies' article. 'However,' he wrote, 'the dilemma remains: as there has been so little counteracting publicity regarding the Regiment (in spite of my efforts) we must rely mainly on word of mouth to clear the Regiment and myself from slander.'

Stirling cared not a jot for the good name of the Special Air Service. He was its pimp in the 1960s and 1970s, degrading its reputation for his own personal gain, so that by 1979 many in Britain regarded the SAS as a cross between a paramilitary unit and a band of mercenaries, not too dissimilar to the soldiers of fortune depicted in the 1978 film *The Wild Geese*.

The regiment's name, and that of Stirling, was arguably at its lowest ebb as the 1970s drew to a close. In March 1979 Stirling was back in the courts, this time taking legal action against the *New Statesman* after an article in which they exposed his plan to transform Loch Morar – where he had holidayed as a boy – into 'a paradise for paying sportsmen'. The locals weren't happy, according to the *Daily Express*, but Stirling didn't give a damn, saying he found it 'perfectly reasonable' to charge people to fish in the loch. He blamed his family – in other words, Bill – for having been 'idle about controlling the loch over the years and people have got used to fishing for free'.[36]

Was there ever an anecdote that captured the essential difference between the two brothers: one generous and affable and the other grasping and mean-spirited?

32

In the same month as Stirling was suing the New Statesman, March 1979, Maj Gen Peter de la Billière, Director of the SAS, took the unprecedented step of writing a letter to the *Daily Telegraph*. He was 'disturbed' at the way in which the SAS was being portrayed in the media, 'as if it were some secret undercover organisation'. It was, he stated, a corps of the British army, 'subject to both military and civil law in exactly the same way as any other corps'.[1]

A little over a year later, on 30 April 1980, six terrorists belonging to the Democratic Front for the Liberation of Arabistan burst into the Iranian Embassy in London's Prince's Gate.

De la Billière was summoned to Westminster for an emergency meeting with Willie Whitelaw, the Home Secretary who, forty years earlier, had been a junior officer with David Stirling in the Scots Guards. Over the following days, a tense siege unfolded before the lenses of the world's media. Then, on 5 May, the terrorists tossed the body of the murdered Embassy chief press officer out into the street. There were more shots from inside the building, and although they weren't fired into a hostage, it was enough for Margaret Thatcher to send in the SAS.

The siege was lifted in seventeen minutes. None of the hostages were harmed and all but one of the terrorists were killed. It was an operation, said de la Billière, performed with 'surgical precision'.[2] Broadcast live around the world, the SAS had been transformed from shady bandits into supermen. 'The Siege Busters' screamed the front page of the *Daily Mirror.* 'SAS to the rescue in the heart of London.'

After the social conflict and economic depression of the 1970s the new decade had brought a morale boost to the British public. A letter from a Mrs Stewart of Aberdeen to her local paper, praising the news cameras and the soldiers, captured the mood. 'The "instant" coverage of the storming of the Iranian Embassy was brilliant,' she exclaimed. 'The atmosphere was terrific. Nothing seemed to escape them, from the activity on the ground to the impassive marksmen and dark figures of the SAS. It was all so British.'[3]

The world wanted to know more about these black-clad British Bulldogs. Philip Warner's history of the regiment was updated and reissued, and several new books were published in the early 1980s. There was a film, *Who Dares Wins*, starring action-man actor Lewis Collins, and there were countless magazine features, all far different in tone from what had appeared in *Time Out* in 1979.

The SAS's involvement in the Falklands War in 1982 further reinforced the growing cult of the regiment. 'SAS Storm South Georgia' was the headline across a two-page spread in the *Liverpool Echo*, and when the war was over the *Sunday Mirror* ran an exclusive with the boast, 'The amazing bravery and endurance of our SAS men in the Falklands campaign is revealed today.'

No one enjoyed the attention more than the regiment's founder.

'We don't hear much from him these days,' lamented the LRDG newsletter of David Stirling in its 1982 edition, 'but a paragraph in the *Daily Mirror* ... reported that an unnamed retired army officer had left him £100 in his will in the hope he would use it to buy cigars.'

Stirling had rarely attended LRDG reunions, even when he lived in Rhodesia in the 1950s, where there was a thriving Salisbury branch. He accepted an invitation to attend the 1970 LRDG reunion in London, a special event to make the twenty-fifth anniversary of the unit's association, but that was the last one.

The *Daily Mirror,* however, was one of several papers that kept Stirling's name in the news in the 1980s. In February 1981 he told the paper what he thought of his secretary, Sabrina Guinness, a girlfriend of Prince Charles in the 1970s: she was 'hardworking, efficient and capable'.

In January 1982 the same paper reported that Britain's coldest winter in years had forced 'that fierce old warrior Colonel David Stirling to make a strategic withdrawal'. On a slow news day the paper remarked: 'The 66-year-old founder of the Special Air Service has flown off in search of some warmth. Stirling, dubbed the Phantom Major by the Germans during the war because of his desert exploits, is just as coy about his plans as the present-day SAS "phantoms".'

Stirling, who talked to the *Mirror*'s journalist while 'sipping his favourite golden liquid from a glass adorned with the SAS winged dagger emblem', didn't reveal his destination, although he confessed that the south of France had an appeal.

Bill Stirling died on the first day of January 1983. His death was largely unreported in the British media. *The Times* carried a short obituary: 'William Stirling was the brother of Lieutenant-Colonel David Stirling who had founded the SAS Regiment in the wake of the disbanding of Commando forces in North Africa. David Stirling proved the value of the SAS to Auchinleck in a series of extraordinarily effective raids and after his own capture by the Germans in Tunisia William virtually assumed his mantle in equally daring exploits in Italy.'

There was no mention of his having founded the Inverailort commando training school, his work for SOE or his command of the Small Scale Raiding Force. It was as Bill would have wanted. When, in 1946, the SAS compiled their 'War Diary' in which they catalogued their achievements and fleshed out some of the personalities within the Brigade, Bill was described as 'the man from the shadows'.[4] Nonetheless the Diary was aware of his role in founding the SAS, stating that 'he was in Cairo in the crucial months of 1941 when David was developing his ideas for what would become SAS. The two brothers spent time discussing this.'

The SAS was less well informed about the origins of 2SAS Regiment, claiming it was formed at the beginning of 1943 in order to work with David's unit. Bill's cousin Simon Fraser, the 15th Lord Lovat, didn't mention Bill's role with the Small Scale Raiding Force or 2SAS when he wrote his memoir, *March Past*, in 1978, either because he was ignorant or because he was asked not to. And when Martin Gilbert wrote his voluminous biography of Winston Churchill in the 1980s, he mistook Bill for David when examining the Prime Minister's response to a 2SAS raid organised by 'Stirling' on the island of Lampedusa in May 1943.

Bill had never even told his children what he got up to in the war. He compartmentalised his life, reflected his eldest child, Archie, and was someone who preferred to look to the future rather than dwell in the past.

In the last quarter of his life Bill had experienced success and failure. He met both with equanimity. During Ascot week in 1959 he lost the staggering sum of £174,500 (approximately £4 million today) playing chemin de fer during a single all-night gambling session. He signed an IOU and then the 'Colonel waved to a waiter and quietly asked for a plate of scrambled eggs. There was no sign of distress and he ate his eggs quite quickly. He had to be off – he had a busy day.'[5]

He cleared the debt in a few weeks, by which time everyone in London knew of his loss, and a legend began that Bill Stirling was Britain's most inveterate gambler. 'I fear he has ruined himself at cards,' said Evelyn Waugh in a letter to Nancy Mitford in June 1961, rueing the fact because he 'was a very indulgent commander to me at one stage of the war'.[6]

In fact, Bill hadn't ruined himself. He was only an occasional visitor to the Clermont Club and gambling was never an addiction. But people liked to boast that they been at the gaming table with Bill Stirling to burnish their own credentials among London's smart set.

His favourite pastime was horse racing, and in Sing Sing – from Sandy Scratchley's stud – he had one of the fastest colts in Britain. In 1959 Sing Sing won all six of his races, beating the best of his age at Ascot, York and Doncaster, but shortly before the 1960 July Cup at Newmarket Sing Sing was doped by a gang that had been active for a while. In Sing Sing's case, they administered too much dope and Bill Stirling was forced to retire him, although he had a successful stud career. His horses continued to enjoy success on the racecourse throughout the 1960s, including Celtic Song, ridden by Lester Piggott.

Bill's business empire had grown to all corners of the globe, and in 1972 he floated his oil company, KCA (Keir & Cawder Arrow) Drilling Group, on the Stock Exchange, selling more than one million shares at ninety-eight pence each. KCA, which owned twelve rigs worldwide, was Britain's only drilling company. Today it is KCA Deutag, based in Aberdeen and employing nine thousand people in twenty countries. Despite his prestige, Bill Stirling didn't appear in *Who's Who*, the 'manual of the old Establishment', unlike David.[7]

Bill had bankrolled Peter's business in Iran but when the Shah was deposed in 1979 they lost everything. David had been determined to make his own way, but the three brothers met occasionally for a shoot. There appeared to be no rancour, certainly not on the part of Bill, who didn't brood or bear grudges, or ever ask David to settle the debts incurred by the Capricorn Africa Society. He embodied the Stirling motto: Gang Forward.

In 1977 Bill sold Keir to the ambassador of the Arab Emirates to raise more capital for his business interests. He forgot to tell his wife and there was something of a kerfuffle, but it was smoothed over and the new owner was happy to allow Mrs Stirling to carry on living in a wing of the house.

Bill spent much of his time at his flat on Park Lane in London, and it was there that he fell and broke a leg in late December 1982. According to the *Daily Telegraph*, 'he was not found until 36 hours after the accident and was taken to the hospital'.[8] He died at a few days later at the King Edward VII Hospital for Officers in Marylebone.

An obituary was published in the *Ampleforth Journal*, which said 'his war record was notable'. It continued:

> After the capture of his brother David, founder of the SAS, Bill took over command of the 2nd SAS regiment [*sic*], operating with brilliant success in daring raids in Tunisia, Sicily and throughout the Italian campaign. Mention of these years was rare* and reminiscence light-hearted: as a first move when planning a raid the enlistment of Adam, the stalker, 'to look after him'; the submarine voyage to make a raid and the ignominious return on the surface, unable to submerge. Readiness to take risks and their consequences were a part of his make-up that inevitably drew him to commando-type operations. Success and failure were equally things to be made the best of. Reticence appeared in other contexts. Only by accident would one learn something of the help he was always ready to give. Instances abound: his concern with the Flying Doctor service in that part of East Africa, his help to the church in Dunblane as well as maintaining the chapel at Keir; or going round the farms one might miss a familiar face, of a man who, it would emerge, had been both encouraged and substantially helped by his employer to set up on his own.

* Bill's reticence may also have been a consequence of his having signed the Official Secrets Act during the war when he worked for SOE.

The brief obituary in *The Times* was augmented by a eulogy from an unidentified friend. Praising Bill's modesty, courtesy, compassion and leadership, the author mentioned in passing that he had suffered tragedy and experienced setbacks in his life, but he had accepted these vicissitudes without complaint or bitterness. The eulogy ended:

> Beyond lay the rock of his personality strong, overshadowing, perpetually at odds with the trivialities and meanness of modern life and – perhaps his fundamental weakness – in personal conflict with powers too strong to overcome. But when all is over the final judgment of any man is the memories and opinions of his contemporaries. Bill Stirling will be remembered not for his virtues or failures rather for an intangible core of nobility which lay inviolate at the heart of his nature.

Bill recognised before anyone else in Britain that a new age of warfare had dawned, one that harnessed a man's initiative and boldness to the advancements in communications, transport and ordnance. He founded the commando training school and through its gates in the summer of 1940 passed many men who would graduate to become Britain's greatest wartime guerrilla fighters: Mike Calvert, Freddie Spencer Chapman, Jack Churchill, Peter Kemp, Tommy Macpherson, Geoffrey Appleyard, George Jellicoe, Gus March-Phillipps and David Sutherland.

Subsequently Bill took command of the Small Scale Raiding Force, encouraged, facilitated and advised both Roger Courtney's Special Boat Section and George Jellicoe's Special Boat Squadron, and, as commander of 2SAS for twelve months, he planned and implemented a series of small-scale operations by parachute, submarine and vehicle that have become the template for post-war special forces operations. He ended the war with one medal, the Africa Star with the 1st Army clasp.

Bill was buried in the family plot at Keir, and ten months later his wife was laid to rest at his side. In 2002 a statue of David Stirling was unveiled a couple of miles to the north. It is right that one of the Stirling boys should have been honoured so; but they got the wrong one. Bill Stirling was the intellectual force behind the Special Air Service, and Paddy Mayne the physical force. David Stirling was its salesman.

On 30 June 1984 David Stirling gave the address at the opening of the newly refurbished SAS base in Hereford. Bradbury Lines had been renamed Stirling Lines and an audience of many hundreds listened as the regiment's founder modestly told them, 'Almost to the day 43 years ago as a second Lieutenant [*sic*] and known to be something of a "cheeky laddie", and of dubious value to the army, I submitted to Field Marshal Auchinleck's [*sic*] Chief of General Staff [Arthur Smith] a paper setting out in my own nearly illegible handwriting the SAS proposition.'[9]

He then acknowledged the role of the LRDG and expressed his 'deep debt of gratitude' for their help.

Stirling briefly referenced George Jellicoe and his Special Boat Squadron, and 2SAS under the command of 'my brother Bill'. He then said that he felt 'uneasy' at being known as the founder of the SAS and in his view there were five co-founders: Jock Lewes, Paddy Mayne, Georges Bergé, Brian Franks and John Woodhouse.

He listed members of the supporting cast, including Mike Calvert, Pat Riley, Bob Bennett, Johnny Watts, Peter de la Billière, Fitzroy Maclean, Johnny Cooper, Roy Farran and the commanders of the Belgian and Greek SAS units.

Stirling had rightly honoured most of the men whose courage and determination and resourcefulness had carried the SAS through some challenging times. There were, however, two remarkable omissions. The first was Bill Fraser, who nine years earlier had died almost destitute. He and Mayne had kept L Detachment going throughout the winter of 1941 and into 1942. When Peter Davis joined the SAS in December 1942 he was more excited at his first glimpse of Fraser than of Stirling, describing the former as the 'terror to the Germans in the desert and with a whole string of operations to his credit'.[10] Fraser was awarded a bar to his MC for leading a three-month operation in Occupied France in the summer of 1944, for which the citation praised his 'untiring leadership [which] kept his men alert and their morale high, and kept the enemy guessing and continually harassed'.[11]

Why did Stirling persistently overlook Fraser's magnificent contribution to the SAS? Because he was working class; because he succumbed to the bottle after the war; and because he was homosexual.

In contrast, Jock Lewes's contribution to the SAS has been exaggerated. It wasn't his idea in May 1941 to plan a parachute raid on an enemy target, it was Col Bob Laycock's. He invented the Lewes bomb, but he and Stirling had little idea about parachute training, and their methods resulted in several broken limbs for a unit already low on manpower. Alf Card, an RAF parachute instructor at Ringway in England, arrived at Kabrit in January 1943 to teach the new SAS recruits. He was appalled at their methods. 'Stirling had formed the SAS out there and his idea of training his people was to … jump off the backs off lorry to teach them landing because he had read in a book somewhere that this is what they were doing,' he said. 'They had very little in the way of flight technique and it was lucky, really, that they survived to do a parachute descent at all because they used to tear this lorry around 30 mph and hurl themselves off it, which is nothing like a parachute landing at all.'[12]

Nor was Lewes innovative in their physical training. He drove L Detachment hard, but these were commandos who had endured months of punishing route marches in Scotland the previous year. Meanwhile, the lectures he gave on demolitions, navigation and signals were nothing new for those soldiers who had been through Lochailort. Furthermore, Lewes was not a particularly effective guerrilla fighter; more Stirling than Mayne or Fraser in that regard.

To cite Georges Bergé as a co-founder was extraordinary; the Frenchman arrived at Kabrit with his men in January 1942 but in a memo dated 3 May 1942, entitled 'The Future of "L" Det.', Stirling stated that Bergé 'feels that his unit is not sufficiently an integral part of "L" Det', an assessment that he shared. The two men wondered whether it wouldn't best if Bergé 'be allowed to disband his unit'. He didn't, but the following month he was captured on Crete.

As for John Woodhouse, he hadn't even served in the wartime SAS, but as CO of 22SAS in 1963 he had turned a blind eye when Stirling corrupted the regiment by obtaining the release of three soldiers so they could operate for him as mercenaries in the Yemen. In an interview in 1993, Woodhouse justified his participation in the Yemen by saying it was in Britain's national interest. He then said with what can only be described as excruciating hypocrisy, 'The question of ex-SAS soldiers becoming mercenaries and being involved in military activities all over the world is one that has concerned the SAS certainly since my time, and probably a great deal more since my time. It is obviously very undesirable that ex-SAS soldiers should become involved in mercenary activities.'[13] Woodhouse had been a partner in Stirling's Watchguard International before its demise in 1972.

As for Brian Franks, he merited recognition for his drive in re-forming the regiment in 1947, but the man who had handed him the baton was the man who had run the toughest leg of the relay: Bill Stirling.

This was the second name that should have been listed as a founding father of the regiment. It was he who spent that year fighting the powers that be to keep the SAS out of the clutches of the Airborne Corps. He won that battle, as he did his next, preventing the deployment of the SAS to the Normandy front in June 1944, but ultimately Bill made too many enemies and he was ousted as 2SAS CO.

Bill, of course, possessed an 'intangible core of nobility', but at the heart of his brother was a bitter envy. Even after Bill's death David denied him the recognition he deserved.

Stirling used his address at Hereford to create the myth of 'The Originals', the sixty-six men who were recruited to L Detachment in the summer of 1941. 'Most survivors of the original SAS foundation unit – and I understand we are known in the regiment as the Dirty Dozen – are here today, and in spirit alongside me,' he said. Later in the day the 'Dirty Dozen' (there were in fact only eleven present) posed for a photograph: Stirling, Cooper, Almonds, Riley, Bennett, Kershaw, Byrne, Brough, Bond, Evans and Trenfield.

In fact, there were several more Originals still alive, including Jimmy Storie, Jeff Du Vivier, Ralph Lazenby, Fred 'Chalky' White and Reg Seekings. Some of them were popular among other wartime veterans of the regiment, notably Cooper, Almonds and Bennett.*

Others weren't. Because they were Originals, they considered themselves a cut above those who came later. This clique caused resentment among some veterans, particularly those who joined the regiment in 1942 and fought their way from North Africa through Sicily and Italy into France and then Germany. One of those was Bob Lowson, a veteran of the Norwegian campaign in the spring of 1940, who subsequently served with the SAS from late 1942 until shot by a German sniper in April 1945. At one post-war reunion he approached a table with a beer in hand to be told by Chalky White to 'fuck off' because he wasn't an Original. Another soldier who resented this preciousness was Bob McDougall, who had joined the SAS in 1942. 'All those Originals could be a bit full of themselves,' he reflected. 'Riley, Seekings, Lilley, a lot of the Originals were unpopular. Not Johnny Cooper.' McDougall also mentioned that during the battle of Termoli one of his pals 'came close to shooting Pat Riley', such was his unpopularity after he had been commissioned. As for Stirling, McDougall summarised him as 'an arrogant bastard'.[14]

Several of the Originals who attended the annual reunions had been captured on the first raid in November 1941 and spent the rest

* So was Jeff Du Vivier, but after the publication of *The Phantom Major*, to which he had contributed, he disappeared off the radar and many veterans assumed he had died. I tracked him to the west of Scotland in 2002 and interviewed him several times. He died in 2010.

of the war as POWs. Their contribution to the SAS was negligible, certainly in comparison to those who joined later and fought with the regiment in southern and northern Europe.

The Originals' conceit was tacitly encouraged by Stirling. They were his men; veterans such as Lowson and McDougall were Mayne's. Yet Lowson, like his comrades, could be critical of Mayne. Virtually flawless in combat, he had his weaknesses as a man: he could be brusque, quick-tempered and capricious, and on the matter of berets, pedantic; they had to be worn straight. If Mayne saw a man wearing his beret at an angle he was in trouble. In contrast, the Originals didn't seem to have any criticism of Stirling. This might have been because they didn't actually know him at all well; he made only fleeting visits to Kabrit and had a small coterie of favourites for his raids. But there was also a protective tone to their comments about Stirling. They knew he was no commando, but they respected his physical courage in trying to be one.

In the early 1980s Stirling had assembled some of the Originals for a film project called 'The Birth of a Regiment'; it never came to fruition, but in 1987 they gathered once more to give a series of interviews to the documentary-maker Gordon Stevens and the historian Tony Kemp. Both subsequently turned the interviews into books, Kemp incorporating their important testimonies into a wartime history of the regiment, which was published in 1991.

The jacket of Stevens's book, *The Originals*, carries a quote from Stirling: 'We've been approached something like twenty-five times since the war. I kicked each out the window because they weren't going to make it with the integrity we require the story of the SAS to be told.'[15]

The interview with Stirling is now at the Imperial War Museum. It is a fascinating audio tape; some of it is accurate, some of it is not.

He talked warmly of Jock Lewes and Paddy Mayne, although he strays into psychobabble in attempting to describe the latter.

But Stirling had to be gracious in acknowledging their contribution to the SAS because it had been well publicised over the years.*

The extent of Bill Stirling's influence in establishing the SAS was unknown, and David was determined to keep it that way. He acknowledged briefly what Bill had done in the early part of the war. 'He and Bryan [Mayfield] succeeded in persuading the authorities to let them go in the submarine to Norway on a raid – I wasn't involved – and on that occasion he recruited his stalker … who wasn't in the army but who was allowed to go along as Bill trusted him in field craft,' he said.

Stirling then made a brief reference to the commando special training centre that his brother had established in May 1940, saying: 'I was involved with Bill when he was chief instructor at Lochailort.'

David mentioned the Yak Mission of which Bill was a member. He knew that they had sailed in the same convoy as the Layforce Commando on 31 January 1941, but told his interviewers that his brother 'came out originally to Cairo, just as I was forming L Detachment. He came out on a mission with Peter Fleming and it was set up by SOE.'

An honest chronological error? David then started to talk at length about the power struggle between GHQ and SOE in the summer of 1941, a fight in which Bill – not David – was prominent. 'The local arm of SOE in Cairo, which gave me a lot of bother, because they always tried to take over my outfit, saying we'd make a very handy operational team, which I had to resist, but they weren't a very competent lot,' said Stirling. 'I didn't know very much of them but I resisted their taking over … I was always determined to keep SAS out of the control of SOE because it had been poaching our functions and they were quite separate, quite different.'

* A biography of Mayne was published in the 1960s – and reissued in 1983 – called *Colonel Paddy: The Man Who Dared*. It is sensationalist and factually inaccurate. In an interview in 1965 its author, Patrick Marrinan, claimed to have been a contemporary of Mayne's at Queen's, playing rugby in the university XV. But Marrinan was four years younger and Mayne had left by the time he enrolled.

That struggle had been won by GHQ by the time L Detachment was formed, thanks to Bill who, with the help of Hermione Ranfurly, had smuggled documents out of SOE that were used to build a dossier revealing the extent of their disarray. This led to a restructuring of SOE Cairo.

Stirling then introduced Orde Wingate into his fantasy world, telling Stevens and Kemp: 'General [*sic* – he was a colonel at the time] Wingate had tried, made a bid, to take me over. He wrote me a long letter after he came back from Ethiopia, inviting me to join up with him or would I like to go under him in some capacity. But again his technique was quite different from ours in SAS. He didn't understand the SAS and so I refused absolutely.'

This wasn't the first time Stirling had made such a claim. In 1959 Christopher Sykes, an intelligence officer in 2SAS during the war, had written a biography of Wingate and Stirling had provided him with his recollection of the summer of 1941. Consequently, Sykes wrote: 'Colonel [*sic*] David Stirling was at that time attempting to organise the first Special Air Service unit in the face of all the opposition that had confronted Wingate from the beginning. It had been suggested to him, in good faith, that he and Wingate might usefully combine since they shared many ideas. But Stirling was quite as much of an individualist as Wingate and for this reason he resisted the suggestion, so much so that he had even avoided meeting the other.'[16]

Wingate was indeed in Cairo in the early summer of 1941, but on 4 July – weeks before L Detachment was raised – he slit his throat in a suicide attempt. He spent several weeks in hospital, ill and depressed, before being shipped back to England in September. Wingate remained in the UK until February 1942, when he was posted to the Far East, where he raised the Chindits, and where he remained until his death in 1944.

David Stirling then discussed how 2SAS came into existence. '[Bill] had a unit called the Special Small Scale Raiding Force [*sic*] and

I wrote to him saying what about turning it into, using it as a base for 2SAS Regiment because I had a full regimental status by then and he thought that was a good wheeze and the last letter – I think it was the only two letters we wrote to each other because neither of us were very good correspondents – saying that it was being confirmed and he'd got 2SAS established ... then I was captured.'

Again, the distortion of the truth, portraying Bill as David's malleable underling. It was a falsehood he repeated when discussing the contretemps that erupted in the spring of 1944 concerning the deployment of the SAS in France. According to David, word had reached him in his prison camp that 'there was a danger the Airborne [Corps] were trying to put the SAS under their command and I wasn't quite sure Bill would have the arguments'. He then implied that he sent word to the SAS on how best to fight their corner, 'but I don't know what validity that had'.

The idea that Bill Stirling or Paddy Mayne needed any guidance from David in the late spring of 1944 is laughable. The pair were guerrilla fighters par excellence, the former a strategic mastermind and the latter a tactical genius. L Detachment would have been far more effective in North Africa had Bill and not David been in charge, with Mayne his second-in-command. As a result of David's poor leadership, the SAS never came close to fulfilling its potential in 1942, until Mayne, free from Stirling's interference, took A Squadron raiding in Libya in October.

Frankly, the best place for David in 1944 was a prison camp – as Bill had suggested to their mother shortly after his brother's capture. Not only was he now incapable of endangering his own life, but more importantly those of the men under his command. Although even a POW camp wasn't enough to prevent Stirling imperilling British soldiers.

An intriguing 'what if' is to consider what might have happened to the SAS Brigade in the summer of 1944, had David Stirling been in command. How would he have responded to 21 Army Group's order to parachute in parties of SAS men a few miles inland from the Normandy beachhead to delay the German armour reserves?

Stirling had gambled with his men's lives on several occasions in the first year of L Detachment, so on the balance of probability one must conclude that he would have accepted the order and the SAS would have been annihilated in Normandy in the summer of 1944.

33

David Stirling was a busy man in the 1980s, a decade that ended with his receiving a knighthood for services to the military. As something of an expert on Everest he made a financial contribution to and chaired the 1986 expedition, a fourteen-strong party's attempt to become the first to summit via the north-east ridge. Six former SAS men were among the group and Stirling, now preferring to be addressed as Col and not Mr, was at Heathrow to see them off. 'This is arguably the finest team of mountaineers ever assembled,' he told the press. 'They are hand picked and I think they have a very strong chance of reaching the top.'[1] Severe weather thwarted their ambition.

He also contributed to *Soldiers and Sherpas* by Brummie Stokes, a former SAS trooper and renowned mountaineer who had summitted Everest in 1976, losing all of his toes in the process. Stokes was the real deal, unlike the man who wrote the foreword. 'His fascination, that too I can understand,' wrote Stirling. 'When I was young and Everest still unclimbed, I dreamed of being the first to reach its lonely summit … I trained in the Swiss Alps and the Rocky Mountains but after two years my plans were interrupted by the outbreak of war. By the time the war was ended, my life had taken a different turn and Everest could no longer be a part of it.'

What turn was this? After the disbandment of the SAS in October 1945 Stirling returned to civilian life and drifted through the next year. He had plenty of time on his hands but, as Evelyn Waugh recorded in his diary, Stirling spent much of 1946 drinking in the company of the novelist and his coterie of glamorous friends. The truth is that the youthful Stirling had never dreamed of climbing Everest; it was the ageing and embittered Stirling that created this legend.

In 1987 Stirling was hired by Prince Bernhard of the Netherlands, the former international president of the World Wide Fund for Nature (WWF), to 'gather intelligence on the international trade in rhino horn by infiltrating the market and buying rhino horn to trace the dealers'. Stirling had set up another mercenary organisation, KAS Enterprises, staffed by many former SAS men, and the company received £500,000 from Prince Bernhard to fund 'Operation Lock' in southern Africa. The project was short-lived. The Prince withdrew his support in 1989 and the following year KAS Enterprises ceased trading. A report in the Independent in January 1991 stated that 'the company went out of business – having failed to account for the equipment, the rhino horn or its funds, which included a large slice of Sir David's personal fortune'.[2]

Throughout the 1980s Stirling was in demand by authors hoping for an endorsement for their book. In 1985 he wrote the foreword for William Seymour's history of Britain's special forces, and in the same year he did the same for Fraser McLuskey, MC, chaplain of 1SAS in 1944 and 1945. McLuskey's book was entitled *Parachute Padre* and was predominantly concerned with the three months he spent in Occupied France in 1944 with Bill Fraser's A Squadron. *Parachute Padre* had originally been published in 1951 and was dedicated to 'Paddy and his men'. Mayne had a chapter to himself, such was McLuskey's admiration for a man he described as one of the most remarkable thrown up by the war. He praised Mayne's 'tender-heart' and his solicitude for his soldiers. 'What impressed his men even more than his skill and courage was his sense of responsibility for those under his command,' wrote McLuskey.

It was an odd choice to ask Stirling to write the foreword to the new edition. He hadn't known McLuskey during the war and he hadn't operated in Occupied France, a theatre that veterans of the Desert War found far more claustrophobic and exacting than the open spaces of North Africa. Stirling's piece was brief and he mentioned neither Mayne nor Bill Fraser.

In 1987 Stirling penned another foreword, this time for *Rogue Warrior: The Blair Mayne Legend* by Martin Dillon and Ray Bradford. The biography was an artful assassination of Mayne's character, praising on one page, damning on the next. A warrior, yes, but cold-hearted and psychologically flawed – not like the cavalier and romantic Phantom Major.

It was claimed, for example, that at the function after the 1939 Five Nations rugby international between Wales and Ireland in Swansea, a furious Mayne had thrown a teammate out of the window; the match was played in Belfast. Haydn Tanner, who played for Wales against Mayne in 1937, 1938 and 1939, and was a fellow Lions tourist to South Africa, had no memory of Mayne being a violent player. Nor did Vivian Jenkins. Both remembered him as aggressive but controlled, as he was on SAS operations.[3]

The book then stated that Mayne 'ran amok' in the officers' mess of No. 11 Commando with a rifle and bayonet, chasing everyone out of the building, including Geoffrey Keyes, whom he later punched unconscious. Neither incident occurred, according to Tommy Macpherson, a fellow officer in No. 11 Commando.

It was claimed in January 1943 that Mayne had sought out Richard Dimbleby in Shepheard's Hotel because he was so enraged by the quality of his reporting from North Africa. But Dimbleby had been back in Britain for six months. So instead Mayne assaulted the provost-marshal and two of his military policemen and was placed under close arrest. The actual story was less dramatic and happened months later, as brigadier George Davy recorded in his post-war memoirs. Towards the end of June 1943, shortly before the Special Raiding Squadron embarked to Sicily, Mayne was embroiled in a fracas in Cairo with Lt Colonel NGF Dunne, the Provost Marshal, who as an officer in the 8th Hussars, had gone by the nickname 'Punch'. Mayne was taken into custody and word was sent to Davy. 'John Crystall, who commanded Cairo area, was an old friend of mine from before the war, a 13/18th Hussar,' recalled Davy. 'I went straight round to him and gave him all the facts and he agreed at once that we must let Mayne go . . . Harry [Cator] then brought the contrite Paddy into my office to apologise to me for causing so much trouble. I thought that a bit unfair and turned the interview into a good laugh.'

In pursuing this agenda, the authors also on occasion deviated from what they had been told by some of their interviewees. David Lloyd Owen was particularly aggrieved and said so in the 1988 edition of the LRDG newsletter. 'When I find in a book two departures from the facts as I recounted them to one of the authors, I ask myself how much else might have been embroidered in the telling,' he wrote. 'Many of us worked with David Stirling and Paddy Mayne in the desert. We all so much admired Paddy's inspired leadership and his tremendous courage.'

Bob Lowson, who served under Mayne for nearly three years, described the book as 'shit', with numerous inaccuracies. He said this with authority because he had been present at the incidents in question.*

The most illuminating sentence in *Rogue Warrior* is in the acknowledgments: 'From the list of many brave and distinguished soldiers we single out one for special mention' wrote Dillon and Bradford. 'Col David Stirling DSO, OBE, "father" of the SAS and President of the SAS Regimental Association, who has kindly written the Foreword.

* Lowson arrived at our interview in 2002 with a copy of *Rogue Warrior*, several pages of which he had flagged as inaccurate and he explained in detail why this was.

His approval opened all doors, in a sense, and made our task considerable easier.'

In his foreword, Stirling talked as much about himself as he did Mayne. He said they were kindred spirits in a sense; he the 'painter manqué' who, to compensate for his failure as an artist, was driven to take on the greatest physical challenge left to man on earth – climbing Mount Everest. Mayne, for his part, was tormented by the 'extreme frustration' of having no outlet for his creative energy. No outlet? He was an international sportsman, who each week experienced the adrenalin rush of performing in front of thousands of raucous spectators. Stirling, who disliked competitive sport, had no understanding of the joy, excitement and meaning it can give to a man.

It was this frustration, claimed Stirling, that was responsible for his 'satanic ferocity', which on at least one occasion caused the Irishman to push 'ruthlessness to the point of callousness'.

This was an oblique reference to the raid on Tamet in December 1941 when Mayne kicked open the door of the pilots' mess and opened fire. There was nothing callous about his action; it was that of a guerrilla fighter. The aircrew were a legitimate target as enemy combatants, and some may have had side arms. It was easier for the enemy to find replacement aircraft than it was the men to fly them. Mayne's only regret was that he had killed them before sabotaging the aircraft; that had been imprudent. Better to silently plant the bombs and then shoot the aircrews.

Stirling's snide barb overlooked the fact that he himself had done something similar at Benina, although when he threw the grenade into the enemy guardroom most of the occupants were in their bunks. That is callous, killing men as they slept. Mayne looked men in the eye when he took their lives.

Rogue Warrior was the book Stirling wanted written about his nemesis. It undermined Mayne and overstated Stirling. A typical sentence (describing the Fuka/Bagush raid of June 1942) ran: 'Then

Stirling had another of his inspirations, as always so shiningly simple that anyone, in theory, might have thought of it. They would drive on to the field and shoot up the planes.'

The LRDG had thought of it eighteen months earlier and executed the tactic at Murzak. Stirling the imitator, not the innovator.

Rogue Warrior repeated Stirling's fallacious stories about the origin of L Detachment, including springing Mayne from a military prison and his breaking in to GHQ to push his memo into the hands of Neil Ritchie.

It portrayed Stirling as the fearless devil-may-care swashbuckler and Mayne as the cynical, brooding rogue warrior touched by depression. There was the odd clue, however, to why – or rather who – was behind this characterisation. Between Stirling and Mayne, wrote the authors, 'there was always good-humoured but intense competition, an almost schoolboyish desire to claim the bigger "bag"'.

There was no competition on Mayne's part. Why would there be? There was only one winner. As Bob Bennett remarked, 'The funny thing was that all the operations, the big success ones were Paddy's, and David, as much as he tried, couldn't get those planes.'[4]

Mayne didn't take Stirling seriously as a guerrilla fighter, and it embittered Stirling for the rest of his life. Again, there are clues in *Rogue Warrior.* 'I was more fond of Paddy than he was of me,' wrote Stirling. The authors countered this claim by citing a comment in a letter written from Mayne to Bill Stirling, in which he said: 'I only wish that DS was around.' That is likely to have been an ironic joke between the pair, the only two men in the SAS who understood the extent of Stirling's incompetency.

As to why Mayne wasn't honoured with a Victoria Cross, Stirling told the authors that there was 'considerable prejudice' against Mayne because of his reluctance to take orders from superiors; one such example was in 1944, when he was placed on a 'hit list by Hitler' and therefore ordered to remain in London. But in defiance of this command he parachuted into France. There was no such list and Mayne had dropped into France with Capt Mike Sadler, now the 1SAS intelligence officer, to liaise with the various SAS commanders in the expectation they would be providing reconnaissance for a forthcoming large airborne operation codenamed 'Transfigure'.*

Mayne never exhibited a reluctance to take orders, and he was held in high regard by Gen Dempsey, Field Marshal Montgomery, Gen Alexander and Brigs McLeod and Calvert. The fact he was denied a VC in 1945 was not because of these officers but someone higher up, perhaps the Prime Minister, who was a friend of David Stirling. While there is no evidence that Stirling used his influence both within government and at Buckingham Palace, one cannot rule out the possibility that he had a small but significant say in the decision to deny his rival Britain's highest military honour.

It was also claimed in the book that Mayne had an 'antipathy' towards women and felt very uncomfortable in their presence, which was untrue. There are numerous instances of his enjoying female company, such as during his recuperation from malaria in July 1941, and again in 1946. Forced to withdraw from an expedition to the Antarctic with a back injury, he spent two weeks in hospital in the Falkland Islands and appreciated the attention of a nurse. 'Quite enjoyed my stay,' he wrote in his journal. 'The matron was pleasant, Joan Treize her name.'[5] He brought home a photograph of her.

Mayne had an old-fashioned view of women, regarding them as the weaker sex, but he recognised and appreciated their strengths, and welcomed their company in the appropriate setting.

What he didn't like was women weakening the *esprit de corps* that he had so diligently cultivated since taking command. Duncan Ridler, who was part of 1SAS's intelligence section, recalled that one night in the spring of 1945, when the regiment was based at Chelmsford, Mayne

* Before Transfigure could be put into effect, German resistance finally broke and Gen George S. Patton led his Third Army out of Normandy.

walked into the officers' mess and saw his second-in-command, Harry Poat, entertaining a lady friend. 'Paddy ordered Poat to get her out and said, "come and have a proper drink with me",' Ridler recounted.[6]

Mike Sadler and Mayne spent a week enjoying the charming hospitality of several Parisian women in the autumn of 1944. 'But he didn't like them in the mess when his boys were there because they interfered with the dynamic,' said Sadler.[7]

It was Stirling who had the misogynistic streak, the man who in a schoolboy debate had argued for the motion that 'women are taking too great a part in public life'.[8]

Rarely seen in the company of women, apart from those who had a family connection, such as Hermione Ranfurly, or those who served a function, such as Virginia Cowles, he admitted he didn't like coquetry and implied that women didn't provide him with 'mental stimulus'.[9] Virginia Nicholson, who was the first wife of Orson Welles before they divorced and she married Jack Pringle, loathed Stirling. She found him cold, hostile and arrogant.

Stirling preferred men and his favourite haunts were exclusive London clubs.

It was around the time of *Rogue Warrior*'s publication that scurrilous rumours began to circulate about Mayne's sexuality. Whispers, innuendo, scuttlebutt. When the book was reissued in 2012 it contained a postscript, written by Martin Dillon (Ray Bradford had since died). Admitting that an assessment of Mayne's sexuality was superficial speculation based on 'very limited data provided by those who knew him best', Dillon insinuated that Mayne had been a homosexual and this was withheld when the book was first published. He had raised the subject with Stirling over late-night drinks at his office but he 'gently sidestepped my questions by quickly moving the topic to his private business interests … that was Stirling's way of evading issues'.

Johnny Cooper did not sidestep the question when I raised it with him in 2001. He had been bemused and angry to learn of the rumours;

he had never seen any evidence that Mayne was homosexual, but he had witnessed Mayne's heterosexuality during the war. Another veteran who rubbished much of what was written about Mayne in *Rogue Warrior* was Arthur Thompson, who joined L Detachment in early 1942 and served with the SAS for the rest of the war. 'Some have tried to say he was gay: that was wrong,' he told me. 'Some people have said that Paddy Mayne didn't like Catholics. I saw no evidence of that; Irishmen were Irishmen to Paddy and nothing was complicated.' Asked to describe Mayne, Thompson replied: 'Paddy was a quiet man, but he was very hard. He loved a booze-up and a punch-up. I remember being at Kabrit ... you were having a beer about ten at night, and Paddy would walk in at eleven and it was an unwritten rule that nobody left till he did and that was two in the morning. But in the morning you had to be up at six. He'd be there, and he would expect you to be there.'[10]

If Stirling was reticent about Mayne's sexuality he readily portrayed what he alleged was his bigotry towards Catholics. After the war, Stirling explained, he had invited Mayne to dinner at the home of the Duke of Norfolk and the pair got on well. Later Stirling ribbed Mayne for having enjoyed the company of one of Britain's most prominent Catholics. 'Blair was furious,' said Stirling, 'and to punish me insisted that I do the "test of courage"'.[11] This entailed Stirling standing up straight, arms at his side, and then falling backwards, whereupon Mayne might or might not catch him. He did, but Stirling was so unnerved by the experience he didn't introduce Mayne to any more of his Catholic friends.

A few months later Stirling repeated this anecdote to another author, Alan Hoe, who had been commissioned to write the authorised biography of the Phantom Major. This time, however, the scene took place at the home of Sandy Scratchley, and it was after the Duke of Norfolk had departed that Mayne conducted his test of courage; in this instance it was Scratchley who fell backwards.

Mayne had no animus towards Catholics. His best friend had been Eoin McGonigal, and he had admired Bill Stirling. The only Catholic he didn't like was David, but that had nothing to do with religion.

One of the most remarkable features – perhaps skills is a better word – of David Stirling was how he corrupted the common sense of fine and intelligent men. He literally bewitched them. George Jellicoe and David Lloyd Owen admitted they were under his spell. Julian Amery, who had a distinguished war before entering politics, was also an admirer, although he was able to recognise his idol's imperfections. 'Persuasiveness was his stock in trade,' he said of Stirling. 'He could flatter brazenly, brush aside difficulties and exercise very considerable personal charm to achieve his ends.' He was extravagant and 'utterly careless about husbanding his resources', added Amery, 'and even close friends could be worried at being touched by him for a loan knowing that his powers of persuasion were irresistible and repayment uncertain'.[12]

Jellicoe was unrestrained in his adulation of Stirling, claiming that he had earned the Victoria Cross 'ten or fifteen times' and was 'by common consent one of the most under decorated officers in the British army'.[13] The only people who thought that were Stirling's minions.

In 1957 Lloyd Owen published *The Desert My Dwelling Place*, an evocative account of his time with the LRDG in North Africa. But one passage was invented, presumably to ingratiate himself with his idol. 'The moment I met David in the early light of dawn on 20th November 1941, I was captivated by his charm and self-assurance,' wrote Lloyd Owen. He claimed that it was he who encountered Stirling and Bob Tait in the aftermath of the inaugural L Detachment parachute operation. '"My name's Stirling,"' he said, almost as though we were meeting for the first time outside his Club in London. "Have you seen any of my chaps?"'[14]

Lloyd Owen told him that Paddy Mayne and his section had arrived some time earlier. They then drank a mug of tea, and during the course of their conversation 'suddenly an idea came to me'. What if in future the LRDG transported Stirling and his men to their objectives?

It was a tall tale, told for literary effect. Jake Easonsmith, who was killed in 1943, was the officer responsible for collecting L Detachment, and Stirling and Tait arrived at the rendezvous *before* Mayne's section. And the partnership between L Detachment and the LRDG was formed later, not in this eureka moment. Why did Lloyd Owen, a gallant and perceptive commander in the war, spin this yarn? Embarrassingly for Lloyd Owen, when *The Phantom Major* was published a year later Virginia Cowles described how Stirling and Tait were greeted at the rendezvous by the 'smiling face' of Easonsmith.

Lloyd Owen's version was more romantic, however, so Stirling picked up the thread and weaved it into his web of deceit, recounting it to Alan Hoe.

The foreword to the authorised biography was written by Gen Sir Peter de la Billière, KCB, KBE, DSO, MC, who had recently commanded the British forces in Operation Granby, the first Gulf War, in 1990. He likened the book's subject to Robin Hood, called him a visionary, a legend in his time, and said it had been his privilege to serve for twenty years in a regiment that had been fed by Stirling with a 'diet of inspiration and innovation'.

Stirling was not a visionary. Nor, as Philip Warner wrote in his history of the SAS, was he a military genius who 'devised a brilliant plan for helping to win the war'.

Wilfred Thesiger, who served with Stirling for a matter of weeks at the end of 1942, claimed in his autobiography, *The Life of My Choice*, that David Stirling's 'material contribution to the victory in the desert was certainly comparable to Wingate's in Burma ... both Stirling's and Wingate's concepts of operations were original'.

This statement does not stand up to scrutiny. Wingate achieved success as an innovative guerrilla fighter in the British Mandate of Palestine in the 1930s, and in helping defeat Italy in Abyssinia in

1941. His contribution to victory in Burma was negligible: a two-month guerrilla campaign in early 1943 diminished his unwieldly and poorly trained force of three thousand men by a third, a heavy toll for a few blown bridges and cut railway lines. Undoubtedly, the principal success of his Chindit long-range penetration force was its propaganda value for Winston Churchill when he met President Roosevelt at the Quebec Conference in August 1943. Churchill was as smitten with Wingate as he was with Stirling: he was a sucker for self-confident, swashbuckling poseurs.

So was Thesiger. Although he recognised Wingate's incorrigible conceit, he claimed that the Phantom Major 'shunned affectation … he avoided all self-advertisement'.[15]

Leaving aside the fact that it was Bob Laycock who first came up with the idea of dropping a small team of parachutists behind enemy lines to attack airfields, the proof that Stirling was neither a genius nor a visionary is contained in three documents, two written in 1941 and one seven years later, and all by David Stirling. The first was in fact a joint effort with Bill, from July 1941. It was headed 'Training of Parachute Troops (Suggestions from Lieut. D. A. Stirling, Scots Guards)' and its salient points are as follows:

With the final disbandment of Layforce there is now no organisation left for prosecuting raids on enemy lines of communication, aerodromes, oil dumps and other enemy dispositions on which damage can be inflicted … if, then, in the Near East, raids of this nature cannot be seaborne I suggest the immediate establishment of a parachute training centre to supply the answer by air.

While the enemy in Libya and elsewhere labour under the present restriction of reinforcements of material and men, the landings of small parties at night on a wide range of objectives will produce maximum effect. The enemy will be forced to withdraw from the front considerable bodies of men to protect these activities and the material successfully sabotaged he will find harder to replace.

It will be necessary to gain the cooperation of the SNO [senior naval officer] commanding submarines. The withdrawal of parties after operations will usually have to be by submarines. Therefore the operations must always be on a scale to warrant the use of a submarine's time.

The document then outlined how he envisaged dividing the training into two phases.

> 1st phase: The period in which a small training centre is established which will be instructional and operational. The instruction at this stage will be designed to enable the original personnel to carry out within two weeks of establishment small scale operations at night.
>
> 2nd phase: The expansion of the training centre to an establishment which could look after the training of recruits on a scale to make possible the night landing of 15 to 20 parties at the same time.[16]

There was nothing visionary about this proposal to form a small airborne raiding unit, as Stirling himself explained in the document he drafted with Bill: 'The Germans have demonstrated with huge losses of personnel (in Crete) that the tactical landing of parachutists is not practicable except in the face of wholly unorganised opposition. On the other hand they have emphasised with many successes, notably in Greece, the results to be gained by small scale strategical landings.'

The only innovation Stirling championed in the document was night parachute operations, which, when he put it into practice in November 1941, ended in disaster.

A few months later – the exact date is unknown, but Stirling signed himself 'Captain', which narrows it from 22 July 1941 to February 1942 – he submitted a second memo to GHQ. This one was titled 'Training of parachutists in Middle East. Most secret.'[17]

It was in response to an idea of a parachute battalion mooted by GHQ. Stirling was enthusiastic and said 'it is practicable to train a Bn or a Bde [brigade] within a short period'. The training facilities and instructor were already available, 'or could be quickly made sufficient to train 200 parachutists in a 5 weeks course'.

He advocated 'the abandoning of the volunteer system' as it 'adds very greatly to the time required for such a formation to become operatively effective'. Instead, an existing battalion should be taken over and trained as parachutists, comprising '4 Coys of 100 men each, a small operative HQ group and a non-operative Administrative Coy of 100 men'. He acknowledged that because of the grave shortage of manpower in the Middle East it may be regarded as unfeasible to permanently appropriate to the parachute unit a brigade. In other words, Stirling believed that any soldier could be trained to be a guerrilla fighter; this displayed a surprising ignorance of the psychological aspect of irregular warfare. It was an incomprehension shared by Orde Wingate when, in 1943, he raised the Chindits to fight in Burma. The men of the 13th King's (Liverpool) Regiment had no say in whether they wanted to become Chindits, and most did not rise to the challenge, not through want of trying but because they were not equipped for special forces soldiering, physically or mentally.

As to the role of the proposed battalion or brigade, Stirling wrote that it could be deployed on a combined operation for the purposes of forming a bridgehead for a combined landing; dropped behind the enemies lines for the harassing of enemy lines of communications, raids on enemy HQs and nerve centres, aerodromes etc., or used in small groups for sabotage and light demolitions.

The third document was written in November 1948 at the request of Roderick McLeod, who had commanded the SAS Brigade in 1944 and who played an influential role in the dismissal of Bill Stirling. McLeod was the Assistant Commandant at the Camberley Staff College in 1948 and asked David Stirling for a memorandum on 'The Origins of the Special Air Service'.* What Stirling wrote in a key paragraph bore little relation to what he had proposed in 1941:

> I argued [with GHQ] the advantages of establishing a unit based on the principle of the fullest exploitation of surprise and of making the minimum demands on manpower and equipment. I argued that the application of this principle would mean in effect the employment of a sub-unit of five men to cover a target previously requiring four troops of a commando, i.e., about 200 men. I sought to prove that, if an aerodrome or transport park was the objective of an operation, then the destruction of 50 aircraft or units of transport was more easily accomplished by a sub-unit of five men than by a force of 200 men. I further concluded that 200 properly selected, trained and equipped men, organised into sub-units of five should be able to attack at least thirty different objectives at the same time on the same night as compared to only one objective using the commando technique; and that only 25% success in the former was the equivalent to many times the maximum possible result in the latter.

At no point in the two documents submitted in 1941–2 had Stirling talked about sub-units of five men attacking thirty different targets. On the contrary, by late 1941 he was warming to the idea of L Detachment's expansion to a battalion or even brigade. Furthermore, if

* This was the memorandum that he sent to Maj Pat Hart in 1950 when Vivian Street had the idea to write a book about the SAS.

Stirling had been truly committed to parachuting why did he abandon the concept after the first raid, a failure of his own making when he ignored the advice of Brig Galloway to heed the storm warning?

He did approach Peter Oldfield, his contact in the RAF, in December 1941 about the possibility of another parachute operation but his failure to go through the proper channels infuriated the Eighth Army, which led to a combined army and RAF memorandum dated 25 February 1942. This laid out the procedure for planning minor operations involving parachute droppings. Stirling could be petulant when thwarted and, rebuffed by the RAF, he abandoned the idea of any future parachute operation. Yet GHQ continued to regard L Detachment as an airborne special force. On 10 March 1942 Lt-Gen Arthur Smith, the outgoing Chief of the General Staff in Cairo, had told Lt-Gen Neil Ritchie that 'Stirling's chief value is that of commanding a parachute force'.[18] The following month, on 22 April, Ritchie had written to his commander-in-chief, Claude Auchinleck, about the possibility of Stirling subsuming the Middle East Commando into L Detachment, but he acknowledged that 'this may not fit in with your need to have him in connection with parachutist training'.

It clearly didn't because less than a fortnight later, 3 May, Stirling wrote to GHQ about the future direction of L Detachment, arguing against the prospect of his unit being 'broken up to provide instructors' for a proposed parachute force recruited from the Indian formations in the Middle East. This was understandable, and it would have been an unforgiveable waste of fighting talent to turn the likes of Paddy Mayne, Reg Seekings and Bill Fraser into instructors.

But why didn't L Detachment conduct any more parachute operations? Parachute instruction remained a core component of training at Kabrit, although Stirling himself does not appear to have made any more jumps after the debacle of November 1941. He may have lost his nerve.

Above all, Stirling concluded that desert parachuting was impractical. Even if they were dropped accurately, the men and the containers of arms, explosives and precious water were scattered over a wide area and – particularly at night – took time to recover. Then there was the challenge of navigation, never a strong skill within L Detachment. It made far more sense to hitch a lift on the back of an LRDG truck. Stirling claimed in his memo to GHQ on 3 May that he and his men could attack as many as thirty targets simultaneously 'by the method of staggering the dropping of parties by LRDG near the targets'.

However, when Bill Stirling raised 2SAS in May 1943 he immediately began planning a series of parachute drops into Italy, land far easier to live off. His intention was to saturate the north of the country with small units of two to six men so that the Germans' lines of communications and transport were severely disrupted. 'Bill was a great strategic thinker,' said Roy Farran in a 1987 interview. 'He did realise that if you dropped small parties way behind enemy lines you could cut their lines of communication and cause panic. All military tactics are: you either break them from the front or you go to the left or the right, but a new flank is opened with aircraft and you can go over the top, and if you bust their lines of communication, they are liable to panic and yield the field.'[19]

Between them in July 1941, David and Bill Stirling created the idea for a parachute unit to operate in the desert, attacking enemy airfields and coastal installations. The thinking was Bill's and David would put the idea into practice. But then on 3 November Bill was recalled to Britain and without his big brother David was lost because he was neither a visionary nor a genius; he was a gifted salesman and then, after the war, a plagiarist who stole Bill's ideas and passed them off as his own.

'He wasn't quite like David in that David Stirling had the opportunities to lead people in actual action in the field,' said Farran of Bill. 'When Bill came along [as CO of 2SAS] it was a different proposition. It was in Europe, more fixed lines of defence of the enemy, and you hadn't these huge open flanks that you had in the desert. Bill was more of a planner than a leader on the ground, but all the same he was a very, very great soldier and he played a great part in Britain's eventual victory in the war.'

That was Bill's contribution to the war, described by an officer who perhaps knew him better than anyone in 2SAS, and one who finished the war with a DSO and MC and two bars; only Mayne could boast a more distinguished SAS career than Farran.

Carol Mather, who served in Layforce and then L Detachment/1SAS for several months, described David's contribution: 'One thing David Stirling did bring to the face of modern war, by this time so entrenched and mechanized, was an erstwhile spirit of chivalry in the very gaiety and dare-devilry of his operations ... his operations often had that touch of humour about them that mystified our enemy.'[20]

It took an American, Virginia Cowles, to see in David Stirling the quintessential British character: the plucky romantic, the endearingly incompetent, but always game to go on. The Charge of the Light Brigade, Isandlwana and the defence of Rorke's Drift, Gordon of Khartoum, Mons, Dunkirk: no country romanticises military defeats as enthusiastically as the British.

It also explains why the blundering and amateurish Captain Scott was immortalised after his death in Antarctica in 1912. Roald Amundsen, in contrast, the ruthlessly efficient professional whose journey to and from the South Pole was fairly straightforward, received far less acclaim.

So was it for Bill, the Amundsen to David's Scott.

Contrary to Peter de la Billière's claim in his foreword to Alan Hoe's biography, David Stirling had not inspired the post-war SAS; what he had done, as de la Billière knew full well, was drag the regiment's name through the gutter, to the point where de la Billière had felt compelled to defend the honour of the SAS in a letter to a newspaper.

But de la Billière was a member of the Establishment, as was David Lloyd Owen, who had remained in the army after the war and risen to the rank of major general. So were most of the people who contributed to Hoe's book: the 16th Earl of Dalhousie, Field Marshal the Lord Bramall, Gen Sir John Hackett, Sir Stephen Hastings, the Earl Jellicoe, Sir Fitzroy Maclean, the Duke of Richmond, the Earl of Scarborough, Margaret Thatcher, Viscount Whitelaw, Lady Susan Wood and Lt-Col John Woodhouse.

Stirling tried to portray himself as an outsider, a born rebel, but as *The Times* had said in its review of *The Phantom Major* three decades earlier, he had always been an Establishment man from top to toe. He took tea with the Queen, dined with the Prime Minister and in 1975 wrote to Lord Hailsham suggesting Britain should have a written constitution.

The maverick was Bill Stirling.

It was one of the many fallacies in a book that was less a biography and more a hagiography.

Alan Hoe was well intentioned but he was in awe of his subject – never a good starting point for a biographer. Stirling's health was failing and the book was his last will and testament, his final attempt to control the narrative of his life.

An inordinate amount of space was devoted to the Capricorn Africa Society as Stirling sought to convince the world it had played an important role in shaping the continent. He may have regretted his blunt (and honest) assessment to the *Observer* interviewer Gavin Young in 1974, when he described the Capricorn Society as 'a total failure'.

Stirling must also have been hurt by his friend Laurens van der Post's recollection of Capricorn in *Yet Being Someone Other.* In a case of the biter bit, van der Post inflated his role by implying that he and Stirling had been equals in the society and had both 'nearly ruined ourselves financially'. Van der Post had contributed little in that regard; he had 'liberalised' and enlightened Capricorn. In describing the 'failure' of the enterprise, van der Post emasculated Stirling, recalling how the stress of the venture left him 'dangerously ill' with 'almost lethal physical depletion'. Mentally, too, Stirling had suffered, and here van der Post revealed how close he had been to Stirling spiritually, close enough to detect the anguished child within the arrogant man. Stirling was worn down by Capricorn's foundering, wrote van der Post, adding: 'I was more protected than he because I did not have his inner sense of defeat.'[21]

Ironically, there were parallels between van der Post's autobiography and Stirling's authorised biography. The former's biographer, J. D. F. Jones, remarked in his 2001 book, *Storyteller*, that van der Post's 1982 memoir was best described 'as a fiction, or, better, a romance'. Despite this, continued Jones, few of van der Post's associates disputed his version of his life even though they knew that much of what he had written was a fabrication. Why the silence? A misguided sense of loyalty or 'had Laurens become so famous and distinguished, so close to the English Establishment, that he seemed immune to correction?'

The same question can be asked of David Stirling. The most insightful analysis in Hoe's biography came from Peter Stirling, who said his brother 'could sell anything, but he had to be controlled'. He admired David's energy and initiative, and his ability to launch an idea, but unfortunately sometimes 'he was a bit short on finishing them'.[22]

Hoe admitted in the preface that he had been inspired to join the SAS in the 1960s after reading *The Phantom Major* and when he came face to face with Stirling he, like so many others, fell under his spell. Hoe wasn't totally uncritical, and one must bear in mind that before the advent of the internet it was harder for a biographer to verify the minutiae of his subject's life.

He questioned Stirling's decision to proceed with the parachute operation in November 1941 against the advice of Eighth Army HQ and he described as improbable Stirling's claim that he charmed de Gaulle into releasing the French paratroopers into L Detachment.

He challenged his assertion that he had been a peripheral figure in GB75 and teased out the complex relationship between Stirling and his mother (but not Bill, who hardly features, although David is said to have disparaged the commando training at Inverailort, describing it as 'wrong' and 'unwieldly'), and Hoe gently probed his bachelor status. Fear, replied Stirling, when asked why he had never married. He had been in love – what fully grown man has not? – but he didn't elaborate on the sex of his paramour.

As Hoe wrote cryptically on the last page of his book, there was a side to Stirling that 'no one was allowed to know'.

Stirling's first serious love affair was when he lived in Salisbury in the 1950s, with a Rhodesian man. There must have been other boyfriends and other affairs – perhaps, for instance, with Cecil Beaton and Mark Ogilvie-Grant – but Stirling guarded his private life with a rigour that he never displayed when it came to protecting military secrets. Who can blame him, a Catholic aristocrat and war hero? One can only feel compassion for what Stirling must have suffered; he was of a generation brought up to regard homosexuality as an evil, with its practitioners to be punished. And they were: two of his contemporaries, Mike Calvert and the codebreaker Alan Turing, were destroyed because of their homosexuality. Stirling was more careful, even though his inner circle knew the truth.

Others were less discreet. Reg Seekings, for example, who after the war emigrated to Southern Rhodesia and became an inspector in the police anti-terrorist unit, sometimes regaled his colleagues with wartime tales, including his description of Stirling as an 'arsehole' and a 'queer'.[23]

A man's sexuality is his own business, but Stirling's – and his struggle to come to terms with it as a young man – was the very essence of his character. He admitted to Alan Hoe that he was a mess as a youth because of the grinding pressure he felt on the subject of sex; what adolescent don't suffer some angst? But Stirling's misery was visceral. How much did his mother suspect?

Margaret Stirling had a deep Catholic faith and an intimidating exterior but beneath she was warm, loving and broad-minded. Did she ask David why he avoided her dances, which doubled as marriage markets? Perhaps packing him off to America in 1938 was her way of trying to help. Maybe rumours had started to circulate about David even then.

Stirling called his puberty 'totally confused, guilt-ridden years'[24] and he never fully accepted his sexuality. It remained a source of shame, and it was one of the reasons he didn't acknowledge Bill Fraser's outstanding contribution to the SAS: Fraser was gay and a constant reminder to Stirling of his own great secret.

Ultimately the shame drove Stirling to concoct an alter ego, that of the bold and fearless action man. It was a sham that slowly sucked him into an orbit of falsehoods and fantasy to the point where, towards the end of his life, in his mind he became Paddy Mayne and Mayne became David Stirling.

Mayne may well have guessed that Stirling was homosexual. Reg Seekings knew, so there is a strong possibility that Mayne did too. It might have affected his attitude towards Stirling as he viewed homosexuality as did most people of his generation. Jimmy Storie recalled that in the sergeants' mess at Kabrit, Mayne occasionally picked on Bill Fraser 'because he thought he was that way inclined'.[25]

In his biography, Stirling claims that he understood what drove Mayne. It was an inner torment, a depressive streak, a destructive fury that made him unstable and unsuitable as a leader. Stirling was talking about himself.

Many thousands of words have been written about Paddy Mayne. Most have been wide of the mark; he was neither a 'psychopath' nor a 'social misfit'.[26] Only those who saw Mayne up close, in the stress of combat, grasped the real essence of the man. None more so than Malcolm Pleydell.

Pleydell said that Mayne enjoyed war and went into the desert in search of 'some good killing' within the rules of the game.[27] For most people – particularly in the soft, safety-obsessed West of the twenty-first century – that is unfathomable. But Mayne saw guerrilla warfare as an extension of sport; man against man, a battle of mind and muscle. Blowing up an aircraft or shooting a sentry gave him the same thrill as scoring a try or tackling an opponent.

The Stirling who understood Mayne was Bill. They were similar men. They abhorred the 'trivialities and meanness of modern life' and yet within them was an 'intangible core of nobility which lay inviolate'.[28]

The same could not be said of David.

Stirling claimed that what brought him and Mayne together was a boozy night in Kabrit when they talked of life before the war. He said that Mayne had first forgiven him for being a Catholic, a bigotry that existed only in Stirling's imagination.

Stirling then said he told Mayne about his failure as an artist, and how it led him to take on the challenge of climbing Mount Everest. At this moment, Mayne became animated.

It was during his 1987 interview with Gordon Stevens that Stirling first made the claim that he was a 'painter manqué'. There was no mention of it in the blaze of publicity that surrounded the Phantom Major's exploits in 1942, nor in the book of that name, which said that after flunking Cambridge he 'passed some months in idleness' before telling his mother he was going to climb Everest. Nor did Carol Mather make any allusion to it when he wrote the first draft of his war memoir in the late 1940s; he did, however, mention that François Martin, the French officer who was with Stirling shortly before his capture in Tunisia, had before the war 'been an art student in Paris'.[29]

Stirling claimed that his teacher had been André Lhote, the French Cubist painter, who died in 1962, four years after the publication of *The Phantom Major*, in which Stirling made no mention of his artistic bent.

Stirling told Alan Hoe that he had spent a year and a half in Paris, enjoying the avant-garde lifestyle of the Left Bank and its pavement cafés in Montmartre while studying under André Lhote, who ran an academy in rue d'Odessa near Montparnasse railway station. Montparnasse is on the Left Bank but Montmartre is on the Right Bank, several miles from Montparnasse. That can be ascribed to a geographical error, common enough, even though Stirling was a regular visitor to the city. The archivist at the André Lhote Association in France has no record of David Stirling having studied at the academy.

More of a puzzle, however, is the chronology of Stirling's movements in the mid- to late 1930s.

Stirling left Ampleforth at Easter 1934 and matriculated at Cambridge on 5 December that year. He spent three terms at Trinity in total: Lent (January to March) 1935, Michaelmas (October to December) 1935 and Lent 1936. He then had a few months working in the office of an Edinburgh architects. On 25 July 1937 he was attached to the 1st Battalion Scots Guards for a month's preliminary training; on 4 July 1938 he spent another four weeks training with the battalion. In September 1938 he had tea with Queen Mary at Keir and on 11 November he sailed for the United States.

Not only did Stirling tell his biographer he spent eighteen months painting in Paris, but once that dream was shattered he embraced the new challenge to climb Everest, and with that goal in mind spent twelve months in the Swiss Alps.

But the longest unaccounted gap between Stirling leaving school and going to America is a ten-month period from September 1937 to early July 1938. But if he was in Paris then, when did he spend a year in Switzerland?

The short answer is that he never went to Paris. He made it up, just as he made up the story of Mount Everest.

He did a spot of climbing, like his brother Bill and thousands of other Britons in the 1930s, who took the Alpine air on their holidays. Stirling went to America to ranch, not to climb; that's why he described himself as a rancher on arriving in New York and on his return to Southampton.

Stirling reached New York on 20 November. Surely a man in training for Everest would have headed straight to the mountains? Not Stirling. He spent three months enjoying the high life and left the city only when his mother despatched Margaret across the Atlantic to take her dissolute brother in hand. By the time he headed west, therefore, it was early spring.

Additionally, why go all the way to the United States – where the highest peak (excluding Alaska) is the 14,505ft Mount Whitney in California – when there was the 15,774ft of Mont Blanc to scale in France?

Stirling was vague in describing his time in America, and Hoe admitted that his movements were indeterminate. One anecdote Stirling recounted was of his frequently telephoning his bank manager in Scotland – reversed charges, naturally – to request an extension to his overdraft to cover his losses on the gaming tables. But a transatlantic call in the 1930s took hours to organise because there were only a few times of the day when conditions were right at both ends of the radio path. As for the idea of Stirling reversing the charges, it's pushing the bounds of credibility to believe that international telephone service operators would agree to waste precious 'talk time' brokering a deal over who was paying for the call.

Then there was Stirling's story about visiting Las Vegas. He left his horses in Los Alamos and took a train to the mecca of gambling, where he emerged a winner. It was a yarn spun to enhance the legend of the light-hearted Stirling, as was the telephone tale. Vegas in the late 1930s was a dusty backwater of a few thousand people with a handful of seedy brothels and casinos. It wasn't until the 1940s that the glamorous 'Strip' sprang up, with the first resort hotel and casino. Furthermore, a train journey from Los Alamos to Las Vegas was an arduous undertaking; it entailed changing at Santa Fe onto a train to Lamy, New Mexico. Then west to Kingman, Arizona, transferring onto a train to California, changing at Barstow and finally heading north-east to Las Vegas.[30]

But all this is superfluous detail. Stirling was never anywhere near Las Vegas. When he heard that war was declared he was in Montana, having driven his horses south from Bella Coola.

En route, boasted Stirling, he made a detour to summit Mount Stimson, at 10,000ft the second highest peak in Montana's Glacier National Park.

Described by J. Gordon Edwards in his 1960 book *A Climber's Guide to Glacier National Park* as 'truly a monster of a mountain', Stimson is guarded by a long, difficult approach, and six thousand feet of vertical climb. Edwards and his wife, Alice, made the first recorded summer ascent in 1951, although they did find evidence suggesting that someone had beaten them to it. Could it have been Stirling? No. It was a peak far beyond his capabilities. Even today few people have soloed the mountain; in 2009 experienced mountaineer Jason Robertson finally managed the feat at the ninth attempt (six failures in winter and two in the summer). Stirling would have us believe he knocked off Stimson on his own without any problem, and then forgot to mention this significant mountaineering first for half a century.

From Mount Stimson, Stirling said he headed south to the Lewis and Clark Range, and from there rode east to the Fort Belknap Indian Reservation, a 350-mile round trip. In fact it's nearer 450 miles, a long way to go just to indulge Stirling's fascination with Native American folklore. Apparently the Stirlings had played a role in the Indian Wars of the nineteenth century. Stirling didn't elaborate on what this was.

Stirling told Hoe that while he rode back and forth across the western States he was constantly working out the logistics for his impending expedition to Everest, right down to the smallest detail.

Alas, he had overlooked one crucial fact: in 1939 one couldn't just head off to Everest on a whim. There was a procedure, which entailed an approach to the Mount Everest Committee. They met on 14 June 1939 and voted to launch expeditions in 1940, 1941 and 1942. None involved Stirling. Finally, if his dream in 1939 was to climb Everest why did he not resurrect it after the war? The peak was still there, waiting to be conquered.

The lies kept coming. On learning of the outbreak of war, Stirling said he was ordered home by his mother by the cheapest means possible but he cocked a snook at her and flew home first class. No. He sailed home on the SS *Manhattan* and on arriving at Southampton he gave his 'Occupation' as 'Rancher', and his address not as 'Dunblane' but as 'Dumbland, Scotland'. An infantile joke from an immature young man.

There were other deceptions, and exaggerations and manipulations of the truth. The odd inadvertent confession too, such as the cause of the car crash that killed Arthur Merton in May 1942. In his letter to his father in June 1942, Randolph Churchill had blamed the crash on the inattention of a truck driver. But Stirling revealed to Hoe that he was at fault. Speeding through the darkness in his haste to reach Cairo, Stirling misjudged the distance between himself and the last truck in the column and caught its rear wheel. Hoe described the injuries suffered by Stirling's friends but did not mention that a man had been killed by his impetuous driving.

So narcissistic was Stirling, he was in the habit of claiming a friendship with anyone of importance: Evelyn Waugh, for example, was a wartime confidant; he wasn't. But Bill Stirling was one of the few people Waugh genuinely admired and respected. He considered David an amusing wastrel.

A sad picture comes to mind in the post-war years, as numerous high-ranking figures published their memoirs, of Stirling rushing to a bookshop and frantically scanning the indexes in the hope of seeing his name. None mentioned him.

His disappointment must have been acute when Winston Churchill released *The Hinge of Fate* in 1950. It covered 1942, a year that ended with the Allies on top in North Africa and in the Pacific. It was a momentous year, and yet not one small reference to Stirling, the man who had apparently enchanted Churchill on 8 August and again the following evening.

Instead, Churchill described how he spent 8 August with the Yeomanry Division before returning to Cairo at around 5 p.m. with a heavy heart, for he had to relieve Auchinleck of his command. He wrote a letter for Brig Ian Jacob to deliver to the Auk by hand, and then he wrote to President Roosevelt to inform him of his decision.

When Jacob returned he found the Prime Minister asleep, but on waking Churchill asked how Auchinleck had taken the news. He was then joined by Gen Alan Brooke, Chief of the Imperial General Staff. There is no mention of a dinner party at which Smuts, Alexander, Stirling and Maclean were present. Indeed, by 9 August Smuts was on his way back to South Africa as Alexander arrived in Cairo.

Alexander and Churchill conversed in the morning, and in the evening the instructions for the change in command were put in writing.

These few days in Cairo were among the most important of Churchill's premiership; the fate of the war in North Africa hinged on the decisions he was taking. But according to Stirling, Churchill devoted two evenings of his brief stay in the Egyptian capital to the military genius that was the Phantom Major, and the upcoming Benghazi raid was at the centre of the discussion.

Stirling also apparently furnished the Prime Minister with one of the most memorable phrases of the war, that of Italy as 'the soft underbelly of Europe'. Oddly, though Stirling bragged of this fact to Alan Hoe, he had forgotten to mention it to Virginia Cowles.

In reality Stirling's brief encounter with the PM was over lunch, a spot of light-hearted relief from the pressure of top-level conferences, as the latter described in a letter he wrote to his wife, Clementine, on 9 August: 'I have had all Randolph's friends to lunch with me,' he explained, naming Lords Lansdowne and Cadogan, and Col Edmund Kellett, the MP for Birmingham Aston, who was killed fighting with the Armoured Corps in 1943. Churchill was particularly intrigued by Stirling, 'who strolled in from behind the German lines, a tall, slim, dandified figure, recalling Don Juan, "he was the mildest mannered man that ever scuttled ship or cut a throat".'[31]

Stirling had a specific purpose for lunching with the PM: he knew that plans were afoot in GHQ to bring L Detachment under greater control, and he couldn't bear the thought of having his influence reduced. In the short time available to him, Stirling implored Churchill to consider his view on the subject. The PM, recognising he owed his lunch guest a favour for having taken his son under his wing, acquiesced and told his private secretary, Sir Leslie Rowan, to attend to the matter. 'I have been asked by my chief to ask you to let me have, for him, without further delay the short note for which he called on what you would advise should be done to concentrate and coordinate the work you are doing,' he informed Stirling in a memo. 'I have been asked to make sure that this in [*sic*] my hands to-day. I can be got at the Embassy.'[32]

Stirling replied on the evening of 9 August, in what was a desperate attempt to assume command of all combined operations. He advised the PM that:

> (i) The scope of 'L' Detachment should be extended so as to cover the functions of all existing Special Service Units in the Middle East as well as any other Special Service tasks which may require carrying out.
>
> (ii) Arising out of this, that all other Special Service Units be disbanded and selected personnel absorbed, as required, by 'L' Detachment.

(iii) Control to rest with the Officer Commanding 'L' Detachment and not with any outside body superimposed for purposes of co-ordination, the need for which will not arise if effect be given to the present proposals.

(iv) The planning of Operations to be carried out by 'L' Detachment to remain as hitherto the prerogative of 'L' Detachment.[33]

In short, Stirling was exhorting the PM to put him in charge of all special forces in North Africa, including the LRDG, which was to swallowed whole by L Detachment.

Stirling never got his wish. Even with the backing of Churchill, GHQ refused to countenance the idea of Stirling in command of Raiding Forces. They had Lt-Col Henry Cator in mind for the task, an appointment that eventually came to pass after Stirling's capture.

That lunch was the extent of the face-to-face communication between Stirling and the Prime Minister in Cairo. There were no long, high-spirited dinners stretching into the wee small hours. The evidence? Brooke and Alexander did not mention meeting Stirling in their war memoirs.

Nor did Richard Casey, the Minister of State in the Middle East, reference Stirling in his memoirs (published in 1946), or the Ambassador in Cairo, Sir Miles Lampson, although he did mention Peter Stirling. Churchill's physician, Charles Wilson, a garrulous and name-dropping diarist who attended the Embassy dinners, passed no comment on the presence of Stirling or Fitzroy Maclean. It is instructive that when Stirling contacted Brig George Davy in 1967 about his libel suit against the *Sunday Times*, Davy expressed his ignorance of these dinners. One might have expected the Director of Military Operations in GHQ at the time, instrumental in the planning of the Benghazi raid, to have been informed of these important discussions between Stirling and the Prime Minister.

To conclude, it is preposterous to imagine that Churchill, in a week when he was embroiled in one of the biggest crises of his premiership, spent two evenings in earnest discussion with David Stirling, a major in command of a small and inconsequential commando unit that had achieved mixed results.

Why has Stirling been able to get away with his fantasies for so long? There are several reasons. The British Establishment is easily hoodwinked by charisma, status and self-confidence: Ignatius Trebitsch-Lincoln,* Anthony Blunt, Guy Burgess, Donald Maclean, Kim Philby, Laurens van der Post and David Stirling bear witness to their collective gullibility.

Stirling – himself duped on several occasions by silver-tongued imposters – was at the heart of the Establishment; he was a very powerful, influential and litigious man, who had friends in high places and associates in dark ones. People were scared of David Stirling. Even in the course of researching this book it was difficult to find anyone who had known Stirling after the war who was willing to be interviewed. The fear lingers.

As Virginia Cowles acknowledged, there is scant documentation about the raising and formation of L Detachment; Paddy Mayne wrote a few reports about the early raids but Stirling could not be bothered with administration. This worked in his favour when it came to recounting the history of the regiment. Often it was his word against whose? Not Lewes or McGonigal, killed in 1941, or Bonington, captured on the first raid, or Fraser, a working-class man who ruined himself through drink. Would *The Phantom Major* have been published in Mayne's lifetime? No. While he was alive, Mayne was the custodian of SAS honour. Stirling took himself off to Africa

* A Hungarian con artist who befriended the Archbishop of Canterbury, defrauded his wealthy friends and was elected Liberal MP for Darlington in the 1910 election. He later became a German spy.

after the war and, as he told Peter de la Billière in the 1960s, rather lost interest in the SAS. He returned after Mayne's death.

Stirling was helped in creating the myth of the Phantom Major by a conspiracy of silence among his upper-class circle of friends. They knew the truth but they shielded him; some out of fear, some out of sycophancy, some out of sympathy for a man they pitied. There was also an element of reflected glory. It was flattering to one's ageing ego to be associated with Stirling. He had become a mythical figure and what man doesn't wish to boast to his friends and his family that he had had the distinction of serving with the Phantom Major in the SAS?

One cannot over-emphasise how the public perception of the SAS changed – literally overnight – after the 1980 Iranian Embassy siege. 'I can only say thank God for the marvellous men of the SAS who did such a magnificent job at the Iranian Embassy,' ran a letter in the *Daily Express*, typical of the nation's sentiment.

Now, wartime members of the regiment took an understandable pleasure in reliving their daring of decades earlier. For men of social distinction – Jellicoe, Mather, Maclean and Hastings – the cachet was of inestimable value for their political and diplomatic careers. Mather, in particular, was acutely aware of Stirling's flaws but perhaps out of self-interest he always offset them with an inflated assessment of his achievements. 'A bit of a gambler, a bit of a drinker,' he said after Stirling's death. 'A very amusing companion but we never saw him really in the role of a great leader, which he turned out to be. The reason for his leadership powers was the utter daringness of his plans ... There was a large element of the practical joke in the whole thing; he liked to play practical jokes on the Germans and Italians.'[34]

Of course, Mather et al. were Stirling's men, not Mayne's. Jellicoe remained enchanted by Stirling till the end of his life, but he was also unstinting in his admiration for Mayne, whom he described as 'an extraordinary tactical genius and as brave as ten lions'.[35]

The real historical victim of the cult of the SAS is the Long Range Desert Group. They were never re-formed after the war, and slowly they faded from memory, their Arab headdresses and leather chaplis relics of a romantic bygone era, replaced in the public imagination by balaclavas and Heckler & Koch submachine guns.

No one conspired more in mythologising Stirling than Fitzroy Maclean, who married into the Stirling/Lovat family in 1946 when he took as his wife Veronica, the daughter of the 14th Lord Lovat, David Stirling's uncle. There was now kinship.

In 1949 Maclean published his memoir, *Eastern Approaches*, which included a section about his brief time in L Detachment. Serialised over four issues of the *People* newspaper, Maclean was described as 'The Second Lawrence of Arabia'.

Tabloid sensationalism aside, *Eastern Approaches* was an expressive and balanced memoir, in which Maclean lauded Stirling's audacity and imagination, and described Mayne as possessing an agility of mind and body, who 'inspired absolute devotion and confidence in those he led and utter terror in the hearts of those unfortunate enough to encounter him in battle'. Maclean mentioned only in passing the car crash in May 1942 as they returned from the unsuccessful raid on Benghazi. He described his injuries, but neglected to state the cause of the crash or the fact it cost Arthur Merton his life.

It was also in *Eastern Approaches* that mention was first made of the dinner at the British Embassy in Cairo in August 1942. Curiously, however, when Virginia Cowles wrote *The Phantom Major* in 1958 (in which Maclean collaborated), she said that when Maclean and Stirling flew from Cairo to Kufra on 6 September prior to launching the Benghazi raid, Maclean was still a little rusty because he had 'been in the hospital ever since his car accident'.

Maclean did dine at the Embassy on 8 December 1943, an evening Alan Brooke recorded in his diary. Also present were Winston and Randolph Churchill, Smuts, Gen Wilson, Maclean and George

Jellicoe. Did Maclean get the two evenings confused in his memory, or did he create a fictitious dinner, at which Stirling was present, at the request of his friend?

On 20 February 1963 Fitzroy Maclean gave a lecture at the Royal United Services Institution about guerrilla warfare. Once more he waxed lyrical about Stirling, comparing him – as he had in his memoir – to Lawrence of Arabia. 'He is a most unaccountable person, and it was largely his unaccountability that bewildered the Germans in the desert,' he told his audience. 'They did not have an idea – neither for that matter did our own High Command – of what he was up to. But whereas it was often worrying and bewildering to our own Headquarters, it was very much worse for the enemy.' But what had Stirling been up to, and why was it worse for the enemy? Maclean did not elaborate. He left the statement hanging, inviting the audience to use their imagination. Not so when he came to Paddy Mayne. Along with Marshal Tito, Mayne was one of two examples cited by Maclean to demonstrate how guerrilla warfare can 'produce decisive results'. Mayne, he explained, 'drawing on a captain's pay, and using a smallish quantity of plastic high explosive, did succeed in destroying on the ground one hundred enemy aircraft in one year'.[36] Maclean was always purposely evasive about Stirling's exploits, resorting to whimsical characterisation, but with Mayne there was no need for sophistry.

Maclean wrote Stirling's entry for the *New Oxford Dictionary of National Biography* but got off to a bad start by stating his subject had been born at Keir. Stirling was born in London. How did this small but significant error occur? Maclean should have checked the records, but probably it was what David had told him, and Maclean believed everything Stirling said, including his trip to America in 1938 to climb Mount Stimson and the success of Capricorn which, according to Maclean, 'attracted wide support and made an enduring impact'.

Reviewing the new edition of the *DNB* for the *Observer* in July 1996, Richard Ingrams, erstwhile editor of *Private Eye*, remarked that on the subject of sex some biographers were explicit. But, 'the founder of the SAS, David Stirling, six foot six inches tall [*sic*] with "a strong personality" never married, for reasons that his biographer, the late Fitzroy Maclean, chooses not to elaborate upon'.

The criticism would have touched a nerve with the editors of the *National Biography*; having commissioned Maclean to write Stirling's entry they asked him prior to publication why the subject had never married as 'we are reluctant to state the fact baldly without some explanation. Do you know why he never married?' Maclean replied: 'I imagine because he never found anyone he wanted to marry. My wife, who was his first cousin, agrees with this.'[37] There was always a reluctance to delve too deeply into Stirling's life and instead to simply accept his version of events. Some of his devotees purposely distorted the truth to curry favour, such as his former commanding officer, Robert Laycock. Writing the foreword in 1954 for Charles Foley's book *Commando Extraordinary*, Laycock said of Stirling: 'More than once he would have won the highest military honour the Sovereign can bestow were it not for the rule that a senior officer must be present to vouch for the circumstances of the citation – and senior officers were never well placed to witness Stirling's raid behind the lines.'

Laycock knew this was untrue. A recommendation for a VC has to be supported by three witnesses, although on occasions this rule has been waived, such as in November 1941 when Lt-Col Geoffrey Keyes was awarded a posthumous VC. He and two other men had attacked Rommel's HQ in Libya, but Keyes was killed in a shootout and another officer, Capt Robin Campbell, was wounded and captured. Only Sgt Jack Terry managed to make it back to the support party waiting on the rendezvous beach – under the command of Bob Laycock.

On 7 February 1991, three months after Stirling's death at the age of seventy-four, Fitzroy Maclean gave the address at a memorial service at the Guards' Chapel.[38] It is worth reproducing some of his eulogy to illustrate how he navigated the facts away from the truth to fit the image of his late friend as the Phantom Major:

> By the latter part of 1941, the war in the desert had settled down into a slogging match between the two opposing armies, swinging this way and that in the narrow coastal strip between the Mediterranean and the Qattara Depression, while to the south the desert stretched endlessly away. Ahead of anyone, David saw the unique opportunity this offered for a small, well-trained, well-led force to carry out surprise attacks on the rear of the formidable, but fully extended, Afrika Korps, while using the empty desert to the south as Lawrence used the Arabian desert, to emerge out of and then fade back into. What is more, possessing, as he did, quite exceptional powers of persuasion and being by nature immensely determined, he somehow succeeded, as an unknown subaltern, in winning the personal support of the Commander-in-Chief, General Auchinleck, and then in placing himself directly under the latter's command – in itself a very shrewd tactical move … David's claim to greatness lies in grasping this idea ahead of anyone else, in securing, single-handed and against all probability, the backing he needed for it and then putting it into execution with such astonishing success.

Had Maclean forgotten about the Long Range Desert Group, a small, well-trained and well-led force who were engaged in guerrilla operations in the summer of 1940 when David Stirling was being instructed in the art by his brother at Lochailort?

Maclean knew full well how Stirling had 'somehow succeeded' in convincing Auchinleck as to the merits of L Detachment – because Bill Stirling was the personal assistant to his Chief of Staff, Gen Arthur Smith.

Epilogue

David Stirling died at a private London clinic on 4 November 1990. The causes of death were a) cerebral vascular insufficiency; b) general weakness and frailty; c) asthma, osteoporosis and atrial fibrillation. The death certificate also listed an 'injury sustained during the 1939-45 war', presumably the spinal injury sustained during Stirling's first parachute descent in June 1941. The death certificate stated incorrectly that Stirling had been born in 'Keir, Stirlingshire'.

Stirling had chosen not to be buried in Lecropt Old Churchyard, in the grounds of Keir, where his mother and father, his eldest brother and his wife had been interred, and where a memorial cross honoured Hugh (and where Peter would be buried in 1994).* Instead he was buried more than a hundred miles north, in Beoraid Cemetery in Morar, a short drive from Our Lady of Perpetual Succour & St Cumin's Church, built by his grandfather. It a beautiful spot, wild, remote and lonely. Fifteen months after Stirling was laid to rest in Beoraid he was joined there by his younger sister Irene. She had never married. She had been in love once, with a Jewish man, and

* His elder sister, Margaret, the last of the Stirling children to die, was buried next to her husband in Edzell Churchyard, Angus, in 1997.

for many years had sought permission from the Catholic Church to marry her admirer. When permission was finally granted, the man had lost interest.

So Irene devoted much of her life to David's various enterprises, working for many years to promote the Capricorn Africa Society, and in the final months of her brother's life she was his faithful nurse.

One can only speculate as to why David chose not to be buried with the rest of his family at Keir.

Eight years after Stirling's death I visited Malcolm Pleydell at his Oxfordshire home. He had suffered a stroke a few years earlier and was in a wheelchair. He signed my copy of his wonderful book, *Born of the Desert*, and we talked for a while. I told him I was researching the life of Paddy Mayne and at the mention of that name Malcolm's eyes lit up and he described his pride in having served with him.

The next veteran I interviewed was Johnny Cooper, in 2000, and for the next eighteen months we corresponded regularly. He spoke affectionately and indulgently, almost protectively, of David. His tone changed when he talked of Mayne; there was a reverence, a warrior describing his beloved chief.

It was Johnny who suggested I write a wartime history of the Special Air Service through the eyes of the men. There's been a lot of books written about the wartime SAS, he said, but they were the work of the officers; it would be good if the men had a voice. With the help of Johnny I was introduced to scores of wartime SAS soldiers in the next few years and something struck me: to them, Paddy Mayne embodied the regiment. He was, to use a modern vernacular, Mr SAS.

'From the very day I joined the regiment Mayne always appeared to be the man in charge,' said John Randall. 'He had a very physical presence. He didn't shout and yell, had a quiet voice, but when he spoke you knew jolly well he meant what he said. He expected people to work hard at being good soldiers and expected them to behave as gentleman because he was one himself. He understood people who got drunk, that was fair enough, but what he couldn't bear were louts and bad manners ... he led from the front and people admired him. We always felt that he would never commit any member of the regiment to an operation he felt didn't have at least a 50/50 chance of succeeding, and he would never ever commit to an operation that he wouldn't be prepared to undertake himself. With a leader like that you had the basis for a fantastic regiment and that's what we were.'[1]

Alex Muirhead, who joined the SAS in late 1942, said: 'He was not everyone's cup of tea and he made some enemies. I had several disagreements with him during my years of service. But I always found him ready to accept a reasoned argument even in the heat of battle. There is no doubt in my mind that Paddy Mayne was a great leader, and if we had not been successful under his leadership I doubt the SAS would have been re-formed.'[2]

Few men knew Mayne better than Mike Sadler, who first encountered him in December 1941 when he navigated his party to Tamet airfield, and who served under the Irishman for the rest of the war. 'Paddy felt his true vocation in war,' Sadler told me. 'He was well suited to war and he enjoyed it. He was very good at fighting the Germans, but he wasn't totally fearless. There's this slight impression around that he wasn't at all scared. He was well aware of the risks at any particular moment – and I don't think he fancied the idea of being shot more than anyone else – but he had a very good control of himself.'[3]

The last time I saw Mike Sadler was in 2017, when we were seated together at a lunch of the LRDG Association in London. Mike's eyesight was failing but not his humour or his memory. We talked more of Paddy Mayne and he told me of a week he and Mayne had in Paris not long after its liberation in 1944. 'We had a lot of fun, particularly with women,' he said with a chuckle. I asked him to sum up Mayne. Mike thought for a few seconds and replied: 'He wasn't the hard-drinking, fearless mad Irishman of popular myth. He was intelligent, sensitive and warm underneath.'

There were two other curiosities that impressed me during my encounters with wartime SAS soldiers: several spoke with deep affection and respect for Bill Stirling, a name I had encountered only in passing. 'I was very fond of Bill,' said Tony Greville-Bell. 'Bill was cleverer than David. David was more charismatic and more physical, the younger brother, and was outwardly very good at dealing with higher-ups and getting what he wanted. Bill was much quieter and more intellectual, and in terms of dealing with authority I think he was better than David. I don't think he ever went on an op with us and that was the right thing to do.'[4]

In contrast, few veterans had much to say about his brother. Many, of course, had joined the SAS after David's capture and knew him only by name.

Even among Originals and men who joined L Detachment in early 1942 the memories of David Stirling were often dispassionate. 'He could be aloof,' said John Wiseman. 'But on the whole he was quite acceptable.'[5]

He was respected, no doubt, but there wasn't the bond formed in battle as there was with Mayne. Du Vivier's outstanding memory of Stirling was of his telling them at some point in the desert that 'when the war was over and we were back in "civvy street" we would all be dying to tell our friends and family some of the hair-raising things we experienced; but you might as well not bother because no one will believe you'.[6]

Mike Sadler gave the best insight: 'Stirling had a very good social manner and also had a compelling personality ... he knew all the right people. He could talk you into anything, but he didn't have to do much talking. He managed to make one feel you were the only person who could possibly do it, that kind of effect. But I also slightly felt he was thinking of something else at the same time.'[7]

Sadler recounted a story from the summer of 1942, when he had been navigating for Stirling in a jeep along a coast road and they encountered some Germans. They made good their escape with Sadler operating the twin Vickers and Stirling behind the wheel. 'Once we got out of range he said "oh, you drive now, Mike" and he got into the other seat and curled up asleep. I was left with the task of finding the way back. But he was rather like that.'

It took me a few years to process this information. When, as a young man in 2003, I wrote *Stirling's Men* I added to the hagiography, unquestioningly accepting all that had been written in previous general histories of the regiment, and in particular the two biographies of David Stirling. But as I matured, I began to re-examine the Stirling legend.

And the more I did, the more puzzled I became. Why had Bill been diminished and David deified, and who had demonised Paddy? The answer, as I delved deeper, was clear. David Stirling was the man responsible.

The death of Stirling didn't break the spell he had cast over so many, but it weakened it, so that the odd voice began to speak out, if not critically then at least with more honesty. Johnny Cooper, who hadn't contributed to Alan Hoe's biography, published a memoir in 1991, *One of the Originals*. He was complimentary about Stirling but didn't shy away from his flaws and mistakes.

In 1994 Stephen Hastings, MP, published his autobiography, *The Drums of Memory*. 'Postwar, David's life was not so successful,' he wrote. 'He started some remarkable initiatives ... most ran into the sand. David was never one for the patient follow up, or indeed for patience as a virtue at all.'

A long-standing sceptic had been David Hunt, the intelligence officer at GHQ at the time of the Benghazi raid in September 1942. He wrote a memoir in 1966, entitled *A Don at War*, in which he sardonically described *The Phantom Major* as 'a most entertaining book'.

He was critical of the 'private armies' that sprang up, remarking that there were too many of them and most in his opinion were of dubious strategic value. His primary complaint was that their proliferation, particularly in North Africa, led to many regiments losing their best officers and men 'for special but infrequently occurring tasks'.

There was one exception, the LRDG: 'This magnificent organisation had all the virtues and none of the faults of the private armies. It had a useful job to do, it knew how to do it perfectly and it did it quietly. The members were geniuses at navigation and were experts at crossing all types of desert surface. Their aim was to be unspectacular both on active service and between times.'[8]

In October 1993 Hunt was asked to review Hoe's biography of Stirling for *Intelligence and National Security*, an academic journal. He described it as 'a work of unabashed hero-worship, based extensively on material derived directly from the hero himself. It could to a large extent be described as an autobiography.'[9]

As *The Phantom Major* had done, the biography tickled Hunt because of its 'engaging gasconading'. Several times in the book Stirling had proclaimed his revulsion for 'pomposo', but his polished false modesty didn't fool all of the people all of the time.

But Hunt also made grave criticisms. Stirling was careless about security and Virginia Cowles was 'misleading' in writing about the Benghazi raid. Indeed. In a shameless book, one of the most despicable paragraphs was the attempt to blame the failure of the entire operation on Lt-Col John Haselden, MC and bar, of the Intelligence Corps. A brave and resourceful man, he was portrayed in *The Phantom Major* as an incompetent egomaniac. But as he had been killed during the simultaneous raid on Tobruk he had no right of reply.

It was Stirling who throughout his life was the incompetent egomaniac. As Hunt pointed out, he was captured because of his 'insubordinate obstinacy' and 'bravado'. He also mocked Stirling's warning to the Eighth Army in September 1942 that the next offensive was doomed unless the SAS were injected. 'The next offensive was the battle of Alamein,' Hunt wrote. 'History records that it went off quite reasonably well without the SAS being injected.'

Two years after the review, Hunt corresponded with Carol Mather, who was preparing to publish his own memoir based on material he had written immediately after the war. Hunt had sent Mather a copy of his review because it contained his recollection of the Benghazi raid. Carol Mather replied, saying how much he had enjoyed reading Hunt's analysis of Hoe's biography, 'which as you say was at the dictation of the subject himself'. He also appreciated Hunt's description of Stirling's 'gasconading tactics'.[10]

The pair exchanged further letters about the Benghazi raid and Hunt said that, contrary to what Stirling had claimed, 'there was no breach of security, though no thanks are due to David Stirling who … was extravagantly careless'.

According to the dictionary, 'gasconade' means to boast excessively. The word originated in the eighteenth century and comes from the French word *gasconner*, to chatter or boast like a Gascon. One of its earliest appearances in the English language was in Daniel Defoe's novel *The Fortunate Mistress*, published in 1724. Five years earlier Defoe had written *Robinson Crusoe*, in which the eponymous hero was credited as the author, leading many readers to believe Crusoe was real.

From David Stirling's gasconading was born *The Phantom Major*, which led many readers to believe he was a special forces legend and the terror of the Germans. In fact, a more accurate title for the book would have been 'The Phoney Major'.

Bibliography and Other Reference Sources

Alanbrooke, Field Marshal Lord (ed. Alex Danchev and Daniel Todman), *War Diaries 1939–1945* (London: Weidenfeld & Nicolson, 2001)

Alexander of Tunis, Field Marshal Earl, *The Alexander Memoirs 1940–1945* (Barnsley: Frontline, 2020)

Amory, Mark (ed.), *The Letters of Evelyn Waugh* (London: Penguin, 1962)

Appleyard, J. E. A., *Geoffrey: Being the Story of 'Apple' of the Commandos and Special Air Service Regiment* (London: Blandford Press, 1946)

Armstrong, Stephen, *War plc: The Rise of the New Corporate Mercenary* (London: Faber & Faber, 2009)

Asher, Michael, *The Regiment: The Real History of the SAS* (London: Penguin, 2008)

Axelrod, Alan, *Mercenaries: A Guide to Private Armies and Private Military Companies* (Washington DC: CQ Press, 2014)

Bagnold, Ralph, *Sand, Wind & War: Memoirs of a Desert Explorer* (Tucson: University of Arizona Press, 1991)

Beaton, Cecil, *Near East* (London: B. T. Batsford, 1943)

Beaton, Cecil, *The Years Between, 1939–44: Cecil Beaton's Diaries Volume Two* (Leeds: Sapere Books, 2018)

Beaton, Cecil, *Theatre of War* (London: Imperial War Museum, 2012)

Beevor, Antony, *Crete 1941: The Battle and the Resistance* (London: John Murray, 1991)

Bierman, John and Colin Smith, *Alamein: War Without Hate* (London: Penguin, 2003)

Byrne, J. V., *The General Salutes a Soldier: With the SAS and Commandos in World War Two* (London: Robert Hale, 1986)

Calvert, Mike, *Fighting Mad: One Man's Guerrilla War* (London: Jarrolds, 1964)

Cherry-Garrard, Apsley, *The Worst Journey in the World* (London: Constable, 1922)

Churchill, Winston S., *The Second World War*, volume 4: *The Hinge of Fate* (London: Cassell, 1950)

Clutton-Brock, Oliver and Ray Crompton, *The Long Road: Trials and Tribulations of Airmen Prisoners from Bankau to Berlin, June 1944–May 1945* (London: Grub Street, 2014)

Connell, John, *Auchinleck: A Biography of Field Marshal Sir Claude Auchinleck* (London: Cassell, 1959)

Cooper, Artemis, *Cairo in the War 1939–1945* (London: Penguin, 1989)

Cooper, Johnny, *One of the Originals: The Story of a Founder Member of the SAS* (London: Pan, 1991)

Cooper, Pamela, *A Cloud of Forgetting* (London: Quartet, 1993)

Cowles, Virginia, *Winston Churchill: The Era and the Man* (New York: Harper, 1953)

——————, *The Phantom Major* (London: Collins, 1958)

Crichton-Stuart, Michael, *G Patrol* (London: William Kimber, 1958)

Davie, Michael (ed.), *The Diaries of Evelyn Waugh* (London: Weidenfeld & Nicolson, 1976)

Davis, Peter (ed. Paul Davis), *SAS – Men in the Making: An Original's Account of Operations in Sicily and Italy* (Barnsley: Pen & Sword, 2015)

Davis, Wade, *Into the Silence: The Great War, Mallory and the Conquest of Everest* (London: Vintage, 2012)

de Guingand, Sir Francis, *Operation Victory* (London: Hodder & Stoughton, 1947)

de la Billière, General Sir Peter, *Looking for Trouble: SAS to Gulf Command* (London: Harper Collins, 1994)

Dillon, Martin and Ray Bradford, *Rogue Warrior of the SAS: The Blair Mayne Legend* (Edinburgh: Mainstream, 2012)

Dimbleby, Richard, *The Frontiers Are Green* (London: Hodder & Stoughton, 1943)

Dorril, Stephen, *MI6: Inside the Covert World of Her Majesty's Secret Intelligence Service* (New York: Free Press, 2000)

Eade, Philip, *Evelyn Waugh: A Life Revisited* (New York: Henry Holt, 2016)

Edwards, J. Gordon, *A Climber's Guide to Glacier National Park* (San Francisco: Sierra Club, 1960)

Fairbairn, W. E., *All-In Fighting* (London: Faber & Faber, 1942)

Farran, Roy, *The Winged Dagger: Adventures on Special Service* (London: Collins, 1948)

Fenby, Jonathan, *The General: Charles de Gaulle and the France He Saved* (London: Simon & Schuster, 2010)

Foley, Charles, *Commando Extraordinary: Otto Skorzeny's Remarkable Exploits and their Urgent Meaning for Us Now* (London: Longmans, Green & Co., 1954)

Foot, M. R. D., *SOE: The Special Operations Executive 1940–46* (London: London Bridge, 1984)

——————, *Memories of an SOE Historian* (Barnsley: Pen & Sword, 2009)

Gilbert, Martin, *Winston S. Churchill: Road to Victory, 1941–1945* (London: Heinemann, 1986)

Gordon-Creed, Geoffrey and Roger Field, *Rogue Male: Sabotage and Seduction behind German Lines with Geoffrey Gordon-Creed, DSO, MC* (London: Coronet, 2011)

Guss, David M., *The 21 Escapes of Lt Alastair Cram* (London: Macmillan, 2018)

Haarr, Geirr H., *No Room for Mistakes: British and Allied Submarine Warfare, 1939–1940* (Barnsley: Seaforth, 2015)

Hackett, General Sir John, *I Was a Stranger* (London: Chatto & Windus, 1978)

Hancock, Ian, *White Liberals, Moderates and Radicals in Rhodesia 1953–1980* (New York: St Martin's Press, 1984)

Hart-Davis, Duff, *The War That Never Was* (London: Century, 2011)

Hastings, Stephen, *The Drums of Memory* (Barnsley: Pen & Sword, 1994)

Hoe, Alan, *David Stirling* (London: Little, Brown, 1992)

Hughes, Jimmy Quentin, *Who Cares Who Wins: The Autobiography of a World War Two Soldier* (Liverpool: Charico, 1998)

Hunt, David, *A Don at War* (London: Routledge, 1966)

Huntford, Roland, *Scott & Amundsen* (London: Pan, 1979)

Hyam, Ronald, *Empire and Sexuality: The British Experience* (Manchester: Manchester University Press, 1990)

James, Malcolm (Malcolm James Pleydell), *Born of the Desert: With the SAS in North Africa* (London: Greenhill, 1991)

Jenkins, Roy, *Churchill* (London: Macmillan, 2001)

Johnston, Charles, *Mo and Other Originals* (London: Hamish Hamilton, 1971)

Johnston, Erika, *The Other Side of Kilimanjaro* (London: Johnson, 1971)

Jones, J. D. F., *Storyteller: The Many Lives of Laurens van der Post* (London: John Murray, 2001)

Kemp, Anthony, *The SAS at War 1941–1945* (London: Penguin, 1991)

——————, *The SAS: Savage Wars of Peace, 1947 to the Present* (London: John Murray, 1994)

Kemp, Peter, *No Colours or Crest* (London: Cassell, 1958)

Kennedy Shaw, W. B., *Long Range Desert Group* (London: Collins, 1945)

Keyes, Elizabeth, *Geoffrey Keyes, VC of the Rommel Raid* (London: George Newnes, 1956)

Killearn, Lord (ed. Trefor Evans), *The Killearn Diaries, 1934–1946: The Diplomatic and Personal Record of Lord Killearn (Sir Miles Lampson), High Commissioner and Ambassador, Egypt* (London: Sidgwick & Jackson, 1972)

Kindersley, Philip, *For You the War is Over* (Tunbridge Wells: Midas, 1983)

Labour for Africa Group, *Africa's Challenge* (London: Labour for Africa Group, 1953)

Lett, Brian, *The Small Scale Raiding Force* (Barnsley: Pen & Sword, 2013)

Lewin, Ronald, *The Life and Death of the Afrika Korps* (Barnsley: Pen & Sword, 2003)

Liddell Hart, B. H. (ed.), *The Rommel Papers* (New York: DaCapo, 1982)

Lloyd Owen, David, *The Desert My Dwelling Place* (London: Cassell, 1957)

——————, *The Long Range Desert Group 1940–1945: Providence Their Guide* (Barnsley: Pen & Sword, 2001)

Lodwick, John, *Raiders from the Sea: The Story of the Special Boat Service in WWII* (London: Greenhill, 1990)

Lownie, Andrew, *Stalin's Englishman: The Lives of Guy Burgess* (London: Hodder & Stoughton, 2015)

Lovat, Lord (Simon Fraser), *March Past: A Memoir* (London: Weidenfeld & Nicolson, 1978)

Mackenzie, S. P., *The Colditz Myth: British and Commonwealth Prisoners of War in Nazi Germany* (Oxford: Oxford University Press, 2004)

Maclean, Fitzroy, *Eastern Approaches* (London: Jonathan Cape, 1949)

Macpherson, Sir Tommy with Richard Bath, *Behind Enemy Lines: The Autobiography of Britain's Most Decorated Living War Hero* (Edinburgh: Mainstream, 2012)

Marriott, Sir John, *Military Memories* (privately published, 1960)

Mather, Carol, *When the Grass Stops Growing: A War Memoir* (London: Leo Cooper, 1997)

McHarg, Ian, *Litani River* (n.p.: SHN, 2011)

McLuskey, J. Fraser, *Parachute Padre* (London: SCM Press, 1951)

Mead, Richard, *Commando General: The Life of Major General Sir Robert Laycock, KCMG, CB, DSO* (Barnsley: Pen & Sword, 2016)

Messenger, Charles, *The Commandos: 1940–1946* (London: HarperCollins, 1985)

Michie, Allan, *Retreat to Victory* (London: George Allen & Unwin, 1942)

——————, *Honour for All* (London: George Allen & Unwin, 1946)

Millar, George, *Horned Pigeon* (London: Heinemann, 1946)

Montgomery of Alamein, Viscount, *The Memoirs of Field-Marshal the Viscount Montgomery of Alamein* (London: Collins, 1958)

Moorehead, Alan, *The Desert War: The North African Campaign 1940–1943* (London: Hamish Hamilton, 1965)

Moran, Lord, *The Anatomy of Courage* (London: Constable, 1945)

——————, *Churchill at War: 1940–45* (London: Robinson, 2002)

Mortimer, Gavin, *Fields of Glory: The Extraordinary Lives of 16 Warrior Sportsmen* (London: Andre Deutsch, 2001)

——————, *Stirling's Men: The Inside History of the SAS in World War II* (London: Weidenfeld & Nicolson, 2004)

——————, *The Daring Dozen* (Oxford: Osprey, 2011)

——————, *The SAS in World War II* (Oxford: Osprey, 2012)

——————, *The SBS in World War II* (Oxford: Osprey, 2013)

——————, *The Men Who Made the SAS: A History of the Long Range Desert Group* (London: Constable, 2015)

Moynahan, Brian, *Jungle Soldier: The True Story of Freddy Spencer Chapman* (London: Quercus, 2009)

Niven, David, *The Moon's a Balloon* (London: Hamish Hamilton, 1971)

Ogden, Alan, *Master of Deception: The Wartime Adventures of Peter Fleming* (London: Bloomsbury, 2019)

Oldham, J. H., *New Hope in Africa* (London: Longmans, Green & Co., 1955)

Palmer, Mike, *SOE CD1: The Life and Times of Sir Frank Nelson* (Torpoint: Palmridge, 2018)

Pearson, John, *The Gamblers: John Aspinall, James Goldsmith and the Murder of Lord Lucan* (London: Century, 2005)

Peniakoff, Vladimir, *Popski's Private Army* (London: Harper & Collins, 1975)

Phiri, Bizeck Jube, 'The Capricorn Africa Society: A Study of Liberal Politics in Northern Rhodesia/Zambia, 1949–1972', doctoral thesis (Dalhousie University, 1991)

Pincher, Harry Chapman, *Dangerous to Know: An Autobiography* (London: Biteback, 2014)

Pitt, Barrie, *Special Boat Squadron* (London: Corgi, 1985)

Pittaway, Jonathan and Craig Fourie, *LRDG Rhodesia: Rhodesians in the Long Range Desert Group* (Durban: Dandy Agencies, 2006)

Pittaway, Jonathan, *Special Air Services: The Men Speak* (Durban: Dandy Agencies, 2009)

Pringle, Jack, *Colditz Last Stop: Eleven Prisons, Four Countries, Six Escapes* (n.p.: ISIS Large Print, 1998)

Pritchard, 'Race, Identity, and Belonging in Early Zimbabwean Nationalism(s), 1957–1965, doctoral thesis (University of Cambridge, 2019)

Public Record Office, *Special Forces in the Desert War 1940–1943* (London: PRO Publications, 2001)

Ranfurly, Hermione, *To War with Whitaker: The Wartime Diaries of the Countess of Ranfurly 1939–45* (London: Heinemann, 1994)

Rankin, Nicholas, *Ian Fleming's Commandos: The Story of the Legendary 30 Assault Unit* (New York: Oxford University Press, 2011)

————, *Churchills Wizards: The British Genius for Deception 1914–1945* (London: Faber & Faber, 2009)

Reid, Jamie, *Doped: The Real Life Story of the 1960s Racehorse Doping Gang* (Newbury: Racing Post, 2015)

Ross, Hamish, *Paddy Mayne* (Stroud: Sutton, 2003)

Roberts, Andrew, *Churchill: Walking with Destiny* (New York: Viking, 2018)

Rotberg, Robert I., *Black Heart: Gore-Browne and the Politics of Multiracial Zambia* (Berkeley: University of California Press, 1977)

Royle, Trevor, *Orde Wingate: Irregular Soldier* (London: Weidenfeld & Nicolson, 1998)

Sandbrook, Dominic, *Seasons in the Sun: The Battle for Britain, 1974–1979* (London: Allen Lane, 2002)

Schmidt, Heinz Werner, *With Rommel in the Desert* (London: Constable, 1998)

Seymour, William, *British Special Forces: The Story of Britain's Undercover Soldiers* (London: Sidgwick & Jackson, 1985)

SAS Regimental Association (ed.), *SAS War Diary 1941–1945* (London: Extraordinary Editions, 2011)

Spencer Chapman, F., *The Jungle is Neutral* (London: Chatto & Windus, 1949)

Stewart, Andrew, *The King's Private Army: Protecting the British Royal Family during the Second World War* (Solihull: Helion, 2015)

Steyn, Richard, *Churchill's Confidant: Jan Smuts, Enemy to Lifelong Friend* (London: Robinson, 2018)

Stokes, Brummie, *Soldiers and Sherpas: A Taste for Adventure* (London: Michael Joseph, 1988)

Strawson, John, *A History of the SAS Regiment* (London: Secker & Warburg, 1985)

Sutherland, David, *He Who Dares: Recollections of Service in the SAS, SBS and MI5* (London: Leo Cooper, 1998)

Sykes, Christopher, *Orde Wingate* (London: Collins, 1959)

——————, *Evelyn Waugh: A Biography* (London: Penguin, 1977)

Sweet-Escott, Bickham, *Baker Street Irregular* (London: Methuen, 1965)

Thesiger, Wilfred, *The Life of My Choice* (New York: W. W. Norton, 1980)

Thompson, Douglas, *The Hustlers: Gambling, Greed and the Perfect Con* (London: Pan Macmillan, 2008)

Thompson, Julian, *The Imperial War Museum Book of War Behind Enemy Lines: Special Forces in Action, 1940–45* (London: Sidgwick & Jackson, 1998)

Timpson, Alastair with Andrew Gibson-Watt, *In Rommel's Backyard: A Memoir of the Long Range Desert Group* (Barnsley: Pen & Sword, 2010)

Tudor, Malcolm, *SAS in Italy 1943–1945* (Stroud: Fonthill, 2018)

Vambe, Lawrence, *From Rhodesia to Zimbabwe* (London: Heinemann, 1976)

van der Post, Laurens, *The Dark Eye in Africa* (London: Hogarth Press, 1955)

——————, *Yet Being Someone Other* (London: Hogarth Press, 1982)

Verney, John, *Going to the Wars: A Journey in Various Directions* (London: Collins, 1955)

Wainwright, Robert, *Sheila: The Australian Ingenue who Bewitched British Society* (London: Allen & Unwin, 2014)

Warner, Philip, *The Special Air Service* (London: William Kimber, 1976)

——————, *Auchinleck: The Lonely Soldier* (London: Buchan & Enright, 1981)

White, Luise, *The Assassination of Herbert Chitepo: Texts and Politics in Zimbabwe* (Bloomington: Indiana University Press, 2003)

Wilkinson, Peter, *Foreign Fields: The Story of an SOE Operative* (London: I.B. Tauris, 2002)

Windmill, Lorna Almonds, *Gentleman Jim: The Wartime Story of a Founder of the SAS and Special Forces* (London: Constable & Robinson, 2001)

——————, *A British Achilles: The Story of George, 2nd Earl Jellicoe, KBE, DSO, MC, FRS* (Barnsley: Pen & Sword, 2006)

Wise, Michael T. (ed.), *Joy Street: A Wartime Romance in Letters, 1940–1942* (Boston: Little, Brown, 1995)

Wood, Lieutenant J. E. R. (ed.), *Detour: The Story of Oflag IVC* (London: Falcon, 1946)

Wood, Susan, *A Fly in Amber* (London: Collins, 1964)

Wyllie, Neville (ed.), *The Politics and Strategy of Clandestine War: Special Operations Executive, 1940–1946* (Oxford: Taylor & Francis, 2006)

Young, Desmond, *Rommel* (London: Fontana, 1989)

Publications

Ampleforth Journal, 1923 to 1994

LRDG Association newsletter, 1945 to 2000

Calvert, M., 'The characteristics of guerrilla leaders and their rank and file', *Practitioner*, 211:266 (December 1973)

Campbell, D., 'The pedigree dogs of war', *Time Out*, 21–27 July 1978

Herman, Michael et al., 'Book reviews', *Intelligence and National Security*, 8:4 (October 1993)

'What makes the Special Air Services special', *Time Out*, 7–14 December 1978

'The "private armies" of 1974 re-examined', *Lobster*, 11 (April 1986)

O'Hara, Larry, 'Notes from the underground, British fascism 1974–92', *Lobster*, 23 (1992)

Wilson, N. H., 'Populism in Rhodesian politics', *Rhodesian History*, 6 (1975)

Television

The Mayfair Set: Who Pays Wins, episode 1, 1999. Directed by Adam Curtis

Men of Action, episode 1, 1959. Presented by Brian Horrocks

Author interviews

SAS/SBS/LRDG/Afrika Korps

Roger Boutinot, L Detachment and 4SAS, 2002–4

Mike Carr, LRDG, 2014–18

Roy Close, 1SAS, 2002

Johnny Cooper, DCM, MM, L Detachment, 2000–1

David Danger, MM, L Detachment and 1SAS, 2002–3

George Daniels, MM, 2SAS, 2002

Ronald Grierson, 1SAS, 2002

Jeff Du Vivier, MM, L Detachment and 1SAS, 2003–8

Sid Dowland, L Detachment and SBS, 2002

Bob Francis, 1SAS, 2002–4

Tony Greville-Bell, DSO, 2SAS and 21SAS, 2002–3
Alex Griffiths, L Detachment and SRS, 2002
Charlie Hackney, L Detachment and 2SAS, 2002–4
Dick Holmes, MM, SBS, 2002–14
Augustin Jordan, L Detachment, 2002
Keith Killby, L Detachment and SBS, 2002
Bob Lowson, MM, 1SAS, 2002–11
Bob McDougall, 1SAS, 2002–3
Alain Papozow, L Detachment and 4SAS, 2002
Jim Patch, LRDG, 2013
Sid Payne, 1SAS, 2002–10
Malcolm Pleydell, MC, L Detachment, 1998
Cyril Radford, 2SAS, 2002–3
John Randall, 1SAS, 2002–3
Reg Redington, DCM, 2002–4
Duncan Ridler, MM, 1SAS, 2003
Alex Robertson, 2SAS, 2003–5
Bill Robinson, 2SAS, 2003
Mike Sadler, MC, MM, LRDG, L Detachment and 1SAS, 2003–17
Rudolf Schneider, Kampstaffel, Afrika Korps, 2013–14
Bill Stalker, L Detachment and 1SAS
Jimmy Storie, L Detachment, 2002–3
Arthur Thompson, L Detachment and 1SAS, 2002–3
Harry Vickers, DCM, 2SAS, 2003
Denis Wainman, 1SAS, 2003
Bob Walker-Brown, DSO, 2SAS, 2002–3
John Waterman, SBS, 2014–16
Cyril Wheeler, 2SAS, 2002–3
John Wiseman, MC, L Detachment and 1SAS, 2002
Doug Wright, MM, SBS, 2002
Albert Youngman, MM, 2002–11

British Lions

Vivian Jenkins, Wales and British Lions, 1998
Hayden Tanner, Wales and British Lions, 1998 and 1999

British Library

'Evelyn Waugh, a Study of his Life and Character', BBC 1968

'In Defence of the British Empire', audio debate, 1957

W6/6148 Africa's Challenge: Containing the Declarations of the Capricorn Africa Society, Salisbury

Churchill Archive

CHAR 1/369/3-4

CHAR 20/65/106-145

CHAR 20/205/49

Churchill Archives Centre, Cambridge University

The papers of Leopold Amery

The papers of Brig Ralph Alger Bagnold

The papers of Randolph Churchill

The papers of Lord Hailsham

Imperial War Museum

Audio interviews

Doug Arnold

Bob Bennett

Bertram Boucher-Myers

Mike Calvert

Alf Card

Brig George Davy

Brian Dillon

Roy Farran

Archie Gibson

Christopher Hutchinson

George Jellicoe

Thomas Macpherson

Daphne Maynard

Peter McAleese

Brian Scott-Garrett

James Sherwood

William Smallman

Peter Upcher

Robert Waygood

Peter Wilkinson

John Woodhouse

Private Papers

Mike Calvert, SAS Brigade

Richard 'Doc' Lawson, LRDG

David Lloyd Owen, LRDG

Carol Mather, L Detachment

Tony Simonds, SOE

Charles Haydon

Liddell Hart Centre for Military Archives, King's College London

Private papers

Maj Gen James Gavin

Maj Gen Sir Robert Laycock

Capt Sir Basil Liddell Hart

Gen Sir Roderick McLeod

Maj Peter Oldfield

Maj Vivian Street

John Rylands Research Institute and Library, University of Manchester

Papers of Field Marshal Sir Claude Auchinleck

SAS Regimental Association archive

Peter Davis, 1SAS, unpublished memoir

David Sutherland, scrapbook

Mars and Minerva, SAS Regimental Journal, 1946 to 2005

Scots Guards Archives

Service records of David and Bill Stirling

Margaret Thatcher Foundation

David Stirling letter to Margaret Thatcher, February 1983
Lord Hailsham diary, November 1974

The National Archives, Kew

Selected files

ADM 116/5112 Review of policy concerning operations of Small Scale Raiding Force
CO 1015/70 Activities of the Capricorn Africa Society, 1951–52
CO 822/1422 Activities of the Capricorn Africa Society, 1957–59
DEFE 2/1093 Small Scale Raiding Force: policy, formation, responsibility
DEFE 2/957 Small Scale Raiding Force: procedures, responsibility
FO 372/8204 State visit by King Faisal of Saudi Arabia to UK
HS 9/1418/6 Bill Stirling SOE File
HS 9/930/2 Daphne Llewellyn SOE File
HS3/192 Bill Stirling's report into SO2
KV 2/626 Douglas Berneville-Claye
KV2/77 Court martial of Theodore Schurch
PREM 16/450 Home Office file on David Stirling and GB75
WO 71/1109 Schurch, T. J. W. Offence: Treachery
WO 201/721 Brief history of L Detachment, SAS, 1941–42
WO 201/728 Reorganisation of Special Service
WO 201/732 Desert organisation 1942
WO 201/753 Small combined operations 1942
WO 201/754 LRDG operations July 1941 to December 1942
WO 201/773 Formation of SAS in PAIC (Persia and Iraq Command)
WO 201/785 L Detachment history
WO 201/808 LRDG narrative and war diary December 1940 to 31 March 1941
WO 201/811 LRDG narrative and war diary November 1941 to February 1942
WO 201/2261 Criticism of Stirling in 1942 by GHQ
WO 203/3774 Special Air Service in South East Asia: organisation
WO 204/7960 SAS operations in the Mediterranean Theatre
WO 205/40 Operation Husky (invasion of Sicily)
WO 208/3288 Colditz POW files
WO 218/96 SAS war diary October 1942
WO 218/97 SAS war diary 1943
WO 218/98 SAS war diary 1943

WO 218/169 8 Commando ('B' Battalion, Layforce) May to June 1941

WO 218/170 8 Commando ('B' Battalion, Layforce) January to March 1941

WO 218/173 L Detachment: formation and training

WO 218/176 2SAS: reports of operations in Italy

WO 218/177 2SAS, Operation Speedwell, September 1943

WO 218/252 LRDG war diary October to December 1941

WO 309/244 Oflag 8F, Marskova Tsebova, Czechoslovakia: killing of British officers

WO 311/1200 Gavi POW files

Miscellaneous

Alex Muirhead, 1SAS. Muirhead family

John Comyn unpublished memoir. Courtesy of Monte San Marino Trust Archives

Reg Seekings interview. Courtesy of John Kane

Acknowledgements

This book has been brewing for best part of twenty-five years, since a November day in 1998 when I interviewed Malcolm Pleydell, the medical officer of L Detachment, SAS in 1942. Since then I have had the inestimable privilege of meeting nearly 150 wartime veterans of the SAS, SBS and LRDG. Each interview has been an enriching experience and my gratitude to these men – all but two of whom are dead – is eternal.

That I am able to tell for the first time the truth of the wartime SAS is because of the bold foresight of my publisher, Andreas Campomar at Constable. I thank him and my editors for their sound judgements, Riana Dixon and, in particular, Zoe Gullen. I have greatly appreciated her assiduous input over several drafts of the book, all of which enhanced the end result.

My father, David Mortimer, whiled away some of his time during lockdown (in years to come will the shuddering horror of that word diminish?) reading the initial manuscript and his honesty was appreciated. My brother, Mark Mortimer, a former infantry officer, was a good resource for my queries about obscure military minutiae.

I also required help with minutiae of other kinds and was fortunate to track down specialists in several areas. Andy Emmerson , the former

Technical Press Officer of British Telecom, and Bob Freshwater, both came to my aid in answering questions about transatlantic telephone calls in the late 1930s, which allowed me to unpick one of David Stirling's many tall tales, while Randy Hees, the Director of the Nevada State Railroad Museum in Boulder City, performed a similar function in dispelling the myth of Stirling's 'jaunt' to Las Vegas. Thank you, gentlemen.

Merci to Dominique Bermann Martin, the guardian of the André Lhote archives in France, who searched their records for any trace of Stirling the art student.

Other people who gave of their time to aid my research are Geoff Simmons, John Kane, Grenville Bint, Chris Rooney, Robert Wilson at the British Yemini Society, Alan Orton and Angela Bamberg, daughter of Jack Pringle, and one of the few people post-war not afraid to air their opinions on David Stirling. I salute your courage (and your father's).

Dai Richard at Rugby Relics generously granted me permission to reproduce the photograph of Paddy Mayne playing for a British Army XV in 1940 and Janine Mitchell, a PhD researcher at Stirling University, and the custodian of the Peter Mackay archive, answered some questions about the Capricorn Society.

I found the Ampleforth College archive a rich mine of information, and Anselm Cramer, Archivist at Ampleforth Abbey, and Bron Bury, Ampleforth Society Coordinator, patiently fielded my questions and also allowed me permission to reproduce the photograph of David Stirling the schoolboy.

As ever the staff at the National Archives, Kew, were a model of swift efficiency, and I also benefited from the assistance of the staff at the Liddell Hart Centre for Military Archives, King's College, the Imperial War Museum Reading Room, Ms Jacqueline Cox at the Cambridge University archives and Tony Richard at the John Rylands Research Institute and Library

I owe a great debt to David Guss, author of the superb *The 21 Escapes of Lt Alastair Cram*, for which I have promised him a slap-up meal in a Paris bistro when he is next in town. And Jonathan Pittaway in South Africa is also in line for a culinary reward on account of his generosity in providing several photos for the book, and also being an invaluable and candid correspondent in all matters SAS.

Finally, I would like to thank Archie Stirling, eldest son of Bill. We first met in January 2020 and although Covid prevented my fulfilling his invitation to visit Keir, we kept in contact and his insights and recollections of his father were of priceless value. We talked far less of David, but Archie remembers his uncle with affection.

Bill has been marginalised and maligned in recent decades. I hope this book will go some way to remedying that injustice. He and his brother David were remarkable men, but one never got the credit he deserved for his immense contribution to the development of Britain's special forces during the Second World War.

Notes

Prologue

1 *Belfast Telegraph*, 15 December 1955.
2 Ibid.
3 McLuskey, *Parachute Padre*, p. 148.

Chapter 1

1 Stirling's birthplace is given as Keir in his entry written in the *Oxford Dictionary of National Biography*, Wikipedia, Britannica.com and in Ben Macintyre, *SAS: Rogue Heroes – The Authorized Wartime History* (London: Viking, 2016).
2 Hoe, *David Stirling*, p. 16.
3 Margaret Stirling obituary, *The Times*, 14 August 1973.
4 *Kintilloch Herald*, 20 April 1910.
5 Cowles, *The Phantom Major*, p. 17.
6 *Ampleforth Journal*, Autumn 1922.
7 Douglas Brown, 'Looking Forward to the Past', *Ampleforth Journal*, 1981.
8 Lovat, *March Past*, pp. 98, 100.
9 *Ampleforth Journal*, Autumn 1928.
10 *Ampleforth Journal*, Autumn 1930.
11 Brown, 'Looking Forward to the Past'.
12 Ibid.
13 *Ampleforth Journal*, January 1943.

Chapter 2

1 Hoe, *David Stirling*, p. 29.
2 *Nottingham Journal*, 12 October 1936.
3 *Dundee Evening Telegraph*, 5 March 1937.

Chapter 3

1 *Northern Whig*, 13 October 1936.
2 *Northern Whig*, 5 April 1937.
3 *Belfast Telegraph*, 19 May 1938.
4 *Belfast Telegraph*, 30 March 1945.
5 Author interview with Vivian Jenkins, November 1998.
6 *Belfast News-Letter*, 5 April 1939.
7 *Belfast Telegraph*, 28 June 1939.

Chapter 4

1 Hoe, *David Stirling*, p. 44.
2 Gibson, IWM audio interview.
3 Ranfurly, *To War with Whitaker*, p. 13.
4 Jellicoe, IWM audio interview.

Chapter 5

1 Foot, *The Special Operations Executive 1940–46*, pp. 4–8.
2 Ibid., p. 14.
3 Ibid., p. 66.
4 Kemp, *No Colours or Crest*, p. 12.
5 Bill Stirling obituary, *Ampleforth Journal*, 1983.
6 Hutchinson, IWM audio interview.
7 Moran, *Churchill at War 1940–45*, p. 67.
8 Hutchinson, IWM audio interview.
9 Lovat, *March Past*, p. 176.
10 Kemp, p. 16.
11 Ibid.
12 Contained in a memo entitled 'Report on Certain Aspects of SO2. Middle East by Capt. W Stirling. 23/5/41'. The National Archives (TNA): HS 3/192.
13 Lovat, p. 102.

14 Spencer Chapman, *The Jungle is Neutral*, p. 6.
15 Niven, *The Moon's a Balloon*, p. 223.
16 Kemp, p. 18.

Chapter 6

1 Lovat, *March Past*, p. 102.
2 Macpherson, IWM audio interview.
3 Lovat, p. 188.
4 Spencer Chapman, *The Jungle is Neutral*, pp. 5 and 18.
5 Smallman, IWM audio interview.
6 Niven, *The Moon's a Balloon*, p. 234.
7 *Stirling Observer*, 3 October 1940.
8 Minute to General Ismay, 6 June 1940. Reproduced in Winston S. Churchill, *The Second World War*, Volume II: *Their Finest Hour* (London: Cassell & Co., 1949), p. 217.
9 Jellicoe, IWM audio interview.
10 Eade, *Evelyn Waugh*, p. 97.
11 'Memorandum on LAYFORCE', in Davie (ed.), *The Diaries of Evelyn Waugh*, p. 491.
12 Eade, p. 98.
13 Amory (ed.), *The Letters of Evelyn Waugh*, p. 149.
14 Ibid., p. 150.

Chapter 7

1 Macpherson, IWM audio interview.
2 In Ross, *Paddy Mayne*, p. 32.
3 Tommy Macpherson, quoted in ibid., p. 31.
4 Gerald Bryan's recollections of Blair Mayne and the battle of Litani River form part of Graham Lappin's research that can be found at https://www.combinedops.com/Black%20Hackle.htm.
5 Rankin, *Churchill's Wizards*, p. 360.
6 Ross, p. 36.

Chapter 8

1 Beevor, *Crete 1941*, p. 25.
2 W. J. Stirling, Scots Guards, RARO: Posting Order BM 9168, 21 January 1941. TNA: HS 9/1418/6.
3 Ogden, *Master of Deception*, p. 42.
4 Johnston, *Mo and Other Originals*, p. 5.
5 Ranfurly, *To War with Whitaker*, p. 83.
6 'Certain Aspects of SO2 Middle East by Capt. W. Stirling', TNA: HS 3/192.
7 Saul Kelly, 'A succession of crises? SOE in the Middle East, 1940–1945', in Wyllie (ed.), *The Politics and Strategy of Clandestine War*, p. 136.
8 The original war diary of the Scots Guards is housed in The National Archives, Kew, but a digitised version has been uploaded on the website http://ww2talk.com/index.php?threads/war-diary-2nd-battalion-scots-guards-jan-dec-1941.57752/.
9 Ranfurly, p. 96.
10 TNA: HS 9/1418/6.
11 Ranfurly, p. 99. No exact date is given for this remark in Ranfurly's diary but it comes under the dates 11–31 May 1941.
12 Palmer, *SOE CD1*, p. 139.
13 All quotes from the dossier have the reference 'Certain Aspects of SO2 Middle East by Capt. W. Stirling', TNA: HS 3/192.
14 Sweet-Escott, *Baker Street Irregular*, p. 83.
15 Palmer, p. 139.
16 Wilkinson, IWM audio interview.
17 Mortimer, *The Men who Made the SAS*, p. 41.
18 Thompson, *War Behind Enemy Lines*, p. 17.

Chapter 9

1 Laycock papers, Liddell Hart Centre for Military Archives (LHC).
2 Michie, *Retreat to Victory*, pp. 186, 187.
3 Mather papers, IWM.
4 Michie, p. 186.
5 Sykes, *Evelyn Waugh*, p. 292.
6 'Raid on Benghazi', Mather papers.
7 TNA: WO 218/169.
8 Jock Lewes's letters to his father are among the private papers of Carol Mather, IWM.
9 Wise (ed.), *Joy Street*, p. 194.
10 Ibid., p. 222.
11 Ibid., p. 224.
12 The cable from Laycock is contained within the Laycock papers.
13 Mather papers.
14 Cooper, *Cairo in the War*, p. 128.
15 Peter Oldfield's diary, among the Laycock papers.
16 TNA.

17 Peter Oldfield diary.
18 TNA.
19 War Office telegram to the Hon Mrs Stirling, 20 September 1942, quoted in Hoe, *David Stirling*, p. 55.
20 Wise (ed.), p. 240.
21 Ranfurly, *To War with Whitaker*, p. 101.
22 Johnston, *Mo and Other Originals*, p. 3.
23 'Change of Command of LRDG', LRDG war diary summer 1941, TNA. Bagnold papers, Churchill Archives Centre.
24 LRDG war diary, TNA.
25 Hoe, p. 71.
26 Mather, *When the Grass Stops Growing*, p. 23.
27 Michie, p. 260.
28 Crichton-Stuart, *G Patrol*, p. 99.
29 Michie, p. 272.
30 Ibid., p. 260.
31 Ibid., p. 271.
32 Memorandum by Col David Stirling, written for the Camberley Staff College, 1948.
33 I heard this joke from veterans that I interviewed, and it is also referenced in *Commando Extraordinary* by Charles Foley, p. 209, and *A History of the SAS Regiment* by John Strawson, p. 77.
34 Jock Lewes letters, Mather papers.
35 Wise (ed.), p. 277.
36 *Ampleforth Journal*, 1928.
37 Sir Chris Bonington, 'How two risk-taking parents inspired the pioneering spirit of climber Sir Chris Bonington', *Mail on Sunday*, 30 September 2017.
38 *Maryborough Chronicle, Wide Bay and Burnett Advertiser (Qld)*, 4 September 1936.
39 *Courier-Mail*, 18 July 1940.
40 *Ampleforth Journal*, 1942.

Chapter 10

1 Ross, *Paddy Mayne*, p. 33.
2 'Army Estimates, 1941', Hansard, vol. 369, 6 March 1941.
3 McHarg, *Litani River*.
4 Ross, p. 52.
5 Ross, p. 54.
6 Jellicoe, IWM audio interview.
7 Peter Davis, unpublished memoir, SAS Regimental Archive.
8 John Kane interview, 1998.
9 Windmill, *Gentleman Jim*, p. 10.
10 Ibid., p. 11.
11 Author interview with Jimmy Storie, 2002.
12 Wise (ed.), *Joy Street*, p. 292.
13 Hoe, *David Stirling*, pp. 84–5.
14 Windmill, p. 72.
15 Ibid., pp. 16 and 17.
16 Jeff Du Vivier diary, quoted in Mortimer, *Stirling's Men*.
17 Hoe, p. 86.

Chapter 11

1 Hoe, *David Stirling*, p. 71.
2 Keyes, *Geoffrey Keyes VC*, p. 190. The letter was undated but appears to have been written in the late summer of 1941.
3 Courtney letter to Bob Laycock. Laycock papers, LHC.
4 Laycock papers.
5 The cables about Bill Stirling's whereabouts are in TNA: HS 9/1418/6.
6 Hoe, p. 95
7 Wise (ed.), *Joy Street*, p. 330.
8 Mather papers, IWM.
9 Peter Oldfield diary, Laycock papers.
10 LRDG War Diary September–October 1941, TNA.
11 Timpson, *In Rommel's Backyard*, p. 16.
12 Jeff Du Vivier diary.
13 Cowles, *The Phantom Major*.
14 Jeff Du Vivier diary.

Chapter 12

1 Jeff Du Vivier diary.
2 Bob Tait's account of the first operation is housed in The National Archives.
3 Jeff Du Vivier diary.
4 I am grateful to Alan Orton, the son of Cpl Johnny Orton, for sharing with me his father's reflections of the contretemps that erupted when Stirling decided to split the party.
5 TNA.
6 Recollections of Mike 'Lofty' Carr, Y Patrol first navigator, as told to the author in 2014 and reproduced in *The Men Who Made the SAS*.

7 PRO, *Special Forces in the Desert War*, p. 98.

8 Jeff Du Vivier's memories of the inaugural raid were recorded in his diary and repeated to the author in interviews in 2003.

9 TNA: Special Services Diary.

10 PRO, p. 98.

11 Jim Almonds's diary, and reproduced in Windmill, *Gentleman Jim*, p. 82.

12 Auchinleck papers, John Rylands Research Institute and Library.

13 Letter from Auchinleck to Cunningham, ibid.

14 Warner, *Auchinleck*, p. 109.

15 Marriott, *Military Memories*, p. 60.

16 Cowles, *The Phantom Major*, p. 51.

17 TNA: WO 218/252.

18 Ibid.

19 'Minutes of a Conference held at HQ Eighth Army on 29th Sept. 1941', LRDG war diary, TNA. Among those who attended the conference were Col Bagnold, Lt-Col Guy Prendergast and Brig Sandy Galloway.

Chapter 13

1 Cecil 'Jacko' Jackson's recollections are featured in *LRDG Rhodesia* by Jonathan Pittaway and Craig Fourie, pp. 47–72.

2 Mayne's account of the raid is quoted in *Honour for All* by Allan Michie, p. 30.

3 Cooper, *One of the Originals*, p. 34.

4 Jackson, in Pittaway and Fourie, p. 65.

5 Cowles, *The Phantom Major*, p. 66.

6 Windmill, *Gentleman Jim*, p. 99.

7 Jimmy Storie's recollection of Lewes's death was told to the author in 2002.

8 Windmill, p. 105.

9 David Stirling letter to Arthur Lewes, 20 November 1942, Laycock papers, LHC.

10 TNA.

Chapter 14

1 Bill Kennedy Shaw politely referred to them as 'Parashots' in his book, *Long Range Desert Group*, but several LRDG veterans have told me the actual nickname was 'Parashits', as did Johnny Cooper in his book, *One of the Originals*, p. 37.

2 The correspondence between Lt-Col M. B. Jennings and Col Roy Thurburn is contained in WO 201/2261, TNA.

3 Sherwood, IWM audio interview.

4 Sutherland, *He Who Dares*, p. 52.

5 Ranfurly, *To War with Whitaker*, p. 126.

6 Author interview with Roger Boutinot, 2003.

7 Author interview with Augustin Jordan, 2002.

8 Lodwick, *Raiders from the Sea*, p. 28.

9 Cooper, p. 39.

10 Gibson, IWM audio interview.

11 PRO, *Special Forces in the Desert War*, p. 317.

12 TNA.

Chapter 15

1 TNA: WO 201/731.

2 Bagnold papers, Churchill Archives Centre.

3 TNA: WO 201/731.

4 Sutherland, *He Who Dares*, p. 58.

5 Cecil 'Jacko' Jackson's recollections are in *LRDG Rhodesia* by Jonathan Pittaway and Craig Fourie, p. 66.

6 PRO, *Special Forces in the Desert War*, p. 136.

7 Pitt, *Special Boat Squadron*, p. 23.

8 Bennett, IWM audio interview.

9 Jellicoe, IWM audio interview.

10 Lodwick, *Raiders from the Sea*, p. 35.

11 Memo from Gen Neil Ritchie to Auchinleck, 22 April 1942, Auchinleck papers, John Rylands Research Institute and Library.

12 Martin Francis, 'Cecil Beaton's Romantic Toryism and the Symbolic Economy of Wartime Britain', *Journal of British Studies*, 45:1 (January 2006), pp. 90–117.

13 Beaton, *Near East*, p. 43.

14 Beaton, *Theatre of War*.

15 Jellicoe, IWM audio interview.

16 Lloyd Owen, *The Desert My Dwelling Place*, p. 112.

17 Mather, *When the Grass Stops Growing*.

18 Maclean, *Eastern Approaches*, pp. 190–1.

19 Ibid., p. 194.

Chapter 16

1 Laycock papers, LHC.

2 Michie, *Honour for All*, p. 331.
3 Jellicoe, IWM audio interview.
4 Randolph Churchill papers, Churchill Archives Centre.
5 CHAR 1/369/3-4.
6 Ibid.
7 Author interview with Arthur Thompson, 2002.
8 Author interview with Roger Boutinot, 2003.
9 Peter Stirling obituary, written by Maclean, *Ampleforth Journal*, 1994.
10 Cooper, *One of the Originals*, p. 41.
11 James, *Born of the Desert*, p. 131.
12 Fitzroy Maclean's account of the Benghazi raid is told in *Eastern Approaches*, pp. 216–24.
13 Cooper, p. 44.
14 Randolph Churchill's account of the raid was told in a letter to his father. CHAR 20/65/106-145.
15 Rose's account of the Benghazi raid is reproduced verbatim in James, pp. 68–76.
16 TNA.
17 Maclean, p. 226.
18 Obituary, *The Times*, 29 May 1942.
19 James, pp. 38–9.

Chapter 17

1 Prendergast's views on the Benghazi raid are described in the LRDG war diary, The Fifth Phase, 19 April to 26 May 1942, TNA.
2 Timpson, *In Rommel's Backyard*, p. 15.
3 TNA: WO 201/756.
4 Upcher, IWM audio interview.
5 Randolph Churchill papers, Churchill Archive Centre.
6 CHAR 20/65/106-145.
7 Cooper, *One of the Originals*, p. 54.
8 CHAR 20/65/106-145.
9 Randolph Churchill papers, Churchill Archive Centre.
10 TNA: WO 201/756.
11 Pitt, *Special Boat Squadron*, p. 25.
12 Translation from a German captured document. Laycock papers, LHC.
13 George Jellicoe report, 'Raiding Operations in the Middle East in July and August 1942', Laycock papers.
14 James, *Born of the Desert*, p. 36.
15 Ibid., p. 80.
16 Ibid., p. 136.

Chapter 18

1 PRO, *Special Forces in the Desert War*, p. 332.
2 TNA: WO 201/728.
3 CHAR 20/65/106-145.
4 Stirling's account of his meeting Churchill in Cairo and his claim that he first coined this phrase in his biography by Alan Hoe, pp. 197–8.
5 Brooke's account of his stay in Cairo is described in Alanbrooke, *War Diaries 1939–1945*, pp. 290–5.
6 Churchill, *The Hinge of Fate*, p. 423.
7 Laycock papers, LHC.
8 Diary entry of August 1942 (undated), Davie (ed.), *The Diaries of Evelyn Waugh*, p. 525.
9 Dillon, IWM audio interview.
10 Gordon-Creed and Field, *Rogue Male*, p. 97.

Chapter 19

1 Sherwood, IWM audio interview. Sadler's description of the raid as a 'nonsense' was made to the author during an interview in 2003, as were his other reminiscences of the Benghazi action.
2 Mather papers, IWM. Mather wrote an account of the Benghazi raid shortly after the war that was later turned into part of his memoir, *When the Grass Stops Growing*.
3 Mather papers.
4 Pittaway and Fourie, *LRDG Rhodesia*, p. 67.
5 Hunt, *A Don at War*, p. 91.
6 Peniakoff, *Popski's Private Army*, pp. 162–5.
7 Fitzroy Maclean's account of the Benghazi raid is in *Eastern Approaches*, pp. 228–62.
8 Mather papers.
9 Ibid.
10 PRO, *Special Forces in the Desert War*, p. 165.
11 Upcher, IWM audio interview.
12 Hunt, p. 133.
13 Ibid., pp. 133–4.
14 Sherwood, IWM audio interview.

15 Scott-Garrett, IWM audio interview.
16 Pittaway, p. 67.
17 Scott-Garrett, IWM audio interview.
18 Sherwood, IWM audio interview.
19 Pittaway and Fourie.
20 Ibid.
21 Andrew Maxwell's letter is among the private papers of Carol Mather, IWM.

Chapter 20

1 Correspondence between Churchill and General Alexander, The Churchill Archive, CHAR 20/65/146-148.
2 Headed 'Combined Signal Board Middle East', TNA: WO 201/756.
3 TNA: WO 201/754.
4 Memo titled 'Maj. Stirling', TNA: WO 201/756.
5 Memo titled 'Note for meeting regarding plans for Lt-Col Stirling's force', TNA: WO 201/756.
6 Kemp, *The SAS at War*, p. 74.
7 Wiseman, IWM audio interview.
8 Author interview with John Wiseman, 2002.
9 Mather papers, IWM.
10 The letter is quoted in Dillon and Bradford, *Rogue Warrior of the SAS*, p. 63.
11 Kennedy Shaw, *Long Range Desert Group*, p. 222.
12 Lloyd Owen, *The Long Range Desert Group 1940–1945*, p. 103.
13 Johnston, *Mo and Other Originals*, p. 20.
14 Ranfurly, *To War with Whitaker*, p. 157.
15 Author interview with Bob Lowson, 2002.
16 Maclean, *Eastern Approaches*, p. 263.
17 TNA: WO 201/773.
18 Fitzroy Maclean letter to David Stirling. TNA: WO 201/773.
19 Correspondence between Stirling and Laycock in the autumn of 1942, Laycock papers, LHC.
20 David Stirling letter to Arthur Lewes, 20 November 1942, Laycock papers.
21 Laycock papers.
22 Thesiger, *The Life of My Choice*, pp. 370–5.
23 Hackett, IWM audio interview.
24 Thesiger, p. 379.
25 James, *Born of the Desert*, p. 303.
26 The exchange of signals between Stirling and Eighth Army HQ is in PRO, *Special Forces in the Desert War*, p. 360.
27 James, p. 315.
28 Peter Davis, unpublished memoir, SAS Regimental Archive.

Chapter 21

1 Laycock papers, LHC.
2 George Jellicoe letter to Mountbatten, 6 January 1943, Laycock papers.
3 TNA: HS 9/1418/6.
4 Maynard (née Llewellyn), IWM audio interview.
5 TNA: HS 9/1418/6.
6 Kemp, *No Colours or Crest*, p. 52.
7 Ibid., p. 60.
8 The minutes of the series of meetings held at COHQ in the winter of 1942/3 are to be found in the Laycock papers.
9 Account of Captain Lord Jellicoe, 27 November 1942, Special Services War Diary, TNA.
10 Author interview with Mike Sadler, 2017.
11 Laycock papers.
12 Author interview with Mike Carr, 2014.
13 Jellicoe, IWM audio interview.
14 Author interview with Bob Lowson, 2002.
15 Johnny Cooper's account of Stirling's capture is in *One of the Originals*, pp. 67–76.
16 Author interview with Reg Redington, 2002.
17 Cooper, p. 68.
18 Author interviews with Mike Sadler, 2002–3.
19 Sgt Heinrich Fugner's account of capturing Stirling is in *LRDG Rhodesia* by Jonathan Pittaway and Craig Fourie, pp. 109–12.
20 Author interview with Reg Redington, 2002.
21 Author interviews with Mike Sadler, 2002–3.

Chapter 22

1 Cowles, *The Phantom Major*, p. 283.
2 TNA: DEFE 2/957.
3 Bill Stirling letter to Bob Laycock, Laycock papers, LHC.

4 Peter Stirling letter to the Hon Mrs Stirling, 15 February 1943, Laycock papers.
5 Johnston, *Mo and Other Originals*, pp. 4–5.
6 Lodwick, *Raiders from the Sea*, p. 54.
7 Author interview with Duncan Ridler, 2002.
8 Appleyard, *Geoffrey*, p. 149
9 King's College London: Liddell Hart Centre for Military Archives, GB0099 KCLMA, Papers relating to Maj Gen Sir Robert Edward Laycock (1907-1968).
10 Vivian Street's letter to his father is among the private papers of Carol Mather, IWM.
11 Ross, *Paddy Mayne*, p. 158.
12 Lovat, *March Past*, p. 234.
13 Peter Davis, unpublished memoir, SAS Regimental Archive.
14 1SAS war diary, TNA.
15 Peter Davis, unpublished memoir.

Chapter 23

1 Cowles, *The Phantom Major*, p. 298.
2 Liddell Hart (ed.), *The Rommel Papers*, p. 393.
3 Michie, *Honour for All*, p. 38.
4 Author interview with Reg Redington, 2002.
5 Oldfield papers, LHC.
6 Report on trial, *Dundee Evening Telegraph*, 17 September 1945.
7 Stirling's statement to the War Office, 13 August 1945. TNA: WO 71/1109.
8 Liddell Hart (ed.), p. 393.
9 Moorehead, *Desert War*, pp. 531–2.
10 'SAS founder "betrayed his men to German double agent"', *Sunday Times*, undated *c.* 1992.
11 Moorehead.
12 'SAS founder "betrayed his men to German double agent"'.
13 Hoe, *David Stirling*, p. 230.
14 The correspondence between the Stirlings, Jellicoe and Bob Laycock concerning Stirling's capture in the spring of 1943 is among the Laycock papers, LHC.
15 Ross, *Paddy Mayne*, p. 224.

Chapter 24

1 Macpherson, IWM audio interview.
2 Pringle, IWM audio interview.
3 Millar, *Horned Pigeon*, pp. 93 and 102.
4 Pringle, IWM audio interview.
5 Guss, *The 21 Escapes of Lt Alastair Cram*, p. 122.
6 Ibid., p. 46.
7 Pringle, *Colditz Last Stop*, p. 67.
8 Millar, p. 137.
9 Ibid., p. 138.
10 Guss, p. 77.
11 Ibid., p. 127.
12 Ibid., p. 134.
13 Millar, p. 137.
14 Ibid., p. 136.
15 Pringle, p. 98.

Chapter 25

1 John Comyn's recollection of his time as a POW are available to view at the Monte San Martino Trust Archives, https://archives.msmtrust.org.uk/.
2 Pringle, *Colditz Last Stop*, p. 106.
3 Ibid.
4 Ibid., p. 105.
5 Kindersley, *For You the War is Over*, p. 149.
6 Private papers of G. C. Williams, IWM. Microfilm documents 6445.
7 Guss, *The 21 Escapes of Lt Alastair Cram*, p. 258.
8 Ibid., p. 260.
9 Pringle, p. 126.
10 Kindersley, p. 149.
11 Guss, p. 267.
12 Ibid., p. 277.
13 In John Comyn's recollections, Monte San Martino Trust Archives.

Chapter 26

1 Kindersley, *For You the War is Over*, p. 166.
2 Wood (ed.), *Detour*, unnumbered page.
3 Pringle, *Colditz Last Stop*, p. 136.
4 Kemp, *The SAS at War*, p. 226.
5 Ross, *Paddy Mayne*, p. 141.
6 Eisenhower's letter to Brigadier McLeod is reproduced in Mortimer, *The SAS in World War II*, p. 186.
7 Calvert, IWM audio interview.
8 SAS signals 1945, TNA.

Chapter 27

1 Farran, *Winged Dagger*, p. 161.
2 Peniakoff, *Popski's Private Army*, p. 350.
3 Memo titled 'Training Instructions No. 8 Commando', Laycock papers, LHC.
4 Author interview with George Daniels, 2002.
5 Appleyard, *Geoffrey*, p. 170.
6 Memo quoted in Strawson, *A History of the SAS Regiment*, pp. 90–1.
7 Farran, IWM audio interview.
8 Strawson, p. 95.
9 Farran, IWM audio interview.
10 Quoted in Ross, *Paddy Mayne*, p. 158.
11 TNA.
12 Foot, *Memories of an SOE Historian*, p. 82.
13 Sykes, *Evelyn Waugh*, p. 326.
14 Author interview with Tony Greville-Bell, 2002.
15 Author interview with George Daniels, 2002.
16 Davie (ed.), *The Diaries of Evelyn Waugh*, p. 551.
17 Ibid., p. 555.
18 Bill Stirling's first-hand account of how he wangled Waugh the time to complete *Brideshead Revisited* was recorded in an audio interview with Christopher Sykes in 1968 for a programme entitled 'Evelyn Waugh, a study of his life and character', which was broadcast on BBC audio is held in the British Library.
19 Amory (ed.), *The Letters of Evelyn Waugh*, p. 210.

Chapter 28

1 TNA: WO 203/3774.
2 Ibid.
3 TNA: KV 2/626.
4 'Note of Interrogation of Lt-Col Waddilove', 2 May 1945, TNA.
5 TNA: KV 2/626.
6 TNA: WO 71/1109.
7 A memo issued from the office of the Judge Advocate General, 14 July 1945, which forms part of the file relating to the court-martial of Theodore Schurch. TNA: KV 2/77.
8 Guss, *The 21 Escapes of Lt Alastair Cram*, p. 337.
9 Oflag 8F, Marskova Tsebova, Czechoslovakia: killing of British officers. TNA: WO 309/244.
10 Reg Seekings audio interview 1998. Recorded in Northern Ireland and given to the author.
11 TNA.
12 *Observer*, 15 December 1946.

Chapter 29

1 Letter to H. de Villiers, 12 February 1952. Privately held.
2 Davie (ed.), *The Diaries of Evelyn Waugh*, pp. 644 and 656.
3 *Kirkintilloch Herald*, 28 July 1948.
4 'Central Africa: Apartheid Goes North', *Time*, 21 December 1962.
5 *Truth*, 2 April 1954. *Truth* was a British periodical founded by the Liberal politician Henry Labouchère in 1877. It later became more associated with the Conservative Party, and it ceased publication in 1957.
6 TNA: CO 1015/70.
7 Ibid.
8 *Daily Express*, 5 July 1952.
9 TNA: CO 1015/70.
10 Ibid.
11 Hancock, *White Liberals, Moderates and Radicals in Rhodesia 1953–1980*, p. 31.
12 Johnston, *The Other Side of Kilimanjaro*, p. 102.
13 Ibid., p. 101.
14 H. Wynn Jones, 'The Capricorn Declaration – where does it go from here?', *Truth*, 2 April 1954.
15 Hancock, p. 42.
16 Bill Stirling's letter to David is reproduced in Hoe, *David Stirling*, p. 315.
17 Ibid., p. 315.
18 Jones, *Storyteller*, p. 186.
19 Hoe, p. 305.
20 van der Post, *The Dark Eye in Africa*, p. 222.
21 *Belfast News-Letter*, 4 May 1956.
22 Jones, p. 151.
23 Hancock, p. 48.
24 Rotberg, *Black Heart*, p. 297.
25 Ibid., p. 298.
26 *Time*, 2 July 1956.

27 Vambe, *From Rhodesia to Zimbabwe*, p. 90.
28 TNA: CO 1015/70.
29 Quoted in Pritchard, 'Race, Identity and Belonging in Early Zimbabwean Nationalism(s), 1957–1965'.
30 The Peter Mackay archive is held at Stirling University and much has been digitised and can be accessed at http://petermackay.online/index.php. His letter to his mother describing Stirling's stalk of him is in his biography.

Chapter 30

1 Kennedy Shaw, *Long Range Desert Group*, p. 121.
2 TNA: WO 218/223.
3 Ibid.
4 Ibid.
5 This two-page document, entitled 'Suggestions for Book describing SAS activities 1941–43' is among the private papers of Carol Mather, IWM. It is undated but the fact Paddy Mayne was still alive (and several other Second World War titles are referenced) dates it to some time between approximately 1949 and 1954.
6 Amery papers, Churchill Archives Centre.
7 Michie, *Honour for All*, p. 32.
8 Foley, *Commando Extraordinary*. His conversation and impression of David Stirling is in Chapter 17, pp. 216–26.
9 Cowles, *The Phantom Major*, p. 5.
10 Amory (ed.), *The Letters of Evelyn Waugh*, p. 505.
11 *Singapore Free Press*, 23 May 1958.
12 'Reviews of Books', *RUSI Journal*, 103:611 (August 1958), p. 456.
13 Liddell Hart's cuttings are housed among his papers in the Liddell Hart Centre for Military Archives at King's College London. *The Phantom Major* was serialised in the *Sunday Times* between 20 April and 18 May 1958.
14 Foley, p. 203.
15 TNA.
16 Cowles, p. 283.
17 Author interview with Archie Stirling, 2020.
18 Hoe, *David Stirling*, p. 17.

Chapter 31

1 Hancock, *White Liberals, Moderates and Radicals in Rhodesia 1953–1980*, p. 86.
2 de la Billière, *Looking for Trouble*, p. 89.
3 Cooper's account of the Yemen operation is relayed in *One of the Originals*, pp. 157–86, and Peter de la Billière describes it in *Looking for Trouble*, pp. 202–11.
4 The three-page document that Stirling sent to Duncan Sandys and the letter Stirling sent to Bob Laycock, dated 2 March 1964, are among the Laycock papers, LHC.
5 Dorril, MI6, p. 692.
6 A comprehensive account of the Yemen incident is in ibid., pp. 683–95.
7 Hansard, vol. 699, 21 July 1964.
8 Woodhouse, IWM audio interview.
9 Dorril.
10 Said Aburish quoted in television documentary series *The Mayfair Set*, episode 1, 1999.
11 David Stirling's involvement in the 'Prince Margaret' aircraft incident is included among documents under the file FO 371/185484, TNA, and available to view at https://www.agda.ae.
12 *Guardian*, 8 June 2007.
13 David Stirling letter to Bob Laycock, 31 October 1967. This letter and all the correspondence relating to the Len Deighton article are among the Laycock papers.
14 A translated copy of the speech was reproduced in the SAS Regimental Journal, *Mars and Minerva*, under the heading 'A speech by Colonel David Stirling'. When I copied the page many years ago, I did not include the date of the magazine issue.
15 John Aspinall's recollection of David Stirling was broadcast in *The Mayfair Set*, episode 1, 1999.
16 McAleese, IWM audio interview.
17 Dorril, p. 738.
18 Hoe, *David Stirling*, p. 477.
19 Sandbrook, *Seasons in the Sun*.
20 Hailsham papers, Churchill Archives Centre.
21 *Peace News*, August 1974.
22 *Birmingham Evening Post*, 23 August 1974.

23 Stirling's essay was reproduced in the *Ampleforth Journal* following his death, 1991.
24 *Newcastle Evening Chronicle*, 8 April 1975.
25 *The Times*, 23 August 1974.
26 *Daily Express*, 23 August 1974.
27 *Guardian*, 4 September 1974.
28 Mark Frankland, 'Footloose, unusual – and such a talent', *Observer*, 21 January 2001.
29 *The Times*, 7 April 1975.
30 Obituary, *Independent*, 1 April 2009.
31 Hailsham papers, Churchill Archives Centre.
32 Amery papers, Churchill Archives Centre.
33 The court case and Stirling's victory were reported in *The Times*, 10 April 1979.
34 *Yorkshire Evening Post*, 5 February 1943.
35 Pittaway and Fourie, *LRDG Rhodesia*.
36 *Daily Express*, 15 March 1979.

Chapter 32

1 Asher, *The Regiment*, p. 446.
2 Ibid., p. 17.
3 *Aberdeen Evening Express*, 10 May 1980.
4 SAS Regimental Association (ed.), *SAS War Diary 1941–1945*.
5 Thompson, *The Hustlers*, p. 138.
6 Amory (ed.), *The Letters of Evelyn Waugh*, p. 568.
7 Michael Crick, 'How to Get into Who's Who', *Spectator*, 10 July 2004.
8 Quoted in *New York Times* obituary, 6 January 1983.
9 Hoe, *David Stirling*, pp. 471–3.
10 Peter Davis, unpublished memoir, SAS Regimental Archive.
11 TNA.
12 Card, IWM audio interview.
13 Woodhouse, IWM audio interview.
14 The reflections of Bob McDougall and Bob Lowson were told to the author together in 2002.
15 The quote from Stirling can be found at https://www.penguin.co.uk/authors/1016679/gordon-stevens.html.
16 Sykes, *Orde Wingate*, p. 333.

Chapter 33

1 *Reading Evening Post*, 30 July 1986.
2 *Independent*, 8 January 1991.
3 Author interviews with Haydn Tanner and Vivian Jenkins in 1998 and 1999 as part of my research for *Fields of Glory: The Extraordinary Lives of 16 Warrior Sportsmen*, one of whom was Paddy Mayne.
4 Bob Bennett interview with Gordon Stevens, now in the IWM Sound Archive.
5 Quoted in Ross, *Paddy Mayne*, p. 237.
6 Author interview with Duncan Ridler, 2002.
7 Author interview with Mike Sadler, 2003.
8 *Ampleforth Journal*, 1929.
9 Hoe, *David Stirling*, p. 32.
10 Author interview with Arthur Thompson, 2002.
11 Dillon and Bradford, *Rogue Warrior of the SAS*, p. 243.
12 Julian Amery, 'An Appreciation of Sir David Stirling', 7 November 1990. Amery papers, Churchill Archives Centre.
13 Jellicoe, IWM audio interview.
14 Lloyd Owen, *The Desert My Dwelling Place*, p. 112.
15 Thesiger, *The Life of My Choice*, p. 375.
16 Mather papers, IWM.
17 Laycock papers, LHC.
18 TNA: WO 201/731.
19 Farran, IWM audio interview.
20 Mather, *When the Grass Stops Growing*.
21 van der Post, *Yet Being Someone Other*, p. 329.
22 Hoe, pp. 352–3.
23 These comments relating to Reg Seekings were made by a Rhodesian cadet in the Police Anti-Terrorist Unit and were posted in response to an article in December 2020 by a former Rhodesian SAS soldier, Hannes, entitled 'David Stirling: How Great Was He?' on www.africaunauthorised.com.
24 Hoe, p. 477.
25 Author interview with Jimmy Storie, 2002.
26 John O'Sullivan, 'Paddy Mayne: The bravehearted Irish Lion who joined the SAS', *Irish Times*, 2 June 2017.

27 James, *Born of the Desert*, p. 51.
28 William Stirling obituary, *The Times*, January 1983.
29 Mather papers.
30 I am indebted to Randy Hees, the Director of the Nevada State Railroad Museum in Boulder City, for enlightening me about the railway network in California and Nevada in 1939 and also about the growth and development of Las Vegas as a gambling mecca.
31 Gilbert, *Winston S. Churchill: Road to Victory* p. 169.
32 TNA: WO 201/728.
33 Ibid.
34 *Of One Company: The Beginning of the SAS*, BBC Radio 4, 22 November 2001. Quoted in Michael Vestey, 'The Art of Deception', *Spectator*, 1 December 2001.
35 Jellicoe, IWM audio interview.
36 *RUSI Journal*, 108:3 (August 1963).
37 Sir Fitzroy Maclean papers, Albert and Shirley Small Special Collections Library, University of Virginia.
38 Maclean's eulogy was reproduced in the *Ampleforth Journal*, 1991.

Epilogue

1 Author interview with John Randall, 2002.
2 Letter from Alex Muirhead to John Slim, Second Viscount Slim. Muirhead Family Collection.
3 Author interviews with Mike Sadler, 2002–03.
4 Author interview with Tony Greville-Bell, 2002.
5 Author interview with John Wiseman, 2002.
6 Jeff Du Vivier, letter to author, 19 January 2003.
7 Author interview with Mike Sadler, 2003.
8 Hunt, *A Don at War*, pp. 130 and 132.
9 Michael Herman et al., 'Book reviews'.
10 The correspondence between Mather and Hunt in 1995 is among the private papers of Carol Mather, IWM.

Index